THE FORT BRAGG CARTEL

I done two tours of duty in Vietnam
I came home with a brand-new plan
I take the seed from Colombia and Mexico
I just plant it up a holler down Copperhead Road
And now the DEA's got a chopper in the air
I wake up screamin' like I'm back over there
I learned a thing or two from Charlie, don't you know
You better stay away from Copperhead Road.

STEVE EARLE,
"Copperhead Road"

For Oscar Medina and Ramon Ojeda

VIKING
An imprint of Penguin Random House LLC
1745 Broadway, New York, NY 10019
penguinrandomhouse.com

VIKING is a registered trademark of Penguin Random House LLC.

Grateful acknowledgment is made for permission to reprint lyrics from
"Copperhead Road." Words and music by Steve Earle. Copyright © 1988 by
Cypark Songs (ASCAP), Duke of Earle Music (ASCAP) and Warner-Olive
Music LLC (ASCAP). All rights on behalf of Cypark Songs and Duke of Earle
Music administered by WC Music Corp. All rights for Warner-Olive Music
LLC (ASCAP) administered by Universal Music Corp. (ASCAP). Exclusive
worldwide print rights for Warner-Olive Music LLC (ASCAP) administered by
Alfred Music. All rights reserved. Used by permission of Alfred Music.

Image credits: page 11: courtesy of Army HRC; page 25 and 90: courtesy of
Tammy Mabey; page 119: courtesy of Army HRC; page 172: by Donnie Roberts
for *The Lexington Dispatch*; page 181: courtesy of Sampson County, NC; page
191: courtesy of Cumberland County, NC; page 215: courtesy of FBI Charlotte;
page 225: courtesy of Forsyth County, NC; page 240: courtesy of Army HRC.

Portions of this work originally appeared, in a different form,
in articles published in *Rolling Stone*.

Designed by Amanda Dewey

ISBN 9780593655085 (hardcover)
ISBN 9780593655092 (ebook)

Printed in the United States of America
1st Printing

Some names and identifying characteristics have been changed to
protect people's privacy.

The authorized representative in the EU for product safety and
compliance is Penguin Random House Ireland, Morrison Chambers,
32 Nassau Street, Dublin D02 YH68, Ireland, https://eu-contact.penguin.ie.

THE
FORT BRAGG
CARTEL

**DRUG TRAFFICKING AND MURDER
IN THE SPECIAL FORCES**

Seth Harp

Viking

CONTENTS

PART IV

PART V

Part I

Part I

I KILL PEOPLE FOR A LIVING

Two veteran Special Forces soldiers, still drunk from the night before, their brains fried from a days-long binge on cocaine, MDMA, prescription pills, and a grab bag of mind-altering chemicals commonly sold in smoke shops as "bath salts," were driving home from Walt Disney World the morning of March 21, 2018, when Sergeant First Class Mark Leshikar, riding in the passenger seat, developed an unshakable conviction that their car was being followed. Leshikar's hard blue eyes, cracked with bloodshot veins from lack of sleep, studied the side-view mirror. He could have sworn that he saw shadowy pursuers on their tail, flitting in and out of the hazy lanes of traffic behind them on the Dixie Highway.

The driver of the car, Master Sergeant William Lavigne II, a member of the U.S. Army's top-secret Delta Force who had been trained in evasive driving and countersurveillance, told Leshikar that he was hallucinating. They were northbound on Interstate 95, headed for Fort Bragg, North Carolina, where both men were stationed. Lavigne, the older and more highly ranking of the two, had been keeping a close watch on the rearview mirror for miles. There was no one on their six o'clock, he insisted. But Leshikar wouldn't listen.

Two little girls, Lavigne's daughter and Leshikar's, were in the back of the car, tired and sunburned after days of exploring the theme parks in and around Orlando, Florida. They were too young to understand what the tense bickering in the front seats was about. All they knew was that their daddies were starting to scare them.

According to Leshikar's mother, sister, and wife, he had been acting strangely for the last six months. The trouble began, they said, in late 2017, as a result of an ambiguous mishap that he sustained while on deployment to Tajikistan, a remote and mountainous narco-state that the United States used for many years as a staging ground for the war in Afghanistan. What exactly happened to Leshikar in Tajikistan, a global hub of international heroin trafficking, is a mystery. An anodyne Pentagon press release states that he and his Green Beret teammates were there to train the Tajik military on standard infantry tactics like target practice, rock drills, and first aid. Everyone in the accompanying photograph looks pretty bored. But upon Leshikar's return to the United States, he didn't seem like the same person. His appearance had changed, too. "When he came home," said his mother, Tammy Mabey, "notably, you could see a droopiness in his eye."

Leshikar told her and his wife, Laura, that he and his team had come under attack in an ambush and that a roadside bomb had rocked the truck he was in, leaving him with a traumatic brain injury. But a spokesman for the United States Army Special Operations Command, known as USASOC, said that no American soldier has ever been killed or wounded in Tajikistan. Nor do Leshikar's personnel records reflect that he was awarded a Purple Heart, a decoration given to soldiers wounded as a result of enemy action.

Whatever the cause of Leshikar's injury, a military doctor had prescribed him tramadol, an opioid painkiller that was freely distributed to elite troops during the wars in Iraq and Afghanistan and became a popular drug of abuse among special operations soldiers. Leshikar also came back from Tajikistan with a steady supply of the benzodiazepine Xanax, which he took along with tramadol to treat anxiety associated with his supposed PTSD, another claimed effect of the fictitious ambush. On top of this volatile pharmaceutical cocktail, which, in addition to suppressing the central nervous system, can cause bizarre episodes of uninhibited behavior, Leshikar had taken up snorting cocaine. He tried to rationalize it, telling Tammy that he and his fellow Green Berets regularly used the stuff to stay awake during night operations. "It's just like taking an antidepressant," he'd said.

Tammy, a single mother who had worked for a succession of small-town police departments in the Pacific Northwest, first as a jailer and dispatcher, later as a patrolwoman, wasn't convinced. Cocaine is illegal, not something prescribed by a doctor, she reasoned. But it was her son's alcohol consumption that concerned her the most. "Marky always acted perfectly fine when doing cocaine," she said. "When Marky would spiral was if he drank too much."

In the past, Leshikar had been a proud, stoic, taciturn man, not given to displays of incontinent emotion. Now, after no more than two or three alcoholic beverages, which combined poorly with the medications he was on, a maudlin gloominess would overtake him, a sullen and wounded sort of machismo. He would turn to his wife and say things like "You know I'm a bad person, right? I kill people for a living."

IN A PHOTO TAKEN at an American base in Afghanistan, where he served six months in combat from 2015 to 2016, Leshikar wears wraparound Oakley sunglasses, a thick beard, and a pleased grin while getting pinned with a Bronze Star medal and a Combat Infantry Badge. In other photos, he sports a custom skull patch on the front of his body armor, a Confederate battle flag on his left shoulder, and an oversize belt buckle shaped like a fanged demon with ram's horns.

"Such a pigheaded, egotistical man," was the first impression that he made on Laura, a paralegal originally from Hawaii whose dad was a marine. She initially scoffed at his swaggering boastfulness and the ridiculous lies he told. He was rather tall and handsome, though: six feet four, with light blue eyes and a jawline as well defined as a carpenter's square. "Over time," said Laura, "he grew on me."

Leshikar was born in 1984 in rural Idaho and joined the active-duty Air Force at age eighteen. He served in the Air Force Honor Guard, a ceremonial unit in which he felt left out of the real action entailed in America's escalating wars. In 2010, after an aimless period in civilian employ, he secured a Special Forces slot in Washington state's Army National Guard and was sent to Fort Bragg for Green Beret training.

Assigned to the 19th Special Forces Group, a National Guard formation that has teams of part-time Green Berets stationed all over the country, Leshikar went on to patch together a career as a so-called guard bum, a reservist with no other regular source of employment who jumps from orders to orders, picking up deployments, temporary duty assignments, and paid training gigs as often as possible. He deployed for a year to the Philippines, worked for a time as a SWAT trainer and private security guard, then did his tours in Afghanistan and Tajikistan.

"His deployments were pretty kinetic," said Jordan Terrell, a paratrooper in Fort Bragg's 82nd Airborne Division, originally from Chicago, who was friends with Leshikar. "I know he threw a bunch of incendiary grenades on a villager's hut and burned a couple of people alive," Terrell said. "He showed me videos. It was pretty fucked up."

Shortly after returning from Tajikistan in 2017, Leshikar suffered a severe clonic-tonic seizure, resulting in his hospitalization. A computed tomography scan of his brain, as well as magnetic resonance imaging, failed to disclose any physical trauma. There was no clear etiology for the seizure, but the doctor who examined him surmised that it had something to do with his heavy use of prescription drugs, as well as chronic insomnia.

In February 2018, about a month before the ill-fated trip to Disney World, Leshikar's little sister Nicole Rick and her husband, a Navy submariner, stayed with Mark and Laura for two weeks while closing on a house in Chesapeake, Virginia. Whenever a babysitter could be found to look after their children, the group of four young parents, all in their mid-thirties, went out on the town together, invariably joined by Leshikar's best friend, Billy Lavigne, the Delta Force soldier. "Full disclosure," Nicole said, "me and Billy and Mark all did coke together."

Before hitting a bar or club, they would stop at Lavigne's house, a cookie-cutter tract home at the end of a cul-de-sac in a newly constructed subdivision of Fayetteville, the moody military town, a low-slung sprawl of suburbs and strip malls, studded with billboards, that surrounds Fort Bragg on three sides. Lavigne had recently divorced, and now that his wife and daughter had moved out, the three-bedroom house was often full of his fellow operators from Delta Force, a highly classified unit a cut above the ordinary Special Forces.

No less secretive than the Central Intelligence Agency, Delta Force exists to carry out covert actions, defined under federal law as overseas operations "in which it is intended that the role of the United States government will not be apparent or acknowledged publicly." Wearing civilian clothes or operating in disguise under false identities, soldiers from Delta Force infiltrate foreign countries and commit clandestine acts of sabotage, espionage, and assassination, often on direct orders from the White House. Behind a heavy curtain of government secrecy, twenty-plus years at war in Afghanistan, Iraq, Yemen, Libya, Somalia, Syria, the Philippines, and elsewhere has given rise in this ultra-elite unit to a toxic culture of addiction, criminality, madness, violence, and impunity.

"The unit guys kind of separate themselves into two groups," said Terrell, who, like Leshikar, aspired to join Delta Force but failed to meet the rigorous and often arbitrary selection criteria. "You have the teetotalers, the guys who are super Christian, warriors for God. No drugs, no alcohol, super goody-goody, by the book. Then you have the guys who are just complete fucking derelicts, constantly doing nefarious shit."

Lavigne definitely belonged to the latter category, as did his buddies who congregated at his house. Laura and Nicole described his core group of friends from the unit as half a dozen tall white men, grizzled and bearded and heavily tattooed, ranging in age from their late twenties to early forties. In between shots of liquor and lines of cocaine, they joked about the operations they had been on and boasted of their exploits in combat, indefatigable in their attempts to one-up each other. "You got 42 confirmed kills?" said Laura, imitating a man's deep voice. "Well, I got 120."

Laura, Nicole, and Terrell, who himself sold marijuana and psilocybin mushrooms on Fort Bragg, all attested to the flagrant and continuous use of cocaine as well as MDMA and other drugs by a regular procession of active-duty Delta Force operators at Billy Lavigne's residence. "They've done coke in front of me," said Laura. "Other operators that were there. Sometimes when I would walk into Billy's house, it was just everywhere."

Lavigne was the one who dealt the cocaine. He collected the cash, went off someplace to meet with somebody, and when he came back, doled out the coke to those who partook. "Billy coordinated it," said Nicole. "All the money that was pulled together was given to Billy."

"Drugs are just the culture there," Terrell said of Delta Force. "Everybody knows it, everybody is complicit in it, and nobody does anything about it."

BILLY LAVIGNE was born in 1983 in Gladstone, Michigan, a small town on the shores of the Green Bay that's more northerly in latitude than Ottawa or Quebec. His father was a tire salesman and his mother worked in a nursing home. In February 2001, he enlisted in the active-duty Army cavalry, not out of any surfeit of patriotic fervor but to get free corrective eye surgery, a little-known perk of military service. Then the terrorist attacks of September 11, 2001, happened, touching off the longest period of war in American history. "He fell in love with what he was doing," said his father, William Lavigne Sr., "and decided to make a career out of it."

Lavigne did an early tour in Iraq as a cavalry scout, then got taken up the pipeline of the 1st Special Forces Group. He made it past the Delta Force selection board in 2009, at a time when the unit, despite its virtual invisibility to the American public, was emerging as the dominant force in the United States' burgeoning special operations complex, waging a ruthless manhunting and assassination campaign in Iraq and Afghanistan, and across the whole Islamic world, from the snowy passes of the Hindu Kush to the desert scrublands of Somalia, often in partnership with the CIA. By the age of thirty-four, Lavigne had spent a total of forty-one months and twenty-two days in combat. "Pretty much anywhere the U.S. had anything going on between 2006 and 2018," said his dad, "he was there."

Trained in the recondite methods of targeted killing by expert Israeli assassins, Lavigne had most recently deployed in support of the war against the Islamic State of Iraq and Syria, where he had most likely belonged to a secret "expeditionary targeting force" dedicated to liquidating the ranks of ISIS commanders in covert hit jobs carried out under cover of night, often in denied areas deep behind enemy lines. Unlike Leshikar, who had a propensity to exaggerate his inner turmoil and psychological darkness for dramatic effect, Lavigne really did kill people for a living.

In his official military portrait, in which he is attired in a blue dress uniform replete with rows of multicolored campaign ribbons, the red arrowhead of USASOC on his breast pocket, and the glittering regalia of a master free-fall parachutist, Lavigne's buzzed head looks like a big white egg, and his ashen face has the pale and drawn appearance of a man who has just shorn off a beard and shaved to the skin. "It's a horrible photo," said Nicole. "Like he's already dead." In real life, Lavigne wasn't bad-looking: tall and bald, with blue eyes and neatly trimmed facial hair. "Him and my brother had similar features," she said.

Lavigne initially made a positive impression on Nicole, a spiritual life coach and Reiki energy healer keenly attuned to the auras that people exude. "Billy was the oddity amongst the Special Forces guys that I was introduced to," she said. "I'm tenderhearted. I would rather see peace than war. He seemed to have ideals that matched mine."

Nicole's tough-talking brother, who'd seen far less combat than Lavigne, was of the opinion that the United States ought to simply nuke the Middle East and be done with it. Lavigne, whose demeanor she describes as "thoughtful" and "introverted," as well as "depressed," disagreed with those belligerent sentiments, speaking up in favor of peace and tolerance toward Muslim countries. "They have a different society," she recalled him saying, "and while I don't agree with it, we shouldn't be doing what we're doing over there."

Ben Boden, Lavigne's best friend from high school, saw his views on the post-9/11 wars evolve over the years. "During the 2005 to 2011 time frame," said Boden, "he was all about kicking ass and taking names." Later, "he was questioning what they were really accomplishing," and "wasn't as gung ho."

To Nicole, Lavigne seemed weighed down by "sadness or guilt," partly on account of his recent divorce, but mostly because he was "tormented by elements of his job." A "soulless" look would come over him, she said, "almost like he was looking through you, as he was talking about the things he had inflicted."

One night at his house, Lavigne confessed to Nicole that he had once shot and killed a child. "He was just a little boy," he told her, "but he had a gun." He also introduced her to his dog, a tautly poised, hyper-alert Belgian Malinois named Rocky that had been one of the unit's working animals. Nicole wanted to know why it had no teeth. Lavigne told her that its titanium dentures had been surgically removed upon retirement because the dog had been trained to attack and had grown accustomed to feeding on the flesh of people killed in special operations raids, including being allowed, "as a treat," to eat human brains. "Oh my God," said Nicole, watching the dog gulp down its supper of wet mush. "That's disgusting."

Like many other Delta Force operators, Lavigne had been prescribed dextroamphetamine early in his career to help him cope with sleep deprivation. Legal meds given to him by an Army doctor were what originally engendered his taste for the clean, cold rush of euphoric confidence that stimulants trigger in the brain. By the early 2010s, he had begun using cocaine. By 2018, he was smoking crack on a daily basis and regularly ingested MDMA, smoked crystal methamphetamine, snorted powdered heroin, and had even taken to inserting speedballs—a dangerous mixture of heroin and cocaine—into his rectum in a dissolvable capsule to get a quicker and more powerful high. "It was out of control," said Laura, who resented how much time her increasingly addled and erratic husband spent with Lavigne. "Every time I saw Billy, he was strung out on something."

William J. Lavigne II in official dress
uniform, December 2018.

———

ON THE NIGHT of February 26, 2018, after his wife's thirty-sixth birthday party at a bar called Paddy's Irish Pub, Mark Leshikar got so drunk that he nearly threw Nicole off the balcony of an apartment complex in a fit of irrational rage. "He thought I was trying to get in between him and Laura," said Nicole, who had merely suggested that her brother be a little nicer when speaking to his wife. Master Gunnery Sergeant Jens Merritt, a comrade of Lavigne's and friend of the group, had to step in to restrain Leshikar and make him unhand Nicole. "It was scary," she said.

To play the peacemaker in this way was characteristic of Merritt, who joined Delta Force out of the Marine Corps rather than the Army. "Jens was a sergeant major and a unit operator," said Terrell. "I don't know what his direct correlation was with Billy, but he was his senior." Nicole, Laura, and Tammy, who all met Merritt, were under the impression that he was Lavigne's immediate supervisor, a "direct boss to Billy," in Nicole's words.

The next day, once he'd sobered up, Leshikar was shaken by what he'd almost done to his little sister, to whom he'd been a father figure in high school. The time had come, he decided, to get clean. "We had a long discussion," recalled Nicole. "He knew that alcohol and drugs were getting in the way of the father and husband that he wanted to be. Both him and Laura were going to get sober together."

Then came the trip to Walt Disney World. The occasion was to celebrate the sixth birthday of Leshikar's daughter, Melanie, and the upcoming birthday of Lavigne's daughter, Ava, custody of whom he shared with his ex-wife. The Leshikars, joined by a female friend of Laura's, drove down from North Carolina with the two children and rented a house in Orlando. There they were met by Lavigne, who arrived from a nearby special operations base in Tampa, where he had been leading a Delta Force training mission in the role of a troop sergeant major.

Unfortunately for Leshikar's newfound commitment to sobriety, alcoholic beverages are available for purchase throughout the Magic

Kingdom. Also, it was Saint Patrick's Day. To commemorate the Irish holiday, he and Lavigne got duly inebriated. Nicole spoke to her brother for a final time that night. "It was his last hurrah," she said. "He was getting clean."

The weather in Orlando over the weekend was muggy and wet, the sticky humidity alleviated by short-lived downpours. During the daytime, the adults discreetly sipped from liquor-spiked thermoses while the kids rode the rides and explored the theme parks. At night, with thunder rumbling in troubled skies, they stayed up late partying on the patio of the rented house.

Cocaine is a drug known for being hard to keep on hand. Supplies of it have a tendency to run out sooner than anticipated. Laura and her friend said that Lavigne repeatedly snuck off throughout the weekend and into Monday to rendezvous with sketchy military dudes, and that on the way home he stubbornly insisted that he and Leshikar stay a night in Savannah, Georgia, by Hunter Army Airfield, home of an elite Army Ranger battalion, in order to meet some guy at a hotel "in the bad part of town," as Laura's friend recalled. She figured that the purpose of the detour was to procure more drugs.

The geographic corridor from Tampa and the Florida Panhandle into southern Georgia and along the coast of the Carolinas includes some of the densest nodes of the United States' global special operations complex, the beating heart of which is Fort Bragg. The tangle of interstates that runs through this stretch of the southern Atlantic coast, collectively known as the Dixie Highway, is also among the busiest drug-trafficking routes in the world, because it connects the ports of Florida to a string of voracious drug markets, including Washington, Baltimore, Philadelphia, New York, and Boston, with Fayetteville lying at the precise midpoint. Between these two clandestine worlds, there is significant overlap.

In July 2018, for instance, Florida police officers arrested a Fort Bragg paratrooper, Master Sergeant Martin Acevedo III, in a bust-up of a heroin deal by the railroad tracks in downtown Orlando but released him after learning that he was in the Army. Master Sergeant Acevedo, an Iraq veteran who belonged to the 82nd Airborne Division, would later be convicted of trafficking kilogram quantities of cocaine through the international postal service from Puerto Rico directly to his home on Green Heron Drive in Fayetteville, just fifteen doors down from where Billy Lavigne lived on Anhinga Court.

All throughout the first half of 2018, another of Lavigne's near neighbors, Sergeant First Class Henry Royer—a Green Beret originally from Hong Kong and who, like Leshikar belonged to 19th Group—together with his partner in crime, Master Sergeant Daniel Gould, a legendary 7th Group team leader who'd won a Silver Star for heroism in Afghanistan, were actively smuggling million-dollar quantities of cocaine into the United States on military flights from Bogotá, the capital of Colombia, to a small special operations base near Pensacola, Florida, called Duke Airfield. "Elite soldiers have access to whatever they have the balls to get into," Gould wrote me in a letter from federal prison in Safford, Arizona, where he was serving time for trafficking cocaine. "Whores, guns, drugs, you name it," he wrote. "We are far from the flagpole and expected to be incorruptible."

ONE OF THE LAST PHOTOS of Leshikar ever taken shows him and Melanie resting with Lavigne and his daughter on a park bench beside the Jungle Cruise attraction at Disney World, in front of some fake boulders and real plants. Leshikar and Lavigne are dressed in tattered baseball caps, cargo shorts, and flip-flops. Both look haggard and slightly sunburned, their eyes blurry, bloodshot, and unfocused, but their bodies give an impression of relaxed strength and vigor with their long limbs draped all over the wooden seat back. Two months earlier, Lavigne had recorded a perfect score on the Army's physical fitness test, and Leshikar looks even leaner and stronger. "Anywhere we went," said Nicole, who's shorter than her brother by a foot, "they were generally the biggest people."

Laura didn't stay in Savannah the night of March 20, but drove on to North Carolina to drop her friend off at the Raleigh-Durham airport. When she left the girls behind with their reprobate fathers, Laura thought that sticking them with babysitting duties would make them behave. In this, she was sadly mistaken.

Lavigne and Leshikar were coming and going from the motel room all night. In the morning, when they set out on the four-hour drive to Fayetteville, Leshikar in particular was wrecked. On top of the alcohol, cocaine, MDMA, tramadol, and Xanax in his system, he had the un-regulated Russian pharmaceutical phenazepam, plus pentylone and N-ethylpentylone, so-called bath salts that are often cut into poor-quality coke and ecstasy and can cause paranoia, agitation, heart palpi-tations, and hallucinations.

Ever since his deployment to Afghanistan, Leshikar had carried within him a shadow being, a tenebrous doppelgänger that Nicole thought of as his "dark passenger." Dark Mark was "harder, shorter, and more mean in how he would talk," and also more "outwardly physically ag-gressive," she said.

Now something had gotten into Leshikar, a monomania that he couldn't shake loose of. He was convinced that they were under surveil-lance. Through whispers and hand signs, he intimated to Lavigne that they should keep their voices down. He was adamant that the interior of the vehicle was bugged. His trembling hands moved all over the dashboard and glove box, in which a handgun was locked, in search of imaginary electronic eavesdropping devices.

Around noon, Lavigne sent several text messages to Laura, warning her that Leshikar was acting strange and that his manic behavior was putting the girls at risk. The word "unsafe" jumped out at her from one of the texts. Alarmed, she placed a video call to her husband. "Are you acting weird?" she demanded to know.

"Weird how?"

"Do you seem paranoid?"

"About what?" Leshikar asked, seemingly unperturbed.

Laura figured that Mark and Billy were playing some kind of joke on her. "Those two would always pull some shit," she said. "I could never take anything serious."

Leshikar's antics, which Lavigne found increasingly irritating, continued all the way home. At times, Leshikar's delusions had to do with his failed attempt to pass Delta Force selection, which hadn't deterred him from hopes of trying again. "The unit has a bucktail on me," he raved, referring to a type of electronic tracking tag. "I feel like you think I'm a threat," he said to Lavigne, "and I'm not going to be able to assimilate into the organization, so you're here to take care of me if shit goes bad."

"No, dude," Lavigne replied. "That's not what's happening. I'm your friend."

When they arrived around five o'clock in the afternoon at Lavigne's gray two-story house at the end of Anhinga Court, Leshikar stepped out of the car, popped the hood, and began to disassemble the motor while it was still hot. He was certain that innocuous parts of the Honda were actually hidden microphones. Lavigne tried to explain to him that they were ordinary engine components, even doing image searches on his phone to show him photos of automotive fuses, but Leshikar refused to be dissuaded.

The situation escalated from there. Lavigne attempted to take the screwdriver from Leshikar's hands, which led to a physical fight. As the two children looked on in terror, the grown men grappled on the driveway, toppled over into the front yard, and wrestled in the patchy grass, burned over from the dry winter. Leshikar had two inches and twenty pounds on Lavigne, but Lavigne had been trained in a syncretic brand of martial arts unique to the Army, drawn from Muay Thai, Brazilian jiujitsu, Krav Maga, and plain old American-style boxing. Despite being the smaller man, he managed to subdue Leshikar. He grabbed hold of both girls, bundled them into the house, and locked the front door, leaving Leshikar panting, red-faced, and enraged.

Two

THEY DO WHAT THEY WANT

L avigne sent the girls upstairs to play with Ava's tablet and walked around the house making sure that the garage door, the sliding glass door to the patio, and all the windows were locked. He placed a last-ditch phone call to Jens Merritt, who he hoped could intercede before things turned violent.

Merritt, the forty-three-year-old Delta Force operator from the Marine Corps who had prevented Leshikar from throwing his sister off a balcony, was not especially alarmed, at first, by the call for help. Whatever Lavigne and Leshikar were fighting about, it was nothing a couple of cigars and a round of whiskey couldn't fix, he figured. He grabbed a handful of stogies from his stash and jumped in his truck.

In spite of his mild manner and apparent level-headedness, Lavigne's fifteen years at war had imbued him with a profound capacity for explosive rage. By going inside the house, locking the door, and calling Merritt to come over, he had given himself and Leshikar both a chance to cool off. But he'd taken Melanie with him, separating the girl from her father. That gave Leshikar the right to seek entry into the house to retrieve his daughter.

Lavigne, who must have been securing the back door or talking to Merritt on the phone, ignored Leshikar's incessant knocking at the front entrance and failed to take into account the possibility that Melanie, just six years old, would naturally come downstairs in response to her dad calling her name. He didn't seem to realize how easy it would be for Leshikar to prevail on his own kid to unlock the door from the inside.

When Lavigne came around the corner of the kitchen, he was greeted by the unexpected sight of the front door wide open and Leshikar coming straight toward him, across the foyer. Leshikar had nothing in his hands. He was unarmed. But Lavigne was so startled and angered that he drew his sidearm, a Colt 1911 that he carried concealed on his person at all times.

Melanie, who witnessed what happened next at close range from the bottom steps of the stairwell, was struck dumb for more than a year afterward. When she recovered enough to speak, she gave an account of the shooting to her grandmother, mother, and aunt.

"Her daddy and Uncle Billy had been arguing," said Grandma Tammy. "Uncle Billy locked her daddy out of the house. And she heard her dad knocking at the door and yelling for her to come open the door. And when she opened the door, that's when he was mad at Uncle Billy."

Next, said Laura, "she got pushed to the side," back into the carpeted stairwell, as Leshikar instinctively acted to protect his daughter by shoving her out of the way. "She looked up and saw Billy pointing the gun at her daddy. And she looked at her daddy and it was like he was dancing."

While relating these facts to the grown-up women, Melanie acted out the so-called dance moves that her father had performed, pirouetting and ducking as if to avoid the muzzle of a gun. "Then she heard a shot," said Laura, "and her daddy was on the ground."

Melanie dropped to her knees and covered her head with her hands, imitating what her father had done. "Then she heard another boom," said Nicole. "She crinkled her little body like how Marky was found," said Tammy, "and rolled into a fetal position." Then, said Laura, "Billy was over him and shot him more times."

Forensic evidence corroborated the child's version of events, including the delivery of a final coup de grâce. Diagrams drawn in conjunction with Leshikar's autopsy show that the trajectories of the gunshots that killed him were various combinations of front to back, back to front, upward, downward, and right to left, indicating that Lavigne had circled around and shot him from multiple angles, or that Leshikar had been gyrating wildly as he was being shot.

Only one bullet impacted him from the front, hitting him square in the neck above the clavicle. Another bullet, whose seemingly backward path investigators were at a loss to decipher, inflicted a superficial graze wound to the left side of his neck, detaching a slender piece of flesh, four inches in length, that was found stuck to the ceiling of the kitchen. A third shot, which by itself would have been fatal, hit Leshikar in the right side, penetrated his lung, impacted his spine, and left his thorax filled with more than a liter of hemorrhaged blood. Two bullet fragments found lodged in the soaked carpet beneath Leshikar's body indicate that Lavigne, unable to stop himself once reflexes and muscle memory took control, had stood over his best friend and finished him off with a kill shot to the rib cage at nearly point-blank range.

JENS MERRITT GOT a second call from Lavigne a short time after the first, while he was still negotiating crosstown rush-hour traffic. Merritt would later claim that due to the noise of the highway he couldn't be sure that he understood Lavigne correctly. But initially there was no ambiguity. Lavigne told him, in a panicked lie, that Leshikar had committed suicide.

"Mark just shot himself," Lavigne said, according to the notes of the Army detective who interviewed Merritt. "What should I do?"

"Call the fucking cops," Merritt responded. He hung up the phone and floored the accelerator.

Lavigne dialed 911 and, quickly changing up his story, told the dispatcher that he'd shot an intruder, a stranger. He didn't know the man, he said. He'd never seen him before.

Joshua LaFave, a Cumberland County sheriff's deputy, was the first law enforcement officer to arrive at the scene, at 5:29 p.m. "Upon my arrival," Deputy LaFave wrote in his incident report, "I made contact with William Lavigne (suspect) who was standing on the front porch with his hands up above his head." He ordered Lavigne to turn around and put his hands behind his back. "While securing Lavigne in the back of my patrol car," LaFave wrote, "he asked me to check on the two children that were inside of the residence."

Additional sheriff's deputies and police officers and an ambulance pulled up with their lights flashing and cut their sirens. Among the first responders was a medical examiner who noted in his preliminary report that Leshikar was found lying prone on the floor of the foyer of the house in an awkward, twisted position, with one arm beneath him. No weapons, or objects of any kind, were near his body.

Merritt was already at the scene by then, inside the yellow police tape. As the police went about securing evidence and taking photographs, Merritt discreetly retrieved Leshikar's cell phone from where it had fallen to the floorboard of the Honda Accord. Instead of turning it over to investigators, he held on to it for several days, then gave it to Laura Leshikar, who reset the device to its factory settings, erasing all its data.

Around sundown, Lavigne was taken to the Cumberland County jail in downtown Fayetteville. On the police report that names him as the sole suspect in Leshikar's murder, his employer is simply listed as "U.S. Army," and his occupation, "soldier." But it wouldn't have taken detectives long to realize that they had a Delta Force man on their hands.

Across Worth Street from the detention center, on an industrial lot hidden behind tall fences and overgrown kudzu, was a metal warehouse that a group of motorcycle-riding Delta Force soldiers used as an after-hours speakeasy where they threw parties often attended by local cops. "It's like a clubhouse for unit guys," said Terrell of the location, which lies within the county jail's no-drone zone. "They go there and drink and do drugs and party and stuff."

Just a few weeks earlier, in February 2018, lawyers for the Special Forces command had persuaded the district attorney to drop rape charges against Lavigne's good friend and Delta Force teammate Cristobal Lopez Vallejo, also known as Cris Valley, over an incident that had occurred at the warehouse after a drunken fundraiser hosted by a military-affiliated biker club called Coast x Coast. The evidence against Vallejo was damning, but the Army's lawyers had persuaded the DA to move the trial onto Fort Bragg, where it could be quietly carried out under the auspices of USASOC. Lavigne, a charter member of Coast x Coast, had been present at the warehouse the night of the alleged rape and was to be a key witness in Vallejo's stage-managed exoneration. But now he had turned up in handcuffs, accused of an even more serious offense.

At the Cumberland County jail, Lavigne was given special treatment from the beginning. The handcuffs were removed, and he was never officially placed under arrest. He was not booked, photographed, fingerprinted, or taken before a magistrate for a bond hearing. He was subjected to no rougher treatment at the hands of detectives than a gentle, informal questioning.

He had already given contradictory accounts of the shooting to different people, first claiming that Leshikar had shot himself, then that Leshikar was a stranger who had broken into his home. Now Lavigne settled on the story that he would stick to henceforth. In this new telling, Leshikar had come at him with a screwdriver, and Lavigne had shot him multiple times in an act of self-defense, and to protect the children.

It was a self-serving tale that he would later repeat to Leshikar's mother and sister. "I let him tell me his side of the story," said Nicole, who spoke to him by phone a few months later. According to Lavigne, the screwdriver that he had supposedly spotted in Leshikar's hand was the same one that Leshikar had been using to disassemble the engine of the Honda Accord. "All he could think of was the screwdriver going through one of the kids' heads," Nicole said, paraphrasing Lavigne. "And he knew that Mark had to be 'put down.' That's how he worded it. That's what really bugged me. Such a horrible way to say it: 'I knew he had to be *put down.*'"

She asked Lavigne why he hadn't attempted to perform cardiopulmonary resuscitation, or any other emergency lifesaving procedure, on her dying brother. "I've shot enough people," Lavigne replied, "to know that he was gone before he hit the ground."

Cumberland County officials pretended to believe Lavigne's phony story, even though it was definitively contradicted by the physical evidence. The medical examiner's report established that no screwdriver was found anywhere near Leshikar's body. The tool that he'd been using to disconnect the battery of the car was found right where he'd dropped it in the driveway.

Likewise, an Army major who conducted an administrative inquiry to determine, for life insurance purposes, whether Leshikar had died "in the line of duty" shredded Lavigne's claim of self-defense. "There is no evidence to support the assertion" that Leshikar came at Lavigne "in a threatening manner," wrote the major, noting that no weapons were found on or around Leshikar's body, and that Lavigne initially told someone, presumably Merritt, that Leshikar had shot himself. Ultimately, the major wrote, "I determined that [Lavigne] is NOT credible."

Even if Leshikar had been brandishing a screwdriver when he entered the foyer of the house, Lavigne had no need to respond with deadly force. The field manual for the course he'd completed in hand-to-hand fighting, known in the Army as "combatives," specifically prepares unarmed soldiers to face an attacker with a knife, spike, shiv, or shank. Trainees are taught to grit their teeth, be "mentally prepared to be cut," and then use a "check and ride" or "check and lift" technique to gain the upper hand over an inrushing assailant. "Billy wouldn't just forget how to disarm somebody," said Nicole. "He was trained for that. If Mark ended up dead, Billy had to want it."

Had there been the prosecutorial will to charge Lavigne, the evidence would have supported a count of first-degree murder, which requires not lengthy premeditation but only a specific intent to kill another person, even if formed a split second before the act. If Lavigne had been a civilian or an ordinary Joe in the 82nd Airborne Division, he would have been extremely lucky, with the services of a skilled attorney, to get the charges against him reduced to manslaughter. Instead, county investigators feigned satisfaction with his flimsy claim of self-defense and immediately closed the case. The office of the district attorney, Billy West, deemed Leshikar's killing a justified homicide within a matter of hours. "They did the bare minimum of investigation," said Nicole. "Obviously, higher-ups had cut Billy some kind of deal."

Lavigne wasn't even subjected to a drug test. The authorities, intent on remaining willfully ignorant of his intoxicated state, omitted the normally routine step of administering a urinalysis or blood draw. "That's where the cover-up started," said Nicole.

Laura, who knew firsthand that Lavigne had been drinking and doing drugs all weekend, later confronted the sheriff of Cumberland County, Ennis Wright, and questioned him about this. "I asked him why no tox screen was done," Laura recalled. "He basically avoided the question."

Lavigne was allowed to walk out of the jailhouse a free man that same night. Waiting for him outside, in a menacing convoy of lifted pickups, was a group of his Delta Force teammates. "There were three trucks that pulled up to the street," said Laura. "A lot of team members or operators were out there."

It was a show of support for one of their own, but also a show of force, lest anyone in Fayetteville forget who they were: a covert troop of black-ops assassins that acts on direct orders from the highest echelons of the U.S. government. Their presence that evening was a reminder to anyone who needed reminding that the unit is a law unto itself and, as far as outsiders are concerned, doesn't even exist.

"They are a very hush-hush community," said Diane Ballard, the lone police detective in nearby Vass, the tiny town where many Delta

Force operators, active and retired, own homes. "They do what they want."

THE FOLLOWING DAY, the local NBC affiliate in Raleigh-Durham reported that "a Fort Bragg soldier," identified as Mark Leshikar, "was shot and killed during an altercation" in Fayetteville, but Lavigne wasn't named as the shooter. Lieutenant Sean Swain, a spokesman for the sheriff's office, told the reporter who wrote the story that no charges had been filed and that "investigators do not have a suspect."

In fact, Lavigne *had* been identified as a suspect, in writing, by Deputy Joshua LaFave. No uncertainty existed with respect to the identity of the responsible party, but Lavigne had already been cleared of wrongdoing and released. The case had been closed, but by referring to an unnamed "person of interest," Swain gave the false impression that an investigation remained ongoing.

Leshikar's mother, Tammy Mabey, was utterly contemptuous of the shoddy and aborted pretense of an investigation that the sheriff's office and district attorney did. "I was in law enforcement for eighteen years," she said. "I was never a detective, but even the limited crime scene investigation that I've done tells me that these guys are full of shit. Why in the hell would you just let some guy off on murder?"

Tammy is the first to admit that her son was a troubled man. "Did he have demons? Absolutely," she said. "Did he struggle with drugs, alcohol, tramadol, cocaine? Absolutely." But Mark Leshikar was a patriotic soldier, devoted father, faithful husband, and loving son. He didn't deserve to be killed or to have his death covered up by government officials. The shooting "was not self-defense," she insisted. "There is proof that he was shot from behind."

Laura went in person to the sheriff's office to request a copy of their case file, but they flatly refused to share it with her, citing the sanctity of police investigations and the privacy of victims. "Even though I'm

Mark Leshikar with his mother, Tammy Mabey,
on the day that his daughter was born.

the spouse," Laura said, "they told me to hire an attorney and try to get a judge's order." Otherwise the answer was no.

NOT LONG AFTER HIS DEATH, Leshikar's wife held a wake for him at a Fayetteville restaurant and bar called Carolina Ale House. "Jens was there," said Jordan Terrell, who went with his wife. "Mark's team was there. And they were all pissed."

The Green Berets from Leshikar's unit—A Company, 1st Battalion, 19th Special Forces Group—had traveled to North Carolina from Washington state to be at the memorial service. "They were sitting by themselves," said Terrell, so he went over to their table to offer his condolences. "They all got quiet," he said, regarded him coldly, and met his attempts to engage them in conversation with monosyllabic replies. "We're going to find out who fucking did this," one of them muttered, "and we're going to take care of it our way." The others grunted and murmured in assent.

Terrell awkwardly took leave of the disgruntled group of Special Forces reservists. At the other end of the bar, he saw Jens Merritt, drinking alone, keeping an eye on everything. "He wasn't talking to anybody," said Terrell. "He was just observing."

Terrell went to use the restroom, and one of Leshikar's teammates, drunk and in an aggressive state of mind, followed him in. "Who are you?" he demanded to know.

Terrell tried to play it cool. "Mark was like a mentor to me," he said. "We were friends."

"Are you with the unit?" asked the man from Washington, meaning Delta Force.

"No," said Terrell.

"Is that girl with you in the unit?"

"No," he said. "That's my wife."

"Do you have a bucktail on you? Are you recording this conversation?"

"No," Terrell said for a third time. "I'm in the 82nd, dude. I'm nobody."

This seemed to mollify Leshikar's teammate. Terrell was only twenty-seven and was black. Nine out of ten Delta Force soldiers are white and in their thirties. The man from Washington pulled Terrell in for a "bro handshake," but "when I dabbed him up," said Terrell, "he pulled me in and did a full body sweep while he was hugging me. He slid his hands down my back, and then around my butt, and checked my pockets."

"What the fuck are you doing?" Terrell said, grabbing the man's wrists and breaking free from his embrace. Terrell left the bathroom and told his wife that it was time to go, but before leaving, went over to Merritt and quietly relayed the implicit threats made by the National Guard soldiers. Merritt listened attentively but was inscrutably blasé about the situation. "Jens was a fucking enigma," said Terrell. "The dude's expression would never change. Ever."

At Leshikar's burial service, Merritt stood beside Laura in his Marine Corps uniform, "making sure I was keeping my head high," said Laura. Some of the men from 19th Group who were present grumbled at the usurpation of this role by a member of Delta Force, the organization that had fostered and protected the killer of the deceased, but Laura was grateful for Merritt's companionship. "Jens is one of the good ones," she said.

THE ARMY'S CRIMINAL Investigation Division, a quasi-military, quasi-civilian detective agency with jurisdiction to investigate crimes involving American soldiers, conducted a parallel investigation into Leshikar's death a year after the fact. The CID agents first told Laura, Nicole, and Tammy that they couldn't open their case until Cumberland County had closed theirs, which wasn't true. Then, after an extended period of additional delay, CID blamed the county for failing to collect sufficient evidence of Lavigne's guilt, leaving CID with no alternative but to adopt the district attorney's finding of justifiable homicide. "A waste of paper," is how Nicole described CID's report, which she received in heavily redacted form: block after block of black ink.

A less redacted version of the same document, obtained years later, shows that CID, rather than adopting the county's findings wholesale, rigged together an alternative but equally tendentious theory of justified homicide that hinged on the small handgun that had been locked in the glove compartment of the Honda Accord, a weapon that belonged to Laura Leshikar.

Army investigators noticed that in one photo of the crime scene Laura's gun, a diminutive 9-millimeter Glock 26, was sitting on the counter between the living room and the kitchen. The slide, which had a distinctive engraving of a star and a woman, was locked back, the chamber was empty, and no magazine was loaded. Another photo taken by the sheriff's office and examined by CID showed the Honda Accord's ignition keys inserted into the lock of the glove box. "This would be consistent if prior to his entrance into the residence," a CID agent wrote, "Leshikar obtained the pistol and placed it into his pocket."

The most obvious flaw in this hypothesis was that Lavigne never told anyone that Leshikar had threatened him with a firearm. When exactly the gun made its way from the car to the kitchen, and who moved it, remain a mystery. But at the moment of truth, under pressure to come up with a believable self-defense narrative, Lavigne had invented the story of the screwdriver, the sight of which was fresh in his memory from the fight in the driveway. At no time, then or later, did he say anything about Laura's pistol. So CID contrived to put the necessary testimony into the mouth of a child.

On March 8, 2019, CID agents interviewed Melanie Leshikar, now nearly seven, at the Child Advocacy Center in Fayetteville. The interview was done with Laura's consent, but she wasn't allowed to be present. Nor was she permitted to view the recording afterward. "We've requested that video so many times," said Nicole, "and nobody will give it to us."

The investigators, led by Special Agent Steve Chancellor, came out of the interview claiming that Melanie had told them that her father had been in possession of a gun when she let him in through the front door. "CID tried to say that Melanie told them that Mark had a gun," said Tammy. "And that's why they didn't further the investigation."

But Melanie repeatedly told her mother, grandmother, and aunt that her father *didn't* have a gun. To be precise, she'd said that "my daddy was a Special Forces soldier," and *usually* or *often* carried a gun, but *hadn't* been carrying one that day. "She didn't know why he didn't have a gun, because he always had a gun," Nicole recalled. "From the very beginning, that's all she would tell us."

Unable to view the video and denied access to CID's files, Laura, Nicole, and Tammy surmised that the agents who interviewed Melanie had taken these qualified statements or similar ones and twisted them around to figuratively plant a gun on Mark's dead body. Laura's Glock didn't figure into Lavigne's own narrative of the shooting or the medical examiner's firsthand report of the crime scene, but largely on the basis of Melanie's disputed testimony, CID concluded that "there is ample evidence" to believe that "Lavigne act[ed] in self-defense." On July 22, 2019, a USASOC prosecutor, a female captain, endorsed that conclusion and shut down the investigation.

Chris Grey, a spokesman for CID, said that the agency "rejects any notion that anything but a complete and unbiased investigation was conducted." However, like Cumberland County, he wouldn't answer the most basic questions about that investigation's factual findings, such as whether agents determined that Leshikar had a gun, screwdriver, or another weapon in his hand or on his person when Lavigne shot him.

Lavigne remained an active-duty operator in good standing on Delta Force. And his use and distribution of cocaine, which neither Cumberland County nor CID made any apparent effort to probe, not only continued but greatly increased, as did his mental illness, disillusionment, and propensity to violence. "Had it been properly looked into," said Nicole, "all the other bodies and drugs that have come in the past two and a half years could have been avoided."

Part II

Three

FAYETTENAM

The 1st Special Forces Operational Detachment—Delta, also known as the Combat Applications Group, or CAG, is generally considered to be the most selective organization in the entire Department of Defense. Colloquially known as Delta Force, the unit was founded in 1977 by a small number of Special Forces officers including Colonel Charles Beckwith, a bull-necked college football player from Georgia who took his inspiration from the British Special Air Service, or SAS.

During the Vietnam War, Beckwith served as an exchange officer with the SAS in Malaysia, where the British army waged a savage and indiscriminate war to put down anticolonial and communist resistance to imperial rule. Beckwith's time in Malaysia convinced him that the United States needed its own version of the SAS, which had sabotaged aircraft and blown up railroads behind Axis lines in World War II and evolved into a long-range reconnaissance and raiding force highly adept at ending the lives of problematic guerrilla leaders. Returning to Vietnam on the eve of the Tet Offensive, Beckwith led a prototypical U.S. Army unit called Project Delta, which penetrated deep into Vietcong territory to rescue prisoners of war, select bombing targets, install wiretaps, and emplace mines. The end of the Vietnam War led to a period of directionless malaise in the Special Forces, but the success of a daring raid to rescue hostages from a hijacked airplane in Uganda by the elite Israeli unit Sayeret Matkal in 1976, combined with heightened anxieties around international terrorism, provided the final impetus for American war planners to give the go-ahead to Beckwith's pet project. Delta Force became operational the following year, replacing an interim counterterrorism unit in the 5th Special Forces Group called Blue Light.

Made up of a few hundred select soldiers, many of whom were seasoned Vietnam veterans, Delta Force was originally intended to be a rarely used team of crack commandos to whom the president could turn in the event of a hostage crisis, terrorist attack, loose nuclear weapon, or another international incident requiring a tactically difficult, highly precise military response in which failure was not considered a realistic option. Yet the unit's first live mission, known as Operation Eagle Claw, was a catastrophic debacle that did grave damage to the presidency of the man who ordered it, Jimmy Carter.

After Iranian revolutionaries overran the U.S. embassy in Tehran and took scores of hostages, President Carter sent about a hundred Delta Force soldiers into the country to rescue the captives. But because the Army operators had to be supported by the Air Force, Navy, and Marine Corps for transport and logistics, the mission devolved into confusion and recrimination between commanders from each of the four service branches involved, and ended in disaster when one of the helicopters, blinded by a sandstorm, crashed into a transport plane loaded with jet fuel, causing an explosion that killed eight crewmen.

Six months later, Carter lost the 1980 presidential election to former California governor Ronald Reagan, who went on to preside over a transformation of America's special operations forces that broadened Delta Force's purview and laid the foundations for the secret killing machine that Billy Lavigne, born in 1983, would serve for the majority of his adult life. In retrospect, the creation of this Fort Bragg–based apparatus, the Joint Special Operations Command, or JSOC (pronounced "jay-SOCK"), was the most significant event in U.S. military history since the emergence of a permanent standing army following World War II. But at the time, it escaped all public notice. There was no ceremony to mark JSOC's official formation and no press release to announce the appointment of its first commander.

Delta Force has always been the core of JSOC, its center of gravity, and the source of most of its top officers. In 1980, the Pentagon formed a naval special mission unit called SEAL Team Six, with capabilities broadly similar to those of Delta Force but with more of an emphasis on maritime operations. An obscure Air Force unit known as the 24th Special Tactics Squadron supplied the command with pararescuemen, air traffic controllers, air-strike spotters, and long-range scouts. In addition, two existing Army special mission units were brought under the JSOC umbrella. One was the 160th Special Operations Aviation Regiment, staffed by experienced helicopter pilots skilled at the difficult and dangerous task of flying low to the ground in the darkness of night. The other was a shadowy surveillance and reconnaissance unit that's been variously known as the Field Operations Group, Gray Fox, the Army of Northern Virginia, the Intelligence Support Activity, or simply the Activity.

In the beginning, JSOC's commander was a relatively middling two-star general. Nevertheless, he answered directly to the chairman of the Joint Chiefs of Staff and the secretary of defense, who in turn answer directly to the president. Nowhere else in the armed forces will you find so abbreviated a chain of command, with just two or three links between the White House and shooters on the ground.

Within the military, a kind of creation myth has sprung up to explain the formation of JSOC at the outset of the Reagan administration as a direct response to the failure of Operation Eagle Claw. Cadets at West Point and lieutenant colonels pursuing graduate studies at the Army War College will inevitably learn from their PowerPoint presentations that the mission to rescue the hostages held at the Tehran embassy went sideways on account of the improvisatory nature of the task force dispatched to Iran, with its hasty mix of personnel and lack of a coherent command structure. In place of this unsightly gaggle, the official story goes, JSOC took shape directly under the wing of the secretary of defense to provide the president with a vertically integrated, full-spectrum, counterterrorism strike force ready to deploy at a moment's notice.

This pat narrative, a sort of morality tale intended to illustrate the cherished principle of joint warfare, is not factually inaccurate. But neither does it exclude another, alternative manner of understanding the creation, at this juncture in American history, of a secret military within the military.

In the 1970s, the Central Intelligence Agency's reputation was at its lowest ebb ever. Investigative reporting and congressional hearings revealed that the agency had presided over the Phoenix Program in Vietnam, a ghoulish mass assassination and torture campaign that left tens of thousands of suspected communist sympathizers dead. The epidemic of heroin abuse among American soldiers in Vietnam had also been traced back, in part, to the CIA's secret war in Laos and support for anticommunist proxy forces that funded their operations by trafficking opium. In 1975, the Senate convened the Church Committee, which exposed some of the most egregious abuses in the CIA's history, including murder plots against foreign leaders, domestic spying on antiwar dissidents, torture of prisoners, collaboration with Nazi war criminals, and twisted mind-control experiments with psychedelic drugs. A number of reforms resulted, including the establishment of standing intelligence committees in the House and Senate. The CIA was banned from conducting political assassinations, and henceforth its clandestine actions had to be authorized by a type of executive order known as a presidential finding. New laws also required the CIA to brief certain congressional leaders on its activities, which had previously been kept concealed from the legislative branch.

The Senate Select Committee on Intelligence formed in May 1976. Its counterpart in the House of Representatives formed in July 1977.

Delta Force, which specializes in reconnaissance and eavesdropping as much as it does in lethal direct action, was activated four months later. The Intelligence Oversight Act, which mandates CIA reporting to a group of eight Republican and Democratic legislators, passed in June 1980. Six months later, JSOC came into existence.

Congressional regulation of covert action is a complex legal subject pervaded by ambiguities, but as a general matter the clandestine activities of the military are less subject to scrutiny than those of civilian agencies. Much regulatory legislation is written specifically to apply to the CIA and makes no mention of the Department of Defense, despite the military having robust spying capabilities of its own, not to mention far more money and manpower. In addition, congressional and judicial deference are at their highest with respect to the president in his powers as commander in chief, which some "unitary executive" legal theorists believe cannot be abrogated at all.

These niceties of law and regulation were largely lost on President Reagan, a politician more distinguished by his television presentation skills than the depth of his intellect. But Reagan's vice president, George Herbert Walker Bush, was a canny bureaucratic operator, the ultimate insider in the world of intelligence. In the aftermath of the Church Committee, Bush was the man tapped to implement reforms as director of the CIA, an institution to which he had deep ties. In 1980, he ran against Reagan in the Republican primary and lost, then joined his ticket as vice president. Bush's subsequent tenure in the Executive Building coincided with a transfer of power from the CIA to the military, which, thanks to the creation of JSOC, now had operatives fully capable of carrying out the same skulduggery as civilian spies, but without the added baggage of congressional meddling.

Over the next eight years, as Reagan and Bush waged off-the-books dirty wars in Nicaragua, El Salvador, and Guatemala, and also intervened in Colombia, Haiti, and Grenada, the administration leaned heavily on Delta Force and other undercover soldiers. The militarization of covert action was tied up with the rapidly metastasizing "global war on drugs," another brainchild of George H. W. Bush's, and partially exposed by the hydra-headed Iran-Contra Affair, the essence of which was the use of illegal arms deals and the sale of other untraceable commodities to fund secret operations. A classified White House memorandum that Reagan signed in 1984 reads like a sketchy blueprint to the "global war on terror" that Bush's son and political heir would institute at the dawn of the twenty-first century. Among other things, the memo authorized killing in "preemptive self-defense," so long as the targets were defined as "terrorists."

That same Orwellian year, *The New York Times* belatedly broke the news of JSOC's existence. The article, titled "U.S. Military Creates Secret Units for Use in Sensitive Tasks Abroad," was sourced to members of Congress and intelligence committee staffers. "The worry," concerned lawmakers told the *Times*, was that JSOC might become "a uniformed version of the Central Intelligence Agency," used by the executive branch "to circumvent Congressional restrictions and reporting requirements."

The *Times* learned that JSOC was "mostly a nighttime operation," with "its own weapons procurement and research, as well as communications," and that JSOC operators "dress in civilian clothes," train at unmarked installations on private property, and "are permitted to have long hair and beards."

The black-ops commando units that made up JSOC were created to fight terrorism "but have acquired broader mandates," the article continued. These included participation in "covert operations in Central America," specifically, "aid to Nicaraguan rebels," a criminal rabble of right-wing drug traffickers and hit men known as the contras, who partly funded their fight against socialism in Central America by smuggling cocaine from Colombia through Mexico to the United States, which at the time was experiencing a boom in the consumption of a new form of coke known as crack.

A number of Democratic legislators were said to be disturbed by JSOC's arrogation of secret powers and its apparent willingness to carry out clandestine actions without informing Congress. "We are aware of the existence of the special operations units," the then-senator Joe Biden told the *Times*, "but not sufficiently informed about their activities." He added, "We are trying to learn more."

MAJOR REORGANIZATION of the armed forces continued throughout Reagan's presidency. JSOC is a combatant command, an organization that exists to direct live missions, and in 1987 was placed inside a larger umbrella formation, a stateside administrative body called the Special Operations Command, or SOCOM, based at MacDill Air Force Base in Florida.

At the time, many in the Pentagon resisted the creation of SOCOM. They feared that it would siphon off talent and resources from the Army, Navy, Air Force, and Marine Corps, and that it would become, in effect, a fifth service branch, one that stood head and shoulders above the rest.

The formation of SOCOM consolidated black-ops JSOC at the top of a four-tier pyramid of special operations personnel whose total number started out around thirty-five thousand and has since grown to approximately seventy thousand—the size of the whole British army. SOCOM's second tier is made up of so-called white special forces, who might number ten thousand in total: the Army's seven Green Beret groups, spread across the country; the Navy's active-duty SEAL teams on the Pacific and Atlantic coasts; and the 75th Ranger Regiment, an elite light infantry troop headquartered at Fort Benning, Georgia. The third tier of SOCOM consists of a large number of active-duty soldiers, sailors, airmen, and marines in support roles, especially military intelligence, psychological operations, and civil affairs. Fourth but by no means least numerous are SOCOM's legions of civilian employees and contractors.

At the head of this reorganized military body, the Pentagon placed a civilian official in a newly created assistant secretary of defense position whose power is analogous to but a cut above the secretary of the Army, Navy, or Air Force. The first person to hold the job at the apex of SOCOM was Charles S. Whitehouse, an old CIA hand who had been one year ahead of Vice President Bush at Yale, where both were members of the secret society known as Skull and Bones.

IN 1988, "Poppy" Bush was elected president, becoming the first and only former director of the CIA to command the armed forces. The following year, he ordered JSOC to invade Panama in order to depose and abduct the Panamanian strong man Manuel Noriega, a key broker in the Latin American drug trade who had been an important client of Bush's back when he was head of the CIA, but lost the tacit approval of the Americans to traffic narcotics internationally after he began cozying up to Fidel Castro's Cuba. Delta Force and JSOC took part in the Persian Gulf War of 1991 to drive the invading Iraqi army out of Kuwait, but were kept on a short leash by General Norman Schwarzkopf, the theater commander, a Vietnam veteran who maintained an old-school aversion to Navy SEALs and Green Berets, whom he saw as undisciplined, throat-slitting, ear-collecting rogues with an unhealthy odor of the Laotian jungle still lingering about them.

In 1993, a botched helicopter-borne abduction raid in Mogadishu, Somalia, left six Delta Force soldiers dead. The fallout from the incident, dramatized in the book *Black Hawk Down* and a film adaption by the same name, forever tarnished JSOC in the eyes of President Bill Clinton, the former governor of Arkansas who'd won an upset victory over Bush in the preceding year's presidential election. The only other time that Delta Force attracted any significant press attention during Clinton's two terms as president also occurred in 1993, but stateside, in the midst of the federal siege of a cult compound in Waco, Texas. It was a curious cameo that showcased the unit's deft touch at public relations and ability to get out in front of potentially damaging stories.

The FBI and ATF had surrounded the religious compound, situated in the Texas countryside north of Austin, and demanded that the Branch Davidians, a splinter group of Seventh-Day Adventists, give up a stockpile of weapons that they'd hoarded in anticipation of Judgment Day. After a lengthy standoff in which the members of the apocalyptic offshoot church refused to surrender their guns and ammo, the federal agents moved in with surprisingly aggressive tactics, making use of heavy machine guns, armored personnel carriers, and even tanks. Amid the resulting gun battle, scores of people burned to death, including dozens of women and children.

One of the harshest critics of the government's conduct of the raid was none other than Colonel Charles Beckwith, Delta Force's founder, then in his mid-sixties and retired. "It's crazy to shoot people like this," Beckwith told *The New York Times* while the siege was still ongoing. "I'm just embarrassed that we live in a society where our government allows something like this to happen."

A full six years later, it emerged that, notwithstanding the Posse Comitatus Act, which bars the military from acting in a domestic law enforcement capacity, Delta Force operators had played a key part in the assault on the compound, known as Mount Carmel. The Pentagon said that the commandos had been there only as observers, but a congressional committee began looking into the matter of who fired certain heat-generating gas canisters into the compound before it caught fire. Declassified SOCOM documents showed that the Delta Force contingent had been in Waco for more than a month in advance of the raid. Photos in the custody of the Texas Rangers showed the Army operators wearing body armor and face paint, as if ready for battle.

No sooner had the FBI agreed to an outside inquiry in the first week of September 1999, than *The New York Times* ran an editorial by a wall-eyed former CIA officer named Charles McCarry, who declared that the questions around Waco would remain "forever unresolved." Quoting Alexis de Tocqueville, McCarry advised America's "bluff rustics" not to indulge in "conspiracy theories . . . including unsubstantiated rumors that Delta Force troopers in body armor and camouflage face paint were present," even though there was photographic evidence of just that, and the Pentagon had already admitted it. Nevertheless, Mc-Carry admonished, "enlightenment is not always in the details."

FORMER TEXAS GOVERNOR George Walker Bush, the eldest son of George H. W. Bush, became president in January 2001. Eight months later, a group of nineteen terrorists, fifteen of whom were from Saudi Arabia, hijacked four civilian airliners, crashed two of them into the World Trade Center in the financial district of New York City and steered another into the western face of the Pentagon, while a fourth was brought down over a field in Pennsylvania, killing nearly three thousand people in less than two hours.

The 9/11 attacks were, among other things, a species of blowback from a covert war that President Reagan and Poppy Bush had waged in the 1980s in Afghanistan. The purpose of the CIA-led campaign in Afghanistan, made famous in the book *Charlie Wilson's War* and the film of the same title, was to drive out Russian occupiers who had invaded to prop up a communist regime in the waning days of the Cold War. One of the most consequential figures in this long-running clandestine mission, known as Operation Cyclone, was an Egyptian-born sergeant in the U.S. Army Special Forces named Ali Abdul Saoud Mohamed, an athletic, energetic, and charismatic man fluent in Arabic, English, and Hebrew, who was stationed at Fort Bragg but traveled widely during his U.S. military career.

Ali Mohamed, born in 1952, was an Egyptian special forces officer. In 1980, while attending a program for foreign army officers at the John F. Kennedy Special Warfare Center and School at Fort Bragg, he was approached by the CIA, and soon became an asset of the agency. The following year, he joined Egyptian Islamic Jihad, a radical fundamentalist group led by an Egyptian doctor named Ayman al-Zawahiri. Ali Mohamed would remain a close associate of al-Zawahiri, an infamous terrorist mastermind, for the next seventeen years.

In 1984, with CIA sponsorship, Ali Mohamed moved to the United States on a type of national security visa reserved for aliens whose admission into the country is "essential to the furtherance of the national intelligence mission," and obtained citizenship by marrying an American woman ten years his senior. He then returned to Fayetteville and joined the Special Forces, becoming an active-duty U.S. Army soldier at the age of thirty-four. Despite his relatively advanced age, he reportedly set an Army record for the two-mile run.

While serving on active duty, Ali Mohamed repeatedly traveled to Afghanistan to fight the Russians alongside anticommunist Afghan resistance fighters known as mujahideen, who were armed and funded by the CIA through Saudi and Pakistani cutouts. He also associated with the al-Kifah Refugee Center at the Al Farooq Mosque in Brooklyn, which recruited Muslim immigrants to serve in the CIA's war, and later became a petri dish out of which the anti-American terrorist group al-Qaeda grew. During Operation Cyclone, which was funded in substantial part by Saudi oil revenues, radical Islam was mobilized to motivate the guerrillas to wage war on the godless Soviet army, with Saudi money used to construct religious schools known as madrassas on the border with Pakistan. Bandar bin Sultan, a profoundly wealthy Saudi prince known as Bandar Bush due to his extraordinarily close ties to the Bush family and who for decades served as a D.C. power broker and intermediary in off-the-books American operations, supplied hundreds of millions of dollars and was an equal partner with the CIA in arming and funding the Afghan jihad. Another of the money bundlers was Osama bin Laden, the pious scion of a Saudi construction empire, who had roads built in remote areas to facilitate weapons deliveries.

The Russians withdrew from Afghanistan in 1989, and for the next five years the country suffered under the chaotic misrule of disputatious warlords. Once in control of Afghanistan's major population centers, the formerly CIA-backed mujahideen, chief among them Gulbuddin Hekmatyar and Nasim Akhundzada, turned Afghanistan into a giant plantation for the cultivation of the opium poppy plant, which is perfectly suited to certain hot and dry but well-irrigated regions of the country, notably a vast endorheic basin known as the Helmand. Infighting between the narco-warlords over control of lucrative trafficking routes made them unpopular with the Afghan people, who chafed at being forced into conditions of narco-serfdom in which they were obligated to grow poppy instead of food crops, as well as other systematic abuses, including the kidnapping and rape of children, especially little boys, whom the pederastic warlords kept as cross-dressed sex slaves.

The Taliban, a puritanical movement of Islamic scholars and students of religion, emerged in 1994 as a reaction to the fractious and iniquitous mujahideen, many of whom hailed from Uzbekistan and Tajikistan. After consolidating power over all but the heavily Tajik north of Afghanistan, the primarily Pashtun Taliban implemented a severely intolerant brand of sharia law. The Taliban are rightly condemned worldwide for their restrictions on women's freedoms, but their popularity in Afghanistan mainly stemmed from their tough-on-crime policies. The Taliban forbade poppy cultivation; *bacha bazi*, or boy play; suppressed kidnapping; and in the summer of 2001 completed a countrywide eradication campaign that radically reduced the world supply of heroin. One expert called it "the most dramatic event in the history of illegal drug markets."

Meanwhile, Ali Mohamed had shifted his focus from anticommunist guerrilla warfare to anti-American suicide terrorism. In 1989, he transferred from active duty to the U.S. Army Reserves. For the next five years, while still a member of the American armed forces, he shuttled among the United States, Afghanistan, Kenya, and Somalia, making a total of fifty-eight trips abroad, usually carrying armloads of classified Special Forces manuals and maps from Fort Bragg. "The manuals were issued to him," said a former Delta Force commander, "while he was serving as a member of the U.S. Army Special Forces."

During the 1990s, Ali Mohamed worked tirelessly to provide the nascent al-Qaeda, formed by a merger between Osama bin Laden and

Ayman al-Zawahiri, with expert training in the methods of irregular and asymmetric warfare taken from the Green Berets. Ali Mohamed taught the core leaders of al-Qaeda and their devotees how to create cell structures for operations, use and decrypt codes, kidnap targets, perpetrate assassinations, make bombs, and hijack aircraft by such methods as smuggling box cutters on board. He personally trained Osama bin Laden, and bin Laden's whole security detail, while staying at bin Laden's house in Peshawar, Pakistan. He literally wrote the al-Qaeda training manual, based on the indoctrination he'd received in the pine woods of North Carolina. All the while, Ali Mohamed was regularly receiving money from an unknown source. His movements and phone calls were monitored by an agency of the U.S. government. He was detained in 1993 by Royal Canadian Mounted Police at the airport in Vancouver, but released at the behest of the FBI. In 1997, federal prosecutor Patrick Fitzgerald, the head of a Department of Justice counterterrorism unit in the Southern District of New York, took Ali Mohamed out to dinner and learned from him that al-Qaeda planned to launch an imminent attack on the United States.

In 1998, Ali Mohamed, who at times used the alias Abu Osama, or Father of Osama, was one of the al-Qaeda conspirators who bombed a pair of U.S. embassies in East Africa, an act of indiscriminate mass murder that killed hundreds of people in Kenya and Tanzania. At that point, his American handlers reeled him in, arrested him, secured his guilty plea on charges of conspiracy to commit terrorism in closed-door, anonymized federal court proceedings, then forever disappeared him into the bowels of the U.S. government without his ever having been formally sentenced.

But Ali Mohamed's protégés went on carrying out devastating acts of spectacular violence. Already, in 1993, several of his mentees from the al-Kifah Refugee Center in Brooklyn had bombed the World Trade Center in Manhattan. In 2000, his former Saudi trainee Abd al-Rahim al-Nashiri masterminded a suicide attack on the USS *Cole*, an American naval destroyer moored off the coast of Yemen. The following year, just five months after the Taliban successfully eradicated poppy from Afghanistan, al-Qaeda pulled off its most audacious and destructive attack yet, striking at the very heart of America's military and financial institutions, killing more people than the Japanese had at Pearl Harbor. At least two of the fifteen Saudi hijackers—mostly uneducated young men who spoke little or no English—had received immigration assistance, safe reception in the United States, money, cell phones, transportation, housing, and religious counsel from an intelligence agent and a Saudi diplomat in the employ of Bandar bin Sultan.

In preparing the United States' military response to 9/11, which the Bush administration blamed primarily on Osama bin Laden, Delta Force sent a top commander, a Special Forces officer named Pete Blaber, to interview Ali Mohamed at a secret maximum-security prison "located smack in the middle of a sprawling urban metropolis," Blaber writes in his 2008 memoir, "ten feet from a newspaper stand bustling with businesspersons." Ali Mohamed, whose true loyalties remain a matter of speculation, was not listed in the Bureau of Prisons' registry of inmates, and the case against him was never unsealed. His current whereabouts are unknown.

IT WAS THE AMORPHOUS, peripatetic, nonstate character of al-Qaeda that enabled the Bush administration to declare a global war on terror, as it was branded, unbound from any geographic region and unconstrained by existing laws and norms. The GWOT (pronounced "gee-WATT") was conceived of as an unconventional war, to be waged by the sorts of special operations forces that don't wear uniforms and whose brutal methods might make civilians squeamish. Since al-Qaeda might be hiding anywhere, the thinking went, the United States was justified in deploying covert military operatives to wherever it chose, to do whatever they saw fit in "preemptive self-defense"—in the language of the 1984 Reagan-Bush memo—to eliminate the threat.

In the fall of 2001, President Bush signed a secret order that restored the CIA's authority to carry out assassinations. That October and November, an irregular task force of paramilitary CIA officers, Delta Force soldiers, and other JSOC operators, charged with avenging 9/11, inserted into the rugged north of Afghanistan, hard against Tajikistan, where many of the deposed mujahideen warlords had taken refuge and where poppy growing, opium harvesting, and heroin processing still flourished. Pete Blaber, in command of a Delta Force team, writes in his memoir of being viscerally appalled by some of the lurid thugs and flamboyant pedophiles among the war criminals, ex-communists, smugglers, and drug traffickers with whom the United States teamed up to take on the Taliban. "The guard on my right immediately gave me pause," Blaber recalls of his first meeting with an unnamed Afghan warlord, whose bearing and attire he likens to a heavily armed drag queen. "A black charcoal substance coated his eyelids, and his unnaturally pursed lips were coated with some kind of pink, gooey substance."

With such allies as these, whom Blaber describes as "land pirates," JSOC and the CIA formed a ragtag coalition, the so-called Northern Alliance, which with the backing of Air Force bombers routed the Taliban from Kabul, the capital of Afghanistan, and chased Osama bin Laden and his followers into the steep, icy, nearly impassable White Mountains on the border with Pakistan. Notwithstanding bin Laden's narrow escape, many people in America believed that the war in Afghanistan was effectively over. That one of the first official acts of the newly installed, U.S.-backed Afghan government was to legalize poppy planting went all but unremarked in the Western press.

IN THE SPRING OF 2002, most of the Delta Force soldiers and other Green Berets who had fought with the Northern Alliance redeployed to Fort Bragg. What followed was an early indication of the kind of stateside blowback that would impact Fayetteville at the tail end of the global war declared by the United States, as well as another illustration of Delta Force's signature alacrity in waging information warfare.

That summer, in a stretch of just six weeks, four Army wives at Fort Bragg were murdered by their husbands, three of whom were Special Forces soldiers just back from Afghanistan. Sergeant First Class Brandon Floyd, a thirty-year-old Delta Force operator who had helped overthrow the Taliban, shot and killed his wife, Andrea, then himself, in the master bedroom of their house in rural Cumberland County.

A writer for the Norfolk *Virginian-Pilot* with a knack for regional history wrote of how the spate of killings revived Fayetteville's reputation as "a rough military town with a penchant for bizarre murders." Fatalville, Fatalburg, and Fayettenam were among the nicknames that rueful locals had given their city, he wrote, citing the just-published book *Homefront* by the anthropology professor Catherine Lutz. She described Fayetteville as "a dumping ground for the problems of the American century of war and empire, where the wounds of war have pierced most deeply and are most visible," including elevated levels of poverty, inequality, homelessness, racism, pollution, prostitution, and gender violence, as well as widespread drug use, which many of Lutz's interviewees, who came from all walks of life, blamed on "soldiers or veterans who bring narcotrafficking knowledge and contacts back with them from Asian and Latin American tours."

Andrea Floyd's mother, Penny Flitcraft, told a small-town Ohio paper that service in Delta Force had turned her son-in-law into a violent control freak. "His training," she said, "was such that if you can't control it, you kill it."

A very different narrative took root and spread, though, in the national press. The series of wife killings at Fort Bragg gave rise to an incredibly weird theory, completely without basis in medical science, that the antimalarial drug mefloquine, sold under the brand name Lariam, was to blame. This disinformation, a distraction from the moral cost of the war in Afghanistan and the connection between American militarism and violence against women, was fed to reporters for United Press International by anonymous USASOC officials.

"A source close to members of the secret Delta Force said Wednesday that [Brandon Floyd] had taken Lariam in Afghanistan," read the earliest article on the subject. A rash of subsequent UPI articles, entirely sourced to unnamed Special Forces officers, whose unfounded claims were repeated by the Associated Press, *The New York Times*, the *Chicago Tribune*, *The Boston Globe*, and the *Los Angeles Times*, as well as leading newspapers around the world, strongly implied or stated outright that all four of the Fort Bragg wife killers had undergone dramatic personality changes after being administered mefloquine. "Aggression, paranoia, psychosis, hallucinations," and unusual anger and incoherence were among the spooky effects that Lariam was said to induce. The commander of a Green Beret who had strangled his wife told UPI that "he himself sometimes experienced increased anger because of Lariam."

Mefloquine has been controversial ever since. The manufacturer of Lariam has repeatedly been sued. Australia and Germany are among the countries that no longer administer it to their troops, owing to fears that it could cause homicidal psychosis. The medication's alleged criminogenic properties, however, are a pure figment of media spin, disseminated by expert practitioners of psychological operations. "Fort Bragg's deadly summer," as it was dubbed in a 2002 *Vanity Fair* article, could not be explained away by the effects of a malaria drug. The rash of killings was a manifestation of a dark and complex pattern that would be seen again and again at Fort Bragg in the years that followed.

Four

DON'T CALL ME YOUR HUSBAND

During the very same week that Billy Lavigne enlisted, in February 2001, American warplanes were bombing radar stations across Iraq in preparation for a wider war that many people in government and media devoutly hoped and prayed would soon come about, but the strikes garnered little attention in the press. When Lavigne raised his right hand and swore an oath to defend the Constitution from all enemies foreign and domestic, no particular prestige was attached to the act of joining up, and few new recruits expected to actually fight in a full-scale war.

William Joseph Lavigne II was born and raised in Michigan's Delta County, one of the coldest and most remote regions of the United States. A land of dark winters, abundant lakes, pebbly freshwater beaches, and humid summers ridden with biting flies, known for the taciturnity and self-abnegation of its people, many of whom are of Germanic or Nordic stock, this area of Michigan is called the Upper Peninsula, or UP for short. "Yoopers," said Ben Boden, Lavigne's closest childhood friend, in his strong midwestern accent. "That's what they call people from here."

In a photo taken December 24, 1999, sixteen-year-old Billy stands at the center of his extended family in front of a Christmas tree laden with ornaments. He's tall for his age, with wide shoulders and long limbs, but still a child compared with the corn-fed menfolk in the picture, three out of four of whom have not removed their baseball caps for the holiday portrait.

"He was a great son," his mother said. "He was never a bad kid. Never a disrespectful teenager. He was goofy, he was silly, he was fun. He was all of those things."

The elder William Lavigne was a strict father, stilted but sincere in his rare displays of affection. Asked to describe his firstborn in a single word, he thought for a minute. "Busy," he said. "Always busy. Lots of skateboarding, motocross. Him and his brother," who was two years younger, "were always doing something."

As an adolescent, Lavigne was gangly, awkward, and a slow learner. "We bonded," Boden said, "over both sucking at school." Lavigne was also intensely self-conscious about his physical appearance. "He had something going on with his eyes," said Boden. "They were kind of crossed."

Lavigne could see all right, but was afflicted with a common form of strabismus in which one eye points inward, toward the nose. The condition is easily corrected, but the surgical procedure is costly and his parents lacked the means to afford the services of a skilled ophthalmologist. "People made fun of him," said Boden. "He knew what it was to be picked on."

The Army's Warfighter Refractive Eye Surgery Program was instituted shortly before Lavigne enlisted. The original intent behind the program was to decrease dependence on eyeglasses and contact lenses among service members, but the prospect of free corrective eye surgery, commonly known by the brand name Lasik, proved to be a tremendous recruiting boon in a country where the poor and working class are largely excluded from participation in the medical economy. Opthalmologists working for the Department of Defense have performed some 750,000 eye surgeries under the program in the last twenty years, and Lavigne's was among the very first. The procedure instantly fixed what had been one of his deepest childhood insecurities.

The 9/11 attacks occurred after Lavigne had graduated from boot camp but while he was still in advanced individual training, or AIT, in which soldiers learn the basics of their chosen military occupational specialty. Then a lowly private second class, Lavigne had no way of knowing that the ensuing armed conflict would last for twenty years and span half the globe. But having signed up to be a cavalry scout, a soldier who patrols at the head of a troop formation to reconnoiter enemy movements, he certainly understood that he would soon be going to war, and that he would be on the front lines of the fighting.

A YEAR OR SO LATER, Ben Boden was drinking a beer at a forlorn little sports bar in frozen Gladstone when he felt a tap on his shoulder. He turned around and this huge dude, built like a towering linebacker, was looming over him. "Oh, great," Boden said to himself, thinking he was about to get a beatdown from the burly stranger. Only then did he recognize his old friend, who was on leave from the Army.

"I didn't expect him to have that kind of physical transformation," Boden recalled. Lavigne had bulked up so much that he actually looked to have grown a few inches in height. "I only recognized him," Boden said, "because he had very distinctive eyes."

Cured of strabismus, Lavigne's blue eyes had become his most appealing feature. "He was really cute," said Jamie Carter, a bartender who worked in Tacoma, Washington, outside Fort Lewis, where Lavigne was first stationed. "He had short blond hair," she said, which he wore buzzed on the sides and raked forward in the front, in the style of the early '00s. "He was tall, not skinny, not big," she said, "but built."

Once a thriving rail terminus and mill town, Tacoma is now a rusting old port city on the Puget Sound, deindustrialized and economically depressed, with few major employers apart from the military. "Washington is disgusting," said Jamie, who later relocated to the Southwest desert. "Nine months of rain and cloudy, dark skies. Nothing to do except go to a bar or do drugs."

One of her friends, a fellow bartender, was dating a guy in the Army, and on cold, drizzly evenings in the fall of 2003 he and his crew of fresh-faced, badly dressed, off-duty soldiers—good-looking in spite of their severe haircuts—would crowd into the TGI Fridays to eat potato skins and mozzarella sticks, guzzle beer by the gallon, and attempt to flirt with the hostesses and servers. Lavigne had his eye on blond, buxom Jamie Carter, but was still too shy to talk to girls. "Anytime anyone spoke to him," she said, "you could see the automatic flush of his cheeks."

It was up to Jamie to take the initiative, which she did. A picture taken around this time shows them standing in front of the wet black stones of a dark waterfall, awkwardly hugging. Another dimly lit photo depicts them sitting on a beige couch in a dingy apartment, eating out of a big bag of Fritos. Soon they had become boyfriend and girlfriend.

THROUGHOUT THIS EIGHTEEN-MONTH PERIOD, while Lavigne was learning the muddy ropes as a junior trooper in 1st Squadron of the 14th Cavalry Regiment, the Bush administration, together with its many friends and allies in the Democratic Party, was working to persuade the American people to support a much bigger war than Afghanistan had been. Through their agents and collaborators in the corporate media, they concocted and propagated an elaborate conspiracy theory according to which Saddam Hussein, the dictator of Iraq, was in league with al-Qaeda and actively working to develop chemical, biological, and nuclear weapons.

It was true that the Iraqi regime had had a weapons of mass destruction program in the past but had abandoned it after being routed in the Persian Gulf War. International inspectors searched Iraq and found no active WMD programs, and Saddam Hussein affirmed, truthfully, that the last vestiges of such research and development had been destroyed more than a decade earlier. As for Saddam's alleged collaboration with Osama bin Laden, it was a risible fabrication never supported by the slightest credible evidence. Nevertheless, the American ruling class, hubristically desirous of war on a grand scale, psyched themselves into believing that Saddam was now on the cusp of obtaining an atomic bomb, necessitating urgent action to depose him in "preemptive self-defense" before he carried out or enabled another massive terrorist attack like 9/11. The United Nations declined to put its imprimatur on an authorization for the use of military force, but Congress was an easy sell. On March 19, 2003, Bush ordered the launch of the invasion.

Lavigne's orders to deploy were cut in early November. One week before he was due to ship out, he asked Jamie Carter to marry him. The proposal took her completely by surprise, but she said yes. "That weekend," she recalled, "I got myself a nice skirt and shirt. Monday we made a court appointment."

They went to the Pierce County auditor's office, filled out an application, and received a marriage license. Lavigne wore a white button-up shirt tucked into a pair of khaki Dockers for the occasion, while Jamie wore the simple white outfit she'd bought. In a photo of the swearing ceremony, taken in an office cubicle, she is so overcome with emotion that she has her hand clasped over her mouth. Four days later, on November 11, Lavigne boarded a plane bound for Iraq, not to return again for one year.

A REPORTER FOR THE TACOMA *News Tribune* caught up with a squad of soldiers from Lavigne's brigade in December, in the Iraqi city of Samarra. The cavalrymen complained of being shot at frequently, and also griped about the characteristic "moondust" of the Salah al-Din province, which the reporter aptly described as "blowing dirt that accumulates when it's dry" and "turns into a slippery layer of glop" in wet weather.

The article was pretty typical of American media coverage of the Iraq War at the time. It portrayed the citizens of Samarra as immensely grateful to U.S. troops for liberating them from the cruel tyranny of

Saddam Hussein and was blind to the fierce nationalist resentment that the mismanaged occupation had provoked. The same day the story was published, on Christmas Eve 2003, a roadside bomb killed three American soldiers just outside Samarra.

Insurgents picked off three more U.S. troops in Samarra in April and May, and another six in the first days of July. Occupation forces withdrew to the outskirts of the hot, dusty, trash-strewn city and established themselves in sandbagged bases on the other side of the wide, green, sluggish Tigris, but homemade bombs continued to wreak havoc on their lumbering convoys. Eight more soldiers, including two women, died in the vicinity of Samarra later in July and scorching August, all killed by these remotely detonated explosive devices.

The situation was similar all over Iraq. Armed resistance had arisen across the country. In the Shiite south, militias with ties to Iran tested the ability of American and British troops to maintain control of An Najaf, Karbalā', and Al 'Amārah. In the Sunni heartland of the Tigris and Euphrates Rivers, a guerrilla campaign led by former Iraqi army officers embittered over the dissolution of the Iraqi state inflicted grievous casualties through a strategy of deliberately targeting support troops and civilian contractors, weakening the United States' political will to sustain the occupation.

Twenty-one-year-old Lavigne was caught up in some of the most intense fighting that American soldiers had seen since Vietnam. His squadron of the 14th Cavalry Regiment served as the reconnaissance arm of a mechanized infantry brigade that was based on a new type of armored vehicle known as a Stryker. On September 4, 2004, a troop from his squadron took part in a complex battle to rescue downed helicopter pilots after a rocket-propelled grenade hit a Kiowa in Tal Afar. Five days later, another patrol from his squadron took fire in Mosul, then located and detained the shooters. On October 11, a suicide bomber plowed a truck full of explosives into a Stryker in Mosul, killing a thirty-four-year-old staff sergeant, the fifth of Lavigne's comrades to die during their yearlong deployment.

ONE MONTH LATER, the cavalry regiment's tour came to an end. Lavigne returned to Washington state around Thanksgiving Day. To Jamie Carter, he seemed to be a changed man. "He definitely did not come home the same person," she said. "He was not who I had married."

Lavigne's blushing, boyish demeanor had become harder and more serious. Gone was the goofy half smile that had perpetually lingered around the corners of his mouth. "That innocence was completely wiped from him," Jamie said.

It wasn't just that his external deportment had turned stony and cold. He'd also become inexplicably indifferent, even hostile, toward his wife. Anticipating his return, she had bought belated birthday gifts and early Christmas presents, and chosen a nice outfit to wear to the regiment's homecoming ceremony. But Lavigne, for some unknown reason, wouldn't allow her to attend. Instead, she picked him up that night, after the ceremony was over, waiting in the darkness at the front gate of Fort Lewis with his footlocker and duffel bag.

It was not the joyful reunion that she had imagined. They drove in near silence back to her apartment, where they had sex. Immediately afterward, he turned to her and said, "I don't want to be with you anymore. I want a divorce."

Jamie was dumbfounded. "Here I am, twenty-one years old," she said, "trying to support someone overseas," only for him to come home and say, "Don't call me your husband. I don't know why we got married."

Short-lived marriages are common among lower-enlisted soldiers. Since married men and women receive significantly more in salary and housing stipends than single service members, marriage fraud is widespread throughout the ranks of junior troopers. Sham marriages are especially likely to take place before deployments, because combat pay and exemption from federal income taxation increase the financial stakes.

Lavigne never explained himself to Jamie Carter. The only thing approximating a reason that he gave her for wanting a divorce was that he'd resolved to join the Special Forces. Whatever he'd gone through during the first of what would be at least three deployments to Iraq, he was left with the fixed intention of becoming a Green Beret. To that end, he couldn't have a woman "holding him back as baggage," he told her.

Jamie saw that it was pointless to argue. She didn't beg or vow to follow him to the ends of the earth. It was clear that he wanted her out of his life. But in the month that followed, she avoided him and made excuses so that she wouldn't have to sign the divorce paperwork.

During this interregnum, Lavigne showed his changed personality, which had become more dominant, assertive, and lacking in empathy, by sleeping with one of her friends. "That was out of character," said Jamie. "I don't think he would have done that before." She added, "We were still married."

Jamie had quit her job at TGI Fridays and was now slinging drinks at a nearby pool hall called Longhorn Saloon. One night the other girl, who "wasn't even cute," in Jamie's opinion, came in with a group of Lavigne's buddies and had the effrontery to place an order with her. That was bad enough, but when Jamie served the drinks, her rival for Lavigne's affections declined to add a gratuity to the tab.

Now Jamie was really angry. She grabbed hold of the table and flipped it over. The girl toppled out of her chair and mugs of beer and baskets of gizzards and fries went crashing to the floor. "You can't even tip me," Jamie screamed, "after fucking my husband?"

The next day, she went and signed the divorce papers. A short time later, Lavigne was transferred to Fort Bragg to attend the U.S. Army John F. Kennedy Special Warfare Center and School, where he would spend the next two years undergoing training in A Company, 4th Battalion, 1st Special Warfare Group. When Jamie found out that he was gone for good, she lay down on her bed and sobbed until her sides ached. "I don't think I ever fully recovered," she said.

Five

PIPE HITTERS

Three years after 9/11, JSOC remained a niche organization, nothing like the blood-drenched, amphetamine-fueled killing machine it would later become, but its role in the GWOT was growing. Following the invasion of Iraq, it fell to Delta Force to hunt for the fictitious weapons of mass destruction, but after a few weeks of fruitless searching, the operators turned their attention to the more practical task of hunting down top officials of the former regime. They killed Saddam Hussein's two sons at a safe house in Mosul, then pulled Saddam himself out of a spider hole near Tikrīt. "Go to hell," an Iraqi heckler jeered at the deposed dictator as he was being strung up for execution by hanging at an American base called Camp Justice. Saddam shot back, "The hell that is Iraq?"

With security conditions deteriorating around the country and especially in Baghdad, where a Delta Force interrogation site at the international airport had come under unwelcome media scrutiny amid the Abu Ghraib torture scandal, the special operations task force in Iraq moved its field headquarters to an isolated airbase in the countryside near the town of Balad. There, at a vast logistics and supply hub then known as Camp Anaconda, the operators established themselves in a cavernous concrete aircraft hangar that they transformed into a secret facility whose walls were panoplied with digital screens streaming drone feeds and video links to conference rooms at Fort Bragg and the Pentagon. The giant hangar, spacious enough to park a commercial airliner, was filled with plywood cubicles and rows of field desks for scores of intelligence analysts, operations officers, specialists in surveillance and reconnaissance, aircraft controllers, medical planners, and personnel from half a dozen federal agencies, including a hundred agents from the CIA and about eighty from the rapidly militarizing FBI, whose close working relationship with Delta Force had only deepened since the Waco raid.

Regular American soldiers living and working at Camp Anaconda had no idea that this high-tech headquarters was hidden in their midst. I know because I was one of them. I was about the same age as Billy Lavigne, also in the Army, deployed to Iraq one month after he did, and was stationed at the Balad airbase.

In basic training, some of my drill sergeants had worn Army Ranger or Special Forces tabs on their uniforms, insignia that I recognized as the marks of superior soldiers. I had never heard of JSOC, though. Like Delta Force, its existence was kept cloaked not only from the public but also from conventional troops like my combat engineering battalion. I definitely didn't know that a small army of black-ops assassins and CIA paramilitaries was based right next to the dusty, sun-hammered spot where my road-building, ditch-digging squad slept in a soot-stained trailer while on burn pit detail. "For security and secrecy," General Stanley McChrystal, the JSOC commander, wrote in his 2013 memoir, "we walled off our plot with concrete blocks."

IN JUNE 2006, the Associated Press reported that in just one day shootings and bombings killed twelve people in Baghdad, a suicide bomber killed four and wounded twenty-seven at the funeral of a Shiite soldier, seven bullet-riddled bodies were pulled from the Tigris River, two who had been tortured to death were fished out of the Euphrates, and police found the body of a teenage girl who had been raped and murdered in Kirkuk. Amid this horrible paroxysm of revenge killings, auguring Iraq's descent into outright civil war split along sectarian lines, President Bush and his National Security Council pulled together a host of new advisers in an attempt to revise their failing strategy. It was at this juncture that a number of ambitious officials in the special operations community stepped up to offer a new path forward. The plan of action that they developed, which Bush's successor would adopt and expand in Afghanistan, forever transformed the American way of making war and goes a long way toward explaining how Fort Bragg, even more than Langley, Virginia, came to be the United States' national nerve center of invisible imperial power.

Stanley McChrystal, then a two-star major general, was the most important figure in this revolution in military affairs. McChrystal, a West Point graduate and the son of a distinguished general, had risen through the ranks in the 75th Ranger Regiment and was groomed for some of the Army's most sensitive missions, including a trip that he took to Egypt in August 1987 accompanied by Ali Mohamed, the Fort Bragg soldier who trained up al-Qaeda. Smart, shrewd, charismatic, and press savvy, McChrystal first came to prominence as a Pentagon spokesman and, consistent with the emphasis laid on psychological operations in the Special Forces, the most important war-fighting innovation that he developed was not primarily tactical or strategic but ideological and mediatic.

Although there were relatively few foreign fighters in Iraq and most came from neighboring Syria, McChrystal was the primary proponent of the view, quick to spread among Washington policymakers, that the enemy was not a nationalist rebellion against outside occupation but one node of a global conspiracy of America-hating terrorists. To describe this nebulous and inherently malignant foe, McChrystal and his staff invented the term "al-Qaeda in Iraq," or AQI. At the top of this dubious organization, which they themselves had done more than anyone else to conjure into being, JSOC analysts placed the dopey Jordanian criminal Abu Musab al-Zarqawi, a mysterious Bedouin bogeyman, much hyped by deceitful Pentagon spooks in the run-up to the war, who might not have even been in Iraq at the time. To explain away the paucity of tangible contacts between insurgents in Iraq and Osama bin Laden's organization, the remnants of which were now scattered around Pakistan and Yemen, McChrystal and his aides redefined al-Qaeda as a concentric grouping of decentralized "franchises" operating on a "blind cell model."

In his memoir, McChrystal admits with remarkable if belated frankness that JSOC produced intelligence assessments "that inflated al-Qaeda's role" and "problematically used 'AQI' as a catchall designation for any Sunni group that attacked Americans." This narrative, he acknowledges, was a way to "sidestep the reality" that most Iraqi insurgents were primarily motivated by "earthly grievances," not Islamist ideology. There's no indication, however, that he shared these important caveats with President Bush, who seized upon the imaginary influx of foreign jihadists into Iraq as an after-the-fact vindication of his discredited case for war. By grossly exaggerating Zarqawi's importance, McChrystal and his deputy, Vice Admiral William McRaven, convinced the Bush administration that it was possible for the United States to kill its way to victory in Iraq through a massively stepped-up campaign of targeted assassinations. This was an essential precondition for the rise of JSOC.

Another of the advisers whom Bush called upon to reformulate the war effort in late 2006 was Michael Vickers, the top Pentagon official in charge of SOCOM, the position originally held by Bush's father's old Skull and Bones crony, now known by the comically unwieldy acronym "ASD SO/LIC & IC," for assistant secretary of defense for special operations/low-intensity conflict and interdependent capabilities. In his memoir, Vickers recalls how the Bush administration scrapped its existing playbook and instituted a new policy that put JSOC firmly in charge of the fight in Iraq.

The plan involved a two-pronged approach, the public-facing aspect of which was a temporary buildup or "surge" of conventional forces. But the real escalation took place behind the scenes, where JSOC was quietly tasked with implementing a radically expanded campaign of mass assassinations very similar to the Vietnam-era Phoenix Program, which, in spite of the repugnance it had elicited in the public, was considered a success by the Washington-dwelling national security set. Once limited to former regime officials and leaders of the insurgency, JSOC's hit list, euphemistically known as the disposition matrix or joint prioritized effects list, grew exponentially to include anyone, however youthful or peripheral, suspected of taking up arms against American occupiers. Vickers calls this covert war the "hidden surge."

From now on, Iraq would be a war of targeted killings carried out clandestinely, almost always at night. Swollen with new infusions of money, personnel, equipment, and aircraft, JSOC became "JSOC on steroids," a "counterterrorism killing machine" capable of slaying recalcitrant Iraqis on a scale that both Vickers and McChrystal describe as "industrial." From about ten a month at the start of the war, the number of night raids that JSOC carried out increased to ten per *day* at the height of the surge.

McChrystal called this relentless tempo the "continuous targeting cycle." Fluent in McKinsey-style jargon like "decision cycle," "dynamic process," and "nodal analysis," he was adept at spitting out pithy truisms such as "it takes a network to defeat a network," and a prolific coiner of acronyms like F3EAD, which stood for Find, Fix, Finish, Exploit, Analyze, and Disseminate.

Despite the ungainly initialism, the F3EAD cycle was not a complicated concept. It typically meant tracking down a target, killing him and every adult man and teenage boy in the vicinity, seizing every piece of paper and electronic device found on their persons, and using these materials to come up with more names to add to the hit list, and then killing them too, sometimes just a few hours later.

The hidden surge, in which Delta Force played the leading role, was greatly enabled by the widespread adoption of cell phones in Iraq, a technological development that coincided with the first few years of American occupation. JSOC's screen-filled headquarters at Camp Anaconda received an influx of personnel from the National Security Agency, who found it trivial to intercept unencrypted calls on Iraq's burgeoning mobile networks and could easily transform cell phones into listening devices.

Television and film depictions of the GWOT often portray American operators and spies as able to speak the local languages, suavely lobbing savvy quotations from the Koran at their truculent Islamist antagonists. But in a startling admission with sobering implications, McChrystal states in his memoir that JSOC in Iraq was "hindered by an almost complete lack of Arabic skills within our force," suggesting that nearly all of those whom Delta Force killed were targeted based not on the content of telephonic intercepts but on pseudoscientific "nodal analysis," tips from paid informants, and arbitrary guesswork.

"We were not death squads," McChrystal writes. But armed with NSA intercepts, backed by newly developed Reaper drones, and joined by fierce Kurdish mercenaries called Mohawks, that's exactly what JSOC became during the covert surge in Iraq, which lasted into 2008. The body count from Delta Force's killing spree, and the proportion of Iraq's hundreds of thousands of war dead who were gunned down in JSOC night raids, will never be known because it wasn't recorded in the first place. That these events are lost to the historical and photographic record was by design. What Vickers dubs the "hidden surge" was a side of the Iraq War never intended to be seen by the public, who were fed images of conventional, uniformed troops on patrol, but never any footage of the plainclothes men who did nearly all of the nighttime wet work.

"From 2006 on, 90 percent or higher of insurgent deaths were from targeted, offensive SOF operations," said a former Delta Force sergeant major who served in Iraq during the surge, using an acronym that refers to special operations forces in general. "Going out night after night, on purpose, and getting in firefights with bad guys—that job fell to us."

Instead of mounting patrols and reacting to fire like conventional infantry, Delta Force operators identified their targets from a distance, in advance, and took them by surprise, often making use of perfidious techniques such as disguising themselves as Iraqis, using wigs, brown-face, and prosthetics. They posed as Red Cross personnel, United Nations inspectors, Western businessmen, or European diplomats. With the help of female support soldiers, they passed themselves off as husband-and-wife pairs, masquerading, for instance, as married school-teachers who'd come to teach English to Iraqi kids. They even copied the enemy's tactics and blew up targets with roadside bombs.

Among themselves, the bearded, long-haired operators called each other by their first names, eschewed divisions of rank, and dressed in a mishmash of civilian attire. When they did wear uniforms, the unit patches they sported were purely fictitious: hometown police badges, the seals of various states, Spartan helmets, crusader shields, the Confederate battle flag, or jokey tabs that said things like HATCHET FORCE or FUCK AL-QAEDA.

No camera crews ever went on night raids with Delta Force. Their operations were not the subject of news documentaries, nor do we possess any oral histories, because silence is the unit's chief point of pride. But over time, these strictures inevitably loosen, if only a little. In recent years, many former special operators have gone on podcasts to discuss their military careers in a certain Army "special mission unit" or "compartmented element." And once-rare photos of JSOC operations have found their way onto social media, including images of Delta Force in Iraq under McCrystal's leadership.

"Several of my rotations to Iraq [were] composed of just my team and a small HQ element," a former Delta Force troop sergeant major named Jesse Boettcher wrote in an Instagram post dated February 28, 2022. "While I had the full force of the US government just a radio call away, there were very few of us on the ground getting dirty. Our small element was able to execute and refine the entire F3EAD cycle almost daily, with very little outside assistance."

In the photo accompanying the post, Boettcher, then in his mid-thirties, sits at a table dressed in soiled civilian clothes. In back of him is a whiteboard. Much of the writing on it has been blacked out, but you can still read random words, including "meeting," "explosives," "liaison," "interrogation," and "safehouse." Taped on the wall behind the whiteboard is a grid of fifty-five mug shots of brown-skinned men. Almost all of them have been crossed out with an *X*.

Another picture, posted January 19, 2022, shows the rest of Boettcher's team, a group of seven unkempt white men. "It might look like a ragtag bunch of ruffians, but this crew were straight-up Pipe-Hitters," Boettcher wrote, using an obscure term considered a high compliment in the special operations community that derives from the concept of a soldier who is so fearless, daring, and addicted to war that he can be likened to a smoker of crack cocaine. "The guys in front," Boettcher wrote, referring to three young men kneeling in the foreground, "have killed more people than cancer."

Boettcher's Instagram photos shed light on another spooky Delta Force tactic: cross-dressing and carrying out hits in drag. Two pictures that he posted show teammates of his disguised as women. In one, a burly, bearded operator in a sequined dress and rhinestone hijab carries a sledgehammer over his shoulder. An even freakier photo shows a clean-shaven operator clad in the flowery garb of an affluent Iraqi lady, wearing rouge and mascara, a Heckler & Koch submachine gun in his hand. The evil little smirk on his face exudes pure murder.

Boettcher did three rotations to Iraq during the surge, each lasting about three months. The pace was grueling. Even when there was no good intelligence to go on, McChrystal's philosophy was to go out at night and hit a bunch of targets anyway to create a sense of offensive momentum—that is, to terrorize the Iraqi populace into submission. "Caffeine, nicotine, and rage kept us fueled," Boettcher wrote.

Harder stuff helped too. "During the dark days of Iraq," recalled the retired sergeant major, "the op tempo got real bad." He and his team sometimes had to stay awake for days on end. "Because of the continuous operations," he said, "our own medical personnel became drug dealers."

To help special operators cope with sleep deprivation, keep up their morale, ward off passivity, and suppress empathy, JSOC doctors did what American medics have been doing since the Vietnam War and distributed amphetamines, specifically dextroamphetamine, known by the brand names Dexedrine or Adderall. "Then guys couldn't sleep," said the retired sergeant major, "so they were getting Ambien. Some were mixing it with booze."

McChrystal alludes to his top officers' dependence on sleeping pills in his memoir. "My command team," he wrote, "kept Ambien close at hand." McRaven also writes of his reliance on Ambien, the mind-clouding effects of which he sometimes found difficult to shake off at key moments.

As Billy Lavigne would eventually find out, such habits, once formed, are hard to break. The retired sergeant major, now in his fifties, still takes prescription amphetamines. "I'm on Dex right now," he said. "Ten milligrams for my ADHD."

ATTACKS ON FOREIGN TROOPS in Iraq fell sharply in 2008 as fighting across the country gave way to a tentative calm. This was in part due to a truce that Iran brokered between Shiite militias and the Iraqi client state. The occupation authorities also bought the loyalties of desert-dwelling mafia clans in the Anbar province who resented the insurgents' suppression of their smuggling routes. This alliance with Iraqi organized crime, dubbed the Sunni Awakening in the American media, also helped to quell the violence.

The lull would prove short-lived, but took place just in time to allow President Bush, at the end of his eight years in office, to declare a "major strategic victory." For this, Pentagon officials, Republican lawmakers, Democratic supporters of the war, and the national press corps primarily credited the surge.

General David Petraeus, the top American officer in Iraq, was the public face of this perceived success. McChrystal was less of a celebrity, but the low-profile, hard-as-nails, results-getting JSOC commander was held in the utmost esteem by Washington insiders. The limited, temporary success that Petraeus and McChrystal had had in Iraq was a fluke that would prove impossible to replicate elsewhere, but by the time President Barack Obama took his oath of office in January 2009, the ascent of their stars over D.C. was at its apex.

True to promises made during his campaign, in which he'd harshly criticized the war in Iraq, President Obama presided over a steep drawdown of troops there, with most out by 2011. But he still had to contend with the war in Afghanistan. Those who thought it had concluded in 2002 couldn't have been more wrong.

In public, the State Department and Pentagon issued sunny assessments of the situation in Afghanistan and portrayed the American-backed client state, led by the longtime CIA asset Hamid Karzai, as a nascent democracy. But in private, White House officials knew from classified intelligence assessments that all the opium-producing regions of the country were back under the control of powerful narco-warlords, and that Afghanistan, after eight years of U.S. occupation, was now producing *nine times* more heroin than the rest of the world *combined*. The Taliban, which issued edicts prohibiting its men from using drugs or trafficking them, had regrouped at the head of a popular insurgency and were mounting an increasing number of guerrilla attacks on American bases, decimating the United States' Afghan proxy forces, who were frequently too stoned on opium, heroin, and hash to go out on patrol.

President Obama inherited a war that he and his top advisers knew was on the brink of disaster. There weren't enough American soldiers on the ground to hold back the diverse bands of resistance fighters who had flocked to the Taliban's white flag. What Afghanistan needed, Obama soon decided, was a surge.

Obama promoted Petraeus to the head of Central Command and, in a signal endorsement of McChrystal's covert tactics, awarded him his fourth star. He then put McChrystal in charge of running the whole war in Afghanistan.

The president, a Nobel Peace Prize winner whom antiwar liberals adored, had long sought to dispel the notion that he was a pacifist. "What I am opposed to is a dumb war," he'd repeatedly said on the campaign trail. Now it would become clear what a "smart war" meant to the Obama administration: black ops writ large, an all-covert GWOT.

It was right around this time—November 11, 2009, to be exact— that Lavigne officially became a "TEAM MEMBER/OPERATOR" in the unit demarcated on his enlistment record as "SFOD-D (DELTA FORCE)." Not long after, a military doctor wrote him a prescription for dextroamphetamine.

Six

THE KILLING FEST

ollowing his divorce from Jamie Carter, Lavigne had completed
Special Forces training at Fort Bragg, a lengthy and intensive
program that, although not especially successful in imparting
real fluency to trainees, emphasizes language acquisition and cultural
education in addition to advanced infantry skills. Besides high-altitude
parachuting, urban combat, wilderness survival, and resisting interrogation, Lavigne learned to read and understand rudimentary Tagalog,
the main language of the Philippines, a little-known secondary theater
of the GWOT. In 2007, he was assigned as an intelligence sergeant to
the Pacific-oriented 1st Special Warfare Group at the Torii Station in
Okinawa, Japan, where he served until 2009.

Lavigne did more than a dozen deployments in his military career,
according to his father, but because his enlisted record brief was
abridged to a single page, none of the tours of duty that he did before
2010 are shown. Considering the pace of military operations at the
time, it is likely that he deployed at least once with 1st Group. He also
spent time in Thailand, earning the airborne wings of the Royal Thai
Army to wear on his dress uniform.

"Advanced land navigation" is how Delta Force selection is discreetly
denoted on a soldier's enlisted record. The selection course, which

chews up and spits out the great majority of Green Berets and Army Rangers invited to try out, culminates in a blistering, crippling night-time ruck march of some *forty* miles over rugged terrain with a heavy pack, a physical ordeal that if a man were unprepared for it would reduce the tendons and ligaments of his hips, knees, and ankles to a bloody gelatin.

In addition, a successful candidate must pass an arbitrary and psychologically abusive review board made up of Delta Force officers and sergeants major, who have idiosyncratic preferences for certain personality types. "The best are generally introverts who are able, when necessary, to be extroverted," said James Reese, a retired lieutenant colonel who served in the unit during the surge years and was involved in selection. "People not inclined to be team players. Artistic, creative types. Many Delta operators paint or play music."

Others described the selection process in less mystical terms. "It is very much a good old boys' club over there," said Jordan Terrell, the paratrooper from Chicago who cultivated friendships with Lavigne and Mark Leshikar in hopes of breaking into the insular Special Forces clique. "To be an operator," he said, "you have to fit a certain unspoken mold. You got to look a certain way, act a certain way, be cool with doing certain things."

Leshikar, who tried out for Delta sometime between 2013 and 2016, perhaps more than once, was among those rebuffed at this juncture. His hot temper was the reason, according to Terrell, as well as rumors that he had committed atrocities in Afghanistan. "Mark was really volatile," said Terrell. "We would always have to keep him from trying to fight people."

According to Colonel Reese, the review board ought to have rejected Lavigne at the psych eval stage, too. "He's a guy who slipped through our cracks," Reese said. "Billy had some psychological problems, even back then. There was something off about him. He was out there. His eyes were always moving or shaking, like his brain was never settled."

That jittery, shifty-eyed depiction of Lavigne is not necessarily at odds with the kinder portrait of his personality drawn by his friends in the Army. "Billy was a cool guy," said Terrell. "Kind of soft-spoken, kind of calm. He always had a smile on his face."

Appearances can be misleading, however, when it comes to unit operators. "Whenever you're in their presence, they can be friendly, super professional," said Terrell. "But you know that if somebody flipped a switch, everybody is going to die."

LAVIGNE'S FIRST FULL YEAR on Delta Force coincided with General McChrystal's introduction of the F3EAD program to Afghanistan, another "hidden surge," and a redoubling of the pace of JSOC night raids. As in Iraq, McChrystal's signature innovation was to redefine the enemy by dramatically widening the scope of who could be considered Taliban.

The original Taliban regime, after being deposed by the Northern Alliance, had decamped to the high-altitude Pakistani city of Quetta. In its stead, the United States installed Hamid Karzai, a mercurial monarchist clotheshorse and rumored heroin addict on the payroll of the CIA who exercised power and extended the new government's writ out from Kabul through a patronage network of warlords, police chiefs, militia commanders, smugglers, and tribal mafiosi, many of whom were major drug traffickers. Karzai's government was primarily a military-industrial money-laundering machine for transatlantic security elites, a corrupt conduit through which a trillion U.S. taxpayer dollars flowed, but secondarily and almost as important, it was a massive drug cartel that produced nearly all of the world's illicit opiates. Some of the top narco-bosses included Muhammed Fahim, Karzai's defense minister; Hazrat Ali in Jalalabad, a city whose airport was a gateway to India; Abdul Rashid Dostum on the border with Uzbekistan and Tajikistan; Gul Agha Sherzai in Nangarhar; and Ahmed Wali Karzai, the president's half brother, also a paid CIA asset, who set himself up as the kingpin of Kandahar, through which the illicit riches of the Helmand flowed.

McChrystal writes in his memoir of how the United States restored control over the Helmand to the clan of Nasim Akhundzada, a longtime ally of the CIA whose tribal militia McChrystal frankly describes as a "durable drug cartel." Abdul Rahman Jan, the right-hand man of Sher Mohammad, nephew of Nasim Akhundzada, ruled the Helmand city of Marjah "as his own drug-financed fiefdom," McChrystal writes, "where he and his men stole boys from local families for their sexual pleasure."

At times, McChrystal seems genuinely chagrined by American actions and able to understand why Afghans might take up arms under the banner of the resurgent Taliban. "Too often," McChrystal writes, American proxies were "corrupt and despised warlords whom we paid handsomely." But he showed no such empathy when it really counted.

Before McChrystal took charge in Afghanistan, JSOC had been limited to assassinating foreign fighters with al-Qaeda. But few of these Arabic-speaking jihadists remained, scattered throughout the cave complexes of the inaccessible Hindu Kush and the mountainous border of Pakistan. Once in command of the war, McChrystal quadrupled the number of JSOC operators in-country and authorized them to strike native-born, Pashto-speaking Taliban, which he later admitted was not a unified movement but "a diverse taxonomy of groups we lumped together." This decision exponentially increased the number of people whom Delta Force was green-lighted to kill.

McChrystal pushed JSOC teams to do more night raids, whether or not they had good intel to go on; had his commanders lower the threshold for targeting; and relaxed the already flexible and forgiving rules of engagement applicable to special operators, the exact parameters of which are classified. The pace of night raids increased dramatically as teams of Delta Force soldiers, Navy SEALs, and Army Rangers carried out one surprise attack after another under cover of darkness, killing up to a hundred Afghans at a time and leaving whole villages in smoking ruins.

These night raids, carried out in conjunction with drastically ramped-up drone strikes, were never publicly acknowledged by military officials. The targeting decisions behind them were driven by American analysts' fallible readings of satellite and drone imagery, as well as tips from informants, many of whom were motivated by personal vendettas. As a result, more than half the Afghans killed or abducted by JSOC operators were targeted by mistake. The error rate was around 50 percent.

Violent deaths in Afghanistan rose sharply across the board after McChrystal took charge. To conceal the rising death toll, he directed unit commanders to stop reporting body counts publicly. At the same time, he made a show of lecturing soldiers in the conventional Army—third-tier infantrymen—about the need for *tightened* rules of engagement, and repeatedly allowed credulous reporters to witness scenes of him handing down tough truths to disgruntled troops on the necessity of avoiding civilian casualties.

But McChrystal wasn't in command of the war for very long. His meteoric military career, boosted by an adoring press corps enamored of the glamour of special operations, unexpectedly crashed and burned due to a surprise media blunder that he inexplicably committed. Michael Hastings, a thirty-year-old reporter for *Rolling Stone*, was instrumental in getting him fired.

The profile of McChrystal that Hastings wrote was really not all that hard on the general. It spoke of his "fearlessness" in hunting down "terrorists" in Iraq, and was in many ways a gonzo celebration of how wild and crazy life is at the top of the American war machine. But Hastings described scenes of McChrystal getting drunk with his aides, some of whom made corny jokes about State Department officials and Vice President Joe Biden. Since there was already a public perception, promoted by the Republican opposition, that weak-kneed Obama quailed before his generals, Obama fired McChrystal to save face. McChrystal, the most admired combat leader of his generation, never commanded troops again.

Three years later, Hastings died in a fiery auto crash that was caught on camera. In the soundless, black-and-white video, which leaves much open to interpretation, his small Mercedes sports car streaks past and appears to explode just before or just as it crashes into the base of a palm tree in the median of a Los Angeles street. The wrecked car explodes again in an even larger ball of flame seen as multiple pulses of bright white light.

The incident was ruled an accident, but because of Hastings's history with McChrystal, and his ongoing, adversarial reporting on JSOC and the CIA, conspiracy theories around his death were never fully dispelled. Unproven rumors that Hastings had been murdered resurged in 2017, when WikiLeaks released a document showing that the CIA's Embedded Device Branch had been researching how to infect onboard car computers with remotely operated malware that would enable the agency to carry out undetectable assassinations by steering vehicles into immovable obstacles at high speed.

McCHRYSTAL'S DEPUTY, Vice Admiral William McRaven, succeeded him as JSOC commander. McRaven was a stone-faced, dead serious Navy officer, far less capable of reflection than McChrystal, to whom all those who opposed American military hegemony, regardless of their motives for taking up arms, were al-Qaeda terrorists who urgently needed to die. His first assignment had been as an ensign on SEAL Team Six, and his elevation to the helm of JSOC proved a boost to the naval side of special operations, but only in the short term.

Although the two units' capabilities are fairly comparable, SEAL Team Six, also known as the Naval Special Warfare Development Group, or DEVGRU, occupies a distinctly subordinate position with respect to Delta Force in the JSOC hierarchy, which is dominated by Army personnel. In a reflection of its lagging status, when the Iraq War started in 2003, most of Team Six had been left behind in Afghanistan and had missed out on what was then seen as the real action. But their established presence on the border with Pakistan, plus McRaven's ascent, left the SEAL operators well positioned, in May 2011, to carry out the most famous mission in JSOC history: the assassination of Osama bin Laden.

How the CIA located bin Laden remains controversial. What's not subject to doubt is that the Saudi arch-terrorist, who'd been a client of Pakistani military intelligence since the 1980s, was living as a guest, prisoner, or hostage of Pakistan's spy service in the garrison town of Abbottabad. Once the United States had a fix on his unfortified, unguarded compound, going in and killing him was an easy-breezy turkey shoot, much simpler than any number of complex, multiday operations that JSOC had carried out in the preceding year on the border with Pakistan.

But the killing of bin Laden and the fame that came with it turned out to be a mixed bag. With CIA assistance, the Abbottabad operation was instantly transformed into a dramatic Hollywood film, *Zero Dark Thirty*, which was nominated for five Academy Awards. One operator involved in the mission wrote a book about it, another was interviewed on television, and the public was eventually treated to the ignominious spectacle of various SEALs bickering over who had fired the fatal shots.

Media attention to Team Six turned negative not long after. In 2015, *The New York Times* published "SEAL Team 6: A Secret History of Quiet Killings and Blurred Lines," a lengthy exposé that aired "recurring concerns" about the unit's covert "killing fests" in Afghanistan, which the *Times* explicitly compared to the Phoenix Program. Written by a tag team of six reporters, it was the first real look at the "dirty business" of assassinating a dozen or more people every night for years on end, and provided a vivid glimpse at "fierce" naval operators who wore long hair and earrings and sometimes dispatched their victims with wicked-looking custom tomahawks. The report also hinted at the prevalence of drug use on DEVGRU.

Two years later, *The Intercept* published an article, later adapted into a book, titled "The Crimes of SEAL Team Six." It revealed a penchant on the part of SEAL operators for mutilating and desecrating corpses, including a sickening practice, too gruesome to describe, known as "canoeing." The article also exposed members of Team Six, now firmly established in their role as the sacrificial black sheep of the special operations community, for shooting people in their sleep, making snuff films called "bleed-out videos," stealing government money, using hatchets and axes in combat, not for any tactical purpose, but out of pure bloodlust, and cultivating a grungy, piratical aesthetic reminiscent of a biker gang.

Meanwhile, Delta Force, despite being at all times the lead organization in the F3EAD "killing fest," barely made a ripple in the national press for the entire duration of the wars in Afghanistan and Iraq.

Seven

ALLEGED MEXICAN WHITE

The first Afghanistan deployment that's shown on Lavigne's enlisted record brief began on October 28, 2011. Five months had passed since bin Laden's death and the pace of night raids had doubled again, rising to an average of ten a night, yet the United States was no closer to victory in its campaign to stamp out opposition to the Karzai cartel. It was a perilous time to be in-country, even more dicey than the deadliest days of the Iraq War.

Three months before Lavigne arrived, his teammate Master Sergeant Benjamin Allen Stevenson, aged thirty-six, had been killed by multiple gunshot wounds in the remote Paktika province, the result of a two-day battle at an isolated redoubt of the Haqqani network, another creature of Pakistani military intelligence formerly backed by the CIA. Two other Delta Force soldiers had been killed in Afghanistan the previous year: Master Sergeant Jared Neville Van Aalst, aged thirty-four; and Sergeant First Class Ronald Aaron Grider, aged thirty. The circumstances of their deaths were never made public, but unclassified casualty reports show that both died from multiple gunshot wounds in the northern province of Kunduz, the gateway to Tajikistan.

A total of nineteen USASOC soldiers died in Afghanistan in 2011. Fifteen were Army Rangers and Green Berets killed in combat. A sixteenth Special Forces soldier, an engineer sergeant from Fort Bragg, died of a drug overdose at Camp Montrond, the top-secret JSOC annex, closed to outsiders, at Bagram Airfield. Two years earlier, another Green Beret from Fort Bragg had overdosed on tramadol and died at Fire Base Ripley, near Tarin Kowt—an early indication of spreading drug abuse in the Special Forces.

A picture of Lavigne taken around this time depicts him and his eight-man team. They are dressed in casual civilian clothes and body armor, standing on a dirt road amid featureless desert landscape, a faint moon floating in the purple sky behind them. All are armed with assault rifles except Lavigne, who totes a heavy machine gun. "Mowing the lawn" was the euphemism consistently used to describe the wet work they did.

The extraordinarily rugged terrain of Afghanistan alternates constantly between baked desert plains, jagged mountain ranges, and green valleys richly watered by cold snowmelt. The Delta Force squadron in-country at the time was headquartered in Mazar-i-Sharif, by the border where Afghanistan, Uzbekistan, and Tajikistan converge. One troop was stationed there and the other was at nearby Kunduz. Lavigne might have been assigned to either element, or to a helicopter-borne vehicle-interdiction force based at Kandahar that had a reputation for laying utter waste to the convoys that came into its crosshairs.

Lavigne's four-month rotation ended February 16, 2012. The following year, the military allowed a *New York Times* reporter to pay a rare visit to "a classified commando base" in "a lush valley encircled by frosty peaks about 50 miles from Kabul" on condition that he not reveal the exact location. The reporter disclosed only that it was the base of "a training squadron drawn from the most secretive counterterrorism units fielded by the United States," which could only mean JSOC.

The article reported that there were sixty special operations teams in-country, and fifty strike forces, as well as nine commando battalions and special police units, "scattered among population centers and along the ring road linking Afghanistan's major cities." The JSOC-led special operations task force, which now made up fully one third of the total American presence, had been consolidated under a single command headed by a two-star major general directly under Bill McRaven, a three-star admiral, who in turn answered only to the four-star-general chairman of the Joint Chiefs, the secretary of defense, and President Obama. It was the first time in history that an entire division-sized element of special operations forces had been deployed to a foreign war zone.

The purpose of the *Times* piece was to tout American efforts to train up Afghan commandos. A photo that accompanied the article shows eighteen of these locally recruited mercenaries assembled on a line, wearing black ski masks to hide their identities. NATO officials who spoke to the *Times* commended their "lethal professionalism," but acknowledged the need to "sharpen" their skills. Other photos showed the Afghan commandos doing training drills on newly built ranges, including a half-built office building, a model village marketplace, and "a full-scale mock-up of a heroin laboratory."

UNDER U.S. OCCUPATION, Afghanistan had become the world's leading narco-state, with an economy almost entirely dependent on the drug trade. Within a year of the Taliban's ouster, opium production had returned to record levels. "The significant increase," the DEA reported, "is attributable to the fall of the Taliban, and the Taliban poppy ban."

The amount of Afghan land under poppy cultivation more than tripled from 2003 to 2004. By 2005, heroin production in Afghanistan had increased a mind-blowing 7,514 percent. In 2007, the country's annual output of pure heroin approached a *thousand* metric tons. By way of comparison, Mexico, in a far-distant second place, produced just fifty tons that year, while third-place Myanmar put out a mere twenty-four. Colombia, the only other significant exporter of heroin, barely topped two tons.

The superabundance of highly potent product inundated Pakistan, Iran, China, Russia, all of Europe, Australia, and the whole world. In the United States, street prices went down, purity went up, and opioid addiction took hold in a population primed for it by a decade of loose prescribing practices around pharmaceutical painkillers. "Heroin from Afghanistan is our biggest rising threat," the Orange County Sheriff's Office told the *Los Angeles Times* in 2006. "We are seeing more seizures and more overdoses." The *Times* interviewed addicts across the country who spoke of the recent advent of "a different kind of heroin," clean enough to snort or smoke with no need for needles. "It is very, very strong," and "cheaper than the other stuff," a recovering addict in Portland told the newspaper.

Reams of articles in prestigious medical journals described a rapid rise in overdoses in the United States, resulting from an influx of "China white" heroin—so called for its porcelain color, not its actual origin. Even in the most remote rural counties, especially in New England, Appalachia, and the Midwest, nearly pure heroin was available on the street at prices much lower than what dealers charged for prescription opioids diverted from the licit drug supply. Yet curiously, in 2008, after years of reporting that heroin from southwest Asia was increasingly available in cities like Chicago, St. Louis, New York, and Boston at lower prices than ever before, the DEA began asserting in its annual National Drug Threat Assessment that *Mexico* was to blame. According to the DEA, virtually none of the heroin consumed in America during the surge in usage seen in the 2000s and 2010s came from Afghanistan. Less than 1 percent is the official figure.

This counterintuitive proposition, akin to saying that no oil from Saudi Arabia is ever burned in the United States, was based on the DEA's "heroin signature program," which analyzes samples of seized product to determine its geographic origin, as well as its "heroin domestic monitoring program," which tests samples obtained in undercover buys in select cities. If you read closely, however, you will find that the DEA cautions against confusing the geographic proportions derived from these programs with "actual market share," and acknowledges that "the amount of Asian heroin transported to the United States is relatively unknown."

The DEA declined to respond to several written requests for assistance in reconciling these puzzling caveats with its confident top-line assertions about the near-total exclusion of Afghan heroin from the homeland, but sifting through twenty years of threat assessments, I found that the agency's twin tracing programs are riddled with untenable assumptions and so limited by selection biases as to be virtually meaningless. For instance, the heroin domestic monitoring program excludes any busts involving more than $200 worth of drugs, as well as seizures at airports. Nearly all Afghan heroin imported to the United States arrives by air, while heroin from South America is smuggled overland, across the Mexican border.

Most glaringly, fully 60 percent of the heroin that the DEA analyzed was a highly purified white powder "of an unknown classification" and with an "inconclusive origin component," to which the DEA peremptorily applied the made-up nomenclature "Alleged Mexican White," on the unexplained grounds that it was "most likely made from Mexico-produced poppies," even though Mexican heroin is famously black in color and low in quality.

In 2012, independent researchers working for the White House Office of National Drug Control Policy issued a paper that highlighted statistical anomalies pervading the DEA's estimates of heroin availability in the United States. "There appears to be appreciable measurement error in these estimates," the authors of the paper wrote, noting their high degree of standard deviation. Using purely mathematical methods, the researchers demonstrated that the DEA's approximations of heroin market share by geographic origin were irreconcilable with other known metrics of opioid availability. One possible explanation, the researchers ventured to suggest, was that the DEA was massively underestimating the percentage of heroin coming into the United States from sources other than Latin America.

"The DEA doesn't like to hear that," said one of the authors of the paper, the retired academic Dana Hunt. "They didn't like that we triangulated everything," to derive the telltale measure of standard deviation. "It was always a contentious presentation," Hunt said. "The DEA doesn't like you snooping into what they do."

But the ONDCP paper, which was technically commissioned by the White House, might have had an indirect impact. In 2013, and for the remainder of President Obama's time in office, the DEA's annual threat assessment made no mention of Afghanistan. Statistics on global heroin production were scrubbed from the publication altogether.

IN 2008, *The New York Times* published a report that linked burgeoning Afghan drug production to officials at the very top of the corrupt client state led by Hamid Karzai. The response of American officials to revelations like these, which sporadically surfaced in the national press throughout the occupation of Afghanistan, was to simply blame the Taliban and portray the spreading insurgency and proliferating poppy cultivation as intertwined phenomena.

In fact, there is no evidence that the Taliban, which from the time of its emergence had an antidrug agenda in its ideological DNA, was ever involved in the opium and heroin trade to any significant degree. In a 2018 retrospective on counternarcotics operations in Afghanistan, the Special Inspector General for Afghanistan Reconstruction, or SIGAR, repeatedly noted the absence of hard proof that the Taliban insurgency was financed by drugs, and the wildly fluctuating and conjectural nature of intelligence assessments on the topic of "narco-terrorism."

"The extent to which the Taliban participates in the trade of narcotics is debated," the SIGAR report said. "There was little consistency and in-depth reporting on the estimates of drug trade revenues flowing to the Taliban." Kirk Meyer, director of the Afghan Threat Finance Cell, which was set up to disrupt the Taliban's sources of revenue, told SIGAR, "I personally never believed it was as big a funding source for the insurgency as a lot of people thought." Afghan traffickers held up in the mass media as Taliban-affiliated narcos, such as the Baloch drug lord Juma Khan, turned out to be CIA assets.

By contrast, SIGAR found ample evidence that the U.S.-backed client state was directly or indirectly involved in the drugs business at every level of government and in every region of Afghanistan. The army, police, court system, parliament, and national executive were corrupted by drug money, SIGAR reported. The border police were in on the game, as were customs officials and provincial, district, and municipal governors. "Almost everyone in influential positions in public life was somehow tainted," said the former British ambassador. As a result, the drug trade "eroded the legitimacy of the Afghan state," SIGAR found, and "undermin[ed] the rule of law."

Drug money flows from Afghanistan to Dubai were traced back to people close to President Karzai. The United States' limited, under-funded, half-hearted antidrug programs, which were pawned off on British forces and which Karzai worked to thwart, were a complete failure. The military only grudgingly participated, seeing poppy eradication as "detrimental to its mission," and the CIA flat out refused to take part. "The CIA instead prioritized its relationships with significant traffickers, such as Haji Bashir Noorzai and Haj Juma Khan," SIGAR reported.

In his second term in office, President Obama completely abandoned any remaining effort to counter narcotics in Afghanistan, and it became implicit U.S. policy to allow poppy to flourish unimpeded. The amount of land under poppy cultivation expanded to nearly a quarter million hectares. Major traffickers protected by the Karzai cartel, such as Lal Jan Ishaqzai, became untouchable.

Ever since World War II, illegal drugs have served as a common coin for the purposes of espionage, paramilitary operations, and covert actions, and the foreign entities that choose to work for the U.S. military and the CIA—the twin sentinels of global capitalism—often profit from this most capitalistic of all enterprises. Throughout its history, the CIA has worked to achieve American national security objectives in partnership with known drug traffickers, including the anticommunist Kuomintang, the founders of modern-day Taiwan; France's Corsican mafia syndicates; Cuban exiles opposed to Fidel Castro; Hmong irregulars in Laos as well as the Royal Lao Army; and the contra rebels of Nicaragua. But American foreign policy elites' complicity in the international drug trade was never so substantial, sustained, witting, and consequential as in Afghanistan.

In the English-language press, the world of nonprofits connected to the State Department, network and cable news, and the Democratic and Republican Parties, total silence descended over the topic of heroin production in the Helmand, Kandahar, Nangarhar, and other Afghan provinces where U.S. soldiers were not infrequently photographed patrolling vast fields of poppy. No person in any position of influence dared to suggest that the scourge of opiate addiction then afflicting the poor and working classes across the United States might have resulted from the wartime narcotics bonanza. A willful ignorance toward the subject prevailed in polite society in Washington and New York. "It was rarely mentioned in policy circles either in Afghanistan or in Western capitals," said the SIGAR report.

Eight

THE NORTHERN
DISTRIBUTION NETWORK

On February 25, 2013, Billy Lavigne returned to Afghanistan for his next rotation with Delta Force. It was no less dangerous a time to be in-country than his last tour.

Four months earlier, his good friend Ryan James Savard had become the fourth Delta Force soldier to die in combat since the start of the hidden surge. Sergeant First Class Savard was killed by enemy gunfire at the age of twenty-nine in the northern province of Kunduz, which despite its small size and remote location was the site of three quarters of the unit's casualties in Afghanistan.

Kunduz, adjacent to Tajikistan, is a rural province at the foot of the Hindu Kush with a mostly tribal society. Hardly any roads existed there before the war, but in 2007 the Army Corps of Engineers built a bridge over the Panj River at Sher Khan Bandar, transforming a fly-blown collection of mud huts into a booming border town with hundreds of heavily laden commercial trucks rumbling across daily. The Tajik strongman Emomali Rahmon, who had been in power for more than a decade and whose security forces completely dominated the drug-smuggling business in Tajikistan, presided over the bridge's opening ceremony, flanked by Hamid Karzai and the American secretary of commerce, an anti-Castro Cuban exile named Carlos Gutierrez.

"Everything must be done to ensure that it is not used by drug traffickers," Rahmon told reporters.

"The river used to protect us from Afghanistan's troubles," a Tajik journalist told a BBC reporter who witnessed the ceremony. "It made drug trafficking more difficult," he said. "Now we no longer have that buffer."

The bridge project was part of a regional trade and logistics agreement funded by the United States called the Northern Distribution Network, which in addition to highways and bridges financed the construction of Tajik military bases, police stations, customs houses, and border posts. In order to secure supply lines into Afghanistan, the Pentagon and State Department invested heavily in propping up the armed forces of Tajikistan, whole brigades of which were dedicated to moving Afghan opiates overland to Kyrgyzstan and Uzbekistan, ultimately bound for railheads in Russia and ports on the Caspian and Baltic Seas. The greatest part of the heroin produced in Afghanistan under U.S. occupation made its way to the international black market this way, in an indefatigable ant march over a thinly populated and scantly visited region of the globe known in certain old atlases as "the Roof of the World." At least half of Tajikistan's gross domestic product derived from this economic activity, and Kunduz, an important base camp of Delta Force for the duration of the hidden surge, was the choke point controlling access to the alpine supply route. No wonder it was the site of such fierce fighting.

During the 120-day window that Lavigne was in Afghanistan in 2013, another three Green Berets were killed in action. Eight more would die before the year was out, plus two Army Rangers and three USASOC support soldiers. JSOC continued to implement F3EAD, but at a reduced pace of assassinations due to "the tyranny of distance and terrain," in the words of the retired sergeant major. The cellular infrastructure was more limited than in Iraq, and the Afghan resistance was wise, by this time, to the NSA's surveillance. They stayed off their phones and forced cell towers to power down at night.

Systematic analytical errors continued to mar the shoddy intel that JSOC produced. Enlisted operators reportedly felt frustrated that they were just posting numbers, killing and capturing increasingly insignificant targets for the sake of manufacturing statistics for McRaven to recite to his bosses at the White House. There was a sense that going out and gunning down low-level "suspected Taliban" every night was not doing any good.

Things were getting grimmer on the home front, too. There were fourteen suicides in USASOC in 2013, another fatal drug overdose, and a chilling murder mystery. In October, in Fayetteville, two masked men entered the house of Sergeant First Class Sean Wayne Wells, a Green Beret from 3rd Group who had done two tours in Afghanistan and recently returned from Tajikistan. After forcing his wife and son into another room, the hooded gunmen executed Wells with a shot to the head, then fled in his wife's car without stealing anything else. The crime was never solved.

THE FOLLOWING YEAR, a female support soldier from Fort Bragg, a psychological operations specialist named Valeria Zavala, deployed with Delta Force to one of their bases in Afghanistan. "It was a JSOC deployment," she said. "I was directly attached to the unit."

Lavigne wasn't there, but two of his buddies were. Back home in Fayetteville, Zavala was an integral part of their social circle, which was organized around the Coast x Coast motorcycle club, founded by a group of active-duty Delta Force soldiers, including Lavigne, to honor the memory of Ryan Savard. Zavala's on-again, off-again boyfriend was a core member of the club. "I was with them constantly for years," she said.

Zavala is apprehensive about talking, even on condition of pseudonymity. She is reluctant to antagonize Delta Force, an institution that casts a long shadow over the small North Carolina town where she still lives. "I know how powerful that unit is," she said, adding, somewhat cryptically, "I've seen how much technology they have at their fingertips."

Jordan Terrell, the friend of Leshikar and Lavigne who tried and failed to make it through Special Forces selection, later worked for Delta Force as an internet technology contractor and said that the unit has signals interception capabilities similar to the NSA's. "Anything you can think of in a sci-fi movie," he said, "it all exists in the real world. There is no data that is not accessible to them. Even if you're talking in the safety of your home, if you don't have some kind of device that blocks telecom signal, they're 100 percent able to listen in on that conversation, or view you remotely through your TV."

Afghanistan was not Zavala's first deployment, nor her first exposure to combat. "In my first trip to Iraq," she said, "the entire field next to a hospital got taken out. There were cracks in the walls, ceilings shaking." She was a medic at the time. "We had some Iraqi army guys come in," she recalled. "It seemed fine, dealing with blood and guts. Then we had a U.S. girl. She was sniped in the head. I had nightmares after that. I would open my eyes and still be able to see her."

The JSOC base in Afghanistan was surrounded by concrete blast walls, sod-filled gabions, stacked coils of razor wire, and plywood guard towers with harsh floodlights trained on the perimeter. There was an airstrip long enough for fixed-wing airplanes to land, and a fleet of black helicopters. Zavala never went outside the wire but often observed the strike team's missions on a video feed from inside an operations center crammed with fiber-optic cables and digital screens. "They were on exfil one time," she said, meaning exfiltration, after completion of a raid. As the operators were rallying up at a waiting chopper, one split off from the others. He'd seen a "squirter" run into a tunnel, so he chased after the man and gunned him down, even though it was against orders and cost him a bullet in the leg. "Those guys," Zavala said, "they don't like to be bored." They train for eight months out of the year, and when it's time to rotate in for their four months of combat, they're ready for action. "They get excited about doing their job," she said. "Which is literally going out and killing people." After a pause she added, "That's supposed to be weird, right?"

One day, Zavala was stuck on a long shift, unable to leave the operations center to eat lunch. One of the operators, a friend of hers from the Coast x Coast motorcycle club, came in from an all-night mission, swung by the dining facility, and brought her a sandwich. Zavala was grateful for the favor but lost her appetite when she saw that the man had a gob of gray matter stuck to his shoelaces. "He had a dude's brains on his boot, and just flicked it off," she said. "That's their job. They murder people with zero remorse."

IN DECEMBER 2014, President Obama declared the war in Afghanistan over. Thanks to the sacrifices of thousands of American soldiers who gave their lives, Obama said in a tepid address phoned in from Hawaii, where he was on vacation, "we are safer."

In reality, though most of the conventional surge troops had been withdrawn, the war was far from finished. Nationwide, violence had not been quelled. Hamid Karzai had been replaced by Ashraf Ghani, a World Bank technocrat with an Ivy League pedigree, but roughly schooled narco-warlords like Abdul Rashid Dostum remained in positions of regional power, producing and exporting more opium and heroin than ever. The Kabul-based regime, which most Afghans saw as nakedly illegitimate, would instantly fall to the Taliban-affiliated resistance if not backed up by the JSOC-led special operations task force, which would remain in place for the next seven years, waging war out of sight and out of mind of the American people.

One of the most salient aspects of the JSOC takeover of the war was the blanket exclusion of media that it entailed. After 2014, "it was easier for journalists to embed with the Taliban," said Jessica Donati, a *Wall Street Journal* reporter who lived in Kabul for four years, "than with the U.S. military." Reporting from on the ground all but ceased. For the U.S. government, said Donati, "it's quite convenient to wage the war like this."

Though led by JSOC officers, the main body of the special operations task force was made up of second-tier or "white" Green Beret teams, SEAL platoons, and Army Rangers. Their job was to manage the Afghan army and police and act as a quick-reaction force to beat back Taliban advances into the cities. Though more of them were deployed than ever before, without tens of thousands of regular troops to back them up, they were overstretched, under-supplied, run ragged, and poorly supervised.

Sergeant First Class Mark Leshikar deployed
to Afghanistan in late 2015.

LAUREN GREY, a longtime Army wife who resided at Fort Bragg for more than a decade, said that Afghanistan during President Obama's second term was like "the wild, wild West." There seemed to be no limit to the bad behavior that Special Forces soldiers like her husband, who did a total of eight deployments, could get away with. "Stealing cars," she said. "Running guns. Selling drugs. Fucking Afghan women. Where do you want me to start?"

Her husband is a large man, tall and powerfully built, with a tendency toward corpulence. He is a legend in the Special Forces community, a face seen on plaques at USASOC headquarters. In a picture taken in front of a snowy mountain range in Afghanistan, he and his muscle-bound, mohawked, tattooed buddies from 3rd Group, who wear a motley assortment of skull patches and Gadsden flags, look more like lawless marauders fetched up from some dystopian vision of postapocalyptic warfare than the traditional image of American soldiers. They're the opposite of clean-cut or straitlaced.

"When you start out as a military spouse, you love it," said Grey. "You're proud." Twenty years later, she said, "he's missing a leg and blind in one eye and we're divorced and our kids don't speak and our family's destroyed."

The Greys lived in Southern Pines, a quaint Moore County town with a picturesque post office and railroad station a short distance from Fort Bragg, inhabited by the elite of the Army special operations community. Having a home in Southern Pines rather than Fayetteville lent a certain cachet to their lives, a certain prestige. Grey had a close-knit group of friends, all "team wives." They put patriotism above other values and believed that their sacrifices meant something.

But over time, a sea change took place in the composition of the Special Forces. A good number of those who stayed in the Army for the second decade of the GWOT were animated by baser character traits, including a sheer love of fighting, addiction to the gunslinging lifestyle, and a mercenary attitude toward killing. Theft of government funds, seen as a victimless crime, became commonplace.

"The Army would give my husband and his team hundreds of thousands of dollars to pay to get information," said Grey. "But instead of really giving the money to informants, they brought it home taped to their bodies."

Five Green Berets in 3rd Group were convicted of stealing about $200,000 in "counterterrorism cash" between July 2009 and January 2010 alone. Around the same time, two in 7th Group were charged in the theft of $210,000. More broadly, at least 115 service members were convicted of stealing a total of $52 million in Iraq and Afghanistan between 2005 and 2015. Many other thefts quietly succeeded and never came to light. Whole pallets of shrink-wrapped cash simply disappeared—*billions* of dollars' worth.

Talk to military wives in Fayetteville, Southern Pines, and Moore County for any length of time and these stories will inevitably crop up. So-and-so came back from deployment and paid in cash for a fully loaded Chevrolet Silverado. His buddy opened a bank account in the name of a limited liability company, which he used to buy a fast-food franchise. Another team guy supposedly buried a bunch of money in a plastic pipe in his backyard; he cheated on his wife and she threatened to expose him; then she drowned in their swimming pool, which is weird because she had been a champion swimmer. Such is the tenor of the rumors you hear.

Dan Gould, the Green Beret from 7th Group who trafficked cocaine from Colombia to Florida on military planes, did three tours of duty in Afghanistan between 2007 and 2015, and cited pervasive pilfering of government cash as having been a corrosive influence on his moral compass. "Everyone in the chain of command knows what's going on," he wrote in a regretful letter from prison, "but no one has the balls to fix the OPFUND." He blamed the ethical drift in organizations like 7th Group on a grinding cycle of deployments in "ambiguous environments" or "gray zones" where "morality and ethics are in the eye of the beholder and everything goes so long as the mission is accomplished and your tactics aren't known to the public or explicitly to the higher-ups."

Grey said that she personally untaped $10,000 from her husband's voluminous torso after he came home from his first tour in Iraq. The next time, after a rotation to Afghanistan, it was seven or eight grand.

The amounts varied, but he always came home with cash. "I was so freaked out that this had become our life," she said. "And I couldn't say anything to anyone. Not our children. Not even the other wives.

"This is when I started to look at my husband as not who I married," she continued. "He was not the same man. He had become a full-on conscienceless killer. Greed was his number one thing. And every time he came home, going back to war was the only thing on his mind."

ON MAY 27, 2014, a long-serving quartermaster in the Special Forces named Timothy James Dumas Sr. tested positive for cocaine during a routine unit drug test. The following month, he was summoned to CID's offices on Fort Bragg.

Chief Warrant Officer Dumas thought that he'd been called in to discuss the incriminating urinalysis. But this was a pretense. The CID agents really wanted to talk to him about theft of government property. Thanks to four deployments he'd done to Afghanistan, where he was invariably stationed at the Kandahar airfield, this was a subject that Dumas knew a great deal about.

Dumas was born in 1976 in Birmingham, Alabama, joined the Army at a young age, and was stationed at Fort Bragg, where he got married more than once, fathered children with multiple women, and bought several houses. He was a broad-chested black man with a shaved head and a Punisher skull tattooed on his arm who measured six feet tall and weighed two hundred pounds. He drove a quad-cab Dodge Ram, drank Captain Morgan rum, smoked Camel Crush cigarettes, and always carried one of two handguns: a chrome-plated Smith & Wesson revolver or a Hellcat semiautomatic in desert tan. "My dad was a really good person," said his eldest son, Timothy Dumas Jr. "There was not a motherfucker alive that did not respect that man—or fear him."

A hard worker who had raised himself up from humble origins, Dumas had no tolerance for laziness or excuses. One of his favorite expressions was, "Pull the sand out of your pussy, boy." Another paternal sagacity of his had to do with the provenance of narcotics on American streets. "If the cops really didn't want it to be there," he'd say to his son, "it wouldn't be there."

Dumas was a warrant officer, a niche category of rank earned by advanced training and merit, that exists in between the commissioned officers who command units and enlisted soldiers who staff the ranks. He belonged to the headquarters company of the 98th Civil Affairs Battalion, 95th Civil Affairs Brigade. That may sound like an anodyne unit. It is not.

The 95th CAB is a unique organization, the only one of its kind in the Army, that supports JSOC worldwide. The brigade's vague and shadowy mission, in the words of its plans officer, "is to influence governments and populations through non-lethal actions." In one indication of its proximity to covert military activities in undeclared war zones, two of its men were killed by blast injuries in Timergara, Pakistan, in February 2010. Details around the incident are scarce, but both soldiers reportedly died disguised as Pakistani men in tribal garb.

Personnel from the 95th CAB are often to be found at the periphery of some of the most questionable incidents to befall the Special Forces. In April 2012, for example, a Land Cruiser veered off the Martyrs Bridge in downtown Bamako, the capital of the African nation of Mali, where JSOC had a growing presence, and slammed upside down onto the surface of the Niger River, killing all six occupants. Two of those who died were civil affairs soldiers in the 95th CAB. Three others were Moroccan prostitutes. A third American serviceman who lost his life in the wreckage apparently belonged to the Army special mission unit, even more secretive than Delta Force, known as the Activity.

Though he liked to pass himself off as a commando, Dumas was really a logistics guy, a property accounting technician whose job was to oversee an extensive military supply chain, ensure that needed equipment was on hand, and prevent theft, fraud, and waste. It was his responsibility to manage the OPFUND, also known as the small purchase program, and to supervise the performance of military contracts in the field. Given the large quantities of cash involved, the paucity of oversight, and the limited paper trail, all of these roles require a high degree of honesty and integrity in a soldier. Unfortunately, Timothy Dumas had neither.

Detective Diane Ballard of the Vass Police Department used to rent a house from Dumas in Carthage, another little town on the periphery of Fort Bragg. Shortly after moving to North Carolina in 2013, before she became a cop, she and her husband answered a rental ad that Dumas had posted for a small brick house on Barrett Street, an uncurbed strip of asphalt just off the town square. "He kind of represented himself as an SF operator," Ballard recalled. "He had a strong personality. He was a very hostile individual."

One evening in October 2013, Dumas came over to the rental house to fix an electrical outlet, and Ballard had the distinct impression that he was hitting on her. Repeatedly asked where her husband was that night, Ballard reluctantly informed Dumas that the man, from whom she's now divorced, was at an out-of-state rehab facility. "That's when he made the statement that if I wanted my husband gone, he could take care of it," she told me. "That he would take care of him permanently."

"Do you think maybe he was just joking?" I asked.

Ballard thought for a minute. "I did not get the impression that he was joking," she said. "He was deadly serious." She added, "I don't get intimidated by people easily. But he scared me."

From 2012 to 2013, while still on active duty, Dumas ran a nightclub in Fayetteville, which evidently brought him legal troubles. He was repeatedly cited for possession of untaxed liquor, failure to return rented property, permitting a minor to consume alcohol, and prostitution. But in each case, the charges were dismissed. Ballard says that Special Forces soldiers are afforded an extraordinary degree of leniency by the courts in this part of North Carolina. "I've seen it," she said. "They show up in their Class A uniforms looking great," and more often than not, the judge will dismiss the charges out of hand, adding for good measure, "Thank you for your service. Have a nice day."

According to Dumas's second wife, the nightclub doesn't exist anymore. "The entire building and surrounding area was demolished and built up new," she said. At her home in Pinehurst, a tidy, single-story house with a yard full of pine needles, she refused to open the door. Through the intercom, she denied any knowledge of her husband's criminal activities. "I'm just as clueless as anyone else," she said. "We led separate lives."

"Dad was a businessman," said Dumas Jr. "Dad was always moving. He was a hustler." He had his rental house in Carthage and also did renovations and repairs as a building contractor. He bred and sold pit bull puppies. He even made boots and soap. "He worked deals here and there," said the younger Dumas. "He always had his hands into something," including a side business of illegally converting AR-15 assault rifles into fully automatic weapons. "He liked guns more than he liked anything else," said his son.

"He would talk about all the parts he had access to and all the guns he could get," Ballard said. "You always got the sense from him that he was involved in something illegal, like some kind of crime ring."

In February 2014, the command sergeant major of the 95th CAB, the highest-ranking enlisted soldier in the unit and whom the Army did not identify by name, was relieved of duty amid a misconduct investigation. A short time later, Dumas's fellow accounting technician, the thirty-three-year-old sergeant Christopher Mann, came under scrutiny for misuse of the property book system. Mann eventually pleaded guilty to stealing more than a million dollars' worth of military equipment and supplies from Fort Bragg by generating false requisition memoranda, then smuggling the purloined property off base to be sold to black-market purchasers in Fayetteville. This was the conspiracy that CID had summoned Dumas to discuss that Tuesday in May, using his failed drug test to put the screws to him.

Dumas "denied any knowledge or participation in Mann's scheme," according to CID's record of the interrogation, but was evidently feeling the heat. In an effort to ingratiate himself with the investigators, he volunteered to share information on "schemes regarding HIKMAT trucking company."

Dumas wasn't bluffing. He knew what he was talking about. Two years later, *The New Yorker* published a report on a long-running fraud based at the Kandahar airfield, where Dumas did four tours, that centered on Hikmatullah Shadman, an Afghan trucking company owner known as Hikmat, who in spite of his youth was one of the wealthiest men in Afghanistan. Supply officers working for the special operations task force created fake missions on paper, billed the government for transport convoys that never took place, then paid the money over to Hikmat, who kicked back a fat cut to soldiers like Staff Sergeant Tonya Long, a customs inspector attached to 7th Group who got caught smuggling more than $1 million in cash back to Fort Bragg in hollowed-out electronics.

But at the time, the CID agents who interviewed Dumas seem to have viewed his offer to snitch with disinterest or suspicion, writing in the case file that he provided no credible information. Told that he might have to testify in federal court, Dumas clammed up, stating that he would need to consult with a lawyer. He admitted, however, to using cocaine, and said that he'd bought the stuff at a gas station in a notoriously rough neighborhood of Fayetteville called Bonnie Doone.

Dumas left the CID office a free man, but knew that he remained under a cloud. Aware that he could be discharged from the Army at the discretion of his commanders for unlawful use of cocaine, he did something rather rash. According to his son, he sat down and began to compose a lengthy letter.

This document, the existence of which was corroborated by three other sources, including one who claimed to have read the text in its entirety, was intended to memorialize everything that Dumas knew about a significantly more serious criminal conspiracy than the Hikmat kickback scheme. It had to do with an international drug-smuggling ring based at Fort Bragg and connected to the Kandahar airfield that Dumas's son had heard talk of since he was a young boy.

"One of my dad's buddies told me that's what they do out there," said Dumas Jr., who was born in 1997. "They're bringing the drugs from overseas onto Fort Bragg. They say a group of Special Forces are pushing and selling drugs. They fly it in, put it out on the street. Said they been doing that for years."

Nine

RISE AND KILL FIRST

In July 2013, Billy Lavigne married for a second time, to a woman named Michelle Yuki, a fellow Fort Bragg soldier, born in 1989, whose enlisted record the Army refused to produce on the grounds that she is currently serving on active duty in a sensitive, routinely deployable special operations unit. In their wedding photos, Yuki appears as a dark-haired woman with a thin figure, pretty features, and a beaming smile. Lavigne, now completely bald at the age of thirty and sporting an egregious farmer's tan, wears his formal dress blues, with the chevrons and rockers of a sergeant first class on his shoulder, and so many stripes on his sleeve, each denoting six months of overseas service, that the stack of gold bars reaches nearly to his elbow.

Ava, the couple's first and only child, was born in May 2014. Lavigne's next rotation began little more than a month later, on June 24. This time, he was deployed not to Iraq or Afghanistan but to Niger, an enormous, landlocked country, mostly desert, in the center of the African Sahel.

Although the move was soon to be overshadowed by events in Iraq and Syria, the Obama administration was then in the process of pivoting the GWOT to Africa. The legal and political foundations for this shift, a permutation of the forever-war paradigm that would have enduring consequences, had been laid a decade earlier.

In the early '00s, having redefined the Sunni resistance in Iraq as a decentralized franchise of al-Qaeda, General Stanley McChrystal and others had secured the issuance of secret directives, known as the "Al-Qaeda Network Execute Order" or "Al-Qaeda Senior Leadership Executive Order" or "AQSL ExOrd," that allowed JSOC to covertly infiltrate any nation on the planet in pursuit of other newly discovered al-Qaeda "affiliates," as well as their "financiers," "facilitators," and loosely defined "safe-haven providers." This transformed the hidden surge into a covert operation that spanned the entire breadth of the Muslim world, from Indonesia to Mauritania.

In March 2005, dozens of neoconservative pundits close to President George W. Bush, as if acting on a single cue, had simultaneously begun to speak of their hopes for an "Arab Spring," a populist uprising that would topple or weaken Arab governments across the Middle East and North Africa that were unfriendly to Israel and America. The Bush administration's blunders in Iraq set the project for a new American century back several years, but in the early 2010s, instigated in part by activists and agitators trained and funded by the United States, massive pro-democracy protests convulsed majority-Arab countries from Oman to Morocco.

In Libya, the rebellion targeted Muammar Qaddafi, an idiosyncratic Arab nationalist, Pan-Africanist, and funder of Palestinian militants who had been on America's hit list for decades and remained there in spite of his recent attempts at rapprochement. Capitalizing on popular unrest in Benghazi, Misrata, and Tripoli, the Obama administration dispatched secret agents and spies, backed by NATO airpower, to carry out an astonishingly reckless and unwise regime change.

Aided by a "shadow force of Westerners" on the ground, including agents of the CIA, American and European warplanes bombarded Libyan targets, including a convoy in which Qaddafi was riding. Qaddafi survived the strike but was set upon by a mob of rebels, who sodomized him to death with "some kind of stick or knife," then shot him in the head and chest. "We came, we saw, he died," Secretary of State Hillary Clinton crowed, overjoyed, when she heard the news.

Later, however, the glee in Washington gave way to a more sober sense of chagrin as the Libyan rebels stirred up by the CIA descended into warring factions. In short order, Libya became even more of a failed state than Afghanistan or Iraq. Armed gangs of jihadists, mercenaries, slave traders, human smugglers, and cocaine traffickers ran rampant, looting Qaddafi's arsenals and storehouses. As if a keystone had been removed from an unstable arc of countries across North Africa, plentiful supplies of war matériel, including antiaircraft guns and batteries of rockets and missiles, cascaded across Mali, Niger, Chad, Algeria, Morocco, Mauritania, and Burkina Faso. The region was beset by pillage, banditry, and murder, much of it related to intractable tribal conflicts and ancient ethnic strife. It was, in Obama's own words, "a shit show."

But the war machine, fueled by the defense industry's thirst for hyperprofits, wins even when it loses. Kicking over the Libyan anthill gave rise to a host of roving jihadist bands that American analysts labeled new al-Qaeda "franchises" and "affiliates," providing endless fodder for a special operations task force that was rapidly expanding under the auspices of a recently created geographic command known as AFRICOM.

On May 28, 2014, President Obama delivered a smoothly worded but logically slippery speech to the graduating class at West Point in which he declared that "for the foreseeable future" these "decentralized al-Qaeda affiliates and extremists," despite having "agendas focused in countries where they operate," and no ability to project power abroad, would nevertheless be "the most direct threat to America." Lavigne's deployment to Niger, which had become a booming corridor in the transatlantic cocaine trade, began less than a month later.

Delta Force's mission in Niger, similar to JSOC missions in all the countries surrounding Libya, was to stand up a "counterterrorism battalion" to protect the Nigerien government from anarchic Tuareg and Fulani rebels from the north, whose perennial jihad against French colonizers had taken on a more Salafist aesthetic and acquired a great deal more firepower, in the wake of Qaddafi's downfall. Little is known about JSOC operations in Africa, but the most kinetic zones appear to be Libya and Somalia, while Niger is more of a monitoring station and drone base. Lavigne went there not as an operator but as a trainer and instructor, a tour of duty that lasted a relatively short sixty days, with the result that he went a full year without seeing combat for the first time since he was a Green Beret trainee. But the emptying of Qaddafi's storehouses in Libya, combined with the CIA's machinations in Syria, was about to reignite armed conflict in Iraq, give JSOC its biggest war yet, and plunge Lavigne back into a world of nonstop nighttime kill missions.

ALL THROUGHOUT IRAQ WAR II, from 2003 to 2011, black-ops JSOC teams known as Advance Force Operations, or AFO, had carried out clandestine missions inside Syria, Iraq's neighbor to the northwest. Some were quiet, low-key affairs in which solo soldier-spies from eso- teric units like the Activity went deep into Syrian territory in wigs and disguises, armed only with lock-picking kits and camera equipment, to gather intelligence on the ratlines of Syrian fighters trickling into Iraq to aid the resistance. Others were cross-border strikes in which teams of helicopter-borne Delta Force operators raided compounds and gunned down dozens of Syrians suspected of abetting the insurgency. Mean- while, the State Department channeled funds to some of the most rad- ical Islamist opponents of the secular regime of the Syrian president, Bashar al-Assad, in hopes of engineering his demise.

Washington's efforts to overthrow Assad, who, like Saddam Hussein and Muammar Qaddafi, was an outspoken and belligerent foe of Israel, redoubled amid the Arab Spring protests. One of the most expensive

CIA programs in history, a billion-dollar fiasco code-named Timber Sycamore, plowed thousands of tons of guns and ammo fresh from German and American factories into Syria in an effort to arm the Sunni portion of the population that had long chafed at the brutal and corrupt rule of the house of Assad. Arms traffickers working for the CIA also shipped stockpiles of seized weapons and munitions from the Libyan port of Benghazi to Syria, pouring accelerant onto the flames of a spreading civil war.

Chief among the Sunni extremist groups that benefited from the instability in Syria and the flood of black-market arms into the country was the Islamic State of Iraq and Syria, known by the acronym ISIS. Though said to have descended from the elusive Abu Musab al-Zarqawi's "al-Qaeda in Iraq," the core leadership of ISIS was in reality made up of former members of the Iraqi military who had been held at an American prison called Camp Bucca. Flush with guns and cash of murky provenance and led by men with deep experience in guerrilla warfare, ISIS won repeated battles against Assad's army; absorbed weaker rebel factions in Syria; took control of Raqqa, a provincial capital on the Euphrates River; then drove across the border into Iraq, overrunning Mosul, Tikrīt, and Samarra. Footage of this lightning blitzkrieg, carried out under apocalyptic black banners by wild-eyed, long-haired *takfiri* fanatics who vowed to "liberate" Paris and Berlin next, stunned Europeans and Americans who had long ago tuned out the terror war.

In June 2014, President Obama announced that he would send three hundred military advisers to prop up the weak and imperiled Iraqi government in Baghdad, for which the United States had spilled so much blood and spent so much treasure to establish. Air strikes on Islamic State–controlled areas followed, the opening salvos of a devastating bombing campaign that would last for the next four years. Obama upped the number of special operators in August, and before the year was out, Operation Inherent Resolve, or as I prefer to think of it, Iraq War III, was underway.

Another JSOC-led special operations task force was taking shape, one that would eventually number more than ten thousand service members. Time and again, the White House and Pentagon vowed that these troops would not be used in combat, only to train, advise, and direct Iraqi and Syrian proxy forces. That might have been true, at least in the beginning, for the Army Rangers, Green Berets, and Navy SEALs who made up the middle or white tier of the contingent. But the black-ops man hunters at the top of the pyramid were most definitely going to be pulling triggers.

LAVIGNE DEPLOYED TO IRAQ on March 18, 2015. After a long hiatus, he was back in the country where he had first seen combat as a twenty-year-old greenhorn. In the early morning hours of May 16, a formation of Black Hawk and Osprey helicopters left Iraqi airspace, flew eighty miles up the Euphrates River valley, and touched down inside eastern Syria near a place called al-Amr. The choppers disgorged two dozen Delta Force operators and commandos from the British SAS, who gunned down a dozen Syrian guards as they stormed a compound. They found their target, a man known as Abu Sayyaf, in an upstairs bedroom; the Tunisian was said to be the Islamic State's "emir of oil and gas," making him a "facilitator" or "financier" green-lighted for summary execution. The operators shot him dead, took his wife prisoner, and dragged her out to the waiting aircraft.

Before exfiltrating, they gathered up all the laptops, cell phones, paperwork, and hard drives they could find. These materials would yield more names to add to JSOC's kill list. It was time, once again, to F3EAD the machine.

LAVIGNE LEFT IRAQ two days later, on May 18, arriving home a few days too late to celebrate his daughter's first birthday. In a series of photos taken not long after, he and his wife appear happy. They are at an outdoor concert, smiling behind dark sunglasses. They pose in a pumpkin patch with the baby. But their marriage was already on the rocks.

Michelle had her own demanding schedule of training and deployments, but Billy expected her to play the role of a dutiful housewife, too. "He was hard on her," Lavigne's mother acknowledged. "He spoiled her, but he wanted things done."

Judy also hinted that her son's alcohol consumption contributed to his marital difficulties. "Guys, when they drink," she said, "they're different."

At home, Lavigne was rarely photographed without a beer in hand. He continued to take the Adderall prescribed to him, and by this time had begun to use cocaine, MDMA, and other hard drugs, according to several of his friends. A dozen Fort Bragg soldiers who spoke on the record and off attested to the spreading drug problem in the special operations community during President Obama's second term. "I'm not going to say all those dudes do drugs," said Jordan Terrell, "but a large percentage of them do."

Dr. Jaime Earnest, who worked with traumatized special operations soldiers during her time as an epidemiologist on the Army's staff at the Pentagon, said that substance abuse among this overwhelmingly male population is practically the norm. "Damaged people self-medicate," she said. "It's what they do."

Aside from alcohol, cocaine was the drug most commonly used by soldiers and veterans in the cohort that she studied. "You start using coke because it makes you feel braver," Earnest said. "And like a big man, you can handle the pressure of your job, when you really feel kind of scared inside. Or deeply morally injured because you're not a robot automaton and you're having nightmares about the people you shot."

Casualty reports obtained through public records requests corroborate anecdotal reports of a sharp rise in substance abuse in the Green Berets. Four Army Special Forces soldiers died of drug overdoses in the eighteen-month period beginning November 2014. By comparison, only two fatally overdosed in the first eight *years* of the GWOT.

LAVIGNE WAS PROMOTED to team sergeant on July 1, 2015, putting him in charge of six to eight junior operators. Around this time, while Ava was still a small baby fond of sleeping on his bare chest, he got a cryptic tattoo on his right side, in the middle of his ribs. It was a three-pronged trident, the handle of which consisted of the letters CXXU. The same design appeared on custom patches worn by operators photographed by his side in Afghanistan.

Lavigne's next rotation, beginning November 2, 2015, was not to Iraq, where thirty-nine-year-old Master Sergeant Joshua Wheeler, his Delta Force teammate, had just been killed in an attempt to rescue hostages in Mosul; or to Syria, where fifty special operators, the first of a growing contingent, had touched down a mere three days earlier, but to neighboring Israel. A photo taken during this tour depicts him standing alongside a blond woman and three men of European descent, all apparently in their mid-thirties, at a lookout point on a hill in Jerusalem. In the background are Al-Aqsa Mosque, the Dome of the Rock, and Gethsemane.

For most of the GWOT, the deep and abiding relationship between the American and the Israeli militaries was soft-pedaled for fear of inflaming Arab and Muslim public opinion. For instance, the United States declined to include Israel in its "coalition of the willing" that invaded Iraq while proudly touting the inclusion of much smaller countries like Palau, Macedonia, and Micronesia. But Israeli politicians and Israeli foreign influence organizations lobbied hard for nearly every war in which the United States became embroiled after 2001, and following President Bush's rescinding of the ban on assassinations, JSOC established a cell in Tel Aviv to share intelligence and jointly train with Israeli commandos and spies, who are prolific extrajudicial executioners, notorious for murdering their enemies in hit jobs the world over, often using poisons, car bombs, and strange devices. Time in Tel Aviv became de rigueur for rising Delta Force personnel, who sometimes wore the uniform of the Israel Defense Forces while in-country. The relationship between American and Israeli special operators deepened significantly as a result of the complex, multiphase war in Syria, as the deployment of a relatively low-level enlisted man like Lavigne to Israel shows.

BY THIS TIME, the improvised Delta Force strike team put together to kill the Tunisian oil trader Abu Sayyaf had matured into a standing, company-sized troop known as the Expeditionary Targeting Force. "It's a tool that we introduced as part of the accelerated operations," Secretary of Defense Ashton Carter told reporters in a rare public reference to the ETF's existence. The Islamic State, he said, "has to fear that anywhere, anytime, it may be struck."

Initially made up of a hundred Delta Force soldiers and support personnel called targeting specialists, the secret assassination troop, which was based out of a string of stash houses and depended on a network of paid informants, later doubled in size. In the past, the unit had had between two and six operators under deep cover in Syria at any given time. That number now increased tenfold as the operational tempo surged to levels unseen since 2007. Back at Fort Bragg, some support staff, working in around-the-clock shifts, were pulling down $300,000 or $400,000 in salary and overtime.

Building off lessons learned in Afghanistan, Iraq War III was conducted from the beginning under conditions of unprecedented secrecy. Journalists were not permitted to embed with American troops, and ISIS atrocities, including the beheadings of several reporters, strongly deterred freelancers from attempting to work independently, especially in Syria. The military command occasionally put out formulaic press releases and promotional imagery, but they had soldiers' faces pixelated, name tapes blacked out, and unit patches blurred. This was the zenith of the Obama-era "smart war" paradigm. Everything about it was classified.

A small but steady stream of reporters did trickle in, though. On November 24, 2016, with help from a Kurdish commander who was willing to subvert the blockade imposed on Syria, I managed to slip across the border at Mount Sinjar disguised as a Kurdish militiaman. The Kurds of Iraq and Syria, motivated by a desire to have their own homeland, have long served as American proxy forces in the region and, in the ground war against ISIS, led a multiethnic coalition known as the Syrian Democratic Forces, or SDF, which functioned as the United States' proxy infantry, often with miscellaneous Europeans and Americans, both military and civilian, embedded in their ranks.

The following day, the special operations task force suffered its first casualty when Senior Chief Petty Officer Scott Dayton, a naval bomb disposal technician, aged forty-two, was killed in an explosion near the town of Ayn Issa. I shed my borrowed uniform, hung a press card around my neck, and headed west, but by the time I got to Ayn Issa, the front line had moved farther south, to a town called Tal Saman. There, even the trees were shot up, shorn of upper branches, their bark shredded. The limit of SDF control was a metal bridge over an irrigation canal through which glassy green water gushed coldly. There were no fortifications, only a rangy squad of long-haired, fierce-looking Kurds standing guard, accompanied by a group of six tall and bearded white men wearing no body armor and carrying only pistols, their Land Rovers parked a short distance away. They were operators from the British SAS doing reconnaissance to plan the next phase of an offensive to take Raqqa, the de facto capital of the Islamic State's spurious caliphate.

Along the highways that paralleled the Turkish border and around Hasakah and Manbij, I counted fourteen newly built American bases, including four airfields, the largest of which had a sunken runway so that airplanes seemed to disappear into the ground as they landed. Most of the bases were smaller roadside outposts surrounded by dirt berms and razor wire, with blinding halogen spotlights turned outward. The largest was a massive industrial facility on the road from Kobane to Raqqa, with complex machinery twenty stories tall, that had been a cement plant owned by the French multinational Lafarge.

On the road, I often saw teams of American commandos driving Toyota Hiluxes that each had a machine gun mounted in the bed, a rocket launcher slung behind the cab, powerful-looking antennae on the back bumper, and a roof rack piled with boxes of ammunition, bagged rations, and bottled water. The trucks were invariably covered in dried mud as if splattered with it, but on closer inspection you could see that the mud had been deliberately applied with a sponge for camouflage.

At the time, complex federal regulations capped the number of U.S. troops authorized to be in Syria at exactly 503, and for years that was the number that Pentagon flacks cited to any reporter who asked. But the longer I was in Syria, seeing bearded Green Berets tooling around in muddy Toyotas at every turn, the more I suspected that the true number had to be double, triple, or even quadruple that.

Over time, I gathered that the Department of Defense relies on three main accounting tricks to frustrate congressional safeguards and mislead the American public into believing that its troop levels in certain foreign countries are many times lower than they really are. First, the Pentagon doesn't count contractors, even when they're filling core military functions like gathering intelligence or disposing of explosive ordnance. Second and most significantly, any soldier, sailor, airman, or marine on deployment orders of less than 180 days is excluded from the head count, effectively leaving out *all* SOCOM personnel, who typically deploy for less than six months at a time. And since JSOC's very existence is classified, Delta Force isn't included in any official tallies, nor is SEAL Team Six.

In October 2017, the task force commander Brigadier General James B. Jarrard, who had been the commander of Delta Force during both of Lavigne's Afghanistan rotations, accidentally let slip at a press conference in Baghdad that 4,000 American troops were in Syria. Asked by a reporter to clarify, Jarrard looked confused. A press officer stood up and interjected that the number was actually 503, but the cat was already out of the bag.

BILLY LAVIGNE'S FINAL deployment began on February 26, 2017. That was just thirty-seven days after Donald Trump was sworn in as president, an event central to the breakdown of good order and discipline in the Special Forces that Lavigne's case later came to symbolize.

For the past fifteen years, JSOC and all of SOCOM had been continuously growing in power, autonomy, and impunity. The GWOT stood thoroughly discredited in public opinion, but America's cultural and political infatuation with special operations, and its veneration of the iconic figure of a bearded commando, were at an apex. In a slew of late GWOT cultural products, including big-budget films like *Zero Dark Thirty*, followed by *American Sniper* and *13 Hours: The Secret Soldiers of Benghazi*, the image of a tall, bearded, and roughly handsome white man with a checkered keffiyeh wrapped around his neck and a black rifle in his hands came to embody a venerable old archetype of American masculinity and male identity in all white settler societies descended from European colonies. If the special ops aesthetic looks vaguely familiar, it's because the operator is the twenty-first-century reincarnation of the rugged frontiersman.

The quintessential role of this mythic figure, represented first by the pioneer, then by the cowboy, is to bring law and order to the gritty fringes of empire and to protect the white family from the depredations of brown-skinned natives congenitally incapable of appreciating the virtues of civilization and democracy, whether they be Cherokee, Comanche, Pashtun, Arab, or Somali. The semiotic nexus between the Old West and the terror war was made explicit in the big-budget action movie *12 Strong*, a dramatization of JSOC's partnership with the Northern Alliance in which a group of Green Berets, backed by Apache helicopters, ride into Mazar-i-Sharif on horseback, fight savage Taliban who live by a barbaric code of sharia law, and establish a forward operating base that they call the Alamo.

Trump, whose only qualification to be president was his unerring ability to channel the darkest currents of the American id, had surrounded himself on the campaign trail with some of the craziest people in the special operations community, including Stanley McChrystal's deputy Michael Flynn, who would later pledge allegiance to the QAnon conspiracy theory, and Jerry Boykin, a holy-rolling former commander of Delta Force who had been reprimanded by the Pentagon for describing the GWOT as a Christian war against the armies of Satan. Believing, absurdly, that the military had been made to fight with one hand tied behind its back, Trump loosened the already flexible rules of engagement applicable to special operators and firmly closed the spigot on the meager drip of information dribbled out to the media. The White House announced that the Pentagon would no longer disclose any information at all on the "capabilities, force numbers, locations, or movement of forces in or out of Syria." The picture, already blurry, went completely black.

Under Obama, assassinations had been authorized only where the target was found to pose a specific threat to Americans. Fuzzy as it was, Trump dropped even that requirement, dramatically increased drone strikes, and delegated authority over strategic decisions to officers in the field, some of whom had no business making such momentous calls. The pace of bombing increased by 50 percent in Iraq, where a strike on a building in Mosul killed hundreds of civilians huddled in the basement. The commander of the war in Afghanistan, acting on his own troglodytic initiative, dropped the largest nonnuclear bomb in existence on a cave complex in Nangarhar. And a JSOC raid in Yemen destroyed the whole village of Yakla, which was left in smoking ruins strewn with the bodies of men, women, and children.

There was an underreported drug angle to this terrifying mayhem. A pair of reports issued by the Pentagon's inspector general found that Trump's personal doctor, Ronny Lynn "the Candy Man" Jackson, a rear admiral in the Navy and a veteran of the Iraq War who would later be demoted for his actions, ran an unregulated pharmacy within the White House that dispensed medications to officials and staffers in off-the-books transactions that were free of charge, while he personally drank on the job and misused Ambien. The White House was reportedly "awash in speed," the downer Xanax, and the military go pill modafinil. Records show that in addition to plentiful supplies of these three, Jackson's medical unit ordered shipments of morphine, hydrocodone, diazepam and lorazepam, fentanyl, and ketamine. All of these substances can cloud thinking, impair memory, and distort judgment.

In the field, special operators became more reckless and aggressive. On March 26, 2017, one month into Lavigne's second rotation in the war against ISIS, a small element of Delta Force operators stationed at the Lafarge concrete plant called down a bunker-buster bomb on the Tabqa Dam, a hydroelectric power facility on the Euphrates River upstream of Raqqa. The Delta element, code-named Talon Anvil, requested the strike without seeking permission from their chain of command by falsely claiming an urgent necessity to prevent imminent harm to the SDF, ignoring warnings that bombing the giant structure could cause it to fail. Only a merciful stroke of luck prevented what could have been one of the greatest humanitarian disasters of our time, as the two-thousand-pound BLU-109, one of the biggest munitions in the U.S. arsenal, miraculously failed to detonate.

When word of the Tabqa Dam incident got out, the special operations task force commander, Lieutenant General Stephen Townsend, simply denied that the air strike in question had happened, ridiculing claims to the contrary as "crazy reporting" and Russian propaganda. "If anything happens to the Tabqa dam," Townsend told an audience of American journalists, "it will be at the hands of ISIS."

ABOUT TWO MONTHS LATER, after the SDF had full control of the Tabqa Dam and the nearby town of Tabqa, a twenty-one-year-old American from Arizona named Michael Hogan, who had volunteered to fight in the SDF alongside the Kurds, had a run-in with a group of special operators in Syria whom he believed, not implausibly, to be Delta Force soldiers. At the time, Billy Lavigne was still in-country.

Having been rejected by the Marine Corps, Hogan was one of a few hundred American and European volunteers who came over to fight in the Raqqa offensive. He had a great time doing battle against the Islamic State, he told me. He loved combat, especially the explosions. "The U.S. dropped a bomb on this one complex," he said. "We thought the devil's fist was breaking up out of hell. I've never heard anything louder in my life. It was amazing."

Hogan and his ragtag squad of half-starved amateurs didn't get to Tabqa until the fighting was over and were sitting around with nothing to do when some British commandos showed up. "The SAS were really cool," he said. "They taught us some tricks of the trade," such as aiming shots at a windowsill to force the enemy to get down. "When they pop back up," he explained, "you can peg them."

Later, another group of commandos showed up, Americans who weren't friendly at all. They donated some much-needed field rations to their malnourished countrymen, but otherwise "pretended like we didn't exist," said Hogan. They had come to Tabqa not to make idle conversation but to sort through the rubbish that retreating ISIS fighters had left behind in the buildings, trenches, and tunnels used as fighting positions. Wearing latex gloves, the operators rummaged through piles of trash in search of paperwork, receipts, calendars, journals, letters, notebooks, cell phones, laptops, flash drives, storage discs, and other materials from which they could extract names to add to the ETF's hit list. This was the "data intake" or "exploit" phase of McChrystal's "continuous targeting cycle," the E in F3EAD.

"We'd run into SEALs and Green Berets and Rangers before," said Hogan. "These guys were different. In how they looked, how they talked, how they acted, they didn't give a fuck. We could have sworn they were Delta."

They rode in "souped-up Toyotas," Hogan said, with .50-caliber machine guns mounted in the beds, and were equipped with "all the best kit," but wore no uniforms, only a motley assortment of sweat-stained outdoor apparel. They were older than most soldiers, with graying beards, and Hogan was impressed by the grimy outlaw aesthetic that they cultivated. "Long hair and beards," he said. "Tattoos on their hands and necks, totally out of regulations. They looked like a motorcycle gang."

BY THE END OF JUNE, the battle of Raqqa was fully underway. The SDF, backed by the special operations task force, had the city surrounded on three sides, and American warplanes strafed anyone who tried to cross the Euphrates River to the south. An ISIS holdout force remained in the old city, determined to fight to the end. The electricity and water supply had been cut weeks earlier. The cellular network was dead.

The dismal drumbeat of air strikes was most intense at night but continued at a desultory pace throughout the day. Little ISIS drones rigged to drop grenades were a perpetual peril, but the most terrifying aircraft in the skies were the A-10 Warthogs that ripped up towering billows of earth and dust when they strafed the ground with their guns. The street-level fighting was done by the high-spirited SDF, which included whole platoons of women and teenage girls, backed by groups of ragtag Arab conscripts, many of them barefoot orphans or toothless graybeards. They were sustained by a supply line that continuously provided them with crates of bottled water, boxes of freshly baked flatbread, sacks of tea and sugar, and cartons of cigarettes, as well as daily truckloads of hot meals with meat and rice in Styrofoam containers. Armed with rifles, machine guns, and grenades, as well as sledgehammers, which they used to bash holes in the walls of houses in order to move around without exposing themselves to the ISIS snipers watching the streets, the frontline Kurdish fighters, backed by a cadre of experienced SDF commanders advised by American officers, tunneled through whole blocks in this way, painstakingly claiming every inch of the urban terrain, with gunfights popping off at every other rubble-choked intersection and booby traps exploding right and left. Land mines were everyone's greatest fear.

I saw not one civilian out of doors in Raqqa, but consistently spotted U.S. military personnel on the eastern and western sides of the city, usually one position back from the ever-shifting front line. They acted as ambulance drivers to ferry wounded combatants to overworked first-aid stations on the outskirts of the city, where injured men writhed and groaned in pain on blood-smeared floors and stoic doctors worked around the clock without the benefit of electricity and essential medicines. The Americans also served as forward observers, air strike spotters, and technicians for the massive surveillance apparatus that had Raqqa under its powerful microscope.

At an SDF mortar position next to a disused swimming pool filled with green rainwater, there was a building with an arbor out back. Parked in the shade of the grapevines was a Humvee, and in the front seats sat a couple of bearded white men wearing wraparound sunglasses and stony facial expressions. I ventured to snap a picture, but an SDF minder spoke up to stop me, placing his hand on my arm. "He's saying don't take a photograph," my translator explained. "It's banned, and they will be angry."

LAVIGNE ROTATED BACK to the United States a few days later, on July 1, 2017, while the battle for Raqqa was still ongoing. The SDF took full control of the city in October, effectively ending the Islamic State as a territorial polity, but the Delta Force kill team remained in Iraq and Syria, running the F3EAD assassination program for years to come.

In 2019, Army operators killed the leader of ISIS, Abu Bakr al-Baghdadi, and took out his lesser-known successor, Abu Ibrahim al-Hashimi al-Qurayshi, in 2022. Delta Force's sizable presence in Syria surfaced again in 2023, when ten operators were seriously injured in a hard landing after a helicopter failed to take off due to a malfunction of its rotor. That same year, fifteen hundred Fort Bragg soldiers deployed to support Iraq War III, which did not end when the caliphate fell, nor when Trump left office, but morphed into an undeclared and open-ended Israeli-American shadow war against Assad and his Iranian allies.

They say you're not a real Special Forces soldier, not a true Pipe Hitter, unless you have three things: a Harley-Davidson, a Rolex, and two divorces. Lavigne was a Yamaha guy and favored a digital watch, but true to the stereotype of a hard-living Green Beret had attained his second divorce by the end of 2017. The house at the end of Anhinga Court was his, so Michelle Yuki was the one to move out, taking primary custody of their daughter.

At work, Lavigne was in line to become a troop sergeant major and was even spoken of as a potential command sergeant major. "A good soldier and person," "a great guy and leader," "a quiet guy, but level-headed," who "always looked out for his team members" and "would complete any task" was how his comrades and superiors, always ready to cover for one of their own, described him to CID agents investigating the death of Mark Leshikar.

In reality, after fifteen years of nonstop war, Lavigne was a broken operator, a used-up military part. That was obvious to his father when Lavigne came up to visit him in Michigan following his divorce. "He had severe PTSD," said Bill Sr. "Combat trauma, anxiety, depression. You could tell he had things going on."

During that trip, Lavigne happened to run into his old pal Ben Boden, who was employed as a security guard at a big-box store in Green Bay, Wisconsin. "I was working at Walmart," Boden recalled. "He was picking up a recliner for his dad. I shook his hand and we talked for a bit."

Boden immediately perceived that Lavigne was in a bad place psychologically. He was scruffily bearded and had put on weight, making his face look puffy and exhausted. His demeanor was jittery, restive, and on edge, and his bleary blue eyes, ringed with dark circles, couldn't hold Boden's gaze for longer than a few seconds. "That was kind of unnerving to me," said Boden. "Because he'd always been so cool, calm, and collected."

Boden ascribed Lavigne's downcast demeanor to his disillusionment with the post-9/11 wars, a subject that they texted about from time to time. "I think he was wondering what they were really accomplishing," Boden said. "Anybody with a conscience, which he certainly had, would question it eventually."

On top of it all, Lavigne had money problems. As a master sergeant with advanced training who often deployed, he likely made about $85,000 a year, which wasn't bad for an enlisted man with an associate's degree living in suburban North Carolina. But his cocaine habit was a drain on his bank account. And he habitually splurged on consumer goods, especially guns and ammo, sporting equipment, power tools, electronics, and dirt bikes. He bought himself a new Chevrolet Colorado quad-cab pickup truck with four-wheel drive and a high-end trim, yet a teammate had to lend him $1,500 to cover his divorce lawyer's fees, money that Lavigne failed to pay back in full. "Lavigne needs to start supporting himself," another teammate from whom he'd cadged funds complained to CID. "He does not have any money."

It was around this time that Lavigne began dealing drugs in addition to using them. Jordan Terrell, who was already friends with Mark Leshikar, met Lavigne in late 2017 at Paddy's Irish Pub, a popular drinking establishment located at the end of the undifferentiated strip mall sprawl of Raeford Road, near an Exxon, a Walgreens, and a Dunkin' Donuts. A friend of Terrell's who knew that he aspired to join the Special Forces made the introduction. After a few rounds of drinks, Lavigne invited Terrell to accompany him to the men's room. Once they were alone, Lavigne offered him a small pile of cocaine on the end of a car key. If Terrell wanted to be in Delta Force, Lavigne told the younger infantryman, "I need to make sure you're not a fucking narc."

Terrell inhaled the key bump and wiped his nose. "I did drugs because I wanted to be part of the community," he said. "I felt like it was something I had to do to be accepted."

It worked. From then on, Terrell, with his steady supplies of shrooms and weed, was a regular member of Leshikar and Lavigne's social circle.

At Lavigne's house, there was always "a bunch of coke on the table," said Terrell, as well as MDMA, ketamine, LSD, methamphetamine, and both types of heroin. The bearded, whiskey-swilling CAG guys who hung out there, with their long hair, shaved heads, sleeve tattoos, and yoked physiques, bought and sold or gifted and swapped drugs among themselves as casually as if Lavigne's kitchen and living room had been a Baghdad bazaar. Leshikar took part in the commerce, but Lavigne was the real dealer. Terrell bought cocaine and heroin from him and other Delta Force operators, for resale and personal consumption. "I always got it from guys at the unit," he said. "I don't know who was selling it to them."

The black tar heroin they smoked out of a pipe. The China white they consumed mixed with cocaine by a method called boofing, as a suppository. "All those dudes were smoking weed, too," said Terrell. Those on active duty were unconcerned about the random drug testing to which all military members are subject because the person administering the test "would give them a heads-up," Terrell said. Warned in advance, "they would start sucking down a bunch of water, getting everything out of their system, so that they could pass their piss test. Or they would get someone else to piss for them." With Trump in the White House and regulations slacker than ever, no one was concerned about getting caught.

The off-duty operators' scruffily disheveled style tilted toward the outlaw motorcycle aesthetic, and there were ex-military bikers in the mix, including fully patched Hells Angels. Their beer-drinking marathons usually centered on barbecue cookouts and the male bonding activity of cleaning weapons together. Although the footage was classified, they would also gather to watch helmet camera videos of raids in Afghanistan, Iraq, and Syria. Despite his protestations of moral injury to his family and friends, among his Army buddies Lavigne seemed perversely proud of his military snuff films, especially those that featured his dog, which were gruesome in the extreme. "Here's me shooting this dude in the face," Terrell recalled Lavigne saying while cuing up a clip on his laptop. "Here's my dog ripping this dude's fingers off."

Leshikar's attempts to compete with the other alpha males in the group and his braggadocio tendencies were a source of tension. His overbearing physical presence and loudmouthed one-upmanship irritated Lavigne, who often felt the need to put Leshikar in his place. "They bickered a little bit," said Nicole Rick, Leshikar's sister. "They would tease each other. They would brag to each other about the things that they could do workout-wise. And Billy would pick on him for not being Delta."

Sergeant First Class Mark Daniel Leshikar
served in Afghanistan, Tajikistan,
and the Philippines.

"Billy put Mark down all the time," said Tammy Mabey, Leshikar's mom. "Because he was only a Green Beret and Billy was Delta. Marky actually had a falling-out with him about that."

Insecure over his failure to pass Delta Force selection and secretly hopeful of trying out again, though he professed to prefer the life of a regular team guy, Leshikar overcompensated by raging the hardest in their bouts of drinking and drug taking. "Whenever we would do drugs, we would all do drugs, but Mark would fucking OD if you didn't cut him off and slow him down," said Terrell. "The dude had very poor impulse control. He was like a fucking powder keg waiting to blow up."

Part III

Ten

COVER GIRLS

I n the decades since 2001, the U.S. government has lavished untold billions of dollars building out the modern-day special operations complex, with Delta Force at its fore. The total budgets of formations like SOCOM and JSOC are difficult even for specialists to estimate because so much of the spending is classified, but funding for the Army's Special Forces and the airborne corps has been effectively unlimited since the wars in Afghanistan and Iraq began. And yet, in spite of so much taxpayer munificence, Fort Bragg and surrounding Fayetteville look rougher around the edges than ever. Driving around the dreary and in places dilapidated base, with its moldy barracks, aging buildings, and potholed streets, and seeing the general state of decrepitude and disrepair in which swaths of the installation languish, you have to wonder where all the money goes.

West of Fort Bragg proper, but still within its confines, lies a tract of pine woods one hundred thousand acres in area. On the eastern edge of this expanse of second-growth forest, scarred, scored, pitted, and gouged from continuous military use, at the intersection of Manchester and McKellars Roads, there is an unmarked compound whose neatly landscaped grounds stand in contrast with the rest of the sprawling, tumbledown base. No signs point the way, but this is the headquarters of

Delta Force, which around here is generally known by the discreet met-
onym "the Building."

The five-hundred-acre facility is among the most sensitive and secure installations in the United States and is entirely closed to the
public. But assuming you are an employee of the unit with proper credentials, a contract worker with a security clearance, a visiting digni-
tary, or a special guest—a NASCAR driver, professional golfer, or
football star, let's say, invited to pay a quiet, no-photos visit—you first
pass through two checkpoints with armed guards, then submit to a bag
inspection and surrender your phone. On a weekday, you will find the
parking lot full of late-model sport-utility trucks with government license plates. If the weather is fair, you might see as many as fifty motorcycles, mostly Harley-Davidsons, parked among all the Chevrolet
Tahoes and Jeep Cherokees. Operators love their hogs. So do military
contractors.

You have arrived at the daily workplace of about two thousand people, some 60 percent of whom are civilians. The outbuildings and surrounding facilities include a helicopter pad, running track, shooting
range, portable trailers housing language classrooms, and a dog kennel
that at times echoes with the clamor of ferocious barking. At the center
of the compound is a cluster of windowless buildings made of gray cin-
der block with red metal roofs. As you approach the main building,
pause to study a memorial plaque for a German shepherd killed in
action.

Tall glass doors open with the swipe of a badge. The first thing you
see is a very long corridor, known as the spine, that runs nearly the
length of a football field. At intervals of about fifty feet, behind velvet
ropes, are glass display cases containing memorabilia assembled by the
unit historian. Here are the handcuffs they slapped on Manuel Noriega
when they captured him in Panama. There is a piece of the Black Hawk
that crashed in Mogadishu. Check out the dirty clothes that Saddam
Hussein was wearing when they pulled him out of that spider hole in
Tikrīt.

Be advised that from this point on, you will be recorded by concealed cameras and sensitive hidden microphones. The Building is as hardwired to the United States' global mass surveillance apparatus as the NSA's headquarters at Fort Meade.

The first wing that you come to houses the command group, a suite of offices with wood-paneled walls and leather furniture, including a plush library and a conference room with a digital simulacrum of the sky for a ceiling. These renovations came courtesy of a rich infusion of cash that the unit received when President Obama took office. After his inauguration, Obama broke with tradition and didn't stop by to pay homage to the unit, which a lot of operators took as a snub. The lump sum of money smoothed things over, though, and McChrystal got promoted, and nowadays you hear nothing but good things about Obama from people in the community.

The commander of Delta Force, the reigning personage here, is a full-bird colonel whose identity is classified but can be ascertained through targeted public records requests. When Lavigne was selected in 2009, the commander was Mark J. O'Neil, a New Yorker who came up through the 75th Ranger Regiment and was groomed by the CIA as a Senior Service College Fellow. During Lavigne's rotations in Afghanistan, the commander was James B. Jarrard, a Georgian who cut his teeth as a Delta troop and squadron commander in the latter half of Iraq War II. The next commander, from 2013 to 2015, was the Pennsylvanian Christopher T. Donahue, who had been the officer in charge of Delta selection when Lavigne was chosen; Donahue's other previous assignments included leading a Delta Force squadron at the height of the assassination program in Afghanistan, directing covert operations in Libya after the downfall of Qaddafi, and a fellowship at Harvard University, an institution deeply invested in cultivating ties with military and intelligence elites. In the summer of 2015, at the outbreak of Iraq War III, California-born Joshua M. Rudd assumed command. Before overseeing the formation of the Expeditionary Targeting Force and the reimplementation of F3EAD in Iraq and Syria, Rudd had done two

JSOC tours in Afghanistan during the covert surge, and six in Iraq War II.

There are many lieutenant colonels in Delta Force on staff and in command of squadrons, and a great surfeit of majors, who command troops and fill other staff positions. With few exceptions, there are no captains or lieutenants. Officers serve at the Building only a relatively short time, midway through their careers, before being promoted up the chain. For instance, after Donahue's two years were up, he held a variety of positions at JSOC and the Pentagon and commanded the special operations task force in Afghanistan before becoming commander of the 82nd Airborne Division. In 2022, Donahue took command of the whole XVIII Airborne Corps, making him the highest-ranking Army officer at Fort Bragg.

Past the command group offices is the dining facility, a kitchen and cafeteria, divided between indoor and outdoor areas, with a staff that includes a professional chef, sous-chef, cooking crew, barista, and part-time waiters. The food is excellent, I'm told. If it's a Friday, the tables will be laid with white tablecloths and fine chinaware. On special occasions, there might be an ice sculpture festooned with shrimp cocktail, or a whole hog roasted on a spit with an apple in its mouth. Feel free to grab a soda or a can of beer from one of the coolers, or an ice cream from the soft-serve machine, and head down one level, to the team bays.

The core of Delta Force consists of its four main squadrons of operators, A through D. Each squadron is made up of about seventy-five soldiers divided into a small number of troops. There may also be a squadron of augmentees, or soldiers who didn't quite make the cut at selection but are still useful as backup and for pulling security. Each squadron is commanded by a lieutenant colonel, and each troop by a major, or captain on the cusp of promotion.

Each squadron occupies one wing of the Building, a spacious bay surrounded by team rooms. My sources in the unit gave these testosterone-soaked areas a wide berth, but described them as a combination of locker room, clubhouse, and man cave, equipped with couches, television sets, and foosball and pool tables. The operators' weapons and gear are stored here in large cages.

All the squadrons have their own fully stocked bar, elaborate mahogany affairs carved by local craftsmen. There is no rule against drinking during working hours, and, barring any fire alarms, the tops of beer cans tend to start popping around three or four o'clock in the afternoon.

Smoking is allowed too, but only in the smoking room, which ventilates to the exterior. A blanket ban on smoking in federal workplaces has been in effect since 1997, but no one is going to enforce it here. You might even see a few ornery old sergeants major puffing on cigars at their desks, as little concerned about Executive Order 13058 as they are the Intelligence Oversight Act of 1980.

Past the team bays, the central stairwell takes you down to a fully subterranean basement. This is not the very lowest floor, though. The stairs go down another half level and terminate at the face of a massive portal like the door to a bank vault: the entrance to an underground tunnel system for sheltering in the event of nuclear war.

The basement houses most of the unit's support staff, a mixed military and civilian workforce divided into half a dozen departments, also called squadrons. One of the biggest support squadrons is dedicated to administrative management and logistics. Others are more involved in actual operations, including the intelligence squadron and squadrons dedicated to combat engineering, explosive ordnance disposal, signals and telecoms, and weapons development. There is also a finance troop, including a covert division that essentially launders money for use in denied missions. Commercial banks provide the unit with preloaded debit or credit cards untraceable to the government and are reimbursed through a backdoor channel.

The intelligence squadron is the largest tenant of the basement. One division of intel squad, the Analyst Support Troop, or AST, inhabits the Building's only sensitive compartmented information facility, or SCIF (pronounced "skiff"), a kind of holy sanctum of the national security state, accessible only by those with the most pristine of clearances. It is the role of the AST to receive raw intelligence from the field, and to carry out the "fix" phase of "find, fix, finish," the second *F* in F3EAD.

Another division of the intelligence squadron, housed in a special access zone at the far end of the basement, is the Mission Support Troop, or MST. Because the job of the MST is to create and maintain fictitious cover identities for operators to use on clandestine missions, and because of the widespread perception that most of the troop's employees are women hired principally for their good looks, everyone in the unit refers to them, informally, as the Cover Girls.

COURTNEY WILLIAMS was twenty-four years old when she learned of an intriguing job opportunity at an unnamed special mission unit at Fort Bragg. It was 2010, and she was coming off a four-year enlistment in the Army, in which she'd been an interrogator and Arabic linguist but never deployed. She was recruited at a job fair by K2 Solutions, a contractor in Southern Pines run by former Delta Force members.

The day of her interview, Williams noticed something unusual. All five women being considered for the job looked exactly like her. "We were all young, petite, attractive, well dressed, and blond," she said. The applicants even had on similar outfits: black pantsuits with blue dress shirts and high heels. "What are the odds?" they asked each other, laughing. At the time, it seemed like a coincidence.

One of Williams's former colleagues, Esther Licea, also said that most MST employees fit a distinct physical profile. "The general type," she said, "was white, in shape, with blond hair." In short, "a pretty girl."

Licea herself didn't fit the mold, being bigger and brown-skinned. She was hired not for her appearance but for certain internet technology skills. Back then, she said, "there were only three Latinas in the whole Building."

The unit, which is 90 percent male, has plenty of black and brown men serving as support soldiers. But less than one in a hundred of the actual operators are nonwhite. "It is very, very, very rare," said Jordan

Terrell, who felt out of place simply being a black man in the parachute infantry. The Army as a whole is tremendously diverse, but the infantry is mostly white, the Special Forces is even whiter, and Delta Force is the whitest of all. "I could not believe, mathematically," said Licea, "that there were not more minorities."

For the most ambitious officers, the high-speed West Point studs looking to rise in the ranks, Delta Force is a stepping stone to the highest echelons of the Army and the Pentagon. "All those unit commanders have their paths laid out for them," said Licea. "Next stop is probably USASOC. Then MacDill Air Force Base as some sort of SOCOM deputy CO," she said, using an acronym for commanding officer. "Eventually, they all make general."

In his memoir, Stanley McChrystal obliquely critiques Army special operators for being excessively tribalistic, insular, strong-willed, opinionated, arrogant, and entitled. In a telling passage, he writes of feeling intimidated and eager to make a good impression when he came down from the Pentagon to take command of JSOC. He had risen in the ranks through the 75th Ranger Regiment, not the Delta Force "old boys' club," as he calls it, and was susceptible to the pangs of an inferiority complex.

The imprimatur that the unit leaves on top officers is invisible to outsiders, but looking at photos of known ex-commanders, you begin to develop an eye for the signature steely-eyed, square-jawed look of the generals who came up through the Delta Force mafia. You see the physiognomic continuity, too, when you walk down the spine of the building, past portrait after portrait of former commanders in an unbroken sequence that does not include a single black or brown face. "That makes an impression," said Williams.

Both women said that the unit is even less tolerant of gays and lesbians, who are not represented even in support roles. At work, Licea heard homophobic slurs uttered "all the time." There was one longtime contractor rumored to be gay, said Williams, but "he sure as hell wasn't talking about it."

WILLIAMS'S OFFICIAL JOB title was "signature reduction specialist." For a base salary of $80,000 a year, she served as the custodian of a controlled repository of valid but fictitious passports, identity documents, and financial instruments, which were issued to operators upon deployment and checked back in when they returned from overseas. "Everything is accountable," she said. "Whether it's a passport, driver's license, or credit card, it's all logged. Sign it out, sign it back in, just like you would a gun or anything else that's sensitive, so that the backstory stays consistent."

The State Department, Social Security Administration, postmaster general, credit card companies, and motor vehicle departments of most American states have memorandums of understanding with the military to provide Delta Force with "fully backstopped personas," said Licea, including real passports and Social Security numbers. These enable operators to travel internationally, disguised as civilians and blending in with the populace, without leaving a digital trail traceable back to an actual person.

"The things you see on TV and think they don't exist, they really do exist," said Williams. At first it was "shocking," she said, to see how the government counterfeited its own instruments for the purposes of international espionage and assassinations. But over time, "it becomes day-to-day life," she said. "I've got to get this guy a driver's license. Got to get him a Social. New name, new identity, new backstory, new passport. Sitting at your desk doing paperwork."

Part of her job was to support a compartmented element of the unit called G Squadron, made up of forty or fifty veteran Delta Force men and a very small number of female operators, the only ones in the unit. G Squadron is housed not in a team bay but upstairs, with the command group. "They are the most professional soldiers," said Williams. "The most well rounded and mature. The top tier of operators."

G Squadron's missions are truly covert. They are the blackest of black ops, the dirty deeds that official representatives of the White

House, Pentagon, and State Department will stand behind a lectern and falsely disavow with the utmost apparent sincerity. "High-level, specialized 'read ins' with no ties to the U.S. government," said Williams, describing a process by which participants are granted access to "sensitive compartmented information," which involves taking a polygraph, undergoing a background check, signing a nondisclosure agreement, and being "read in" or indoctrinated about the specifics of an above-top-secret program.

"We worked with DIA, CIA," she continued. "All the agencies worked with JSOC together. We'd get executive-level orders from the White House to either collect information or capture a target, or to kill, depending on what the mission was." She added, "Usually we were going after high-profile targets that nobody knew the American government was after."

Besides fake identities, it was Williams's job to maintain the existence of front companies used by G Squadron operatives as "commercial cover" when they deployed on "alias operations," she said. Her duties included paying rent and utility bills on behalf of spurious business entities used as cutouts, work that often entailed expenditures of her time and taxpayer money that she saw as wasteful. She recalled taking a chartered flight to a small town in Maine simply to check the mail at an empty office. The MST would send people on monthly rotations to a city in Florida merely to be seen walking in and out of a vacant building. They once sent Williams to California with $10,000 in cash to buy a bunch of cell phones straight from the factory—no receipt needed.

Another time, a pipe burst in the untenanted suite of a front company in Washington, causing the landlord to become suspicious because the place flooded and no one was around to open the door. Williams and a co-worker jumped into one of the unit's brand-new sport-utility trucks and drove at top speed all the way to D.C. to deal with the situation. "Sorry," they told the incredulous landlord. "Everybody's away."

WILLIAMS'S TIME IN THE UNIT was a roller-coaster eight years of her life. She was expected to wear a pager at all times and be at the Building within an hour of it going off. She juggled multiple cell phones, and when one would ring, she'd have to remind herself which front company it pertained to, and what role she played in relation to that fictitious entity. "In two seconds," she said, "you have to swap mentally."

Staffers were routinely dragooned into supporting training exercises, and in airline hijacking scenarios Williams was invariably cast in the part of a damsel in distress. "I got shot a bunch of times in the face with a paintball gun," she wryly recalled. The operators were forever playing pranks on the Cover Girls, packing their desks with plastic explosives, for example, or coming down from the team bays with savage war dogs straining against their leashes to frighten the women who were afraid of dogs. "It was not a professional environment," said Williams, and Licea agreed. "Having worked in corporate America prior to going to the unit," Licea said, "this stuff would never fly. You'd be fired."

Fat people on the support staff were relentlessly mocked. A soldier of Asian descent was called a "chink" to his face. The boozing in the team bays inevitably degenerated into obstreperous roughhousing. "That's it, we're not fucking drinking anymore," a sergeant major would bellow in frustration. "You guys are out of control." But the dry spells never lasted long. "It was like they were trying to herd cattle," said Williams, "or take care of a bunch of children."

The operators who came down to Williams's office for paperwork purposes routinely propositioned her for sex. "The comments were just ridiculous," she said. "Don't you think your job would be better," one man said, boldly looking her in the eyes, "if you were under the desk sucking my dick?" Others massaged her shoulders, took big whiffs of her hair, made comments about the size of her breasts, or drunkenly proposed marriage. A besotted sergeant major often seen walking around with a beer in one hand and a tomahawk in the other once punctuated his declarations of affection by hurling his ax into the wall.

On two occasions that both Williams and Licea recalled, aggrieved women came on base and went to the front gate of the unit demanding to speak to the commander. One claimed that an operator had attempted to rape her at his apartment after a date. The other was an operator's wife who had learned that her husband had married another woman while working under an alias identity in Jordan. On neither occasion did the commander grant an audience. The unit sent counterintelligence personnel to placate the women and pretend that something would be done about their complaints.

"There is zero respect for women in that community," said Valeria Zavala, the psyops soldier who deployed to Afghanistan with JSOC. "I know this is specifically about Delta Force," she said, "but it's like this across the whole of USASOC."

Some operators, said Williams, "were more mature" and resented the madhouse atmosphere. Ryan Savard, who was cut down by machinegun fire in Kunduz in 2012, was one of them, she recalled. "He'd come down and talk to me about this a lot. He wanted to start a family and be faithful to his wife" and was annoyed by the unit's aggressively virile culture of philandering, seduction, and conquest. "'I'm so frustrated with this fraternity-like mentality,'" she quoted Savard as saying the last time they spoke. "'This isn't what I signed up for.'

"But no one in their right mind would choose to leave Delta and go back to the regular Army," Williams said. "Because at Delta, you didn't have to be at work at nine. As long as you got your training, paperwork, and predeployment stuff done, you just showed up whenever the fuck you felt like it. So even if they were sick of the culture, they'd vent to me about it, but they'd rather die than go back to the regular Army."

Billy Lavigne, who joined Delta Force one year before Williams was hired, was also the polite type, she said. To loutishly proposition a woman wasn't his style at all. "He was quiet, friendly with everybody," she remembered. "He didn't really have a personality. He just kind of blended in."

DURING HER FIRST DAYS on the job in 2010, Williams was informed that Israel was the only nation in which Delta Force would not do spying missions. "We were told in our training that we could never go to Israel in alias," she said. "We had no reason to collect on them." The operators who went there to work with the IDF were not even allowed to choose their own accommodations. The Israelis "put them in certain hotel rooms that were bugged."

Every other country was fair game for G Squadron's counterintelligence, reconnaissance, wiretapping, and bugging missions. China, including the self-governing island of Taiwan, was the most difficult to penetrate, Williams said. "Asian countries they were super paranoid about. But we had guys that would go there."

An operator on a spying mission would first fly commercial under their real name to a random city somewhere in the United States. It was Williams's job to drive out and meet them with a lockable bank bag full of fake documents. Arriving at their hotel the morning of the day that they were due to fly overseas, again on an ordinary passenger airline, she'd take custody of their authentic identity papers and go through their clothing and luggage in search of any overlooked scrap, such as a dry-cleaning ticket or gas station receipt, that could tie them back to their true self, Fayetteville, or Fort Bragg.

Increasingly, though, by the mid-2010s, it wasn't enough to strip them of these physical vestiges, "because young operators coming out of selection still in their twenties had been on social media for years." Billy Lavigne, for example, joined Facebook in 2006. Instagram launched in 2010, and before long "everybody's face was everywhere," said Williams. The CIA and FBI had the same problem with their youngest cohort of undercover agents, and simply abjuring social media wasn't a solution either, because the complete absence of an internet presence had itself become a red flag for foreign counterintelligence services. "We were all hitting the same walls at the same time."

Williams takes credit for coming up with the fix that she said Delta Force implemented, called True Name. Under this admittedly imperfect protocol, alias identities consisted of the operator's actual legal name, a fake Social Security number, and biographical details that were one step removed from reality. Since her name is Courtney Paige Williams and she was born in 1985 in a suburb of Boston, she might become Courtney Rene Williams, born on the same day but in 1986, in Providence, Rhode Island.

Each case was different. If an operator was named as a hometown hero in an online write-up of a high school football game in Lincoln, Nebraska, for instance, his alias would have to integrate that data point. Cover stories were tailored to square with the information that could not be scrubbed from the internet, but were kept several degrees off-kilter to confuse the picture. Foreign counterintelligence officials, confronted with small discrepancies between what was discernible on the web and an American's physical travel documents, would tend to assume that the passports and credit cards were more accurate than old Facebook pages and defunct Myspace accounts. Even if an operator had in the past posted photos of himself in uniform, "we could control it," she said, by creating a backstory in which he'd done one enlistment in a noncombat unit, then left the military for civilian employ.

Williams said that during her time the State Department, under Hillary Clinton, became very stingy with alias passports. "State didn't like commercial cover at all," she said, and tightly limited the number of fictitious documents that it would issue. "They felt it was a huge liability to the U.S. government for us to be pretending to be who we're not."

An example of the risks involved emerged in 2013, when a pair of American men named Alexander Crabb and Benjamin MacDonald, aged forty-two and thirty-nine, respectively, were briefly detained in Libya after a confused exchange of gunfire near the Roman ruins of

Sabratha. Crabb and MacDonald were carrying embassy credentials, and the State Department claimed that they were in-country to plan evacuation routes for diplomatic personnel. In reality, says Williams, they were Delta Force soldiers on a classified mission that went wrong, resulting in their capture, after which the Libyans posted pictures of their passports online. MacDonald's had been issued just four months earlier.

ONE DAY OVER LUNCH in the dining facility, seated across the table from the commander of the intelligence squadron, Williams raised the possibility of deploying with the unit overseas, as support staff often do, and which would have been a boon to her professionally. Her boss's reaction caught her completely off guard. He started laughing hysterically, hitting the table with his hands. "You're not hired to be deployed with the operators," he told her once he'd regained his composure. "You were hired for your assets," he said, making a hefting gesture at chest level, "and if they want you to deploy with them, it's because they all want to fucking run a train on you."

Williams stood up without a word and walked out of the cafeteria. She managed to get into the hallway before the tears began to flow. "It was like everything that I already knew and feared, he just said to my face," she said. "How I had been made to feel for the whole time that I had been working there. Those were the exact words that he used."

Previously, the same lieutenant colonel had called Williams into his office for a supposed dress code violation. Concerned that her white pants were transparent, he and the squadron sergeant major had directed her to turn around and bend over to assess whether her underwear could be seen through the fabric. Williams had complied, but got the impression that their real intention was to humiliate her. "So that I could walk out of their office," she said, "and make them laugh."

Licea confirmed that both of these incidents took place and that Williams was "unfairly targeted." But Williams made things worse for herself by never backing down from a conflict, Licea said. As a mellow Southerner whose family comes from a Caribbean island, Licea sympathized with Williams's plight, but had trouble relating to her acerbic Yankee pugnacity. "A lot of times I felt like telling her, 'Dude, Courtney, pick your battles,'" she said. "But to Courtney, everything was a battle."

Williams filed a grievance at the squadron and unit level, but nothing was done. The next time she came up for a performance review, she received a mediocre rating. Now she was really angry. "My work," she said, "was immaculate." She appealed the performance review, submitted a complaint with USASOC's inspector general, and eventually filed a discrimination claim with the Equal Employment Opportunity Commission.

"Once she started speaking up," said Licea, "things kept getting worse and worse for her. They came after her hard." If Williams were one minute late, she received a counseling statement. If she rushed home to take care of her sick daughter, she was clapped with an AWOL. Then, in 2016, the unit yanked her security clearance on the grounds that her dispute with the leadership made her a security risk. "From that point on," said Williams, "my life became a living hell."

Still employed but unable to view classified material, she had to wear a big red badge on her arm and be escorted everywhere in the Building, even to the bathroom. They moved her desk into a cramped storage closet and assigned her the task of proofreading a spreadsheet that contained some eight million entries. Such drudgery would have driven another person insane, but Williams's irrational tenacity powered her through the tedious labor for more than a year. "I'm one of those people," she said. "I'm so fucking stubborn. I was not going to let this happen to me."

She was never going to win this battle of wills, though. She was up against a force much bigger than herself. Not wanting to get crosswise of the Special Forces command, no attorneys in Moore County would represent Williams, forcing her and her husband to burn through their savings on out-of-town lawyers. Then the administrative law judge overseeing the EEOC hearing granted a motion to protect classified information contained in the materials at issue, greatly increasing the cost of continuing to prosecute the case. That ruling is what finally broke her. "I was trapped," she said. "I'd exhausted everything. I had lost years of my life and was just completely drained."

Given enough time, anyone who has adverse dealings with an entity like Delta Force will inevitably drift into paranoia. Williams was sitting at a traffic light in Fayetteville when it first occurred to her that she was mired in a rancorous legal dispute with an organization that exists to kill people in secret. The question of whether she was putting her own life at risk necessarily followed. "Am I going to be one of these people," she asked herself, "who dies in a car crash and it's not really a car crash?"

Finally, she agreed to sit down to settlement talks. The unit's lawyers initially offered her pittances in the realm of $5,000 or $10,000, but a changeover in leadership at USASOC in the summer of 2018 resulted in a significantly more amenable offer, a sum sufficient "to buy a small house in North Carolina," she said. She took the money and was medically retired so that she and her kids didn't lose their health insurance.

MARK LESHIKAR'S MURDER occurred during Williams's last days in the unit's employ. She didn't immediately hear of the incident, thanks to the swift and effective cover-up brought about by the authorities. But Esther Licea did.

All the other Cover Girls knew about it, too. The whole unit was aware that Lavigne had gunned down a Green Beret from 19th Group in a bizarre, drug-fueled altercation witnessed only by two little girls, and that "it was immediately ruled a justified homicide," said Licea.

Some support staffers didn't buy the official story. "There were a lot of whispers," Licea remembered, about the command's decision to keep Lavigne on as an operator. "They had him on light duty," she said. "He'd go to the cafeteria and eat lunch with his brothers, and then go back to the team room, maybe work out or go to the range, but he was not punished per se." She added, "It was weird to me, very weird, that something like that can happen and you keep employment. The whole thing was shady, shady, shady."

"It's a very incestuous society," said Williams, referring to the top officers and enlisted leaders on Delta Force, other USASOC generals and colonels, the sheriffs and district attorneys of all four counties that Fort Bragg overlaps, local judges, prominent lawyers, and special agents in charge of the regional offices of federal agencies. "They're basically all friends," she said. "They go hunting together. They all golf together. They're neighbors." Their kids attend the O'Neal School, a private preparatory academy in Southern Pines. "Within Delta and the community," she said, "there's a relationship with Cumberland County police. They liaison with police."

Every time a member of the unit was arrested during Williams's eight-year tenure—usually for minor offenses such as driving under the influence, but sometimes for more serious crimes, including sexual assault—the leadership was there to bail out their boy and quash all word of the incident. "There were protocols that went right into action," Williams said. "When something happened, they would scramble to get to it before it hit the news. It didn't matter if it was 1:00 a.m. They'd be making phone calls, getting people out of bed. It was unbelievable to see how fast they worked. It was like a well-oiled machine."

UPON LEAVING THE BUILDING at the conclusion of a workday, off-duty Delta personnel often decamp to one of several drinking and eating establishments around Fayetteville and Southern Pines. Paddy's Irish Pub, the bar where Jordan Terrell did a key bump in the bathroom with Billy Lavigne and where Laura Leshikar had her birthday party the night Mark Leshikar nearly threw his sister off a balcony, is one of them. Another is a regional chain restaurant off the All American Freeway called Mac's Speed Shop, a barbecue roadhouse and sports bar popular with military biker clubs such as the one that Lavigne and his buddies belonged to, Coast x Coast.

A third locale, code-named Warehouse 13, was another center of Delta Force nightlife during the first Trump administration. Like the Building, the hidden warehouse in downtown Fayetteville, separated from the Cumberland County jail by the terminus of Worth Street, had the benefit of not being marked on any maps. Situated behind several brick buildings on a dusty alley lot next to the train tracks, it was nearly impossible to spot from the street, even when crowded with partygoers.

Eleven

WAREHOUSE 13

For Erin Scanlon, a newly minted Army officer from Scottsdale, Arizona, Fort Bragg was a prime posting for her first duty station. She had secured a lieutenant's slot in an artillery unit of the 82nd Airborne Division thanks to the good offices of one of her ROTC instructors at the University of Arizona. "He was a really good mentor that I looked up to," Scanlon said. "He had been in Delta Force."

In her college graduation photo, Scanlon has long blond hair that reaches nearly to her waistline. In Fayetteville, she lived alone in an apartment off base. A fitness fanatic, she spent her free time running and lifting weights. It was a lonely life at times, but she enjoyed the rigors of leading a company of soldiers and hoped to advance in the ranks. Pretty soon she had been promoted to first lieutenant and was able to shed the demeaning "butter bar" label applicable to the lowliest officers. She was twenty-five years old.

On the evening of September 9, 2016, one of her fellow gym rats, a military wife named Tina Taylor, invited her to a charitable event at Mac's Speed Shop, the barbecue joint popular with military biker clubs. The fundraiser, held to honor five Green Berets recently killed in action in Afghanistan, was hosted by "some SF guys," Taylor texted.

Scanlon poured herself a glass of wine as she got ready to go out. It was a warm night at the tail end of summer, and she chose an outfit that looked like a sundress but was actually a skort. "I'm going braless tonight," she texted Taylor. "In case you wanted to know."

"Sexy," Taylor texted back. "I was dying to know."

They arrived at Mac's shortly before ten o'clock and saw that a line of motorcycles were parked out front, some with the crossed hatchets insignia of the Coast x Coast club. Right as the two women walked into the crowded beer hall, a tall, lean, shaggily bearded, and fiercely hand-some white man who went by the name of Cris Valley stopped them, "tried to flex, laughed, and walked away," Taylor would later recall to a Fayetteville detective.

This was Cristobal Lopez Vallejo, a thirty-four-year-old sergeant first class on Delta Force. He was the founder and leader of Coast x Coast, one of many such clubs affiliated with the Special Forces that proliferated around Fayetteville during the wars in Iraq and Afghanistan. "Tons of operators, guys from USASOC, JSOC, Delta Force, support guys, they're all part of these so-called motorcycle gangs," said Courtney Williams. "I thought it was so fucking ridiculous and lame."

The long and colorful history of motorcycle gangs and the military dates back to the 1940s, when the Hells Angels was founded by a mechanic who had been kicked out of the Army during World War II. In the Vietnam era, the quintessentially American persona of a disaffected outlaw biker, with his scofflaw ethos of militant alienation, was inextricably wrapped up with the mythos of Special Forces forged in the jungles of Laos and Cambodia. In recent years, a new generation of military-adjacent motorcycle clubs, such as the Infidels, a Muslim-hating, Trump-loving biker gang open only to GWOT veterans, is growing like never before. But the Coast x Coast guys, though bearded and tattooed and plenty salty, looked less like Sons of Anarchy than customers in a Bass Pro Shops. As motorcycle gangs go, theirs was pretty tame.

The main purpose of the club, aside from being an excuse to get together and drink, was to conduct an annual cross-country motorcycle ride to raise money in honor of fallen special operators. Coast x Coast convoys set out from Southern California and cross the Southwest, Texas, and the Deep South, ending in Virginia. They make a dozen stops along the way, visiting with Gold Star mothers and hosting events at bars and grills, motorcycle dealerships, and sports arenas. The ride concludes at Arlington National Cemetery, where the riders pay special homage to Ryan Savard among the ranks of their fallen brethren.

Two weeks before he met Scanlon, Cris Valley, dressed in camouflage cargo shorts, had thrown out the first pitch at a Padres game in San Diego. In Colorado Springs, he'd appeared on a talk show aired by the local Fox affiliate, wearing a Coast x Coast vest and accompanied by a military working dog named Gunner. Valley referred only vaguely to himself as a Green Beret and said nothing about Delta Force, but such public appearances, even under a pseudonym, were highly unusual for an active-duty JSOC operator. It's unclear whether Vallejo obtained permission from the unit to go on television or take center stage at sports events. Around Fayetteville, he was known as a gregarious party animal, attention-seeking alpha male, and raunchy ladies' man—to put it mildly. "Throughout the whole night," Scanlon said, "he kind of acted like a celebrity, going around chatting with people like a politician."

"He was the number one CAG guy running around Southern Pines with all these little girls chasing after him," said Lauren Grey, the team wife whose husband's many deployments to Afghanistan and Tajikistan with 3rd Group left their family in shambles. In a picture taken at Spartan Blades, a custom knife store in Moore County, Grey and Vallejo pose side by side. She has an uncomfortable look on her face, like a sick person trying to smile. You can't see it in the photo, but his right hand is cupping her rear end, without her consent. "He was quite good-looking," she said, "but he had a definite bad side. All those guys have bad sides," she added. "They don't do what they do because they're good guys. They do what they do because they're killers."

Born in California in 1982, Vallejo joined the Army shortly before

9/11, one month before Lavigne. He transferred to Fort Bragg three years later and proceeded to rack up practically every qualification an infantryman can attain, undergoing advanced training in parachuting, land navigation, reconnaissance, surveillance, and sniping. He was taught how to survive behind enemy lines and resist interrogation. He learned to read and understand Arabic but could not speak it. By the time he met Scanlon, who was nearly ten years his junior, he'd done three rotations with Delta Force in Afghanistan and Iraq, as well as an earlier tour in Mali with the 1st Special Forces Group.

Lavigne, who had recently returned from his four months of living in a bugged hotel room in Israel, was with Vallejo at the event at Mac's Speed Shop that night. True to his retiring demeanor, he made little impression on Scanlon, who barely remembered meeting him. She never guessed that Vallejo and his buddies were active-duty Delta Force operators. She figured they were run-of-the-mill Special Forces veterans, retired from the Army or otherwise discharged, because regulations forbid active personnel to raise money for a military cause, as the Coast x Coast club was doing all over the country.

Over the next five years, Vallejo would raise $450,943 in untaxed donations through his 501(c)(3), the Coast x Coast Foundation. Of that sum, IRS records show, $187,143 was disbursed to grantees, most of whom were friends of his undergoing pseudomedical treatments like cryotherapy, electrodiagnosis, and gyro-stimulation. The foundation's sloppy and incomplete tax returns, which at one point resulted in the revocation of its nonprofit status, don't specify where the remaining $263,800 went.

THE EVENT AT MAC'S Speed Shop succeeded in raising tens of thousands of dollars from raffling off a donated motorcycle. The Coast x Coast crew, including Vallejo and Lavigne, then relocated to Paddy's Irish Pub, the other main haunt of Special Forces soldiers in Fayetteville. Scanlon, who readily admits that she was drunk and flirting with Vallejo, went with them. Taylor came, too.

Bouncers wearing bulletproof vests stood at the entrance to Paddy's and ushered the group through a metal detector. Inside, the bar was illuminated by a trippy black light that made white shirts glow neon blue. The burly, bearded bartenders wore plaid kilts that showed off their hairy legs, and when Scanlon went to use the restroom, she found that the brass door handle was cast in the form of male genitalia.

That is Paddy's for you. In the men's room, the urinals are shaped like a woman's mouth, with red-painted lips open to catch a stream of urine. The walls are papered with pictures of vaginas.

Some time after midnight, Scanlon posed for a group picture alongside Vallejo. As the camera flashed, he gave one of her butt cheeks a big squeeze. "I didn't say anything when he did that," she said. "Sad as it is, that happens a lot. That's being a girl at a bar."

With Paddy's about to close down for the night, Vallejo invited Scanlon and Taylor to "the after-after-party" at a place he called Warehouse 13. Thinking it was some kind of lounge or club, they took a cab to the location on Worth Street, only to find that it was literally a warehouse sitting on an irregularly shaped parcel of industrially zoned land set back from the street, adjacent to the railroad tracks. "Sketchy looking," said Scanlon, "like a run-down CrossFit gym."

The only entrance to the little black site of a party spot, which Vallejo rented from an out-of-state chemical company, was closed off by a tall gate of cyclone fencing topped with razor wire. "Cris came up with the idea for getting this warehouse," said Valeria Zavala, who spent more nights there than she cares to remember. "They would have these epic parties," she said, "tailgate pool parties, where they would put a liner in the back of a truck and fill it up with water." On one occasion, the Coast x Coast guys "hired midget wrestlers to come out," she said. They outfitted the warehouse with couches, a full bar, foosball and Ping-Pong tables, a stripper pole, and something called a Sybian.

"It's like a saddle vibrator," Zavala explained. "Once people started getting drunk, they would bust it out, and drunk girls would try it and get all hornied up. That was their MO, that was how they operated."

Though the Cumberland County jail, the largest law enforcement facility in Fayetteville, is located directly across Worth Street, the sheriff's office and police department denied all knowledge of the warehouse and the activities that went on there. Other municipal authorities, however, suspected it of being an illegal bar and a fire hazard.

Four months before the night that Vallejo invited Scanlon to the warehouse, Cumberland County's Alcoholic Beverage Control received a tip from a police officer in Hope Mills about "a party occurring in downtown [Fayetteville] in which 'donations' would be accepted," an ABC agent wrote in an affidavit attached to a warrant to search the warehouse and seize alcohol. The tipster "also indicated that drugs would be present."

Two ABC officers went to check it out. "What we noted was a warehouse that appeared to pull double-duty as a gym and party location," one officer wrote in an email to a colleague. There were several people present, and the officers learned that "the men were military with security clearances." Out of deference to their "service of our Nation," the officers let them off with a verbal warning.

Later that day, a city inspector went out to the property and found multiple storage buildings in disrepair, surrounded by junked cars, barbecue grills, piles of wooden pallets, and tiki torches. "This is a very secluded parcel," the fire marshal wrote in an email to the zoning department. "It appears that a lot goes on here."

CREEPED OUT BY the griminess of the location and lack of outdoor lighting, Scanlon and Taylor decided that they would not stay more than twenty minutes. They remained that long only because Taylor, an avid bodybuilder, was famished and there was a folding table laden with party snacks.

Besides Vallejo and Lavigne, there were two other Delta Force soldiers at the warehouse that night, both members of Coast x Coast, plus a retired JSOC explosive ordnance technician. Women made up the rest of the party: two young Army officers from the 95th Civil Affairs Brigade, the sketchy, JSOC-adjacent support unit; the widow of one of the slain Green Berets in whose honor the event at Mac's was held; and a Las Vegas woman who belonged to a traveling troupe of singing, dancing bartenders.

As soon as Taylor had eaten her fill, Scanlon ordered an Uber, which started toward the warehouse at 2:50 a.m. She asked Vallejo if she could use the bathroom, and he directed her to the portable toilet out back. "You're lucky I'm in the Army," she told him jokingly, setting her phone and purse on the table. "Because otherwise I would not be using a port-a-potty."

She went out, crossed the asphalt blacktop under the thin light of a quarter moon, and passed a looming portrait of Ryan Savard painted onto the side of a motorcycle trailer. The chemical toilet was set up against the exterior wall of a metal building, adjacent to an alley filled with rusting cars overgrown with rampant kudzu.

She finished using the toilet, opened the door, and was startled to find Vallejo standing right there. "He just ambushed me," she said. "He didn't let me get past him. He started kissing me, and I was pushing him away. I said, 'No, find someone else. I'm not doing this.'"

Vallejo was seven inches taller than her and fifty pounds heavier. "He literally picked me up off the ground," she said, and set her on the flaking hood of a Saab convertible sunk in tall weeds. He then allegedly "penetrated her vagina with his penis against her will," as the Fayetteville police detective Paul Matrafailo later wrote in his report. After that, she put up no more physical resistance. "Ms. Scanlon realized this was not going to stop," Matrafailo wrote, "and gave up fighting back in the hopes that it would end quickly."

As soon as it was over, Scanlon said, "I jumped up and grabbed my shoes and ran inside to get my stuff. It was right around 3:00 a.m. My phone was blowing up from my friend and the Uber driver, who was there trying to find me."

Taylor saw Scanlon emerge from the warehouse, trailed by Vallejo. Already Taylor could sense that something was wrong because when Vallejo tried to catch up with Scanlon, she "darted off" to the street, where she stood "pacing and shaking." Taylor walked over to see what the matter was. The first words out of Scanlon's mouth were, "I feel like I just got raped."

Scanlon had to order another Uber, because the first one had given up trying to find her and driven away. During the car ride, she looked down at her phone and saw that Vallejo had sent her a text: "How are you? Let me know when your [sic] home safe." To this he appended a heart emoji and a kissy-face.

"Do you realize what you did?" she replied at 4:25 a.m.

He didn't respond.

FIRST THING THE NEXT MORNING, before she showered or changed clothes, Scanlon presented herself at Womack Army Medical Center on Fort Bragg and underwent a sexual assault forensic examination. The nurse who did the rape kit noted that her makeup was smeared, and described her general demeanor as "tearful." She had multiple small lacerations on her vulva, contusions and scratch marks on her left flank and lower back, and DNA that proved a match to Vallejo's in her vagina and cervix.

Scanlon initially went to Fort Bragg CID to report the alleged rape, but after taking her videotaped statement, the agents referred her to civilian police on the grounds that the incident had taken place off base. In the days that followed, Detective Matrafailo reviewed Scanlon's text messages, obtained a warrant, took DNA samples from the hood of the Saab, reviewed security camera footage, visited Mac's and Paddy's, and interviewed Taylor, among other witnesses. His investigation concluded with a finding of probable cause, and on September 30 he placed Vallejo under arrest for second-degree rape, second-degree sex offense, and sexual battery.

In his mug shot, Vallejo appeared freshly shaved, his beard gone. His shaggy head of hair had been neatly trimmed and parted to one side with a comb. Only then did Scanlon learn the true identity of the man she knew as Cris Valley. "This guy's active duty," the detective told her. "He's in JSOC."

VALLEJO, WHO CONSISTENTLY maintained his innocence, pleaded not guilty. A trial was set for February 2018 in Cumberland County court. But the "well-oiled machine" with the power to "make things somehow go away" that Courtney Williams described continued to work its gears in the background.

For a defense attorney, Vallejo retained the ex-marine Kris Poppe, an experienced criminal litigator in civilian practice who had spent most of his legal career in the military and had defended some of the most notorious defendants in Army history, including Colonel Steven Jordan, the only officer charged in the Abu Ghraib prisoner abuse scandal; and Major Nidal Hasan, a military psychiatrist of Palestinian origin who committed a mass shooting at Fort Hood, Texas. In preparing Vallejo's case for trial, Poppe made sure to speak to Billy Lavigne. "We interviewed him as a witness," Poppe said. "He was an eyewitness to the events of that night. It was two females that were eyewitnesses, and him."

Two weeks before opening arguments were set to begin in Cumberland County court, Army staff attorneys known as judge advocates general—military lawyers attached to the Special Forces—convened a "weird meeting," Scanlon said, with her and the district attorney, Billy West. Fort Bragg CID had initially washed its hands of the case, but the JAG officers, a male captain and a female major, claimed to have only belatedly learned that Vallejo and Scanlon were both soldiers, which gave the Special Forces parallel jurisdiction to try Vallejo. They urged

Scanlon to consent to dropping the case against him in civilian court in favor of a military trial on Fort Bragg, which they said offered a better chance to convict, among other reasons because a guilty verdict need not be unanimous under military law.

"It was very frustrating," said Scanlon, "that all these people had waited till the last minute, then were trying to put the decision on me, when I'm not a lawyer, I'm not a police officer. I had no idea why they were making me decide this."

Under pressure, she consented to removal of the case onto Fort Bragg. The records kept by the Cumberland County court were expunged, and all traces of the rape and sexual battery charges against Vallejo disappeared. Another four-month delay ensued. "I was pissed that another obstacle had gone up," Scanlon said. "I wanted this all behind me."

BY THE TIME that Donald Trump was inaugurated in 2017, cases of special operators behaving badly had been mounting for years and reached a crescendo during his tenure in office. Many of the incidents of misconduct and criminality had to do with drug trafficking and went scantly reported in the national press. But the most notorious cases, involving rape and murder, did garner sustained media attention, to the detriment of the SOCOM brand and the prestige that special operators had long enjoyed as the ultimate "quiet professionals."

In 2013, Angel Martinez-Ramos, a Navy SEAL who traveled frequently to Panama, El Salvador, Honduras, Guatemala, and Colombia on official business, was caught at the Miami airport with ten kilos of cocaine in his carry-on. In 2015, James Matthews, a former SEAL, was pulled over in New Jersey hauling a trailer stuffed with $1.4 million worth of marijuana. James Dennis Smith Jr., another ex-SEAL, and a former CIA special agent, was charged in 2017 with supplying hundreds of kilos of marijuana, as well as steroids, to a multimillion-dollar drug ring in South Carolina. Both Matthews and Smith were licensed pilots who trafficked drugs by air.

"I definitely have an extremely addictive personality, to say the least," said Matthews, who told me upon his release from prison that he had smuggled many tons of California-grown bud across the country to New Jersey and New York primarily for thrills, and that his SEAL training had made him an exceptionally successful trafficker for years before he got caught. "My discipline," he said. "My attention to detail. How I dress, cut my hair. How I could talk to cops." In an ambiguous adage that could well apply to the life of Billy Lavigne, Matthews added, "The words 'addiction' and 'discipline' are synonymous with each other."

In April 2016, Rob O'Neill, one of the SEALs who claimed to have killed Osama bin Laden, was arrested for driving under the influence by police officers who found him passed out in a car with the lights on and engine running outside a convenience store in Montana. In February 2017, an Army Ranger out of his mind on a high dose of dextroamphetamine stole a pistol from a Fort Lewis armory, shot and seriously injured a man in Tillicum, Washington, in an attempt to jack his truck, then fled into the woods and covered his body in mud in an effort to evade detection by dogs, but ended up surrendering to police because he could not bear the cold.

In June 2017, two SEAL Team Six operators stationed in Mali, abetted by several Marine Raiders, plotted to assault and sexually humiliate one of their comrades on the AFRICOM special operations task force, a Fort Bragg–based Special Forces soldier named Logan Melgar, who had reported their alleged theft of OPFUND and also looked askance at their practice of bringing prostitutes to the barracks in Bamako. The operators' plan to get revenge was to choke Melgar unconscious and then film while a depraved Malian security guard nicknamed Big Man, shirtless and wearing a dog collar and leash, performed anilingus on him. But in carrying out "Operation Tossed Salad," as the perpetrators called their malicious assault on the straitlaced, teetotaling Green Beret from Lubbock, Texas, they caused Melgar to die of asphyxiation. Managing the fallout from his death and the negative press it gave rise to and ensuring that the two JSOC personnel involved were exonerated of murder and served minimal jail time would preoccupy the Naval Special Warfare Command for the next five years.

Meanwhile, in December 2017, a group of Navy SEALs came forward to report the tramadol-popping enlisted leader of their platoon, Chief Petty Officer Eddie "Freaking Evil" Gallagher, for indiscriminately shooting unarmed men, women, children, and the elderly during the battle of Mosul for no reason but to rack up confirmed kills in a deranged quest to top the body count claimed by dead-eyed Chris Kyle of *American Sniper* fame. Caught on camera about to stab an unconscious teenaged ISIS fighter in the neck with a custom hunting knife, Gallagher was charged with war crimes, but beat the most serious counts, including murder, after one of his teammates who'd already been granted immunity took responsibility on the witness stand—an old mob trick that the prosecution, led by a rookie lawyer who'd never tried a murder case before, walked right into. But Gallagher's three-ring circus of a court-martial, which drew the intervention of President Trump, who had made it a part of his political persona to defend accused war criminals, contributed to a darkening in public perceptions toward the Navy SEALs.

Delta Force, however, is a little more adept at sidestepping scrutiny than its naval counterpart, as is the Army Special Forces. None of the foregoing cases involved Green Berets; nearly all of the perpetrators were Navy men. Delta Force had been implicated in the abuse of Iraqi prisoners in 2004, but ever since then the unit had kept its name completely out of the news. That ability to maintain a low profile and dodge media attention was now tested to the maximum when, less than a month after Cris Vallejo's trial was moved onto Fort Bragg, Billy Lavigne was hauled into the county jail on suspicion of Mark Leshikar's murder.

The Fort Bragg brass was faced with a stark reality in March 2018. Two active-duty Delta Force operators, members of the same regulations-flouting motorcycle club, were simultaneously suspected of the two most serious crimes in the book, and in both cases the alleged victim was a fellow service member. So far the press had not got wind of Lavigne's case, but Vallejo's mug shot had been published on a local news site, which identified him as a "North Carolina soldier." The threat of negative media attention, which can endanger congressional funding and foreshorten the careers of top generals, whom the Pentagon reflexively fires when scandals roil the units they command, came at a bad time for the image-conscious institutions involved. The murder case against Lavigne needed to go away. So did the rape case against Vallejo.

VALLEJO'S COURT-MARTIAL, captioned *United States v. Cristobal Vallejo*, convened on June 25, 2018, at the courthouse on Fort Bragg, a brick building done in the Greek Revival style typical of the Carolinas. While theoretically open to the public, as all criminal trials must be under the Sixth Amendment to the Constitution, there were no reporters in the courtroom. Nor is it known what testimony the witnesses gave, what arguments the lawyers made, or what the judge's oral rulings were, because no transcript was made of the proceeding, and as soon as it concluded, USASOC destroyed the audio recordings. Although this destruction of records would be impermissible under regulations in effect today, Colonel Adam Kazin, chief of Army JAG's criminal division, told me that the deletion of the audio files was "standard practice at the time."

Other than when she was called as a witness, Scanlon was kept sequestered by the prosecution team in a side room for the duration of the trial, an abrogation of her right to be present that no one involved in the case could explain. Fortunately, she had an ally in the courtroom.

Lindsey Knapp used to be an Army officer stationed at Fort Bragg. Later she got her law degree and, in addition to running a women's counseling center and yoga studio in Sanford, North Carolina, worked for USASOC as an advocate for sexual assault victims. She was present for all three days of Vallejo's trial, and what she witnessed left her incensed.

Colonel Kazin rejected any notion that the prosecution took a dive. "We don't take cases into the courtroom with the intent of losing them," he said. "Nobody has time for that." But Knapp said that the prosecution turned in a performance that was conspicuously abysmal. As in the court-martial of Eddie Gallagher, the government's case was presented by a pair of relative novices who struggled to keep up with Vallejo's experienced civilian lawyer. "Those two captains," said Knapp, referring to the junior JAG officers appointed to act as lead prosecutors, "this may have been their first trial ever."

On June 25, Scanlon was called in as the first witness. Nervously she took a look at the jury, which consisted of ten majors and colonels, all of whom served the Special Forces. She was practically the only person in the room who didn't wear USASOC's red arrowhead patch on her shoulder.

Vallejo, seated at the defendant's table alongside Kris Poppe, was dressed in his formal blue uniform, the chest and shoulders of which were adorned with golden braids, rows of ribbons, and silver skill badges that marked him out as a military superstar. In her basic dress blues, Scanlon felt naked by comparison. "I had no deployment stripes," she said. "No unit patch. No awards. Because I had been in for eighteen months. And he's sitting there decked out." She felt diminished in the eyes of the jury. "You want to think they're not comparing?"

Poppe grilled Scanlon on the stand for eight painful hours. In her and Knapp's telling, his line of questioning was intended to demonstrate that she was a promiscuous young woman who had gotten drunk and gone out on the prowl in a revealing outfit, pictures of which Poppe put up for the jury. She had willingly hooked up with Vallejo behind the warehouse, then lied about it in order to avoid charges of "fraternization," the military crime of an officer having sex with an enlisted person—a theory that is difficult to understand, since Scanlon herself had reported the incident to police.

The prosecution's whole case turned on Scanlon's credibility, yet they meekly sat through Poppe's aggressive cross-examination, said Knapp, and allowed him to elicit the details of an unrelated consensual relationship that Scanlon had previously had with an enlisted man. Although such questioning is generally prohibited by Military Rule of Evidence 412, a "rape shield" law intended to prevent rape cases from devolving into trials of the victim's reputation for chastity, the judge, Colonel Jeffery Nance, allowed Poppe to quiz Scanlon on the subject of the past relationship in order to establish her alleged motive to lie about fraternization. Nance cautioned the jury that they were forbidden to conclude that Scanlon, having willingly slept with one enlisted man, was likely to do it again, but to use an old legal cliché, that was a bit like throwing a skunk into the jury box and instructing the jurors not to smell it.

In the days that followed, the prosecution called only five witnesses, compared with nine by the defense, and inexplicably failed to put Detective Matrafailo on the stand, even though he'd gathered the evidence against Vallejo. One of the people whom Poppe summoned to give evidence was William J. Lavigne II. He testified on June 26, at a time when, according to his father, he was suffering the most severe PTSD of his life. Because of the Army's destruction of the audio, there is no surviving record of his testimony. Knapp couldn't recall the questions that Poppe asked or the answers Lavigne gave, only that "the defense brought up folks to say that they didn't see anything, or that it was consensual."

One of the questions of fact at issue in Vallejo's trial was if Scanlon had made inconsistent statements about whether any of the partygoers at the warehouse had directly witnessed the alleged rape. To establish that Scanlon had only belatedly reported seeing the Green Beret's widow walk by the portable toilet, Judge Nance ordered Scanlon's *own lawyer*, Captain Alycia Stokes, to testify against her.

To Knapp, this was the most glaring of a series of questionable rulings

THE FORT BRAGG CARTEL

on the part of Judge Nance, who later made public comments suggesting he believes that sexual assault charges against male soldiers are often trumped up. Captain Stokes resisted the highly unusual order by going on leave so that she wouldn't be available to testify against her own client, but Nance threatened to send federal marshals after her. "Then he berated her on the stand," Knapp said, "for being elusive and not showing up right away."

"They should not have allowed my lawyer to testify against me," said Scanlon. "That was such a crazy ethical mistake."

ON JUNE 27, both sides delivered their closing arguments. Scanlon was called in later that day for the reading of the verdict. She had brought with her a victim's impact statement that she was prepared to read if Vallejo was found guilty. "That night he shattered my whole world," the statement read. "I had to get shots and blood drawn to get tested for sexually transmitted diseases so many horrible times." She spoke of the humiliation of being physically overpowered and the enduring fear that it instilled. "I was too scared to go to stores, the gym, and other crowded places," she wrote. "Because every man with a dark beard or a hat terrified me."

She never got the chance to read these words to Vallejo or the court. As the jury filed in, everyone stood. Scanlon tightly held hands with family members who had come to support her, staring straight ahead and refusing to make eye contact with Vallejo. "I was resolved to be stoic no matter what," she said, "because I knew I had stood up for myself as much as possible. As soon as they said 'not guilty,' my people just kind of quickly escorted me out."

LINDSEY KNAPP SPENT the next month drafting a five-page letter detailing the many irregularities that had marred the investigation and trial, all of which had militated in Vallejo's favor. On August 18, she emailed the letter to Lieutenant General Francis Beaudette, the commander of USASOC.

Outraged by her insubordination, Beaudette immediately sent Knapp home on administrative leave. She spent the next two years under investigation for supposed spillage of classified information—namely, the fact that Vallejo was a member of Delta Force, which she'd included in the letter, emailed over an unencrypted network. On May 1, 2020, she was harshly reprimanded in writing, then fired. She hasn't worked for the military since.

Looking back on the court-martial, "it was a solid case and my testimony was powerful," said Scanlon, who left the military in 2019 and went to work as an aide to a congresswoman. "But I was this lowly lieutenant up against Delta Force and USASOC and JSOC, and all that that entails. Only afterwards did I realize I didn't stand a chance."

BOTH SCANLON AND KNAPP saw their military careers derailed, and Vallejo's came to an end as well. He escaped legal punishment but by his conduct had marked himself out as a black sheep in the unit. Going on television, throwing out pitches at major-league baseball games, and raising hundreds of thousands of dollars at events conspicuously promoted on social media, often using the portraits of fallen Delta Force soldiers to promote raffles and sell merchandise, were against Army regulations and flew in the face of the unit's culture of anonymity and silence. And his indiscriminate womanizing pushed the limits even in the context of an inordinately macho culture that prized sexual conquest. He was kicked off Delta Force in April 2017 and rode out the remainder of his time in uniform as an ignominious "SURPLUS SLDR" in the headquarters company of USASOC.

A civil lawsuit that Scanlon filed against the Army for its handling of the case was dismissed, but the result was an ABC News article, published in January 2020, that amounted to the first negative story about Delta Force in sixteen years. Vallejo wasn't pictured or named, and he was erroneously identified as having been a former member of the unit at the time of the alleged rape, but it still cast Delta Force in a negative light.

Vallejo retired in 2021. He moved to Colorado, where he had spent his first years in the Army, married a woman, and had a kid. But he would not live long enough to enjoy the pleasures of fatherhood and middle age. An unfortunate accident was in his future. The sandman, however, would come for Billy Lavigne first.

Part IV

Part IV

Twelve

HE WAS SEEING BAD THINGS

After Billy Lavigne was absolved of criminal responsibility for the death of Mark Leshikar and released into the custody of his teammates, they dropped him off at his mom's house in Hope Mills, a large suburb south of Fayetteville. Judy had moved to Hope Mills to be closer to her son and granddaughter following a divorce from Bill Sr. and lived in a little blue house with an American flag out front. "He came here that night and cried and cried," said Judy. "He was devastated. I've never seen him more broken."

"Mom, that was my best friend," he said. "Mom, I tried to get someone to come help."

"Billy," she replied, "I know you wouldn't have done what you did unless you had to."

Judy is a tall woman with blue eyes, curly bangs, and buckteeth. The hourly wage she earns at Walmart is meager, the lunch breaks never long enough. Her eldest son, with whom she was especially close, tried to ease her burdens.

"I'd come home from work at ten o'clock at night," she said. "He'd run out to get my groceries. He'd say, 'Come on, Mom, let's watch a movie, make popcorn.' That was Billy. He took me to the ocean. I had never seen it before. He took me to the mountains to ride horses. That's how he was."

One of Judy's prized possessions is an old letter, dated March 11, 2004, that she received from Major Joseph Davidson, the squadron operations officer of Lavigne's cavalry troop during his first deployment. "Our mission here is wide-ranging and at times very challenging," the letter read. "Primarily we are trying to provide Iraq with a secure and stable environment. Tied into that is the need to find and apprehend the Non-Compliant Forces."

The letter is addressed "Dear Ma'am," and in places refers to "William" as "your husband." But Judy was deeply touched. "Major Davidson," she said, "he was so proud of Billy. He knew that there was something special in him. 'Billy's going to go far.' He told me that. And Billy did go far. He dedicated his life to his family and his country. He only had an issue when he got ill with PTSD."

Judy paused to dab tears from her eyes. "Billy didn't get really bad until after Mark died," she said. "That's when we noticed a turn for the worse."

JORDAN TERRELL was on a bus headed back to Fort Bragg from the Special Forces selection course when a friend called to let him know that Mark Leshikar was dead. "That night," said Terrell, "I got fucking obliterated."

Several days later, once he'd recovered from his hangover, Terrell called Lavigne and demanded to know what had happened. Lavigne reacted calmly and in a conciliatory tone. He told Terrell to grab his camping gear and meet him on the beach in Wilmington, North Carolina, about a two-hour drive from Fayetteville.

Crouched before the flickering light of a driftwood campfire, one arm around his toothless, watchful Belgian Malinois, Lavigne told Terrell essentially the same story that he'd given Nicole Rick: Leshikar had disappeared from the motel room in Savannah the night before and had gone out and bought a bunch of uppers, downers, ketamine, and bath salts. On the drive home, he'd developed the paranoid delusion that his failure to pass Delta Force selection had somehow made him an actively surveilled JSOC target, and that Lavigne had been tasked to covertly serve as his minder. At Lavigne's house, he had taken a screwdriver to the undercarriage and engine of the car in a frantic search for hidden transponders. Lavigne had tried to lock him outside, fearing that he posed a danger to Ava and Melanie, but he had burst into the foyer wielding the screwdriver as a weapon.

"Why didn't you disarm him," Terrell asked, "or shoot him in the leg?"

"Well," Lavigne replied, "I didn't want the girls to get hurt."

"The girls were in the other room," Terrell said. "You had them barricaded in the other room."

"Yeah, well," Lavigne said. "I just didn't want to get into a tussle."

"Parts of the story were true," Terrell said, but Lavigne never adequately explained why he had escalated so quickly to the use of deadly force. "That part didn't seem authentic," said Terrell.

"Billy was very good at putting a mask on," he added. "He was always smiling."

ON MARCH 26, 2018, Lavigne failed to check in with his squadron by 1600 hours as required of every soldier every day. His mom called his first sergeant, informed him that Lavigne "was in a bad way," then drove him to the hospital, where he admitted to attending physicians that he'd used cocaine that afternoon. Nevertheless, he remained an active-duty operator on Delta Force.

Lavigne's frayed mental state deteriorated precipitously in the months that followed. "He changed dramatically in a short period of time," said his father, who came down from Michigan's Upper Peninsula to stay for a time in one of his son's spare bedrooms. "I started really noticing a change in his behavior," said the elder Lavigne, who looks like an older, thinner version of Billy, with watery eyes and a long, yellowing goatee. "I would see him staring off into space a lot, thinking."

On July 4, Bill Sr. took Billy to see the Independence Day fireworks show on Fort Bragg in the hopes that the spectacle would cheer him up. The annual event, which regularly draws a crowd of forty thousand, features live music, a flag ceremony, and a skydiving performance by the Army's trick parachuting team, the Golden Knights. But the throngs of people put Lavigne on edge. Pyrotechnic explosions lit up the night sky, strings of firecrackers went off as loud as machine-gun fire, and smoke drifted across the parade ground. "We had to get out of there," said Bill Sr. "He was seeing bad things."

IN MID-JULY, Lavigne called Leshikar's mom, Tammy Mabey, who had been doing everything she could in the last four months to expose the cover-up of her son's murder. In between shifts at the grocery store where she worked in dark and rainy Lynden, Washington, she wrote letters to news outlets including CNN and *Dateline*, presenting the facts, attaching supporting documents, and urging them to investigate. She'd also written emails to top Army officers, including Major General Donna Martin, then the commander of Army CID. None had responded.

When Tammy saw that the call was from Lavigne, her first thought was that it was an attempt at intimidation. In fact, Lavigne was calling to beg her forgiveness. "He was trying to find peace within himself," said Tammy.

But that wasn't going to happen so long as he continued to lie about the shooting. "He was trying to tell me the story about the screwdriver," Tammy said. She coldly informed Lavigne that she had a copy of the medical examiner's report, in which the doctor who first arrived at the scene wrote that no screwdriver had been found anywhere near her son's body. "He hung up on me as soon as I said that," she said.

AS LAVIGNE STRUGGLED to cope with the psychological torments of guilt and regret, his drug dealing grew more overt and the company he kept less selective. On the night of August 31, 2018, Cumberland County sheriff's deputies were called out to his house in response to a neighbor's complaint, went inside, and saw that someone had been cooking crack cocaine. They seized powder cocaine, a crack pipe, a digital scale, a gun belt, and a small arsenal of weapons, including a Ruger Vaquero revolver, a Mossberg shotgun, a snub-nosed Glock, and a Savage Arms sniper rifle. There is no record of Lavigne having been booked into jail that night, but he was charged with manufacturing a controlled substance, as well as the rather more unusual offense of harboring an escapee. The sheriff's office declined to say who the escapee was, or what they had escaped from.

In need of a criminal defense attorney, Lavigne hired Kris Poppe, the lawyer who just two months earlier had gotten Cristobal Vallejo acquitted of rape. "I was Billy's attorney," Poppe said. "Billy was a personable guy. Obviously really highly skilled at what he did. He was very committed to his daughter." After a pause he added, "He was also someone who was dealing with some demons with regard to substance abuse."

Lavigne posted a $2,500 bond, and his court date was set for January 2019. But some time before trial, the case disappeared from the county docket. Once again, the DA had dropped felony charges against Lavigne. It would not be the last time.

"He had been getting into all kinds of legal trouble," said Tammy. "Hanging out with bad people, deep into drugs, and nobody said or did anything. He was still a very active, decorated soldier."

TWENTY-SIX DAYS AFTER Lavigne's arrest for manufacturing a controlled substance, he was finally kicked off Delta Force, which had recently changed its official name to the 3rd Operational Support Group. Like Vallejo, he was transferred to a do-nothing position at the headquarters company of USASOC.

Interviewed by CID in 2021, the commander of the headquarters company used the opportunity to vent his frustrations with his non-combat administrative unit being used as a dumping ground for Delta Force's most damaged operators, half a dozen of whom he had on hand at any given time. "They never come to us under simple circumstances," the commander told investigators. "They have real deep problems that usually involve some type of crime," and may be facing a court-martial, civilian trial, or sexual assault investigation.

"We receive heavily redacted reports on the cause for their arrival," the commander continued, "which limits our ability to properly risk-mitigate. They often do not have a clear understanding of why they are reporting to the headquarters company, which makes them incredibly guarded and disgruntled. We intentionally limit their physical presence as it is a hindrance to the good order and discipline of the company."

The commander went on to voice his concern that an embittered ex-operator might commit a mass shooting. "Having some of the most tactically skilled, physically fit, and intelligent operators in the military coming in on bad terms is dangerous," he warned. "It presents a very real concern from a force protection standpoint. We have no guards protecting this building. We lack the capability to neutralize immediate threats other than dialing 911. The gym is a highly populated place where no one wears a uniform, bags are carried, and 'piggybacking' into the building is easy. In the past," he continued, a profanity-spewing operator angered at having been expelled from the unit "was busted at the gate with a loaded AR-10 in his back seat with a blanket over it."

In Lavigne's case, he came from Delta Force "as a highly trained, disgruntled, and unstable soldier pending separation and a myriad of charges," the commander told CID. Lavigne repeatedly made suicide threats and "on multiple occasions demonstrated erratic behavior such as throwing boxes and coolers at the supply cages and kicking doors."

The other soldiers in headquarters company, many of whom were children when 9/11 happened and had never deployed, "were very intimidated by him," the commander said. "They all expressed a very real sense of fear every time Lavigne was in the company area."

TIMOTHY DUMAS, the quartermaster in the JSOC-adjacent 95th Civil Affairs Brigade who had been questioned by CID about theft of military property after testing positive for cocaine, also saw his military career come to an ignoble end just short of his pension eligibility date. He was issued a reprimand for drug use, refusing a direct order to attend rehab, and disrespect toward superior officers, and was consequently separated from the Army, in March 2016, for moral and professional dereliction.

Dumas's separation packet, which runs to 128 pages, shows that he was repeatedly cited throughout his career for neglecting to properly maintain supply records, failing to report deficiencies, and losing sensitive items. For all of 2012 and 2013, at the height of JSOC's hidden surge in Afghanistan, the property records pertaining to Dumas's battalion were found to be missing in their entirety. "A lot of things," said his son, "were not showing up in the stocking list for Fort Bragg."

Dumas Sr. lodged vociferous, expletive-laden complaints up and down the chain of command, even directly emailing the JSOC commander, Admiral William McRaven. In these manifestos, he mixed diatribes about his fatherless upbringing with recitals of his many deployments and awards, as well as complaints about racial prejudice shown him by his chain of command, certain JSOC files that were stolen from his locked cabinet, and the Army's failure to provide proper funerary honors to Joshua Townsend, the first Green Beret to die of a drug overdose in Afghanistan.

Dumas also alluded to himself as one who kept secrets on behalf of the organization. "I did not expose the truth," he wrote in his rebuttal to the memorandum of reprimand that he received, "when I was questioned by the FBI and CID about crimes committed by high-ranking officials who are serving now in various Special Operations commands."

But Dumas's implicit threats went nowhere, it seems. The bad paper went into his permanent record. He was now confronted, at the age of forty, with the necessity of making a living without the regular supplement of a military income. For a time, the once-proud chief warrant officer, accustomed to being saluted by sergeants major, was reduced to delivering pizzas for Cicis. He became despondent and drank heavily.

"They put him on the couch for a fucking year," said Timothy Dumas Jr., who goes by T.J. "He didn't have no work. He was downing bottles of wine, antidepressants, and all that shit." As an aside he added, "My dad used to have a whole network of getting pills, all from the military."

During this period of unemployment and malaise, Dumas was a regular fixture at Paddy's Irish Pub and Mac's Speed Shop. They don't seem to have been especially close friends, but he and Billy Lavigne knew each other and were often spotted in the same company. "Dumas was an acquaintance," said Jordan Terrell. "I would see him at Mac's and Paddy's, drinking like everybody else. Always with other unit guys," he added.

Estranged from his second wife, Dumas occasionally unburdened himself to a Waffle House waitress ten years his junior named Brianna Woods. Several of her friends bought cocaine from Dumas, but she got the stuff for free. He would bring a few grams over to her apartment by Cross Creek, where she'd have a bottle of Captain Morgan rum waiting, and they'd have sex. Afterward, he'd complain of getting stiffed out of his pension and describe a plot he'd cooked up to blackmail the Special Forces. He had written a letter, he told her, disclosing criminal wrongdoing in the Green Berets, which he meant to use as leverage to get his retirement benefits reinstated. The stratagem struck Woods as an unsafe plan of action, but she knew better than to contradict Dumas. "He was a big old teddy bear," she said. "As long as you didn't cross him."

T.J., who never met Woods, had also heard about the blackmail document authored by his father. "Something happened between the Special Forces and him," said T.J. "He wrote a letter, threatening them. He was going to disclose information. Uncover some shit that they were blaming him for that he didn't do. And I'm guessing it had to be something with drugs."

In contrast to his hulking father, T.J. is of medium stature, with a slight build, a ginger afro, and green eyes inherited from his mother, a white woman. His parents' marital difficulties contributed to his troubled youth; his rap sheet in North Carolina includes arrests for shoplifting, larceny, carrying a concealed handgun, assault on a female by strangulation, assault on a government official, resisting arrest, disorderly conduct, making harassing phone calls, communicating threats, and making a false report of mass violence at a school campus. He was seated on the stoop of his house in Carthage, and on the step beside him was a box of his dad's military records, certificates, and medals, as well as a scrapbook of photos taken on deployment. He paused to hit a crackling vape pen and exhaled a billowing plume of cherry-scented fog. Then he continued with the story.

"I heard about the letter back when I was a kid," he said. "I was a sophomore going to high school. There was only one person Dad trusted enough to give him a copy. But that copy gone. The person that had it is locked up in jail, and he ain't never getting out."

And who, I asked, might that be? "That state trooper that was arrested in Lexington with $3.7 million worth of drugs on him," T.J. said. "Freddie Wayne Huff."

Thirteen

YOU CAN'T MAKE THIS SHIT UP

Freddie Wayne Huff II, a North Carolina lawman born in 1980, never served in the military. All the same, his story of early promise, high achievement, subsequent disillusionment, loss of faith, turning against his former employer, and descent into addiction, drug trafficking, and violent crime closely paralleled the downward trajectories of Timothy Dumas and Billy Lavigne. Although the bare bones of his criminal exploits were reported in a few North Carolina publications, authorities kept his connection to events at Fort Bragg under wraps.

Freddie Huff joined the Lexington police force not long after high school. A self-described "obsessive perfectionist" who worked tirelessly to improve himself during the mania phases of his bipolar disorder, he quickly distinguished himself as a highly motivated young K9 officer with a preternatural ability to find drug money at traffic stops. Many a cartel courier passing through North Carolina lost a five- or six-figure sum to Officer Huff, a tall, solidly built, pink-skinned white man with hooded eyes and a high-and-tight haircut.

In 2009, Huff was deputized as a DEA task force officer and assigned to the El Paso Intelligence Center, or EPIC, the agency's main source of intelligence on Mexican drug cartels. There he became friends with a terminally ill DEA analyst, a bespectacled black man named Karl Culberson, whose long and varied career working for the federal government included a self-reported stint with the CIA. Nearing death from pancreatic cancer, Culberson confessed something that changed the course of Huff's life.

"What you think you're doing is noble," Culberson told Huff. "But *they* want it here. You're a pawn. Everything you're doing is in vain."

Huff was quietly troubled by Culberson's words, which he took to mean that the American government could stop the flow of drugs into the United States at any time but chooses not to. Nevertheless, he continued to work as a narcotics agent.

In 2010, Huff returned to the police force in Lexington, which lies about two hours north of Fort Bragg, and went back to doing what he did best: correctly guessing which passing motorists were carrying drug money, pulling them over, and confiscating the cash. A partial but revealing set of police records show that between 2010 and 2013, Huff seized $1.3 million from twenty-five motorists whom he detained for traffic infractions. All the stops took place on the stretch of Interstate 85 between Charlotte and Greensboro, and every one of the suspects was a nonwhite man whom Huff pulled over for failing to signal, following too closely, going slightly over the speed limit, having obstructed state tags or a broken taillight, or some other minor offense.

On June 17, 2010, for instance, Huff stopped thirty-three-year-old Felipe Fabela for tailgating. Lo and behold, Fabela turned out to have $449,360 concealed in a hidden compartment of his 1998 Mazda minivan. Three months earlier, Huff had pulled over forty-four-year-old Herman Alonso Rojas driving the same inconspicuous model of Mazda, which also had a concealed hiding place, and relieved him of $93,920. Rojas had been doing seventy-five in a seventy.

With the money that Huff brought in, which he said amounted to more than $9 million, the police department built a new training facility in Lexington, bought a fleet of late-model vehicles, and invested in an arsenal of black assault rifles fresh from the factory. Huff moved up to the state highway patrol in 2013 but in spite of his stellar performance lasted scarcely a year on the job.

On March 16, 2014, Trooper Huff pulled over an inebriated insurance executive from Asheville who—he later learned—was a donor to North Carolina's governor, Pat McCrory. Throughout the duration of the stop, the punch-drunk businessman repeatedly warned Huff that he was going to have his job, but Huff ticketed him anyway, for driving under the influence. Before the month was out, Huff had been fired on the petty pretense that he'd lied about having sold a pair of state-issued shoes on the auction site eBay, a trivial breach of department regulations.

Getting summarily canned for ticketing a corrupt crony of the governor's, as Huff saw it, left him embittered toward the law enforcement profession. "When they fired me," he said, "I lost everything. Lost my certifications. Lost my expert witness status. They blacklisted me."

North Carolina state trooper Freddie Wayne Huff,
in 2013, before he was fired, in his view, for
ticketing a corrupt crony of the governor's.

Recalling Culberson's cynical words about the true power behind the global drug trade, Huff vowed then and there that if he ever had the opportunity, he would use his granular understanding of how police detect drug smugglers to make a killing in the game. "I told myself that if anything ever fell in my lap," he recalled, "I was going to use every fucking thing I had known, learned, and taught against *them*."

HUFF'S OPPORTUNITY TO BREAK bad was not long in coming. Thirty-five years old and in need of income to support himself, his wife, his two children, and three adopted kids whom the Huffs had taken in from a household broken by poverty and abuse, Huff found work buying up damaged and defective appliances from a home improvement chain store and shipping them down to the Mexican border to be refurbished and resold. This mundane enterprise turned out to be reasonably remunerative. Huff was making enough money to get by, but sweating on the loading docks behind Lowe's, grunting and grappling with heavy and cumbersome washers and dryers, he couldn't stop thinking like a cop—or a crook.

One of the intermediaries that Huff used to export inoperable appliances to Mexico was an unassuming establishment in Laredo, Texas, called Aguilar Appliance Repair. Through intuition and a little research, Huff ascertained that the import-export shop, housed in a pair of portable trailers on a dirt lot in one of the poorest neighborhoods of hot and sunny Laredo, was owned by relatives of Miguel Ángel Treviño Morales, who, as Huff knew from his time at EPIC, was one of the most notorious drug lords in the world. Until 2013, Treviño Morales had been the ruthless leader of the Nuevo Laredo–based paramilitary cartel known as Los Zetas.

Of all the drug cartels in Mexico, Los Zetas was by far the most feared. They were not just narcos. They were real soldiers, elite ones, trained in the United States. The cartel traced its origins to a joint project between the United States and Mexico to create a Mexican commando unit modeled on the Green Berets, called the *Grupo Aeromóvil de Fuerzas Especiales*, or Airborne Special Forces Group. The original members of the GAFE, as the unit was known by its initials in Spanish, were schooled in irregular warfare at none other than Fort Bragg, North Carolina, as well as Fort Benning, Georgia, and also received instruction from Israeli trainers. Around the year 2000, the majority of the unit defected from the Mexican state and went to work directly for the Matamoros-based Gulf Cartel, a powerful smuggling mafia that controlled the underside of the Texas border, serving as its armed wing and enforcer corps. Not long after, the rogue commandos again betrayed their employers, struck out on their own, and formed a rival cartel. "Los Zetas" was a reference to the alphanumeric call sign used by the group's first boss, a Mexican special forces officer named Arturo Guzmán Decena.

The advent of Los Zetas, who really were narco-terrorists, inaugurated the darkest era in all of Mexican history. Trained in marksmanship, rapid deployment, ambushes, surveillance, and psychological operations, Los Zetas used overt military force to consolidate control over most of the Texas border and the Gulf Coast port of Veracruz. Augmented by the state and local police forces that they co-opted, as well as an endless supply of short-lived hit men recruited from the lumpen class of the northern borderlands, Los Zetas wore paramilitary uniforms, drove around in homemade armored vehicles called *monstruos*, and, to sow terror, filmed themselves committing sickening atrocities. Countless thousands died in their raids, assaults, and sprees of arson. Countless thousands more were abducted and disappeared.

A sophisticated criminal militia that used encrypted communications and had the backing of deep-pocketed investors, powerful lawyers, and many Mexican politicos, Los Zetas leveraged their military control over large swaths of territory to diversify into nearly every illicit enterprise imaginable, reaping *billions* of dollars in profits. The cartel's portfolio included stealing oil and gas from the state petroleum company, extorting mining operations and other industries, running prostitution rackets, smuggling migrants, and taxing legal businesses, in addition to trafficking drugs, which by 2010 included a higher-than-ever percentage of heroin.

Since the early '00s, consumer demand in the United States for cheap and potent opiates had been steadily growing. Much of the heroin trafficked by Los Zetas and other Mexican cartels across the southern border was the "black tar" variety grown in Sinaloa and Guerrero, where poppy cultivation was on the rise to satisfy expanding American demand, but the majority of the product smuggled overland from Mexico was the more highly refined "China white" type whose ultimate geographic origin the DEA found to be such a head-scratching mystery. A potential clue lies in the nickname given to Los Zetas' Nuevo Laredo–born underboss Iván Velázquez Caballero, the right-hand man of Heriberto Lazcano, a psychopathic ex–GAFE commando originally from Puebla, who led the cartel from 2004 to 2012. They called Iván Velázquez "El Talibán." Spanish-language sources offer contradictory accounts of how Velázquez came to go by the alias, but it was apparently some sort of homage to the Afghan insurgency. Los Zetas, which the academic Guadalupe Correa-Cabrera likens to a malevolent transnational corporation with similarities to ExxonMobil, Halliburton, and Blackwater, was a highly entrepreneurial, globalized organization with tentacles in Europe, the Middle East, West Africa, and East Asia, in addition to Central and South America. They and other Mexican cartels had the capacity to move drugs all over the world, and insert them into the United States through distribution networks that reached into the most remote rural counties.

Heriberto Lazcano was killed in 2012. His successor as boss of Los Zetas was Miguel Ángel Treviño Morales, a Dallas-raised drug trafficker, fluent in English, whose family owned Aguilar Appliance Repair in Laredo. What Treviño Morales lacked in military experience he made up with extreme brutality and cruelty, gaining a reputation as a uniquely sadistic crime boss, a mass murderer and diabolical torturer who had personally killed thousands of people. He was captured in 2013, and his brother Óscar Omar fell in 2015, but the larger Treviño Morales clan remained an underworld power in the Rio Grande valley, with extensive real estate holdings on both sides of the border. The used-appliance shop that did business with Freddie Wayne Huff was one of their properties.

WHEN THE PROPRIETOR of Aguilar Appliance Repair came up to North Carolina in 2016 to pick up a load of washers and dryers, Huff invited her over to his house to meet his wife and kids. Though he looked, on first glance, like a big dumb gringo, Huff was cunning, charismatic, and street-smart. Concealing the fact that he had been a state trooper and DEA task force agent, Huff gained the woman's trust, gathered that she really was plugged into the Mexican drug world, and gradually let it be known that he was interested in buying wholesale narcotics. After a months-long courtship in which each side felt the other out, Ruben Treviño Morales, one of Miguel Ángel and Óscar Omar's fifteen-odd siblings, agreed to meet Huff in person.

The improbable rendezvous took place in the parking lot of a Tex-Mex restaurant in McAllen, Texas. "He screamed cartel," Huff recalled of his first look at the lesser-known Treviño Morales brother. "He wore super expensive designer clothes. He had a long pinkie nail," for taking bumps of cocaine up his nose. "He looked like a Mexican Kenny Rogers."

That an Anglo who spoke only broken Spanish and lacked any familial ties to Mexico could simply approach an exceedingly dangerous transnational crime syndicate like Los Zetas and arrange to become one of their distributors in the United States would seem like an implausible plot point in an unrealistic movie, yet that is exactly what Freddie Wayne Huff did. From 2016 to 2021, he was Los Zetas' main man in the Carolinas, with an operation extending into Georgia and Virginia. He went on running his appliance business, which was profitable in its own right, and used it as a cover for trafficking cocaine. He rented a warehouse in High Point, a muggy, traffic-ridden suburb of Greensboro and Winston-Salem; bought moving trucks and tractor trailers; and hired employees. At the peak of his criminal career, Huff was moving fifty to a hundred kilos of cocaine every seven to ten days, putting him in the top tier of all traffickers in the United States. "You're the most badass white boy I ever met," Huff proudly recalled Treviño Morales telling him.

Drawing on his past work as a K9 officer, Huff helped Los Zetas' border smugglers understand how to pack and conceal shipments to thwart drug-sniffing dogs by wrapping the kilos in shop towels soaked in ammonia, vacuum sealing them in plastic, and then repeating the process, enveloping the bricks in multiple fail-safe layers of a sharply pungent chemical that dogs will do anything to avoid. To defeat X-ray machines, he procured a tractor trailer whose rear differential axle had been hollowed out and lined with lead, a custom job that cost $50,000. "It took thirteen bolts to take apart, but it looked much more complicated," said Huff, who understood how to exploit the ordinary human laziness of customs agents, among other weaknesses in the narcotics-interdiction apparatus. He also advised the cartel's couriers on how to hide money in cars. "It was like I was teaching a fucking school," he said.

"Huff used the very information that he had gained as a law enforcement officer to then thwart law enforcement in order to improve his drug-dealing activity," said the federal prosecutor Randall Galyon, an Assistant U.S. Attorney for the Middle District of North Carolina.

For a personal hideout and base of operations, Huff rented a large redbrick house on Peppermill Drive in Lexington that had a four-car garage and a basement, which he converted into a combination game room and home gym replete with hidden compartments operated by means of electric motors activated by magnetic switches, in which stacks of money and kilos of cocaine were stored. There he received gangsters from across the state, as well as southern Virginia and northern Georgia, including Atlanta, as well as hustlers and mobsters from New Jersey, Connecticut, and Illinois. During his first two years in business, before he developed a sales pipeline to Fort Bragg, Huff mainly sold to street gangs in Raleigh, Charlotte, and the Piedmont Triad, a sprawling agglomeration of suburbs, strip malls, and office parks, home to some 1.6 million people, with High Point near its center. Shot callers from the Bloods, Crips, and Gangster Disciples would come to his McMansion of a trap house to buy kilos at the wholesale price of forty grand, product that they broke up and distributed on the street.

For personal protection, Huff carried two identical subcompact handguns that were easy to conceal. "I had two Glocks, .380," he told me. "They were really small. They only held six rounds but were very accurate. That's why I always carried one on my ankle. If I ran out of bullets on top, I could go down on one knee and grab the one off my ankle, and that gave me twelve rounds maximum."

Additional security came from a coterie of trained wingmen, almost all of whom were or had been police officers, sheriff's deputies, marines from Camp Lejeune, or soldiers from Fort Bragg. Huff was effectively Los Zetas' franchisee in North Carolina, and like Los Zetas, his little cartel was made up almost entirely of cops and soldiers. "They were former law enforcement, former military," said Randall Galyon, the federal prosecutor, of Huff's accomplices. "Mr. Huff knew that they provided a set of skills that would be useful to him."

ONE DAY IN 2018, a pair of FBI agents showed up at Huff's warehouse in High Point, an unexpected visit that shot a bolt of fear through his heart because he had $700,000 in drug money stashed in a washing machine in plain view. But it turned out that the agents only wanted to talk to him about one of his warehouse employees, Robert Seward, a bearded black man from Fayetteville who had converted to Islam. A few years earlier, Seward had traveled to Syria and joined the Islamic State, only to become disillusioned with the austere path of jihad, escape from a training camp, and return to America. "You can't make this shit up," said Huff.

The FBI agents seemed to be keeping tabs on Seward, not looking to make an arrest. Huff gave them minimal information and kept Seward on as an employee, because he was well aware of what was packed inside of the washing machines, dryers, dishwashers, and stoves that it was his job to unload. "Robert knew what was going on," said Huff. "He lived in one of the warehouses, and he turned a blind eye to shit. And one day he comes to me and he says, 'I got this friend of mine who used to move a lot of cocaine. Would it be okay if I introduced you to him?'" Huff said yes.

Not long after, a quad-cab Dodge Ram, black with Alabama license plates, pulled up to the warehouse towing a flatbed trailer. In the driver's seat was Timothy Dumas. "He gets out," said Huff, "and he's got on a Thin Blue Line bracelet, and he's a very fit, muscular kind of guy."

Dumas, who woke up every morning around five o'clock to run and lift weights and often wore a three-piece suit, fit the profile of the kind of man with whom Huff liked to work. "I preferred to deal with older, more mature people," Huff said, "not thugs with their pants hanging around their ass." Once they got to know each other, Huff and Dumas became not only business partners but best friends. "He was an amazing man," said Huff. "Probably the most amazing guy I've ever met. No homo," he hastened to add.

It's one thing to traffic drugs internationally and smuggle them across the country undetected. It's another, often more fraught thing to convert stacks of bulk cocaine into cash. What made Dumas such a valuable partner to Huff was that he could liquidate wholesale product at an incredible rate. The secret to his mercantile alacrity was Fort Bragg.

"Tim told me about basically a gang," said Huff, "a drug-trafficking organization within the military," made up of "an unspoken group of soldiers that policed themselves." The bricks of coke that he passed off to Dumas were in turn distributed among the group, a confederation of semi-independent dealers in and around Fayetteville.

The core members of the underground military mafia, in Dumas's telling, were Special Forces soldiers who had gone over to the dark side during deployments to Afghanistan. The main players were "guys that are trained killers, that have already killed people," Huff said. As such, they played by cartel rules. In order to settle debts and resolve disputes, they "would resort to anything," Huff said, "including murder."

Besides dealing drugs on base and off, "they were taking grenades," Huff said, "taking automatic arms," stealing them from Fort Bragg armories, and reselling them on the black market. Dumas's role in the gun-trafficking portion of the conspiracy, before he was kicked out of the Army, was to falsify entries in the property book accounting system to keep anyone from noticing the disappearing items. "That was his job," said Huff. "Maintaining records."

During the second decade of the GWOT, criminal organizations in the United States sourced much of their weaponry from corrupt members of all four branches of the armed forces. The Florencia 13 street gang bought assault rifles from marines stationed at Twentynine Palms, California; a Navy SEAL sold machine guns to the Mongols outlaw motorcycle club; and the Gangster Disciples obtained the pistols used in Chicago shootings from soldiers at Fort Campbell, Kentucky, to name a few cases. American soldiers, sailors, airmen, and marines participate significantly in that clandestine "river of iron" that keeps Mexico's paramilitary cartels, especially Los Zetas and their progeny, better supplied than the Mexican government with military-grade machine guns, grenades, antitank bazookas, helicopter-mounted rotary cannons called miniguns, and plastic explosives, as well as advanced laser optics and night-vision goggles.

In 2018, a pair of Fort Bragg soldiers attempted to sell dozens of stolen assault rifles and blocks of C-4 to men whom they believed to be representatives of Los Zetas in El Paso. In June 2021, the Associated Press published a multipart series, the product of a decade-long investigation, on the Army's massive unacknowledged losses of weapons, and detailed the case of a single pistol stolen from Fort Bragg that was used in four shootings in New York. The soldier who diverted it to the black market was never identified.

Mugshot of Timothy Dumas Sr. taken after his arrest in 2016 on drug and gun charges in Sampson County, North Carolina.

DUMAS INTRODUCED HUFF to two of his closest cronies, both of whom had served at Fort Bragg. One was a Puerto Rican man named David Garcia, whom Dumas presented as his oldest Army buddy. "This is my brother," he told Huff. "I'd do anything for him. I'd kill for him. I'd die for him."

Dumas also introduced Huff to Orlando Fitzhugh, another forty-year-old black man and former soldier. Fitzhugh, a veteran of the 82nd Airborne's 505th Parachute Infantry Regiment, had been investigated for dealing drugs on Fort Bragg in the 1990s and served time in the disciplinary barracks at Fort Leavenworth before being separated in 2000. He would go on to be convicted federally of trafficking cocaine in 2023.

Huff asked Garcia and Fitzhugh about the "military groups that trap narcotics," but neither man was willing to discuss the subject. Huff was left with the impression that they were afraid of the repercussions of naming names. "Which was weird," said Huff, "because these are people who are not scared of anything."

One day in late 2019, Dumas came to the basement, handed Huff a thumb drive, and told him to keep it in a safe place. On the memory stick was the blackmail letter that he had described to his son and to Brianna Woods. So far, Dumas had not carried out his threat to reveal its contents. Now, he told Huff, he wanted to use the letter as a kind of dead man's switch. If anything happened to him, he wanted it made public. "It was like his insurance policy," said Huff.

Huff stashed the thumb drive in the drawer of a minibar in the basement of his house in Lexington. But before doing so, he plugged it into his computer and opened the word processing document. "I read the whole thing in depth," he said. "It was seriously incriminating shit."

Although four sources independently attested to the existence of Dumas's "insurance policy" and described its contents in broadly similar terms, Huff alone claimed to have actually read the text. According to him, the lengthy letter was addressed to a high-ranking general and alleged that "soldiers were involved in bringing opiates from Afghanistan and distributing it on Fort Bragg." The letter specifically identified the service members who were supposedly transporting commercial quantities of occupied Afghanistan's marquee national product into the United States. "It names each one of them dudes," Huff said.

Several years had gone by and Huff was unable to recall any of their identities from memory except one. Subsequent events ensured that he would not forget one particular dealer with whom Dumas worked: a white guy in the Army known to Huff, as well as Dumas, as Will Lavigne. "He was dispersing methamphetamine and cocaine," Huff said of Lavigne, on Fort Bragg itself and "to military personnel in and around Fayetteville."

He added, "Fort Bragg has a lot of secrets. A lot of underground narcotics secrets. It's its own little cartel."

Fourteen

THAT MAN WORKED
FOR THE CARTEL

On February 5, 2019, a thirty-five-year-old black woman with a lengthy rap sheet nearly died of a heroin overdose on the floor of Billy Lavigne's living room. Sheriff's deputies administered naloxone, an opioid blocker that can rapidly reverse an overdose, and left without charging anyone with a crime.

Later in February, Lavigne was sent to an Army drug rehab program at Fort Gordon, Georgia, where troops with substance abuse disorder are sometimes afforded a chance to get clean. He promptly failed out for "refusal to participate."

On March 28, Lavigne was again admitted to Womack Army Medical Center on Fort Bragg, where he again tested positive for cocaine. A few weeks later, he underwent his annual physical exam. Other than some moderate hearing loss, the medical screen noted no serious debilities in his physical condition, but the doctor who did the exam marked him down as unfit for deployment due to an unspecified psychiatric illness.

On August 28, Lavigne sold his house for $179,000, which was slightly less than what he'd paid for it eight years earlier, and moved to a one-bedroom unit of a gray apartment complex between a Dollar General and a Taco Bell. The same day that the warranty deed on the house sale was recorded in the county index, the Coast x Coast motorcycle club started out on its fifth annual Ride for the Fallen, and Lavigne was among the participants.

The Coast x Coast honorees that year included two Green Berets and an Army Ranger recently killed in action in Afghanistan, a Navy cryptologist who lost her life in a bombing in Syria, and a former Delta Force commander who died in a rollover of a riding lawn mower in Alabama. Despite the nonprofit's loss of tax-exempt status, the Delta Force biker club held a series of money-raising events at bars, taverns, and cantinas in San Diego, Las Vegas, Phoenix, Colorado Springs, Dallas, Nashville, and Fayetteville. On September 7, they convened at Arlington National Cemetery. Four days later, on the holiest of holidays for all GWOT warriors, they visited firefighters in New York City.

Cris Vallejo, still the leader of the club, rode on a blacked-out Harley-Davidson with a Mexican blanket behind the saddle and brass knuckles for foot pegs; his future wife was at the event in Las Vegas. Lavigne drove the support truck and did not appear in any of the photos posted to social media.

IN LATE 2019, Lavigne fell into a romantic relationship with an exotic dancer named Amanda Marie Tostado, a thirty-two-year-old white woman who went by the stage name Amanda Panda. "I don't have anything good to say about her," said Lavigne's mother, Judy. "I knew what she did for a living. I heard that she was a dancer. I heard other stories, too. I'm not judging. But she wasn't for him."

Lavigne's father wasn't impressed, either. To him, Amanda Panda sounded like a stripper's name. "I followed her on Facebook," said Bill Sr. "It turns out I was right."

Tostado had been arrested numerous times in Cumberland County for drug and probation offenses. In one mug shot, she has her blond hair up in a messy topknot, gold hoop earrings, and cursive script tattooed across one side of her neck. "She's a little bitty thing, don't weigh ninety pounds soaking wet," said Sharon Shively, a small-time moneylender and underground pawnbroker in her sixties who was acquainted with a wide swath of Fayetteville's criminal class. "She's tiny, looks kind of lost. You feel like you need to rescue her. That's why Will liked her."

Lavigne, who increasingly went by Will rather than Billy in the years after Mark Leshikar died, often hung out at Shively's place in Hope Mills, a ranch-style house that when I visited had four or five late-model trucks parked outside, muted rap tracks thudding from the back bedrooms, and people traipsing in and out of the kitchen to snort lines of something off the countertop. "He was having some mental issues," Shively told me of Lavigne. "He was *always* fucked up."

Shively, a chain-smoker with a puckered mouth and hard eyes who was charged with but not convicted in 2017 of discharging a firearm within city limits, said that Lavigne was good friends with Tostado's cousin, Britton Ray Whittington, as well as her ex-boyfriend Bobby Lee Anderson. Photos of Anderson portray a heavyset white man with a chin-strap beard, diamond earrings, and flat-brim hat turned sideways. His police record in Cumberland County includes arrests for assault by pointing a gun, assault on a female, larceny, and first-degree murder, though only the larceny charge resulted in a conviction. Lavigne often stayed at Anderson's lake house in Fayetteville's Arran Hills neighborhood. "Him and Will were tight," said Shively. "Real good friends."

Whittington, a goateed white man with blue eyes and a sardonic smile who went by Ray-Ray or Big Ray, had been arrested on more than forty occasions in Cumberland County and had served time for trafficking drugs, possession of a firearm by a felon, larceny of a motor vehicle, shooting into an occupied dwelling, and assault with a deadly weapon on a police officer. When not locked up, he lived in a large, isolated house on Marsh Wood Lake, close to the Cape Fear River. "Whittington, he was a big drug dealer," said one of his neighbors. "Been busted multiple times. He's sketchy, very sketchy. He needs to be locked away for life."

In February 2019, Whittington was arrested for shooting at the ground, like Yosemite Sam, to scare off three bail bondsmen who'd come to his rural residence to collect a young woman who had a warrant out for her arrest. That August, he was arrested for human trafficking. "Whittington coerced and forced the victim to engage in prostitution through internet dating sites," the sheriff's office said.

Lavigne was out at Whittington's lake house that summer and accidentally shot off a parachute flare that punched a hole in the side of an aboveground swimming pool, causing all the water to gush out. Enraged, Whittington whipped out a pistol. He would have killed Lavigne, said a witness to the confrontation, but retaliated instead by stealing his truck. Lavigne ended up shelling out two grand to get it back, and they remained friends.

Whittington, now incarcerated in the Pasquotank prison up by the Great Dismal Swamp, told me that he and Lavigne met in the course of "dealing dope." Lavigne was in a bad place at the time, said Whittington, who spoke with a gnarly backwoods accent. "It was terrifying, battling with his addiction. He was going through a lot. He couldn't get over his wife. I was strung out myself and ended up meeting him. I would help him and he would help me. Then things got out of hand. Money got short. It's a real story."

Whittington, Anderson, and Tostado, all of whom would go on to be convicted of trafficking narcotics during the time of their association with Lavigne, were his co-conspirators in dealing drugs to civilians in Fayetteville. Their bulk supplier of wholesale product, according to half a dozen sources including two CID agents, was Timothy Dumas. Freddie Huff, who habitually collected intelligence scrubbed from the internet on those he dealt drugs with, had pictures of the group saved on his phone, including a photo of Tostado taken from her Facebook page. "A bunch of rednecks," was how Huff described the foursome.

Sharon Shively and her associate Skyler Rainsford, a young white man with a buzzed head, manicured eyebrows, and a gold chain, recognized Dumas's photo, knew him by name as well as the nickname Chief, and confirmed that he was the clique's source of coke. "They were buying dope from the cartel," said Shively. "I think Will might have got a little mixed up in that."

Pressed to define "cartel," Shively said, "Somebody that's associated with Mexicans. Who will kill you," she added, "if you don't pay for your shit."

Lavigne had the additional role in the conspiracy, said Rainsford, of acting "as an enforcer for his friends." He provided security for drug deals, escorted loads from city to city, and collected unpaid debts. "Kicking in doors," said Rainsford, and "getting stuff out of them."

Even dope sick, Lavigne cut an intimidating figure. "He had guns all the time," said Shively, who once lent Lavigne $500 and ended up keeping the three Kalashnikovs that he put up as collateral to secure the loan, which he failed to pay back. "I never knew him to not have a gun."

There was another thing that Shively noticed about Lavigne. He had a habit, not atypical for a soldier, of always carrying around a pen and paper. He was often seen "jotting stuff down," she said, "documenting what he had been through and heard" during his time on Delta Force. He told people that he was writing a book about his time in the unit, which struck Shively as a dicey proposition. "There was too much information out there on what Will did," she said. "He should have kept his mouth shut."

ON FEBRUARY 7, 2020, an administrative board charged with determining whether and how Lavigne should be separated from the Army set aside an earlier recommendation from USASOC that he be given a general rather than honorable discharge. The board's decision not to stick him with bad paper had the effect of salvaging his eligibility for a retirement pension. Lavigne texted Ben Boden to say that a weight had been lifted from his shoulders.

One minute after midnight ten days later, Lavigne crashed his souped-up racing truck into a sixty-seven-year-old woman's car somewhere in Fayetteville and sped off from the scene. A warrant for his arrest on hit-and-run charges was sworn out the following day. This time, for whatever reason, the charge stuck.

On March 4, North Carolina reported its first case of COVID-19, a highly contagious respiratory disease that escaped from a U.S.-funded biolab in Wuhan, China. The emergence of the novel coronavirus and its rapid worldwide spread inaugurated a dark era in the United States. The pandemic years coincided with an outbreak of violent crime, a spike in political strife, and widening social isolation. Paranoia ran wild, faith in institutions crumbled, and all across America drug use surged, with accidental overdoses rising to an all-time high that approached 100,000 deaths in a single year.

On March 10, the governor of North Carolina declared a state of emergency. Fort Bragg implemented a travel ban, quarantined soldiers returning from deployments, and limited training exercises. A statewide stay-at-home order, applicable to soldiers as well as civilians, went into effect March 30.

During the loneliness and uncertainty of the lockdowns, many people reconnected with distant family members, friends from whom they'd drifted apart, and old flames. Jamie Carter, Lavigne's first wife, heard from him for the first time in years on April 9. They ended up having a lengthy exchange of text messages.

"How have you been?" he asked.

"Bored," she replied. "Sitting in the house, quarantined."

She asked what he was doing to pass the time.

"I'm working on a book," he said. "Dude already wants to turn it into a movie."

"Is it about you or a fictional story?" Carter asked.

"It's about my life," he said. "I just finished version one."

"That's awesome," she said.

"How's your daughter?" Carter asked. "Are you still married? Do you have any more kids?"

"Not married," he replied. "Bad divorce and custody battle after I was involved in a domestic shooting."

Carter blinked at her phone's screen. A domestic shooting?

Without any prodding, Lavigne went on: "I shot my best friend in front of both of our daughters and killed him. Haven't seen or talked to my daughter since last June."

Carter was stunned. In an effort to make sense of this information, her brain conjured up a scenario in which Lavigne had caught his wife in bed with his best friend and shot the man. "Was he having an affair?" she asked, trying to be tactful.

"No affair," Lavigne replied. "He just had a mental breakdown."

"What happened?" she asked. "Did you feel threatened?" She also asked, "You're not going to jail?"

Lavigne didn't directly answer the first two questions. "The investigation and charges have been dropped now," he texted. "Now it's my turn to hit back," he added in an apparent reference to the score-settling book he was writing.

They went back and forth about his divorce and custody battles. Then she returned to the main question on her mind. "What was the reason for the shooting?"

"I'll call you about it sometime," he replied. "Got to go."

EVERY TIME THAT LAVIGNE failed a drug test, protocol required USA-SOC to refer him to military police for questioning, and twice the interrogation was done by a CID agent named Jeremy Speer, the leader of a Fort Bragg antidrug unit. On his lawyer's advice, Lavigne never made any statements and invoked his right to remain silent, Speer told me. Lavigne seemed "annoyed" that he had to be there, as well as "agitated" and "falling apart," he said. "Clearly, he was struggling with PTSD."

On July 22, 2020, Lavigne was hanging out at a trap house on Enloe Street in Fayetteville, a small brick structure surrounded by a muddy yard littered with hundreds of cigarette butts and swarming with blue-bottle flies. He was smoking crack, and as usual he was armed to the teeth.

"He always had weapons," said Renee Locklear, a Native American woman in her fifties who was at the crack house at the time. "If he didn't have a knife, he would be toting around, like Rambo, some bow-and-arrow-type shit." She described Lavigne as "a big crazy white man" who was "sweet one minute and crazy as hell the next."

Roy Lynn Parker, a heavyset man in his thirties with a scaly rash all over his body, was also present the night of July 22. Somewhere outside was twenty-four-year-old Ian Detar, an inveterate burglar and petty meth peddler. Hearing gunshots, Parker went to the window. A confused scene ensued. Parker ran into Detar, who told him that Lavigne had tried to shoot him. Detar didn't say why. The sound of police sirens approached, and Parker saw Lavigne flee the scene on foot, but he didn't get far. "They picked him up down at the stop sign," Parker said, indicating the pine-needle-strewn intersection of Enloe and Piedmont.

Lavigne was named on a police report as the suspect in a case of assault with a deadly weapon, a Class E felony that under North Carolina law is easily upgraded to attempted murder. Yet once again, his lawyer got him off the hook. No charges were filed against Lavigne in county court. The outstanding warrant for hit and run wasn't executed on him, either. He was simply uncuffed and let go.

"Lavigne was a suspect in a shooting in Cumberland County," said Special Agent Speer. "He'd basically shot at a drug dealer." Speer added, "I don't know if it was a rival or a rip-off. Lavigne was never interviewed for that case."

But Lavigne couldn't stay out of trouble long. On October 30, he blew through a red light on Main Street in Hope Mills and was pulled over by a Cumberland County sheriff's deputy. A check of his name revealed that he had an outstanding warrant, now eight months old, for the February hit and run. He was taken to jail and, for the first time ever, fingerprinted, photographed, and booked.

In his mug shot, Lavigne's balding head is buzzed and his blond beard has begun to gray. His expression is blank, and there is an unsettling glint in his eye. He looks as if he were about to be shot by a firing squad and doesn't even care. He was released on his own recognizance, and a court date was set for April 14, 2021.

Mug shot of Billy Lavigne after his arrest in Hope Mills, North Carolina, on October 30, 2020.

IN THE FIRST WEEK of November 2020, Amanda Tostado changed her Facebook status to "in a relationship." On Thanksgiving Day, Lavigne brought her to his mom's house in Hope Mills for a turkey dinner. Judy was hard pressed not to show her displeasure.

She couldn't understand why Billy spent his time babysitting Amanda's little girls, who were about the same age as Ava, or why he let her drive around in his new truck. Judy wasn't about to turn anyone away from her table on Thanksgiving, but privately took her son aside and whispered, "Why are you helping this woman?"

Lavigne turned up at the house on the Sunday after Thanksgiving to lift weights in the garage with a tall and muscular black man whom he'd never brought over before. Judy's new husband, a man named Gregory Brandt, didn't like the look of the guy, or Billy's erratic behavior lately, and locked them both out of the house. Lavigne left in a huff, annoyed with his mother and stepfather, and his buddy went with him.

"The last time Will's parents saw their son was when my dad came and picked Will up from their house," said Timothy Dumas Jr. "That's what I heard from the CID officer. Will got into a black truck with a black bald man, and that's my daddy."

Throughout Thanksgiving weekend, Lavigne was corresponding with friends and family. He texted Ben Boden on November 27. "I asked him if his ex was letting him see his daughter," Boden said.

"Nope," Lavigne replied.

"That sucks bro," Boden texted.

Lavigne's dad also heard from his son that weekend. "I talked to him Thanksgiving," said Bill Sr. "He seemed somewhat normal." They discussed his imminent retirement from the military, scheduled for February 2021. Lavigne was in line to receive a monthly pension worth at least half of his peak active-duty salary, lifelong medical benefits, and disability payments for hearing loss and PTSD. His financial freedom secure at the relatively young age of thirty-seven, he dreamed of escaping to the peace and solitude of the heavily wooded Upper Peninsula of Michigan, where the winters may be long and cold and buried in snow, but fresh water is plentiful and wildlife still roams in abundance. "He had two months to go," said his father. "He was planning on coming home and building a log cabin on our property. It was the last thing we talked about."

JESSI MARIE LINDSLEY, a tattoo artist and junkyard mechanic with long hair dyed bright red, was one of the last people to see Lavigne alive. She was a friend of his and often did drugs with him. She once inked a tattoo on his chest to commemorate the life of Mark Leshikar.

On November 30, a raw and drizzly Monday, Lindsley and her boyfriend were working on a customer's car at a trailer park in Fayetteville, when she turned around and there was Lavigne. He had on a black ski mask and was carrying a crossbow.

He had come to kill Lindsley's boyfriend, whom she described as an "abusive asshole" who frequently beat her and put her out on the street to turn tricks. Lavigne, with his demented sense of altruism, had decided to do her a favor by putting an arrow bolt through the man's chest. "He thought he was protecting me," said Lindsley. "His brain just didn't work anymore."

Lindsley was born in 1983, the same year as Lavigne. Her rap sheet in North Carolina is sixty-eight pages long. "Jessi was into drugs—using, selling, hustling," said Leona Cain, a childhood friend of hers. In one of her Facebook photos, Lindsley is mounted on a Suzuki motorcycle wearing a Playboy bikini, her body covered in tattoos of crosses, hearts, stars, waves, seashells, and Chinese characters. She evidently loved pit bull puppies, horses, and little kids. In many of the pictures, she's openly carrying a handgun.

"Will was having a really hard time with a lot of things," Lindsley said in the raspy voice of a heavy smoker. "He was a good man with a good heart, but got a lot of damage from his time in the service. He really needed some help from the military. His ability to handle problems was not good. He thought the way to deal with a situation, if someone was doing something wrong, was to kill them."

Lindsley's boyfriend wisely fled the scene, and she managed to talk Lavigne down. She put her hands on his shoulders and made him look at her. "You don't want your daughter growing up thinking you're a monster," she told him. "Because you're not. You're a hero."

"I am a monster," Lavigne said. Overcome with emotion, he got to his knees, put his face in his hands, and wept. "I killed my best friend," he said, sobbing.

Lindsley held him in her arms. "By the end of the conversation," she said, "he agreed that he really needed help to detox from the drugs that he was on, and to try to get some kind of help for his PTSD."

But Lindsley, who dealt drugs herself, knew that Lavigne was involved in more than just using and had problems that went beyond his mental health. He and Dumas, with whom she was also friends, "were working for the cartel," she said. "Will was getting coke from Timothy." Echoing Shively and Rainsford, Lindsley also said that Lavigne "was driving with people that were coming back from their pickup location, making sure they got back safe, and collecting money if somebody was being a problem and not wanting to pay."

"When you say he worked for the cartel," I asked, trying to maintain an appropriate sense of skepticism, "you don't mean that literally, do you?"

"Oh, I definitely mean that literally," she replied. "A lot of military guys that come up from selection or retire from 3rd Group or Delta Force do."

Eleven months after uttering those words, in December 2021, Jessi Marie Lindsley was murdered. She was shot multiple times in the chest, her body dumped in a culvert of Gray's Creek. The shooter, according to the Cumberland County district attorney's office, was an eighteen-year-old Italian American boy, originally from New York City, named Javeeno Jeno Resimo, who used to live with Ray-Ray Whittington at his lake house and was known around Fayetteville for being a protégé of Whittington's—"Ray's little prodigy," in the words of one informant, and "his little guinea pig," in those of another. Jeno Resimo would go on to be convicted of murder in a jury trial and sentenced to life in prison without the possibility of parole.

Fifteen

FREDDIE HAD EVERYTHING UNDER CONTROL

T he first months of the COVID-19 pandemic were a time of record profitability for Freddie Wayne Huff and Timothy Dumas. The cocaine business was booming, especially around Fayetteville. "About half the product we had went to Fort Bragg," said Huff. "The other half was domestic," that is, sold to civilians in the Piedmont Triad and the greater Carolinas.

Huff was moving thousands of kilos of dope, raking in millions of dollars, but a potential problem emerged in the form of an issue that Dumas had with one of his main buyers. Word on the street was that Will Lavigne owed a lot of money for unpaid consignments of meth, diminishing his trustworthiness in the eyes of his fellow traffickers. Of even greater concern was that Lavigne, who couldn't seem to catch a case no matter what he did, was rumored to be an FBI informant. "Sometimes I trust him," Dumas told Huff, "and sometimes I don't."

"Which to me was weird," Huff recalled. "Because if you're dealing drugs, you shouldn't be associating with an FBI informant," even if the person is only rumored to be one. "But Tim still opted to fuck with him. I don't know why."

Huff, who was six feet two, weighed 245 pounds, sported buzz-cut hair, and typically wore a full suit and tie, always with those two little pocket Glocks concealed on his person, struck some of *his* associates as a potential police agent, too. "I'm not racist or nothing, but he looked like a cop since day one," said Jaime Rosado Fontanez, a thirty-three-year-old Florida man who in the summer of 2019 had helped Huff and Dumas develop a second international cocaine connection through a Puerto Rican trafficking organization based in Orlando.

A visit to Huff's trash-strewn stash house in Lexington, which was furnished with little aside from a few couches and tables, some blow-up mattresses, a weight set, and a pool table, instantly disabused Rosado of the suspicion. "He was dealing with all these people in North Carolina, all these black people who were no joke," said Rosado. "The Bloods, the Crips, everybody respected him." Gangsters with street names like Hundred K, Straight Up, Day One, Dirty, and Rise came and went at all hours, toting backpacks and duffel bags. The driveway was full of candy-coated Range Rovers and Cadillac Escalades with chrome rims, spinning spokes, and custom stereos. "He controlled everything in North Carolina," said Rosado. "Charlotte, Winston-Salem, Lexington. Georgia, too. Atlanta. He was big, man. Everybody knew him."

Huff, Rosado soon realized, was a "crazy, crazy dude." He had rented a grand white house with marble floors, a sunporch, and a swimming pool in a gated neighborhood of Charlotte for his family to live in but was rarely at home. He did his first line of cocaine as soon as he got out of bed, before breakfast or brushing his teeth, chain-smoked three packs of cigarettes a day, and tore around in a Lamborghini Huracán that, although only a few years old, had never been washed or vacuumed. "Nastiest car I've ever seen," said Rosado. "Stinking of cigarettes."

Though closely related by blood to certain Puerto Rican mafiosi in Orlando, Jaime Rosado was an atypical narco. He abhorred violence and never carried a gun. He was a pacifistic homebody whose idea of a good time was to smoke weed and chill with his wife and mom. Rather than stay at Huff's chaotic trap house in Lexington, he would post up at a nearby Holiday Inn, where he'd kick off his sandals, recline by the pool, and blaze fat blunts of hydroponic bud. He had seen how careless Huff could be with his piles of cash and didn't plan to be around when a stickup crew broke down the front door.

Rosado also lived in fear of one of Dumas's associates, a hit man in his fifties named Joey Green, a.k.a. Joey Bananas. "He was a black dude, gold teeth with dreads," said Rosado. "He was really crazy. He used to kill people for $5,000."

"Joey Bananas, Joey Green, he was an unofficial bodyguard of ours," said Huff. "He was dangerous. Tim and him would always get in fights with one another. There was a time I can remember when they were actually shooting at each other. Later hugging and crying, right?"

To Rosado, Dumas was no less intimidating, but more stable and reasonable. His big thing was guns. He never went anywhere unarmed. If he got up in the middle of the night to use the toilet, he'd take with him the pistol he kept by his bedside. He owned an arsenal of heavy weaponry, including machine guns, .50-caliber antimatériel rifles, and a cache of grenades stolen from Fort Bragg. He boasted of his special operations background and often related stories of his exploits over-seas, including tales of gunning down foreign drug traffickers, burning their labs, stealing their product, and smuggling it stateside through international transportation networks exempt from customs inspec-tions. "Tim confessed that to me," said Rosado. "He used to bring a lot of kilos on military planes."

BY 2020, Huff had been using cocaine nonstop for four years, and his tolerance was consequently very high. "He was sniffing like an ounce a day," said Rosado. "I was like, Freddie, stop. Oh my God, you need to stop the shit, man. You haven't eaten breakfast, bro."

Dumas was coming unglued from escalating drug use, too. Brianna Woods, the Waffle House waitress whom he used to hook up with, said that his habit worsened noticeably in the spring of 2020. "He didn't seem like the person I met," she said. "His eyes were really big. He'd trip over his words. He was constantly licking his lips. He didn't sleep much. He was staying up for days at a time," often dedicating his sleepless nighttime hours to compulsive art projects such as fabricating papier-mâché death's-heads from seashells. "He was obsessed with skulls," said Woods.

On March 28, 2020, Fayetteville police responded to an incident in which Dumas was suspected of shooting into an occupied dwelling place at an apartment complex near the Cross Creek shopping mall. Ten months later, I went to the location and found four people, two men and two women, living in a first-floor unit of the complex. They spoke Spanish with a Caribbean accent and didn't know any Timothy Dumas. Nor did they recognize his photo. Finally, one woman's face lit up. "El tipo que pegó el tiro aquí," she said, pointing to a small black hole in the wall: "The guy who fired a shot through here."

The other woman, Estella, told me the story in English. It was late at night and she was out front smoking a cigarette. "Out of nowhere," she said, "this tall, bald-headed black dude comes up with a skinny black guy with dreads. He tells me I should go smoke in the back because there's going to be a shooting."

Estella thought he was joking. His rudeness annoyed her. She went into her apartment and, a few minutes later, began to record a video of her godson dancing on the living room carpet. She showed me the brief clip on her phone.

A child about waist high is dancing next to a laundry hamper to music from the television. You can clearly see the moment that a bullet hole appears in the wall, blowing out a cone of gypsum powder. The 9-millimeter round misses the boy by about eighteen inches.

Estella called 911, but doesn't know if Dumas was still on the premises when the cops arrived. She and her whole family had gone into the back bedroom to hide.

Dumas was named as the suspect on a police report, which even details the make and model of gun he used, a Taurus Millennium. Yet court records show that he was not charged with a crime, making it the seventh time since 2013 that he had been arrested but not prosecuted in Cumberland County—a run of leniency that narrowly beat out Billy Lavigne's half a dozen dropped cases.

AT MIDNIGHT ON APRIL 11, 2020, days before protests against North Carolina's COVID restrictions broke out in downtown Raleigh, Huff and Dumas kicked down the door of an apartment in a suburb of Winston-Salem called Walkertown. "Police," they shouted, guns at the ready. "Search warrant."

According to Huff, the break-in was to retrieve certain unnamed goods that had been stolen from Timothy Dumas Jr. In T.J.'s version of events, however, it was Freddie Wayne Huff III, then eighteen years old, who had been robbed. Either way, the victims of the armed home invasion, a young black man and a black woman in her forties, did not report anything stolen, only complained of having been threatened at gunpoint. "Subject kicked in victim's door and threatened to kill them," a Forsyth County sheriff's deputy wrote.

Huff and Dumas almost made a clean getaway, but egress from the Pinecrest Apartments was constrained to a narrow lane with choke points at both ends. "We were surrounded by fucking Forsyth County sheriff's officers," said Huff.

Seven people, including Huff, Dumas, and both of their sons, were thrown into the county lockup. After years of escaping criminal consequences for his actions, Dumas was charged with burglary, communicating threats, and impersonation of a police officer. His arraignment was set for December 17, 2020. But like Lavigne, he would not live long enough to see the inside of a courtroom.

Although equally culpable in the nighttime armed break-in and assault with a deadly weapon, Huff was not charged. "Bobby Kimbrough, the sheriff of Forsyth County, was a super good friend of mine," Huff said. Sheriff Kimbrough would later serve as a character witness on Huff's behalf in federal court.

Such instances of preferential treatment at the hands of law enforcement marked Huff's whole criminal career. He told Jaime Rosado that he had moles in departments of police throughout North Carolina. A Lexington cop identified in court documents as J. W. Wolfe worked as a delivery driver for Huff, and although he denied trafficking drugs, he admitted to flashing his badge to get out of a traffic stop while moving appliances. There is also a reference in court documents to Huff allegedly using a gay sex video of a state trooper to blackmail the trooper into doing his bidding. "He had people in the police that he knew were protecting him," said Rosado. "Freddie had everything under control."

ONE THING HUFF didn't have under control was his finances. "He made millions, but he went broke," said Rosado. "He used to spend a lot of money on stupid stuff. He had a girl problem, a cocaine problem. He had an expensive lifestyle."

In his state trooper days, Huff used to envy the pricey clothes and watches worn by the drug dealers he arrested, even if his sartorial tastes ran in a more conservative direction. Now that he was the cocaine kingpin of North Carolina, he was always dressed to the nines. "Freddie didn't look like a drug dealer," said Rosado. "He looked like a rich man. He looked like a lawyer."

Oftentimes, including the night he got locked up in Forsyth County jail, at Huff's side was one escort or another whom he found on Eros.com, a website based in North Carolina and used by sex workers nationwide. "They were beautiful," said Huff, but their time didn't come cheap. "They were anywhere between $700 and $1,200 an hour." He once lost $50,000 gambling at a casino in Philadelphia with his favorite escort, a woman from Colombia.

An even larger sum of money went missing in the summer of 2020 from a house that Huff and Dumas rented in the Orlando area whenever they went down to Florida to buy cocaine from Rosado's Puerto Rican kinsmen. "A hundred thousand dollars disappeared," said Rosado.

Huff and Dumas mutually suspected each other, but among such men accusations of theft are not lightly broached. "Neither of us," said Huff, "had the balls to confront each other." Rather than risk a potentially fatal showdown, they quietly drifted apart, both nursing acrimonious doubts.

Huff knew about Dumas's upcoming court date, set for December 17. He had a picture on his phone of a letter to Dumas from the clerk of Forsyth County, notifying him that he was due to appear before a judge. Huff also had photos of the front and back of Dumas's USAA credit card and a clear, well-lit, full-frontal picture of Dumas in a restaurant in which Dumas looks wide-eyed and surprised at being photographed.

The silence between Huff and Dumas lasted until the final week of November 2020, when Huff got a text from Dumas saying that Joey Green had disappeared. They spoke on the phone, and Dumas made it clear that he now blamed Green, not Huff, for the loss of the hundred grand. Dumas had already told the same thing to Rosado.

"Joey got killed," said Rosado. "I'm not a hundred percent sure how he got killed. If it was Freddie, or Tim. They never told me that. Because I'm just a businessman."

According to Huff, Dumas killed Green with his bare hands by breaking his neck, then forced Robert Seward, the would-be ISIS fighter, to help him dismember the body, the pieces of which they put in hard plastic cases and buried under Dumas's rental house in Carthage. "Tim told me where Joey was at," said Huff. "He was under T.J.'s house in different Pelican boxes."

One year later, in the fall of 2021, the Carthage Police Department pulled security while the FBI searched the house on Barrett Street, a stone's throw from the Moore County courthouse. They used cadaver dogs to explore the crawl space, but the canines failed to alert, and after a time the agents went away. "I could have told them they weren't going to find anything," said T.J. "From what I know," he added, "Joey's family never got closure."

The elimination of Joey Green from the equation led to a peace-making deal between Huff and Dumas and a resumption of their trafficking activities, but it proved short-lived. "Tim came to the basement," Huff said. "He didn't look good." His eyes were bloodshot, and his face had taken on a waxy pallor. "He looked like someone who had the flu."

Still reeling from the horror of having chopped up and disposed of Joey Green's body, his nerves addled from continuous drug use and sleep deprivation, Dumas told Huff that they had an even more serious problem than a thieving bodyguard. He had come to believe that Will Lavigne really was an FBI informant. "I'm going to kill him," Dumas told Huff. "I don't have a choice."

That Lavigne might have been informing for the FBI was an allegation that a veteran lawman like Huff had no trouble believing. After 9/11, as the FBI militarized and grew to contain within it a sizable spy agency with undercover operatives all over the world, its ranks of informants swelled to more than fifteen thousand people. These freelance generators of intelligence, though not FBI employees, routinely receive five- and six-figure sums of money for providing the bureau with information on terrorist groups, transnational cartels, and other forms of organized crime.

Impunity to break the law can be another benefit of informant status, because police and prosecutors will often exercise their discretion to drop charges against valuable sources of underworld intel. For instance, Darren Griffin, a former Special Forces soldier from Toledo, Ohio, who was trained at Fort Bragg and served in Iraq, continued to use and sell drugs while informing for the DEA and the FBI both, which earned him $350,000 in government payouts.

In a span of less than two years, Lavigne had had at least six felony charges against him dropped, including manufacturing drugs, harboring an escapee from prison, aggravated assault with a deadly weapon, and first-degree murder. And lately, Lavigne had been asking Dumas ill-advised questions about his wholesale supplier of cocaine, whom he somehow already knew by name. "He was asking about me a lot," said

Huff, who acknowledged that Lavigne's probing inquiries made him angry. "Specific, interrogative kind of questions. They were not innocent."

If Dumas was sure that Lavigne was an FBI informant, then Huff trusted his judgment. "Tim was not a paranoid person," he said. "He was realistic." And cartel rules dictated that Lavigne should pay with his life for his suspected treachery. All the same, Huff claimed, he tried to walk Dumas back from the radical path of murdering an active-duty member of the Special Forces.

Huff said that he was packing a suitcase at the time that the conversation about Lavigne took place, shortly after Thanksgiving. Huff was about to fly down to San Antonio, then drive to McAllen to meet with his contacts in Los Zetas, and he urged Dumas to come with him. But Dumas wouldn't be dissuaded, in Huff's telling.

Dumas received four kilos of cocaine from Huff. Then he called Lavigne, said "I got a mission for you," set up a meeting for that night in Fayetteville, climbed into his truck, and drove south. Huff, meanwhile, flew from the Davidson County Executive Airport to San Antonio on Ruben Treviño Morales's private plane.

Such was Huff's alibi for his whereabouts on December 1, 2020. He said that he was in Webb County, Texas, some fifteen hundred miles from Fort Bragg, with the brother of one of the most infamous cartel killers of all time.

Sixteen

UNTIL VALHALLA

Eric Haney, a first-generation Delta Force soldier who published a memoir about the founding of the unit, wrote that while some Army bases "have a real beauty about them," Fort Bragg is "about as drab and unappealing a spot as you can find in North America." Haney held out special disdain for the pine woods west of Fort Bragg proper, more than a hundred square miles of "near-worthless land," he wrote, that is "sparsely covered with straggly pines and stunted scrub oak trees."

To soldiers in training, Fort Bragg's terrain is an aggravatingly irregular plane, shaped like the underside of an egg carton, of loose sand dunes covered in pine saplings. The foamy black-water creeks, which get their dark color from steeping in the tannins of drowned trees, do not improve the mood of the forest, which in wintertime is monotonously orange in hue. But there are some miraculous creatures that thrive here. The Saint Francis's satyr butterfly, whose tan coloration and black eyespots lend the patterns on its wings an uncanny semblance to desert camouflage, has evolved to depend on regular disturbances of the soil caused by troop movements and artillery practice and is found nowhere on the planet but Fort Bragg.

On the evening of December 2, 2020, an off-duty soldier with a permit to hunt deer was stalking along a firebreak trail leading down to one of several artificial lakes in the area. It was nearly sunset, and he was hoping to spot deer creeping out of the forest to drink water at the sandy spit of beach along the edge of the shallow reservoir known as McArthur Lake. But his path was blocked by an unexpected sight. Up ahead, stuck in a rut in the trail, was a late-model gray truck positioned at an odd angle. No one was at the wheel.

Drawing nearer, the deer hunter saw that the vehicle was a quad-cab Chevrolet Colorado with racing wheels and street tires unsuitable for off-road use. A short distance away, a heavyset black man was lying face down on the pine needles.

The hunter's first thought was that the man must have suffered a heart attack while trying to push the truck out of the sandy wallow in which it had foundered. Pine boughs and broken branches had been shoved under the tires to give them greater traction. But cautiously coming a bit closer, he saw that the man had been shot in the head.

The hunter took out his cell phone, found that he still had reception at this remote corner of Fort Bragg, and dialed 911. He was on military land, so the call was routed directly to the 10th Military Police Battalion, the local headquarters of Army CID.

It took the MPs at least ten minutes to drive out to McArthur Lake, which is closer to Southern Pines than Fayetteville, a good ten miles down Manchester Road from the Delta Force compound. While waiting for them to arrive, as the surrounding pine trees were beginning to fade into night and the temperature dropped into the forties, the deer hunter noticed that there was a second dead body in the bed of the truck: a long-legged white man wrapped in a blood-soaked painter's tarp.

ON THE MORNING of December 3, Special Agent Jeremy Speer arrived at the 10th MP Battalion, housed in a squat redbrick building with windows tinted black, and recognized a familiar face taped to a whiteboard.

"Hey," he said to a few of his colleagues, who were milling around drinking coffee. "What's up with Lavigne?"

"You know him?" they asked.

Speer explained that he had twice questioned Lavigne after he failed drug tests. He was an ex-operator with a bad case of PTSD who had recently washed out of Delta Force. The Special Forces had him on desk duty, letting him skate by until his imminent retirement date, but the guy was a loose cannon. He had killed his best friend a couple years back under murky circumstances and over the summer had been involved in a shooting in Fayetteville that went uninvestigated.

Lavigne was dead, Speer's colleagues told him. His bullet-riddled body had been found in the back of his own truck in the woods near McArthur Lake, alongside the body of a former chief warrant officer in the 95th Civil Affairs Brigade, another hard case by the name of Timothy Dumas.

Maegan Malloy, a young undercover narcotics officer, also learned of the double homicide when she arrived at work that morning. "It was an all-hands-on-deck thing," she recalled.

By the time she and Speer arrived at McArthur Lake, the roadside was swarming with Army investigators in CID windbreakers and khaki pants. There was a sharp chill in the air, and the spongy earth underfoot was still damp from a downpour three days earlier.

Crime scene technicians had turned aside the tarp that Lavigne was wrapped in and were taking photos of his dead body. Malloy, who'd never worked a murder case before, came closer to have a look. "I can never unsee that," she said.

Lavigne had been stripped of all clothing except for a pair of running shorts. He had been shot at least three times, Malloy said, in the chest, groin, and leg, and looked to have bled out from the leg shot. His sightless blue eyes, now gone glaucous and cloudy, stared up at the cold winter sky. His gray skin was smeared with still-wet blood. The tattoo on his chest, done by his friend Jessi Marie Lindsley, consisted of the initials M.L., the date March 21, 2018, and a legend that read, "UNTIL VALHALLA."

On the ground a few paces away, Dumas looked to have been killed execution-style. The way he'd fallen face-first after being shot in the forehead was consistent with a scenario in which he'd been on his knees when the triggerman, standing right in front of him, did him in. According to three CID sources who saw Dumas's body, including Malloy and Speer, the fatal wound appeared to be inflicted by a small-caliber gun such as a .22 or .380.

WITHIN A DAY, CID agents had formed a working theory of the double murder. Their tentative narrative of events was based on what they already knew of the two victims' criminal proclivities; the positions of their corpses and the proximity of McArthur Lake; their recent history of text messages; and the absence of any drugs, guns, or money recovered from the scene.

The text messages were especially informative, said Malloy. They showed that Dumas was one of the biggest dealers in the area. "He was pushing kilos and kilos of coke on Fort Bragg," said Malloy.

Lavigne, whose texts also showed that he dealt drugs wholesale, had received messages threatening him over unpaid debts. "He owed a lot of money to some local person here in Fayetteville for drugs," said Malloy. "Because he was an addict. Even though he was in the drug game, he was also a user, a bad user."

The evidence led military investigators to think that Dumas, who was known to offer to kill people for money, had been contracted by someone to murder Lavigne. The job of taking him out would have been entrusted only to an experienced soldier or police officer, the agents figured. "The level of training that Lavigne had, someone would have to be pretty good to get the jump on him," said Malloy, and Speer agreed. "The majority of criminals in Fayetteville," he said, "are not that sophisticated."

The investigators further reasoned that Dumas did not act alone. The big chrome revolver that he normally carried was gone. Lavigne had been stripped of whatever weapons he'd had on his person, too. Dumas and Lavigne could not have killed each other in an exchange of gunfire in the woods. There had to have been a surviving shooter, an as-yet-unidentified Third Man.

The CID agents reached the conclusion that Dumas and the Third Man had tracked Lavigne down somewhere, shot him dead, rolled his body up in the tarp, and put him in the back of his own truck. Then they had driven him out to McArthur Lake, planning to sink his earthly remains in the layer of soggy logs mired at the bottom. But Lavigne's truck had gotten stuck, fouling up the plan.

It was at this juncture that the Third Man betrayed Dumas, according to Malloy and Speer, as well as two other, more senior CID special agents who informed Mark Leshikar's mother, sister, and widow of Lavigne's death. "Tim and somebody killed Billy, wrapped him in a blanket, and were going to take him to dump him," said Tammy, relating what she heard from the investigators. "They got stuck in that deep sand there, and the guy decided to shoot Tim, execution-style, to get rid of any witnesses."

The CID agents who worked the scene presumed that the murder weapon used to kill Dumas was a subcompact handgun. Such a firearm is much less impressive than the hefty magnum revolver that Dumas toted, but a little pocket pistol or ankle gun has its advantages. It's easily concealed, lightweight, lethal at close range, and makes relatively little noise. A muffled pop or snap is all that anyone passing by on Manchester Road late at night might have heard from within the woods.

ARMY INVESTIGATORS were out at Dumas's rental house in Carthage the same day that the bodies were found. They searched the premises, seized a hunting knife, and confiscated a bottle of Captain Morgan rum. They also questioned T.J., but only cursorily. It seemed to the younger Dumas that the agents had already made up their minds about the sorts of people who were responsible for his father's murder. "They were immediately trying to blame it," he said, "on gangsters and cartels."

T.J. had his doubts. "I call bullshit," he said. "I've lived here my entire life. Ain't no cartel or gang member going onto Fort Bragg, killing somebody, and leaving the fucking area."

Dumas's truck was found some forty miles away, in Scotland County, near the town of Laurinburg. The quad-cab Dodge Ram had been stripped of identifiers and firebombed. "Burned to a fucking crisp," said T.J. "They even took his license plates off."

In the movies, they make it look easy to set fire to an automobile. In reality, T.J. pointed out, it's at least a ten-minute job, and a burning car creates a flaming pyre and a column of smoke that can be seen from miles away. "Y'all took a vehicle," he said, incredulously, "drove it all the way from Fort Bragg to Scotland County, Laurinburg, took the license plates off, burned it, and got out of there in time, unseen? Y'all didn't pass by no security cameras, no ATMs, in a big black Dodge Ram?" He refused to believe it. "This was a hit," he insisted.

"I've hung out with gang members," he added. The last thing that they're thinking about is taking your license plates off after killing you. That's something that professionals do."

Dumas Jr. is convinced that his dad was murdered for attempting to blackmail the Special Forces. Someone named in that kompromat letter he wrote describing the trafficking pipeline from the Kandahar airfield to Fort Bragg had to be responsible, he figured. He's unequivocal about it. "I believe the military killed my father."

FOUL PLAY SUSPECTED IN DEATHS OF MASTER SERGEANT AND VETERAN AT FORT BRAGG, read the headline of a CBS News story that ran December 4, 2020. "Both the soldier and the veteran," that is, Lavigne and Dumas, "had been under investigation for using and selling drugs," CBS reported, citing unnamed defense officials. "Shell casings were found

on the ground, leading investigators to suspect that it was a double homicide resulting from a drug deal gone wrong."

Three days later, *The New York Times* published an article in which
officials publicly disclosed, for the first time, that Lavigne was the
shooter in the death of Mark Leshikar. "He was involved, it was determined to be justified and the case was closed," a Cumberland County
spokesman told the *Times*.

"Lavigne proudly served his country with no questions asked," read
his obituary, published in the Southern Pines *Pilot*, a small-circulation
paper often called upon to eulogize Delta Force men. "He was and is an
American hero."

In lieu of flowers, Lavigne's family requested that mourners make donations to the Coast x Coast Foundation. "Billy, we love you and will miss
you," the Coast x Coast club posted to its Instagram page. "RIP, bro."

Lavigne's funeral was held on December 29 at the JFK Memorial
Chapel on Fort Bragg, a church with pine-green carpets and stained-
glass windows in which haloed Green Berets are depicted with rifles in
their hands and Hebrew scriptures at their feet. His ex-wife and daughter, now six years old, were present, as were many of his former comrades from the unit. His friends and family remembered him as "an
amazing father" who "opened his heart and home to all who knew him,"
who "made every minute count," and who "never feared the mountains
in the distance." As the booming strains of Toby Keith's "American Soldier" rang out under the vaulted ceiling, a slideshow of Lavigne's life
played.

Many of the photos showed him with his mom, his grandparents, his
daughter and her mother, his second wife, Michelle Yuki. There were
pictures of Lavigne parachuting, diving, working on construction projects, toying with guns, and camping on the beach with his dog. Mark
Leshikar did not appear in any of the images, but Cris Vallejo did. Iraq,
Afghanistan, Niger, and Israel were among the locales in which Lavigne
was shown in plain clothes and under arms, either packing a pistol or
carrying a sniper rifle, Kalashnikov, or machine gun. In some of the

photos, he and his Delta Force teammates, who once dressed up as the Blue Man Group, throw up a trident-like gang sign.

Lavigne's former comrades did their best to console his mother and speak positively of the departed. "I talked to his guys during his funeral service," said Judy. "They said they wouldn't be where they were if it wasn't for Billy. Because when they hit troubled waters, it was Billy who stepped up and encouraged them. He was a mentor to a lot of people."

Bill Sr., already dissatisfied with the sketchy account he'd heard of his son's murder from Army officials, noticed that Amanda Tostado was not among the mourners. "His girlfriend has been really elusive," the elder Lavigne told me a short time later. "There is something weird there. I think she knows more than what she's said to the investigators."

During the subsequent reception, Bill Sr. made discreet inquiries among the Delta Force men who had come to pay their respects, but they didn't seem to know any more than the police. "Most of Billy's friends or associates I talked to or met," he said. "There was never no mention of this Dumas."

How was it possible, he wondered, that no one could give him any answers? His son had served nineteen years in the military, deployed to many countries, fought in war after war. Now he had simply turned up murdered, on the base itself, the victim of what looked to be a professional hit by skilled assassins, and investigators were stumped?

There was more. On the same day that the murders of Lavigne and Dumas hit the news, the families of both men and the public at large learned of another, equally ominous Fort Bragg murder mystery. Six months earlier, Specialist Enrique Roman-Martinez, a disgruntled junior paratrooper suspected of dealing drugs on base, had gone missing during a camping trip to the North Carolina seashore with seven of his comrades from the 82nd Airborne Division, only for his partial remains to wash ashore a few days later. For half a year, there had been no updates on the investigation into his death. Then, as if Army officials were trying to dump out all the bad news at once, the same *New York*

Times reporters who learned that Lavigne had been Leshikar's killer also obtained a copy of Roman-Martinez's autopsy. It showed that the cause of his death was homicide. Specifically, Roman-Martinez's head had been chopped off with an ax. So far, CID hadn't named a suspect in that case, either.

"It's real strange that something like this can go on at Fort Bragg and nobody seems to know nothing," said Lavigne Sr. "They're covering something up," he said. "That's the way I feel about it."

CID AGENTS CONTINUED to work the case into the first weeks of 2021. They interviewed Jessi Marie Lindsley. They came knocking at Sharon Shively's house in Hope Mills and seized three assault rifles that Lavigne had owned. Malloy, a lowly criminal investigator, not a team chief or warrant officer, was tasked with searching certain storage facilities that Lavigne maintained all over North Carolina and found that they were overflowing with expensive consumer goods. "This dude had hobbies in everything," Malloy said. "It was incredible. Nice-ass North Face jackets. Rock climbing and camping stuff. Hockey gear, every type of outdoor sport. Lots of workout equipment. Real James Bond shit."

"My son had so much stuff," said Judy. "We don't know where it's at. I tried contacting Amanda. I guess she changed her number."

Amanda Tostado had her reasons for lying low. The investigation into Lavigne's death spelled trouble for anyone with whom he had recently discussed drug deals by text message. Six days after the memorial service, Tostado was arrested and hit with state narcotics charges.

While out on bond, Tostado went over to Sharon Shively's house in tears, saying that she'd been attacked by multiple men. "That girl was beat up," said Shively. "She was in pretty rough shape. She laid down and finally went to sleep. I sat there with her, and she was talking in her sleep. There was like three or four of them. She was hollering at them for them to stop. That they were hurting her."

In Tostado's mug shot, she has a black eye, split lip, and bruised cheekbones. The look on her face exudes pure misery. Her probation was revoked, and she was locked up in the North Carolina Correctional Institution for Women. After serving a two-year sentence for possession, she was transferred to the federal system, where she pleaded guilty to trafficking methamphetamine and was sentenced to ten years in prison. Bobby Lee Anderson, named in the same indictment, was sentenced to nearly twenty-two years.

WITHIN THE 10TH MILITARY POLICE Battalion, word was that the lead agents in the Lavigne/Dumas case were onto a sizable drug ring. Other soldiers and veterans from the same units as the two victims were believed to be involved. "It was very large in scale," said Malloy. "A major drug-trafficking operation. Quite a bit of drugs were coming through Fort Bragg."

But CID is an organization with a limited purview. In cases of serious felonies with a nexus to interstate and international drug trafficking, the Army detective agency is liable to get bigfooted by the FBI, which has parallel jurisdiction to investigate crimes on federal land. On February 1, 2021, the FBI stepped in and slammed a lid shut on evidence of organized crime in the most elite echelons of special operations, including the bureau's trusted partner agency, Delta Force. "The FBI came, swept out the office, and took everything we had," said Malloy.

Speer said that the changeover was abrupt and dramatic. The morning it happened, everyone in the Fort Bragg CID office was told that they would turn over their complete files and notes on Lavigne and Dumas. All the whiteboards that they'd used were covered in brown paper and sealed with duct tape. When the FBI team arrived, the feds uncovered the whiteboards, took photos, and then wiped them clean. Next, they took custody of every physical piece of paper related to the case, downloaded all relevant computer files, and deleted the raw evidence from CID's hard drives. "When the FBI comes through," said Speer, "that's what they do."

The FBI, whose former director James Comey was a frequent visitor to Delta Force's headquarters and a personal friend of the unit commander, never provided a single substantive answer to any of the written questions that I submitted, and denied all of my FOIA requests. After CID's file on the Lavigne/Dumas case had been closed for three years, in early 2024, CID headquarters at Fort Belvoir, Virginia, agreed in writing to provide me with a redacted copy. Days before CID was set to produce the records, however, the FBI intervened and blocked their release.

WILLIAM LAVIGNE II was laid to rest in the Sandhills State Veterans Cemetery on Fort Bragg. When I visited on a bright but cold and blustery day in January 2021, after the sod had healed over from his interment, the military graveyard was nearly deserted, and the many American flags on the premises snapped in the wind, their lanyard tackle clanging against metal flagpoles. The steady noise of traffic passing below on Murchison Road contributed to the atmosphere of quiet unrest. An engraving on Lavigne's tombstone read, "LOVED & LIVED & FOUGHT HARD."

"At his core," said Ben Boden, who lacked the financial means to travel to North Carolina to attend the funeral of his best friend from childhood, Lavigne "was definitely somebody that cared about others and was a good guy." He was never cut out for his chosen profession, in Boden's estimation, and the killing that he was called upon to commit in service of his country corroded him from the inside out. "He was forced to be somebody that he wasn't for so long," said Boden, "that it just ate away at him."

"People call him a killer," said Judy, her eyes welling with tears. "I mean, the things I've read have just been unbearable. But he was not a

TIMOTHY DUMAS, SR. AND MASTER SERGEANT WILLIAM LAVIGNE III

Homicide Victims
Cumberland County, North Carolina
December 2, 2020

Dumas, Sr.'s 2015 Dodge Ram pickup truck

Lavigne's 2016 Chevy Colorado pickup truck

Timothy Dumas, Sr.

Master Sergeant William Lavigne III

DETAILS

The FBI's Charlotte Field Office in North Carolina and the U.S. Army Criminal Investigation Command are asking for the public's assistance in creating a timeline around the deaths of Timothy Dumas, Sr., and Master Sergeant William Lavigne III.

Dumas, Sr., 44, and Lavigne, 37, were found dead on Fort Bragg near Manchester Road in Cumberland County, North Carolina, on December 2, 2020. Investigators are seeking to create a timeline of their location and activities on December 1 and 2, 2020. A gray 2016 Chevrolet Colorado pickup truck belonging to Lavigne was found at the crime scene near Manchester Road. A dark-colored 2015 Dodge Ram pickup truck belonging to Dumas, Sr., was found abandoned at another location.

Anyone with information regarding the homicides of Dumas, Sr., and Lavigne, or who may have seen either of them or their respective vehicles on December 1 or 2, 2020, is asked to call FBI Charlotte at (704) 672-6100, or U.S. Army Criminal Investigation Command at (910) 396-8777.

You may also contact your local FBI office or the nearest American Embassy or Consulate.

Field Office: Charlotte

For more than two years, the FBI's only public statement regarding the Lavigne/Dumas murders was this poster.

killer." Or rather, she said, "*they* made him that way." The U.S. government trained her son to be an assassin and then used him as such, again and again, until killing was all that he knew. "I'm sure he didn't like to take someone's life," Judy said. "He didn't go around and kill people for the fun of it. Only when duty called."

"Mark and Billy were both let down by the Army," said Leshikar's sister Nicole Rick. Had authorities investigated her brother's murder properly in 2018, "they would have seen how damaged both of them were." A stint in the penitentiary wouldn't have been the worst outcome for Lavigne. Neither of the SEAL Team Six operators who killed Logan Melgar served more than a couple of years in prison, and Lavigne could have safely counted on similar lenity. An extended stay at a minimum-security correctional institute would have afforded him a chance at rehabilitation and redemption, an opportunity to rectify his failures as a father and repair his role in his daughter's life. As bad as the story of Leshikar's death was for Delta Force, by covering it up, the unit only compounded its public relations problems when Lavigne was murdered in turn. Now it was obvious that something was really rotten in the state of things at Fort Bragg, and in the Special Forces. "After seeing how Mark's story was reported on," said Nicole, "and seeing situations like this, where soldiers are killing each other, it makes me have so little faith in the honest reporting within the military."

Seventeen

THE THUMB DRIVE

Days after the murders of Billy Lavigne and Timothy Dumas, the FBI passed a tip about Freddie Wayne Huff to Homeland Security Investigations, whose remit is to investigate crime linked to the border. The FBI informed HSI that Huff, a former North Carolina state trooper and ex–DEA task force agent, was "obtaining large quantities of illegal narcotics from Mexico."

A task force led by HSI convened, joined by investigators from both law enforcement agencies that Huff had worked for: the Lexington PD and the highway patrol. The task force also included the Forsyth County Sheriff's Office led by Huff's "super good friend" Bobby Kimbrough, the Winston-Salem Police Department, the Davidson County Sheriff's Office, and the North Carolina State Bureau of Investigation.

Huff was oblivious, for a time, to these developments. But he knew that many of his underworld associates held him responsible for the murders of Lavigne and Dumas. "I know that I was suspected," he said, "because me and Tim had a falling-out right before his death."

No third party had witnessed the reconciliation that Huff said took place between him and Dumas in the basement of his house in Lexington in the last week of November. "Nobody knew that we were working together again," he said. "And then Tim shows up murdered. So obviously, anybody would think that it was probably me."

Huff managed to convince some of Dumas's people of his innocence, including Robert Seward, Orlando Fitzhugh, and Dumas Jr. But doubts about Huff lingered in the minds of some members of his set. A courier whom Huff had used to move money and drugs, a man who went by the street name Straight Up, drifted away and was not seen again. An FBI analyst in Savannah, Georgia, whom Huff had relied upon for tip-offs and who'd had a relationship with Dumas, also went dark on him. In February 2021, an unnamed person who had close dealings with Huff approached the HSI-led task force. "I have an idea of who it was," said Huff of the turncoat in his midst. "But I'm not sure."

The confidential informant told federal agents a long story about Huff offering to have someone killed by his bodyguards, a pair of Mexican *sicarios*, and that on another occasion Huff had put a bounty of $40,000 on the head of a person who had stolen five kilos of cocaine. The anonymous source estimated that Huff was trafficking fifty to a hundred kilos of coke every seven to ten days, which comes out to a midrange estimate of three and a half *tons* per year, and that his smuggling innovations had reduced the losses suffered by Los Zetas at the border from about 17 percent to 7 percent. He or she also provided the feds with information on various exotic cars that Huff owned and houses he maintained in North Carolina.

WITH DUMAS DEAD, Huff needed a new partner, and, true to form, the person he chose was a military man. Rahain Antione Deriggs II was a twenty-six-year-old Marine Corps sergeant stationed at nearby Camp Lejeune. His military occupation, that of a supply chain and matériel management specialist, was essentially the same job that Dumas had held in the Army. The Marine Corps confirmed that Deriggs served six years and that he "left active duty" on November 26, 2020—one week before Lavigne and Dumas were murdered. But in response to a public records request, the Marine Corps stated that they had lost Deriggs's personnel file.

"Deriggs, as a marine, would have a lot of skills that would be helpful in the drug-trafficking trade," said Randall Galyon, the federal prosecutor in Winston-Salem. "[Huff] had Mr. Deriggs serve essentially as his bodyguard."

"He was basically my right-hand man," said Huff. "He took road trips with me. He helped me package money. Whatever I needed him to do, he'd do."

Huff is rather harsh in his assessment of Deriggs's character. "He is a big motherfucker, but he wasn't the sharpest knife in the drawer. He would follow directions to a *T*, but if you had to have him make his own decisions, he would fuck it all up."

On March 27, 2021, Webb County sheriff's deputies pulled over Sergeant Deriggs, who is black, while he was transporting money from San Antonio, Texas, to Laredo. In a green military duffel bag in the back seat, the deputies found $210,021. "This type of bulk monies are consistent to be illegal proceeds as part of organized crime [*sic*]," the sheriff's spokesman said in a statement to the *Laredo Morning Times*.

The loss of money meant that Huff and company were unable to purchase their next load of coke from their cartel contacts in Laredo, who required cash on delivery. But they could still buy on consignment from Jaime Rosado's people in Orlando. The Puerto Rican trafficking organization, led by a faceless capo identified in court documents only as Steven, fronted them the kilos on the understanding that if they didn't pay up, Steven would have them all killed.

For the next several months, Huff's crew was back in business. They trafficked hundreds of kilos up to the Piedmont Triad from Orlando, but their leveraged position, combined with Huff's habit of immediately squandering every dollar he made on prostitutes and gambling, made them vulnerable to any stroke of bad luck. This turned into a real problem when Michael Terry, a Winston-Salem gangster known by the street name Hundred K, refused to pay for $150,000 worth of cocaine that he believed to be of inferior quality. "So we owe Steven," said Huff, "and we don't have no money."

The stress he was under added to a long list of health problems that had been dogging Huff since he'd lost his job with the state police. In addition to chronic anxiety, clinical depression, bipolar disorder, restless leg syndrome, gastroesophageal reflux disease, and hyperlipidemia, for which he took "near-lethal doses," he said, of a slew of prescription medications, Huff had been diagnosed with early-onset Parkinson's and generalized idiopathic epilepsy. He regularly checked into the hospital after suffering seizures, and on one occasion reported to doctors that "he was overloaded with stressors, including marital problems, multimillion-dollar business problems, legal problems, and taking in two homeless children."

In this agitated state, exacerbated by his continuous use of cocaine, Huff paced back and forth in the basement of his suburban lair in Lexington, chain-smoking cigarettes and plotting how to strike back at Hundred K, an amateur rapper with a gold grill and beard whose music videos depict him showing off whole garbage bins full of cash. "He was going to kidnap Hundred K's mom first," said Rosado, "because he had her location." But Rosado, ever the peacemaker, persuaded Huff to go after a more legitimate target. They settled on Hundred K's number-two man, Tomont Williams, who went by the hood alias Rise.

Huff and company meticulously planned and executed the abduction mission. First, Huff and Deriggs disguised themselves as U.S. marshals. They bought a blacked-out Dodge Charger from a police auction, left it registered to the state in case anyone ran its plates, and rigged it with strobe lights. Then they bought black tactical uniforms from a military surplus store and stenciled "U.S. MARSHAL" with white spray paint on black body armor.

Rosado, meanwhile, obtained a postal service uniform. Dressed as a mail carrier in short pants, he reconnoitered a house in Winston-Salem where Rise was known to stay. When the gangster left the property in a white Jeep Wrangler, Rosado alerted Huff, who hit the police lights

on the Dodge Charger. Rise submitted passively to arrest by the puta-
tive lawmen.

Hundred K, who drove around in a green Cadillac Escalade with
twenty-inch chrome rims, received a text message with a photo that
showed Rise tied up in the basement of Huff's house, an array of guns,
knives, and one of Dumas's hand grenades held against his head. "We
called Hundred K," said Rosado. "We told him to give us the money. If
not, we are going to chop this boy up."

"Okay, okay," Hundred K replied. "I'll give you the money. All right."

They settled on the parking lot of Hanes Mall on the southwest side
of Winston-Salem. Hundred K paid partially in the form of jewelry, and
could come up with only eighty thousand in cash. But that was enough
for Huff to quash the beef. The two crews parted ways, and Tomont Williams, a.k.a. Rise, "never told the police anything," said Huff.

Believing, naively, that there the matter would rest, Huff agreed to
front Hundred K another four kilos on the understanding that he would
pay interest to make up the seventy thousand that he still owed. But as
soon as Hundred K was safely back in his hood with the drugs in hand,
he placed a taunting video call to mock Huff for his gullibility. "Fuck
you," he crowed. "I wasn't going to pay for the first ones anyway."

The kidnapping of Rise had been for nothing. There didn't seem to
be any easy way out of the predicament. "Steven would have had me
and my whole family and Jaime's family killed," said Huff. "We owed
him like $180,000."

While racking his brain for ideas, Huff had a conversation with one
of his regular buyers, a Latino man who knew to whom Hundred K had
given the stolen cocaine. "I go to a Mexican that I sold to," said Huff,
"and he tells me that Michael Sosa has my shit. I was like, well, this is
my saving grace right here."

MICHAEL SOSA LIVED in a small residential compound at the end of a
shady lane in a rural suburb of Forsyth County. He had a battery of

security cameras trained on his front gate, and five or six dogs that pa-trolled the grounds and would throw themselves against the fence in a frenzy of crazed barking at the approach of any stranger.

Sosa, twenty-nine, a big spender at strip clubs and a wearer of flashy jewelry, knew that some people figured him for a dope dealer. "When you're Mexican and have a lot of money," he told me, "people automati-cally think you're selling drugs. That's what a lot of people think of me." In reality, he said, "I have a construction company."

On the morning of May 28, 2021, Sosa was asleep in bed when he heard something slam, then the sound of shouting. He rolled out of bed and grabbed his strap, ready to start blasting. It was 6:50 a.m.

Still in his pajamas, Sosa came out into the hallway with his weapon at the ready. But the intruders, clad in black commando gear, wearing combat helmets, ski masks, and tactical vests that identified them as federal marshals, already had his mother at gunpoint, her hands bound with zip ties. Sosa set down his gun and put his hands in the air. It had been a mistake to lock the dogs in their kennel the previous evening.

Laser dots played on Sosa's chest. One of the supposed marshals was white and the other was black. Through the front window, in the gray light of early morning, Sosa could see their vehicle, a "blacked-out Charger with police lights." Claiming to have a search warrant, the pair proceeded to ransack Sosa's home, garage, and attic, collecting all the cash, jewelry, and guns they could find. Their haul included $80,000 from a safe that Sosa's brother was forced to open with a gun to his head, a handful of diamonds worth a hundred grand, two assault rifles, a shotgun, and a couple of handguns. Sosa denied that any drugs were in his house, but the loot also allegedly included a bin full of vape car-tridges, three pounds of marijuana, and the bricks of coke that Hun-dred K had stolen from Huff, which were recognizable by a distinctive stamp in the shape of the irrational number π.

In the meantime, Sosa's mother was getting increasingly agitated.

She was breathing heavily, gulping down air. Her anxiety erupted into a full-blown panic attack. Then she fainted.

Not wanting to be responsible for causing the woman's death, the white marshal used a drop phone to call emergency services. On his way out the door, he wiped the device of fingerprints and threw it in the trash. He and the black marshal made haste to load up the Dodge Charger, but the ambulance arrived in record time from a hospital just down the road, and the two groups had an awkward encounter in the driveway.

As soon as the ski-mask-wearing, suspiciously behaved federal marshals were gone, the medics called the real police. The Winston-Salem officers who arrived minutes later traced the 911 call to the burner phone that had already been jettisoned. But with a few keystrokes in a database, they were able to associate it, by dint of geographic collocation, with the personal cell phone of a former state trooper named Freddie Wayne Huff, whose name was flagged on a federal watch list. Within hours, HSI agents in white polo shirts were out at Mike Sosa's house to interview him.

BY MAY 2021, the HSI-led task force had been investigating Huff for five months—the same amount of time that Lavigne and Dumas had been dead. They already had him on tape selling cocaine to an informant and had done multiple controlled buys at his stash house in Lexington. Seeing the recklessness and aggression that he displayed in kidnapping and robbing Sosa and his family, they decided that the time had come to make a move.

An HSI tactical team took Huff down first, at a convenience store near his house. Next, they nabbed Rosado in a traffic stop, catching him with eleven kilos of cocaine in a cardboard box. The task force arrested a total of ten men that day, including Deriggs and Huff's son, whose disgruntled mug shots were broadcast on the evening news.

"That was horrible, man," said Rosado. "That was the worst day of my life." The cops asked Rosado what he thought would happen to him when the Puerto Ricans learned that he had lost eleven of their kilos. "I'm dead," Rosado replied.

At the Davidson County jail, where Rosado was initially held, he ran into Deriggs. The hulking ex-marine was sitting on a bench crying. "I feel sorry for Rahain," said Rosado. "He didn't deserve this. He was a good guy. He was loyal to Freddie, and Freddie was treating him like a dog."

In addition to the cocaine that Rosado was caught with, the task force seized two kilos of heroin at Huff's house on Peppermill Drive and five pounds of marijuana. Huff denied that he ever dealt methamphetamine and also said that he didn't know to whom Billy Lavigne owed money for meth, yet officers seized a whopping sixty kilos of the stuff from his basement. The total quantity of drugs confiscated was worth some $3.7 million, and the crystal meth accounted for the bulk of that estimated street value.

The task force reported seizing $300,000 in drug money from the Lexington trap house, a conveniently round figure that Huff, who in his state trooper days had been an expert in asset forfeiture, dismissed out of hand. He said that more than $1 million had been hidden in the basement. "I don't know what happened to all that money," the judge in Huff's case would later comment. "Somebody's driving a Lamborghini."

The police also confiscated a money-counting machine, six digital scales, four vacuum sealers, and eight firearms. Among them was a sub-compact pocket pistol found on the floor of Huff's Lamborghini Huracán, a Glock 42—the caliber of which was .380.

Finally, the task force swept up all the electronic devices on the premises. In additional to a personal computer and several cell phones, these included the thumb drive that—according to Huff—contained the blackmail letter Dumas had written, purporting to name the members of a drug cartel embedded in the Special Forces at Fort Bragg. None of the cops read what was on the thumb drive. A forensics unit of the Winston-Salem Police Department logged its seizure, then locked it away in their evidence room.

Freddie Wayne Huff II was arrested and charged with trafficking drugs five months after Billy Lavigne and Timothy Dumas were murdered.

Part V

Eighteen

ACID IS LIFE

Specialist Enrique Roman-Martinez, the paratrooper whose autopsy was released simultaneously with the news of the Lavigne/Dumas murders, was a very different kind of soldier from the sort of bearded special operators that Fort Bragg is famous for. Though airborne qualified, meaning he had been trained to jump out of airplanes, Roman-Martinez was a support soldier, a human resources specialist, in a conventional unit. He wore camouflage but sat in a cubicle. He never deployed.

Yet the macabre manner of his death, the timing of its announcement, and the revelation that Roman-Martinez had been an on-post drug dealer greatly aggravated the consternation felt in the community about the double murder by McArthur Lake, and contributed to a sense among the family members of Billy Lavigne, Timothy Dumas, and Mark Leshikar that things had gotten completely out of hand at the Army's flagship installation. That Roman-Martinez was beheaded, a method of killing associated with organized crime in Mexico, inflamed rumors of some kind of cartel on Fort Bragg and led to speculation that his murder might have been connected to the expert hit put on Lavigne and Dumas. The unsettling story of his violent demise, even in a tough military town already known for bizarre unsolved murders, still haunts the Piedmont country of North Carolina, where "Justice for Enrique" flyers were once ubiquitous. His killer is still out there, too.

Enrique Roman-Martinez was born in 1996 in Chino, California, a sprawling suburb of Los Angeles in San Bernardino County where the top employers are Walmart, a for-profit hospital, and the state prison system. "We were really poor growing up," said his big sister, Griselda Roman-Martinez. "Our mom always worked two jobs."

Enrique was a sensitive, angsty kid. Words that his sister uses to describe him include "gentle," "spiritual," and "feminist," as well as "depressed." He spent long hours online reading about alternative medicine and Eastern religions. "He believed in crystals," said Griselda. "He was trying to get into Buddhism. Me and my mom being Catholic, it was hard to understand."

As a teenager, Enrique developed a passionate interest in psychedelic drugs. In high school, he was known as a precocious evangelist for the healing powers of psilocybin mushrooms and LSD and peddled these substances to his classmates. His Instagram handle was Trip-on-Roman. The password to his email account was AcidisLife#$7435. He even got a diagram of the lysergic acid molecule tattooed on his body.

In 2014, at the age of eighteen, Enrique enlisted in the Army, where his matronymic surname, Martinez, was lopped off in accordance with the naming conventions of the English language, and he became known simply as Roman. He made the decision to enlist for two pragmatic reasons, neither of which had anything to do with the GWOT, then well into its second decade. "One was to provide an income for our family," said Griselda. "The other was to go to school to find a cure for depression." His plan was to do one four-year enlistment, then use the GI Bill to go to pharmacy school. "He sincerely felt that hallucinogenic mushrooms were a cure for mental illness."

Roman initially aspired to join the 75th Ranger Regiment, an elite light infantry brigade based at Fort Moore, Georgia, but was disappointed to find that he wasn't cut out for special operations. After boot camp, he washed out of Ranger School. "He didn't have the endurance," says Griselda. "He wasn't super strong. He was a relatively small guy."

Roman did manage to complete the rigors of paratrooper training and was assigned to the 82nd Airborne Division, which functions as a sort of farm team for the Special Forces. But repeated parachute jumps gave him a kind of leg injury known as compartment syndrome, which several surgeries failed to alleviate. Left unable to run well and hobbled by chronic pain, the unlucky young soldier, who was liking military life less and less, was given an unenviable desk job at the headquarters of the 37th Brigade Engineer Battalion, a unit that supports frontline troops by clearing roads, digging fortifications, building bridges, and doing other construction work in combat zones.

In the late GWOT era, such units were as pervaded by drug use as the Special Forces. But rather than cocaine, the most commonly used substance among lower-enlisted soldiers in the conventional Army was LSD. "Everyone does LSD," said Maegan Malloy, the undercover narcotics agent. "On post, it's the main drug."

"Pretty much everybody was doing acid," agreed Jordan Terrell, the Special Forces dropout in the 82nd Airborne Division who sold LSD and shrooms to Billy Lavigne and his Delta Force teammates, and bought coke and heroin from them. "Psychedelics and cocaine were the two biggest."

A gloomy Special Forces base in the pine woods of North Carolina would seem bound to produce a bad trip in all but the most stalwart of psychonauts. But in fact, the history of LSD in the United States is deeply rooted at Fort Bragg. The Army and Navy were part of the CIA's efforts during the Cold War to develop a mind-control drug that they could use to elicit confessions and program assassins. In the 1950s, as part of Operation Third Chance, more than a thousand Fort Bragg soldiers were among the first Americans to be voluntarily dosed with LSD.

Today, soldiers in the market for a recreational high prefer LSD for straightforward reasons. It's among the most difficult drugs to detect by urinalysis, and tiny acid tabs are easy to conceal. Few police dogs are trained to detect it.

Stuck in a cubicle and counting the days until his enlistment ended and he could go to pharmacy school, Roman catered to the large and growing psychedelics market on base as a means of making money on the side. Every time that he went home on leave, he came back carrying a supply of blotters. He developed hookups in Raleigh and the District of Columbia and opened a post office box for ordering high-quality acid off the dark web. He sold the tabs using a dead drop under a trash can in the stairwell of his barracks building, charging $15 a pop.

Roman made minimal effort to conceal his activities, even posting provocative pictures of himself on social media in which he was blatantly dropping a tab of acid on his tongue while wearing the uniform and maroon beret of the 82nd Airborne Division. Informants, including one of his roommates, reported his use and distribution of drugs to his chain of command. The 37th Brigade Engineer Battalion took no disciplinary action, but Roman was quietly placed on a military police watch list, a system called ALERTS, used to track potential dealers in the ranks. He was also directed to attend substance abuse counseling.

ROMAN WAS STRAIGHT and liked girls but had never had a girlfriend and didn't use dating apps. He spent his free time playing video games and reading anime comics, slept with his arms and legs wrapped around a body pillow in the shape of an anime character, and bought so many collectible anime figurines that, in spite of the money he made selling drugs, he had gone into credit card debt.

Though he had trouble relating to girls on a romantic level, Roman easily befriended women. He was always "protective" and "supportive," his sister said, of his many "chick friends," whom he lavished with compliments to boost their self-esteem. In the headquarters company of the 37th Brigade Engineer Battalion, he became close with a cute, tomboyish female soldier, even younger and lower ranking than he was, named Annamarie Cochell.

Private Second Class Cochell, originally from rural Michigan, was a jittery and anxious girl addicted to Juul-brand vape sticks, who was romantically involved with Roman's good friend Specialist Alex Becerra, a handsome and athletic former collegiate soccer player from Texas. Like Roman, Becerra was a devoted aficionado of LSD and had been flagged on the ALERTS watch list.

By May 2020, people across North Carolina had begun to chafe at the pandemic lockdown, which the governor had repeatedly extended. It was a time of stewing discontent and inchoate violence in America. A summer of fiery street protests was on the horizon, and a divisive presidential election loomed.

Before the sun rose on May 22, Roman, Cochell, Becerra, and five others from headquarters company struck out for the coast of North Carolina, a three-hour drive away, in violation of an order than forbade soldiers to travel more than fifty miles from Fort Bragg. Specialist Becerra planned the camping trip. The highest-ranking member of the group was Sergeant Samuel Moore, an Eagle Scout who'd been raised in a strict Christian household. The lowest ranking, aside from Cochell, was Roman's roommate, Private First Class Samad Landrum, a gangly young black man known for his cleanliness, honesty, and good attitude. They were joined by three specialists, all in their early twenties: Joshua Curry, Benjamin Sibley, and Juan Avila.

ARRIVING AT THE SEASIDE TOWN of Davis, the wayward soldiers from Fort Bragg took a ferry to Cape Lookout, a windswept barrier island known for its herds of wild horses. The tomahawk-shaped island, together with an island perpendicular to it called Shackleford Banks, is part of a labyrinthian complex of mazy landforms girding the coast of North Carolina, including Cape Fear, namesake of the Cape Fear River, that once presented a deadly hazard to sailing ships. For centuries, the swampy straits, mucky inlets, and brackish estuaries of this notorious naval graveyard have supplied the setting for ghost stories, tall tales, and nautical legends. The first English colony in the Americas disappeared from Roanoke Island in the late 1580s, leaving behind nothing but the word "Croatoan," an old name for Hatteras Island, carved on a tree trunk. Almost exactly a century before Roman's ill-fated camping trip to Cape Lookout, the next headland south of Hatteras, the entire crew of a perfectly intact schooner called the *Carroll A. Deering* inexplicably disappeared, leaving the ship to founder on the shoals there, a riddle to historians ever since.

The group from Fort Bragg found the north end of the cape excessively crowded that Memorial Day weekend. The National Park Service allows motorists to drive their giant trucks and sport-utility vehicles directly on the sensitive ecosystem of the beach, and many had Trump 2020 banners and Confederate battle flags flying from their fenders and antennas, the sight of which rankled Roman, whose mother had come to the United States undocumented from Mexico. "Fuck you," he shouted at a carful of Trump supporters as they drove past, showing them his middle fingers.

This was a typical gesture on Roman's part. In the headquarters company, he was known for his mordant sarcasm and dark sense of humor. His comrades said that he cursed like a sailor, laughed like a girl, often made light of suicide, and "absolutely hated the Army."

The eight soldiers, riding in a blue Ford Ranger and Becerra's white Jeep Wrangler, stopped midway down the elongated island to toss around a football. Roman, who couldn't swim and feared the open ocean, sat on the sand next to Annamarie Cochell while the other boys waded out into the surf to search for starfish and cast out fishing lines. Cochell's cousin had recently passed away, and they fell into a deep discussion of "why bad things happen to good people, and why people have to die."

Later in the afternoon, they drove several miles farther south and found a campsite at the foot of some sand dunes, within sight of a historic lighthouse. They pitched their tents, ate a hasty dinner of pre-made tuna sandwiches, and built a fire. This work done, they broke out their stores of hard seltzer and light beer and sat back to take in the ocean at sunset.

Roman drank no alcohol that evening, but dropped a quantity of acid that both Landrum and Moore described as a "shit ton." He had brought plenty of LSD to go around and offered to share with the others. Sibley, Moore, Curry, and Avila declined, while Becerra, Cochell, and Landrum each took one of the chits of white paper, which were printed with a curious black design, too tiny to decipher, and placed them to dissolve on their tongues.

RAIN HAD BUFFETED Cape Lookout earlier in the week. Now, around 8:00 p.m., the overcast sky, inflamed by the descending sun, looked increasingly troubled. Distant thunder rumbled, the wind picked up, and thin spits of rain hissed in the coals of the fire. The onset of the storm "set everything in motion," said Moore.

Becerra and Cochell, who were beginning to feel the first psychedelic effects of the drug they'd taken, got up and wandered down the beach a way. "I think they just wanted some alone time," Moore said.

This was the moment when Roman first showed signs of becoming distraught. He started to "freak out," in the words of one specialist. The others couldn't understand why he was so upset. He paced around, mumbling something about how he couldn't find his wallet. He was irrationally convinced that Becerra and Cochell had stolen it. He was so perseverative on this point that Moore went after Becerra and Cochell and persuaded them to come back to the campsite. Roman then found his wallet in the center console of the Jeep and temporarily calmed down.

Again the group settled down around the campfire. Some of the young soldiers, insufficiently entertained by the awesome spectacle of a thunderstorm brewing out over the Atlantic, sat scrolling social media on their phones. Roman showed Cochell a picture of an anime girl on his battered Samsung Galaxy, which was covered in manga stickers. "Would you hit that?" he asked her. It was another of his awkward attempts to relate to her on a sexual level, and she wasn't quite sure how to respond. "She's not my type," Cochell replied.

All four of those who had dropped acid were really tripping now. Rain began to pour down, nearly extinguishing the fire. All of the surviving campers spoke of this violent rain squall, but oddly, it was not captured by nearby weather stations.

Thunder cracked and boomed, and wild bolts of lightning on the horizon starkly illuminated the choppy waves, momentarily freezing them in their turbulent churning. Roman, in the thrall of perception-enhancing LSD, was horrorstruck. He was afraid of water and afraid of the dark, but above all, his mother told investigators through a Spanish translator, he was afraid of thunderstorms.

The other campers scrambled to secure their belongings and disassemble a pop-up canopy before it blew away, and Roman took shelter in the rear seat of Becerra's Jeep. There, while waiting out the rain gale, he had what the others described as a mental breakdown.

A bad trip, also known as a psychedelic crisis, is a state of unrelieved terror and psychic suffering of a potential severity unimaginable to the sober mind. An Army clerk who was unwittingly dosed with LSD in 1961, in an experimental interrogation to determine if he'd stolen classified documents, recalled that he was taken into a dark room illuminated by a bare light bulb. "A man was sitting at a table with his hands hidden," said the soldier. "He asked what I had done with the documents. Then my head exploded, as big as the universe."

Roman was paralyzed with fear one minute, panicked and hyperventilating the next. "I want to go home," he whimpered. Again and again he asked, "Are we going to die?"

"It's just a storm," Sergeant Moore told him. "Nothing bad will happen."

The ferry to the mainland ran only a few times a day, but Roman couldn't seem to accept that they had no choice but to remain on the island all night. Despite his apparently incapacitated state, he unexpectedly got hold of the keys to the Jeep and tried to drive away, forcing Becerra to restrain him in a choke hold. Likewise, the owner of the Ford Ranger had to wrestle down Samad Landrum, who was also having a bad trip and would have driven off too, had he not been held back.

The rainfall lasted only a short time. When it had blown itself out, the campers set about fixing the flattened and overturned tents. Roman alone remained in the Jeep, looking "depleted" or "checked out," as if "nothing was there." Having failed to coax him out of the vehicle, the others decided to let him stay where he was, wrapped in a Grateful Dead blanket. They brushed their teeth with bottled water and bedded down for the night, leaving Roman in the back seat, "fixated on staring at an unknown object."

BACK AT FORT BRAGG, the captain and the first sergeant of the 37th Brigade Engineer Battalion's headquarters company did a walk-through of the barracks around one o'clock on Saturday morning. Finding Roman's door unlocked and slightly ajar, they went into his room.

On the nightstand, the captain noticed a bottle of Percocet, an opiate painkiller that had been prescribed to Roman after the most recent surgery to his legs. There was also a nasal-spray dispenser of Narcan. Not long before, another soldier in the battalion had nearly died of a cocaine overdose, and Roman was evidently prepared to revive any of his comrades who ingested too much heroin or fentanyl. The captain and first sergeant switched off the light and went out, closing the door securely behind them.

Hundreds of miles away, at the campsite on Cape Lookout, Landrum was awakened around two o'clock by the sound of Moore unzipping the tent that they shared. Still slightly tripping, he listened as Moore walked to the edge of the sand dunes and took a long piss. Then Moore returned and they both went back to sleep.

By seven o'clock on Saturday morning, the sun had risen. Becerra woke up at 8:30, emerged from the tent where he'd spent the night spooning with Cochell, and noticed that the door of his Jeep was open. Roman was no longer in the back seat.

Roman had probably gone off on a walk, Becerra figured. Perhaps he had needed to take a dump and had hiked up past the lighthouse to where the bathrooms were. Weirdly, though, he'd left behind his wallet, phone, and glasses. The first two items he could do without. But with 4.25 diopters of corneal astigmatism, Roman was "highly dependent on wearing his eyeglasses during all waking hours," his optometrist said.

This proved to be an important point, because it bore directly on whether Roman had left the Jeep voluntarily. "He would leave his phone and wallet for sure, but not his glasses," said Christian Romero, a childhood friend of Roman's who also joined the Army and was stationed at Fort Bragg, but in a different unit. "Enrique is blind as fuck without his glasses," Romero said. "He loves views, too. He's one of those guys who's into nature."

By 9:15 a.m., Becerra and Cochell had begun to worry. For nearly two hours, they and one of the specialists walked around the south end of the island, past brackish inlets and hard hummocks covered in sea oats and cordgrass, periodically pausing to call out for Enrique. Meanwhile, the two other specialists and Landrum went fishing.

IN THE HOT and sunny afternoon, with Memorial Day recreation on the island in full swing, park rangers stopped by the campsite and asked the group from Fort Bragg to please move their vehicles, which were encroaching on protected sand dunes. Becerra and the owner of the Ford Ranger complied.

For the next three hours, Becerra, Cochell, and Landrum drove around the island's network of hard-packed dirt roads, looking for Roman in a historic village of old wooden houses, around the decommissioned lighthouse, and amid the impenetrable thickets of a bird preserve. He was nowhere to be found.

At 5:00 p.m., Becerra called 911. "We lost our friend," he told the dispatcher. "We are kind of worried that something happened to him." He added, "We have been looking for him all day."

Then Becerra made a misleading statement that would dog him for years. "We were trying to find a park ranger or their offices or anything," he said, omitting the encounter with rangers around noon, at which time neither he nor any of the others had reported Roman missing.

Becerra was also the first person to suggest that Roman could have committed suicide. "He might have hurt himself," he told the dispatcher, unprompted. "He wasn't diagnosed, but he did have suicidal tendencies."

A group of park rangers, including the chief ranger, showed up at the remote campsite at the southern tip of the island nearly an hour later. The rangers were trained to look for red flags indicative of a struggle, such as abrasions and scrapes on the bodies of the campers, but didn't spot anything of the kind. They helped search for Roman until sundown, then suspended their efforts for the night. Twenty-four hours had yet to elapse, so for the moment there was no emergency.

The campers from Fort Bragg were left on their own again. The disobedient paratroopers, now reduced in number to seven, sat glumly around their fire. In a last-ditch effort to locate Roman, they acted on a park ranger's suggestion and called a comrade back at the barracks and asked him to check inside Roman's room. Although it was practically impossible for Roman to have made his way back to Fort Bragg, they had looked for him everywhere else, it seemed.

The soldier called upon to perform this task found Roman's door locked, so he went in through the unlatched window, leaving his fingerprints on the sill. He reported by phone to the campers on the island that Roman wasn't inside. Later, investigators would be unable to find Roman's journal, in which his sister swears he made daily entries.

It was now ten o'clock at night. Although it meant telling on themselves for disobeying the pandemic lockdown order, guaranteeing that they would all get in trouble, the seven campers finally broke down and called the commander of the 37th Brigade Engineer Battalion, Colonel Scotty Autin, to let him know that he had a soldier unaccounted for.

Specialist Enrique Roman-Martinez in the
uniform of the 82nd Airborne Division.

Nineteen

EVIDENCE OF ABSENCE

Six days after Roman's disappearance, around eleven o'clock in the morning on Friday, May 29, 2020, a wildlife biologist in search of nesting sea turtles was riding a four-wheeler along the beach of Shackleford Banks when she spotted an object lying on the sand that she didn't immediately recognize. At first her brain tried to categorize the roughly spherical object lying there in the midday sun, swarming with flies, as a coconut shell. Drawing closer, though, she saw that it was a severed human head, beaten and scraped purple and red, with short black hair.

A portion of the lower face was missing. The left eye was gouged out, the right ear ripped off. Maggots infested the ragged stump of neck. Crab holes had formed in the surrounding sand.

It was obvious to the wildlife biologist, whose job was to study aquatic animals in their natural habitat, that she was not looking at the result of a shark attack. Clearly, this was the work of a person wielding a hatchet or ax. As for the identity of the deceased, he could only be the missing Fort Bragg soldier whom search parties had been looking for since Monday morning, the bespectacled young man from California whose face was all over the local news: Enrique Roman-Martinez.

An autopsy performed on the partial remains five days later at the Brody School of Medicine in Greenville confirmed the biologist's initial impression that Roman was not the victim of an aquatic predator, or a boating accident, for that matter. The medical examiner found evidence of multiple chop injuries, including one especially forceful blow that had shattered Roman's mandible. The instrument used to transect his neck and cervical spine at the seventh vertebrae wasn't necessarily an ax, but it had to have been some kind of hand tool that was sharp on one side and heavy and dull on the other, close examination of irregular skin tags revealed. The cause of death was homicide.

NEWS OF THE GRUESOME DISCOVERY at Shackleford Banks reached CID agents on Fort Bragg later that afternoon, while they were in the process of interrogating Private Annamarie Cochell. Upon returning to base late Sunday night, the six male soldiers who had been on the camping trip had tried to conceal Cochell's involvement by surreptitiously dropping her off at the female barracks. That stratagem had completely backfired, because Roman's failure to turn up in the days that followed set off a full-blown police investigation.

At first, little had happened because Colonel Autin waited until Monday morning to alert Fort Bragg's CID office, said Dustin Collier, an attorney for the Roman-Martinez family. "That gave the seven other soldiers two full days to clean their tracks," he said. The forty-eight-hour delay was "the single most disturbing fact about this entire investigation," Collier said.

Once CID got involved, the agents had quickly learned of the drug use on the camping trip, and which of the campers had dropped acid. Cochell had already waived her *Miranda* rights, declined to retain a lawyer, written out a statement that contained everything she could remember about the trip, drawn diagrams of the campsite and the route taken across the island, given up her cell phone to have its data extracted, and agreed to take a polygraph exam. Meanwhile, the National Park Service and the Coast Guard had been combing the marshes, dune beds, and scrub forests of the barrier islands with cadaver dogs, while patrol boats plied the waters miles out to sea, helicopters went chopping back and forth overhead, and drones buzzed low over the shallow sounds and swampy straits in search of any sign of the missing paratrooper. Now the CID interrogator stepped out of the room and was gone for an interval of time ominous in its duration. When the agent returned, Cochell was asked to sign another *Miranda* waiver, this time acknowledging that murder was among the crimes that she could be charged with. At this, a CID agent recorded, Cochell became "visibly upset."

With the exception of Private Samad Landrum, a young black man, the only African American in the group, whose parents had the good sense to make sure that he was represented by a lawyer, the campers all signed the same *Miranda* waivers as Cochell. They all underwent repeated interrogations unaccompanied by attorneys, surrendered their phones for inspection, and agreed to take lie detector tests. All seven steadfastly denied wrongdoing. Nevertheless, in the eyes of CID, they were the most likely culprits. "CID has told me they're quite confident it's murder," said Collier, "by one or more of the seven other soldiers."

They were the last to see Roman alive, CID agents reasoned. They had failed to report him missing at noon on Saturday when they'd first had the chance, during the encounter with park rangers that Becerra had subsequently misrepresented to the 911 dispatcher. Then they had orchestrated a break-in of Roman's living quarters and perhaps made off with his diary, which might have contained records of drug sales. Taken as a whole, these omissions, evasions, and suspicious actions led CID to suspect that one or more of the campers had killed Roman, cut up his body, and thrown it into the ocean, only for his head to reappear onshore like the finale of some nineteenth-century work of gothic fiction.

Missing in this scenario of their guilt, however, was the critical element of motive. None of the scattershot theories posited by CID and the witnesses they interviewed were very persuasive. Christian Romero suggested that Becerra might have harbored a grudge toward Roman over an incident in which Becerra had been ticketed for driving under the influence of alcohol because Roman failed to perform designated driver duties. Roman's platoon sergeant speculated, even less convincingly, that he might have been killed for selling the other campers an inferior LSD product. The battalion chaplain was a particularly fecund source of sexually charged conjectures concerning the relationship between Cochell and Becerra. Griselda wondered if her brother, always protective of his female friends, might have been killed for standing up for Cochell against some actual or planned depredation by the other boys.

The problem was that no physical or testimonial evidence existed to buttress any of these hypotheses. In the course of their investigation, which turned into one of the most exhaustive in the history of CID, agents cloned the seven suspects' phones and computers, studied their social media accounts, subpoenaed their bank records, and fanned out to states across the country to interview their friends and family, as well as their teachers, principals, coaches, and pastors going back to elementary school, asking these people intrusive questions about the junior troopers' histories of interpersonal conflict, risk-taking behaviors, money problems, religious convictions, and sexuality. Based on hundreds of interviews, CID created detailed personality profiles that were often unflattering but far from incriminating. Cochell, the agents learned, had been ticketed in her hometown for having a broken taillight and had once stolen $5 from her mom. On Landrum they couldn't dig up any dirt at all. People described him as "square," "boring," and "incapable of lying."

BECAUSE ROMAN'S DISAPPEARANCE took place on federal land, the FBI could have intervened and taken over the investigation just as it did the Lavigne/Dumas case. Instead, the bureau sat back and let CID take the lead.

Over the next eighteen months, a task force of federal agents led by CID conducted upward of four hundred interviews, executed more than a hundred warrants and subpoenas, and examined five hundred terabytes of digital data. They returned to the barrier islands seven times, twice with large search parties to pick through the brackish marshes, salt meadows, and tangled forests of juniper and live oak in search of Roman's head-less skeleton, with divers exploring the area all around the rock jetty nearest the campsite, scanning the serried seafloor for any sign of human remains. They took soil samples and studied the drift of tides in the complex currents around the cape. They plastered beach towns with missing-person posters, offering a $25,000 reward for information. Because Roman had jeered at a group of Trump supporters, they consulted with the Anti-Defamation League and the Southern Poverty Law Center, examining maps of the distribution of hate crimes in the Carolinas.

These efforts produced scant clues. A rib bone picked up by a park ranger turned out to be equine. A fisherman found a pair of U.S. Army boots on the beach, but they were too big for Roman, who wore a size 8. Forensic serologists were unable to find any trace of blood in the two vehicles, or on the hatchet, shovel, and pliers stored in the toolbox of the Ford Ranger. A block of wood and scraps of fabric recovered from the campsite also failed to luminesce under blue light, as did the items of clothing the campers had been wearing.

"Prosecutors have been unequivocal with me," says Collier, "that the most likely explanation was that one or more of those seven were involved." Yet repeated interrogations of the suspects went nowhere. The soldiers' stories, consistent from the beginning, never changed over time. None ever cracked under pressure and admitted to facts not disclosed in the first week. And they were able to give plausible accounts of actions that at first had seemed suspicious.

They didn't notify park rangers of Roman's disappearance midday Saturday because only a few hours had elapsed, they were still hoping he would turn up, and they "didn't want to escalate the situation," as Moore put it. "Once we realized that Roman's *missing* missing," Cochell said, "we called 911 and our leadership."

The short-lived effort to hide Cochell's involvement was a misguided attempt at chivalry intended to protect the youngest member of the group, who was also the sole female. And a park ranger confirmed that he was the one to suggest that someone back at Fort Bragg enter

THE FORT BRAGG CARTEL

Roman's barracks late Saturday night, leaving the matter of the missing journal as the only question mark hanging over the impromptu break-in.

FRUSTRATED AT EVERY TURN, CID kept falling back on an early theory that had been excluded by Roman's autopsy: that he had committed suicide. Unable to come up with any more tenable narrative, agents were increasingly convinced that Roman, caught in the grips of existential despair brought on by a psychedelic crisis, had climbed out of the Jeep without bothering to put on his shirt or eyeglasses because he knew he was about to die, plunged into the waves heedless of his phobias of darkness and the water, straggled his way out past the surf in spite of his inability to swim, and drowned himself. Then, hundreds of yards offshore where large watercraft operate, a passing motorboat had struck his floating body, decapitating him.

It was less crazy than other theories that investigators had explored. The only person with any apparent motive to kill Roman, the only person who had ever made statements of intent to do such a thing, was Roman himself. Griselda said that he was excited about getting out of the military, moving back to California, buying a car, enrolling in pharmacy college, and one day visiting Japan. He did not want to die, she insisted. But one soldier after another attested to Roman's tendency to make suicidal comments. These were a reflection of his dark sense of humor, but it wasn't always clear that he was kidding. Griselda herself acknowledged that her little brother struggled with depression all his life.

The obstacle to this line of investigation was the Brody School of Medicine autopsy that had found the cause of death to be homicide. The CID agents sought a second opinion from an expert in Burlington, Vermont, but she concurred with the first doctor's findings. "The possibility of Roman's body coming into contact with a spinning boat propeller was eliminated," the agent who received her report recorded.

Still not convinced, CID consulted with a specialist in "boat versus people incidents" at the U.S. Fish and Wildlife Service. After reviewing pictures of Roman's severed head, this man flatly told the agents that "a boat strike did not cause the injuries." He explained that to fully decapitate a person would require a very large boat propeller, which would not only cut the neck but also inflict massive blunt force injuries to the skull and spine. Fish had eaten Roman's left eye and the passage of his head over beds of mollusks had scraped off patches of hair, but his cranium was otherwise intact. So too were his uppermost cervical vertebrae.

For a time, the investigators seemed to accept these conclusions. Then, with the one-year anniversary of Roman's death on the horizon and no logical suspects in sight, CID had Roman's head disinterred from a cemetery in Chino and flown to Dover Air Force Base for another autopsy.

This time, two CID agents were in attendance, and to assist the doctor in his examination, they had helpfully brought along several sample boat propellers. To their disappointment, however, the medical examiner, a leading practitioner in the field of forensic anthropology, determined "with a great deal of scientific certainty" that Roman's wounds were "not consistent with a boat propeller strike," because "there were no injuries to the skull or vertebrae."

It was just what the Fish and Wildlife man had said. Yet once again, CID obtained a second opinion. They presented both autopsy reports to the chief medical examiner of Pitt County, North Carolina, but this fourth doctor was equally unequivocal and vehement. "There was no conceivable situation," he told the detectives, in which "the head wasn't removed by another person." The agent taking notes recorded that he "would not back off of saying it was a homicide."

Nevertheless, in their final press release, in which they declared the death of Enrique Roman-Martinez to be a cold case, CID backhandedly pushed the theory that he had been accidentally decapitated by a boat propeller. The agency upped the reward for information to $50,000, the largest the Army had ever offered, and urged members of the public to come forward "if you were operating a boat in that area" the night it happened "and recall possibly hitting something in the water."

The statement, issued August 2, 2021, identified the lead investigator as Special Agent Steve Chancellor, the same CID agent who, two years earlier, had been Mark Leshikar's family's point of contact with CID and had tried to tell Tammy and Nicole that according to seven-year-old Melanie, Mark had been armed at the time he was shot by Billy Lavigne. In the press release, Agent Chancellor downplayed reports that Roman's death had been ruled a homicide. "Please understand," said Chancellor, "that homicide basically means that someone's death was caused by someone else."

Expanding on this legally specious contention, Chancellor stated, falsely, that Roman's death "could have been unintentional." Specifically, Chancellor said, contrary to the unanimous opinion of four medical doctors, Roman could have been beheaded by "someone running over someone with a boat while the person was in the water."

Griselda was furious when she read the press release. "It doesn't even make sense," she texted me the next day. "They are trying to deter this investigation from a homicidal one to an accidental one, and in my opinion they look ridiculous and incompetent."

IN *THE DEVIL'S TRAMPING GROUND,* a 1949 book of North Carolina folklore, the author John Harden, a Greensboro newspaperman, tells the story "The Missing Major," about an Army officer named Robert Clark who disappeared on his way from Raleigh to Fort Bragg the afternoon of March 17, 1944. Major Clark's Dodge coupe was found hidden in the woods somewhere between Raeford and Southern Pines. The way the car had been concealed with piles of blankets, pine boughs, and woody vines led CID and the FBI to believe that Clark had been murdered. But an elaborate, long-running, multistate investigation, involving many false leads including rumors that Clark had committed suicide or faked his own death, eventually petered out inconclusively. Clark's body, like Roman's, was never found.

Then there was the Vietnam-era case of Captain Jeffrey MacDonald, a philandering young Special Forces doctor with a Princeton degree whose wife and two young daughters were murdered in their beds the night of February 16, 1970. Army investigators were convinced that MacDonald, deprived of sleep and strung out on amphetamines that he used to keep slim and work long hours, had committed the crime in a fit of spontaneous rage. MacDonald's alibi was that a group of murderous hippies, out of their minds on LSD, had broken into the house where he and his family lived on Fort Bragg, knocked him unconscious, then bludgeoned and stabbed the woman and girls to death while intoning "acid is groovy." The ensuing legal saga, the subject of several mutually contradictory books and a television miniseries, became the lengthiest court drama in North Carolina history, with multiple trials, convictions, reversals, and appeals that repeatedly reached the U.S. Supreme Court.

The death of Enrique Roman-Martinez was easily as bewildering as any Fort Bragg murder mystery that had come before. The baffling fact pattern seemed as if designed to confound all attempts at explanation. Never in the past had CID gone to such lengths to solve a single soldier's stateside murder, yet the investigation ended with demoralized investigators ignobly attempting to gaslight the public into thinking that it had been a boating accident. The bad trip that Roman suffered in the hours leading up to his death, and his eerie premonitions of imminent mortality, lent an unsettling air to the story, like some urban myth used to scare teenagers off LSD.

Ultimately, investigators did not recover one shred of physical, digital, testimonial, or forensic evidence linking Alex Becerra, Annamarie Cochell, Samad Landrum, Samuel Moore, Benjamin Sibley, Joshua Curry, or Juan Avila to Roman's killing, nor were they able to impute a plausible motive to any one of them. But that didn't stop the Army from bringing criminal cases against all seven. "While they don't have enough to charge for homicide," said Collier, "they have ample for lesser offenses that they could use to leverage people to flip."

Each of the campers was charged with disobeying a direct order for violating the COVID lockdown and making false statements for omitting to tell their commander about Cochell's presence on the camping trip. In addition, Becerra, Landrum, and Cochell were charged with illegal drug use.

One by one, over the course of 2022, they were court-martialed for these offenses and conspiracy. They all pleaded guilty to one or more counts and accepted reductions in rank, forfeiture of pay, and expulsion from the military. But even under the pressure of these trials and punishments, none flipped and inculpated any of the others in Roman's murder.

HAVING DECLARED IT a cold case, CID had no choice but to close its file on Enrique Roman-Martinez and move on. The agency's Fort Bragg office was severely overtaxed in those days, its resources and personnel spread thin.

According to the *New York Times* article that disclosed the occurrence of the Lavigne/Dumas murders and the contents of Roman's autopsy, it had otherwise been, until then, a "relatively calm" year at Fort Bragg. That was a regrettable misstatement of fact.

Casualty reports obtained through public records requests show that the base was then in the midst of an unprecedented wave of fatalities, like nothing ever seen before at any other U.S. military base, driven by record numbers of suicides, overdoses, and homicides, many of them drug related, and the carnage was only beginning. Just three weeks after the Lavigne/Dumas murders and the release of Roman's autopsy report, while the Fort Bragg brass still had their hands full managing the media attention and churn from higher headquarters that resulted, yet another murder took place.

Once again, it involved a war-traumatized special operations soldier who dealt illegal drugs on base. And the USASOC organization to which he belonged was none other than Timothy Dumas's old unit: the 98th Civil Affairs Battalion of the 95th Civil Affairs Brigade.

Twenty

ROID RAGE

Lynda Lewis never wanted her son to join the military. Keith Lewis, born in 1989 in Sarasota, Florida, was a sweet, animal-loving kid, thin and not very tall, who doted on his pet cockatoos and parrots. Lynda tried to discourage him from signing up for the parachute infantry, but heedless of her advice, he enlisted at the age of eighteen.

In 2009, Lewis deployed to Afghanistan as a grenadier in a rifle platoon with the 501st Infantry Regiment. Bowe Bergdahl, an earnest, awkward, homeschooled oddball from Idaho who was in the same unit, famously deserted with the intention of walking to Pakistan, but was captured by the Taliban, becoming an object of sustained derision in right-wing media. For Lewis, it was a rough twelve months. "He was in an IED blast," said Lynda. "He saw people die."

A video shot by American soldiers circulated in his platoon. It showed a little Afghan girl getting crushed like a bug beneath a giant armored vehicle. Witnessing such horrors, and being a part of the force that inflicted them, transformed Lewis from the inside out. "He had a huge personality change," said his mom. "He was angry all the time. He was distant. Everything made him jump. He had migraines, horrible nightmares."

Again and again, Lewis had the same dream. He was alone at night on a road somewhere in Afghanistan, surrounded by wild dogs. He could hear them growling in the darkness. Then he'd wake up.

In 2012, Lewis transferred to Fort Bragg, trained as a special operations medic, and was assigned to the headquarters company of the 8th Psychological Operations Group, and later to the headquarters of the 98th Civil Affairs Battalion. It was at USASOC that his use of steroids began. "He was never a muscular kid," said Lynda. "He became huge."

A robust black market for anabolic steroids, which are banned on account of their adverse health effects, invariably forms in the places where elite American soldiers are stationed. Doping to attain an edge in competitive military hierarchies and to conform with the culture of bodybuilding and supplementation that prevails in the Special Forces is widespread. The suppliers of illicit steroids often seem to be support soldiers—medics, supply guys, and the like—who cater to an operator clientele and inject themselves as well.

Take, for instance, the 2021 case of Staff Sergeant David Rankine, an Army information technology specialist assigned to SOCSOUTH, a Latin America–focused outpost of SOCOM in Homestead, Florida. Like Dan Gould and Henry Royer, the pair of cocaine-trafficking Green Berets busted in 2018, Rankine used that duty station, with its frequent overseas flights, as a way station for the importation of a variety of illicit anabolic steroids including boldenone, trenbolone, nandrolone, drostanolone, and clostebol, according to the transcript of a Fort Bragg court-martial that USASOC unlawfully withheld for more than a year until I sued them in federal court to obtain its release. Steroid abuse evidently contributed to Rankine's anger issues and other defects of character, because in addition to trafficking steroids and using cocaine, he was charged with punching a woman in the face with his closed fist and forcing a prostitute to perform oral sex on him at gunpoint.

Keith Lewis, who regularly used the same class of steroids, also had episodes of uncontrolled rage directed at women. On the night of October 24, 2016, after an argument at a bar with a stranger who'd said something supportive of Bowe Bergdahl, he threw his wife, an Air Force veteran named Sarah Lewis, who was three years older than him, against the wall of the rental house they shared on Willow Street in Fayetteville, causing her to cut her head. She called the cops, and he went and got his gun. An armed standoff ensued.

"He called me and said, 'Mom, I've got a gun to my head. I hurt Sarah, and my career is ruined,'" said Lynda. "I talked to him for a long time. He finally put the gun down."

Lewis was arrested for assault on a female and assault by pointing a firearm at a police officer, but the office of district attorney Billy West predictably dropped the charges. "There were no real repercussions," said Lynda. "Life just went on."

Major Dan Lessard, a spokesman for the 1st Special Forces Command, said that Lewis received nonjudicial punishment and was directed to attend counseling, but the disciplinary measures couldn't have been very serious. Lewis was promoted to sergeant that year, attended a special operations combat medic course the next, and made staff sergeant in 2020.

The marriage counseling wasn't effective, either. Even after the birth of his daughter Callie in 2017, Lewis continued to drink heavily, inject steroids, and beat his wife, who became pregnant again in early 2020. On at least two occasions that year, the last being December 11, Sarah called Lewis's unit, "because he had been drinking real bad and using steroids, and asked that he be moved back into the barracks," said Sarah's mother, Rhonda Phillips. Unfortunately for her daughter and granddaughter, "they didn't do anything."

Sarah also told her aunt, Tammy DeMirza, about the phone call that she made in the second week of December, by which time she was nine months pregnant. "She went to Fort Bragg and said he's drinking and taking steroids, and had a gun and was threatening to kill her," Tammy said. "They did nothing."

"So far, we have not been able to determine that that call on the eleventh of December actually happened," Major Lessard said. "We're still looking into it."

ON DECEMBER 22, 2020, a cold and windy day in Fayetteville, around seven o'clock in the evening, Sarah called 911, told the dispatcher that her husband was drunk and wouldn't let her have their three-year-old daughter, then dropped the phone and fled to a neighbor's house. Lewis followed her outside, supporting Callie on one hip and holding a gun in the other hand.

As Sarah pounded on the neighbor's door, screaming for help, her husband opened fire on her with an onslaught of armor-piercing rounds so heavy that it totaled the neighbor's car. "He was holding Callie," Rhonda said, still stunned by the awful fact months later, "the whole time that he was shooting Sarah."

As Sarah lay dying, her infant daughter was born. The baby girl was going to be named Isabelle but did not live. "The most horrific thing I've ever seen in my life," said Aunt Tammy, "was that baby in the casket with her mother."

Either Lewis let Callie go or she slipped free, and went running into the arms of one of the officers who responded to the scene. "A policeman swooped her up," said Rhonda. "Or else she probably would have been killed."

Lewis went back into the apartment, picked up Sarah's phone, and spoke to the 911 dispatcher. "Fuck," he said. "She's dead." His last recorded words were, "Steroids and alcohol don't mix."

Lewis then stepped outside onto the porch. Surrounded by armed officers shouting at him to drop the gun, he raised his pistol to his temple and pulled the trigger.

A FEW DAYS LATER, the property manager of the house on Willow Street caught a pair of uniformed Army officers going through Keith Lewis's car in the driveway. When she asked to see a letter of administration to prove that they were legally the executors of the estate, the officers, one of whom was a captain, bluffed their way past. "They told her that both of Keith's parents were dead," said Rhonda. "So there was no one else to handle the estate. But both his parents are alive."

Every time a special operations soldier dies, his command springs into action and seizes his personal effects, including his computer and phone. Officially, this is to protect military secrets from unauthorized disclosure. In practice, it provides the perfect opportunity to sequester evidence of criminal activity in elite units and keep it out of the hands of family members, who might make a stink in the media, or civilian law enforcement officials, not all of whom can be counted on to strike the appropriately patriotic position of unquestioning deference toward the Special Forces as Billy West.

The officers cleared out Lewis's car, took his uniforms and gear from the house, and seized all electronic devices that they could lay hands on, including two computers and Sarah's cell phone, whose call log would prove that shortly before her death she phoned the headquarters company of the 98th Civil Affairs Battalion and begged them to house Lewis in the barracks before he carried out his threats to kill her and the baby both. Rhonda and her husband, who like many military family members know little of the law and lack the means to hire an attorney, never saw the device again. "I've spoken to the detective for the city of Fayetteville a few times," said Rhonda, her voice faltering with grief and fatigue. "He keeps saying her phone was turned over to the Army."

Sarah's parents, armed with an actual letter of administration, entered the house in February 2021. They found the place in disarray and largely bare of furniture, with no table or chairs and—weirdly—all the photos gone from their frames. But if it had been the officers' intent to get rid of evidence of Lewis's involvement in distributing steroids on Fort Bragg, they were remarkably sloppy and inattentive to detail. Buried in the back of the ransacked closet, hidden in some plastic tubs, were more than a hundred syringes, some bloodstained from use, most still in their plastic packaging.

Rhonda took photos of the drugs she found, which she sent to Tammy, who showed them to me. There was a baggie of unmarked white pills, partially crushed; a bottle of trenbolone acetate, a substance used to stimulate muscle growth in cattle; and a used vial of testosterone propionate, a potent hormone known to lower the threshold for aggressive behavior in men. "Supposedly there's an epidemic going around Fort Bragg," Tammy said. "Steroids are being sold on the black market."

JAMES REESE, the retired Delta Force officer who was on Billy Lavigne's selection board, said that being chosen for the unit "is like becoming a New York Yankee. You're given the best of everything." A stable of professional nutritionists, physical therapists, athletics trainers, and doctors expert at treating sports injuries work full time at Fort Bragg attending to the needs of special operations soldiers, who are routinely prescribed amphetamines to keep them awake, hypnotics to sleep, opiates for pain, and anxiolytics for panic attacks associated with PTSD. To give elite operators an additional edge, SOCOM's directorate of science and technology occasionally floats the possibility of introducing a regimen of performance-enhancing drugs including anabolic steroids, which in the short term are very effective at preventing injuries and speeding up recovery. In the meantime, a command climate of implicit tolerance toward doping prevails in the Army Special Forces no less than in the Navy SEALs.

Jordan Terrell was in pretty good shape when he went through Special Forces selection and couldn't understand why he wasn't able to keep up with his cohort. "They were trashing us every day, from sunup to sundown," he said. "We were running five miles on Monday, rucking five miles on Tuesday, running five miles on Wednesday, rucking five miles on Thursday, doing a twelve-miler every weekend, and then just getting thrashed all day every day, and these dudes were just going, going, going. The unwritten, unspoken secret," he said, "was that they were getting steroids."

On January 28, 2021, a thirty-two-year-old officer in an elite explosive ordnance disposal unit, Captain Robert Sean Latham, a veteran of the wars in Iraq and Afghanistan, was jogging on Fort Bragg when he suddenly dropped dead from "probable cardiac arrhythmia," according to his casualty report. Latham's obituary photos, many of which depict him shirtless, show that he was an active outdoorsman and weightlifting enthusiast who had the ripped physique of a fitness model or an actor in an action movie. You would never expect someone so young and fit to die of a heart attack.

On October 27, a senior Special Forces intelligence sergeant named Calvin Thomas Rockward, a veteran of Iraq and Afghanistan who had done recent stints in Malaysia, Thailand, South Korea, and Indonesia, also died during physical fitness training on Fort Bragg. Again the cause of death was cardiovascular failure, even though Rockward was only thirty-eight and in even better shape than Latham, to go by numerous photos on social media in which he shows off his toothy smile and shredded abs alongside his equally fit, heavily tattooed girlfriend.

Five months later, a Delta Force troop commander, Major Eric Adam Ewoldsen, was found slumped over the steering wheel of his truck on the side of the road somewhere on Fort Bragg, dead at the age of thirty-eight. A West Point graduate who had logged an incredible fifty-nine months in combat since 2008, Ewoldsen had served in an array of leadership positions on Delta Force, including as its executive officer in 2017, its operations officer in Syria in 2018, and a troop commander in Iraq during the time that the unit assassinated Abu Bakr al-Baghdadi.

Both Ewoldsen and his wife, a nutrition and fashion consultant with legions of followers on social media, were fanatically committed to healthy eating and exercise. "He was one of the most insanely fitness-oriented people I knew," said a former officer who served with Ewoldsen early in his career. "He was easily the most physically in-shape lieutenant in our cohort, and my impression was that he stayed that way."

Ewoldsen's wife's posts show that she and her husband planned their austere meals with scrupulous care and did intense daily workouts. Despite being in their late thirties with three children, neither had an ounce of visible fat on their bodies. It's all the more surprising, then, that he should have suddenly keeled over and died from "atheroscle-rotic cardiovascular disease," as his casualty report specifies, two years shy of his fortieth birthday.

It is possible that Latham, Rockward, and Ewoldsen, whose medical records were protected from public disclosure, died of rare illnesses, genetic conditions, any number of freak medical events, or sheer ex-haustion. But they were long-standing members of a community suf-fused in alcohol, hard drugs, and steroids, all of which can cause hypertension, elevate cholesterol levels, harden arteries, greatly in-crease the risk of cardiovascular disease, even in young people, and pre-cipitate severe anger issues.

"Everything that's happening at Fort Bragg is horrible," said Lynda Lewis, whose heartbreak and despair over her son's crimes and his sui-cide were compounded by dismay at being stonewalled by the Special Forces command. She kept Lewis's body in cold storage for months be-cause the Army would not turn over his autopsy report or medical file, and she didn't want to lose evidence that his brain might have been damaged from the explosion that hit him in Afghanistan, or that he'd been medicated for post-traumatic stress. "I have to prove that he was not in his right mind," she said.

But even with the body count on Fort Bragg rising and soldiers drop-ping dead from unclear causes right and left, USASOC made no effort to come clean with the victims' loved ones about the rampancy of drug use on base or confront the resulting rash of criminality and mortality in Army special operations. Toward Lynda Lewis and Rhonda Phillips, the brass adopted the same adversarial, legalistic, and tight-lipped ap-proach as they had taken toward the families of Mark Leshikar, Billy Lavigne, Timothy Dumas, and Enrique Roman-Martinez. "I called ev-ery day for a month," Lynda said. "No one at Fort Bragg will talk to me at all. They say get a lawyer."

Twenty-One

WITHDRAWAL SYMPTOMS

D espite assurances from *The New York Times* that 2020 at Fort Bragg had been "relatively calm," Keith Lewis was the fifty-fourth soldier to die there since the beginning of the year, and not even the last; an artilleryman shot himself in the head a week later, on December 27. The following year, as CID and the FBI were investigating, without much success, the murders of Billy Lavigne, Timothy Dumas, and Enrique Roman-Martinez, another fifty-four Fort Bragg soldiers lost their lives, for a staggering two-year total of 109 fatalities. Only four of those deaths occurred overseas, in Afghanistan and Syria. All the rest took place stateside, mostly on Fort Bragg proper or in Fayetteville.

None of the Fort Bragg casualties in 2020 and 2021 were from COVID-19. The majority were deaths of despair: suicides and overdoses. A shocking number were outbursts of fratricidal, soldier-on-soldier violence, or unsolved murders. And many cases were simply marked "pending determination," to the great frustration of military family members.

"They sit across the table from you. They don't say anything. You ask a question. They look at each other. Then they stare back at you, and give some formal answer," said Heather Baker, an elementary school teacher from the Texas Panhandle whose nineteen-year-old son, Private Caleb Smither, turned up dead in his bunk from ambiguous causes in January 2020, his body in such an advanced state of decomposition that he couldn't have an open-casket funeral. "He looked like someone had beat the shit out of him," said his mom of the putrefying bruises that covered one whole side of his body. Army authorities eventually determined that Smither, who belonged to the same 37th Brigade Engineer Battalion as Enrique Roman-Martinez, died of bacterial meningitis, but couldn't explain how a private second class with a recent head injury had been left completely unsupervised for five days. At one point Baker snapped at them, "I've heard better excuses from fourth graders."

Colonel Adam Kazin, chief of Army JAG's criminal law division, tried to explain away the high number of deaths as a stochastic cluster with no real underlying cause. "These things come in waves," he said. "A lot of it's just coincidence, timing." Because Fort Bragg has fifty thousand soldiers, it's necessary to compare murder, suicide, and overdose rates with "civilian society in a similar-sized city," he said.

But it makes no sense to compare a population that consists almost entirely of young men with a small city that's half women and includes many elderly people, children, and babies. The only appropriate comparison is to other military bases. And no other U.S. military installation, in modern times, has reported fifty or more service member deaths in a single year—not even close.

The nearest equivalence might be to recent events at Fort Hood, Texas, an Army base nearly as big as Fort Bragg, home to a large number of cavalry troops and support units. Thirty-eight soldiers died at Fort Hood in 2020, including a photogenic young woman named Vanessa Guillén, resulting in wall-to-wall media coverage, including at least nineteen articles by fourteen different writers in *The New York Times* alone. Under pressure from multiple congressional subcommittees, the secretary of the Army launched a massive investigation into Fort Hood's "toxic culture," a months-long bureaucratic ransacking that concluded with the unceremonious firing of nearly the entire chain of command, including three major generals, one of whom was the chief of Army CID, which was subsequently reorganized under civilian leadership. The national press treated Fort Hood's "year of heartbreak and bloodshed," in the words of one *Times* headline, as a catastrophic meltdown of good order and discipline, worthy of daily coverage on cable news, while the only article to appear in the *Times* about Fort Bragg, then in the midst of an objectively more dire crisis, was the misleading piece that soft-pedaled the Lavigne/Dumas murders and the disappearance of Enrique Roman-Martinez as troubling anomalies amid an otherwise placid situation.

In reality, soldier deaths had been taking place at Fort Bragg at an average rate of one a week since the beginning of 2020, a dismaying pace that wouldn't relent until 2022, and then not by much. One of the earliest occurred on February 24, 2020, when a captain from Pennsylvania, a former high school wrestling champion who served in the 44th Medical Brigade, somehow committed suicide by shooting himself in the neck with a 12-gauge shotgun, then in the head with a .45-caliber pistol. The rare multiple-gunshot suicide was the first of twenty-one suicides at Fort Bragg in 2020, making self-harm the leading cause of death that year, at a time when suicides, although elevated in the general population, were actually on the decline nationwide. According to the Centers for Disease Control, 13.5 out of every 100,000 Americans killed themselves in 2020. In the military, the rate was 28.7 per 100,000 service members. At Fort Bragg, it was something like 40 per 100,000—triple the national average.

The Defense Department, the White House, and Congress have long recognized that the military has a problem with suicide. Suicide prevention is a frequent topic of discussion at every echelon of military planning, from the Pentagon down to the platoon level. But the second-leading cause of death at Fort Bragg in 2020 and 2021 was accidental overdoses, proof of a growing epidemic of substance abuse, so evident in the lives of Leshikar, Lavigne, Dumas, and Roman-Martinez, that almost no one in the chain of command was willing to discuss or acknowledge, except to falsely portray the scourge of addiction in the ranks as merely a reflection of larger socioeconomic and epidemiological trends.

On February 22, 2020, Specialist Christopher Jenkins, a signals intelligence analyst from West Palm Beach, Florida, died from the combined effects of fentanyl and cough syrup. His unit issued no press release, and his family did not publish an obituary. On March 16, a Special Forces candidate from Ohio named Jamie Boger was "found unresponsive in his barracks room," USASOC announced. No further details were given, but Boger's casualty report shows that he succumbed to an overdose of fentanyl and cocaine.

On August 16, Specialist Cristhiam Gonzalez Pineda, a helicopter repairman originally from Tegucigalpa, Honduras, died from acute fentanyl, cocaine, and alcohol intoxication. Two months later, Private First Class Anthony Savala, a Native American infantryman from Stockton, California, consumed a fatal mixture of cough syrup, benzodiazepines, and fentanyl. On November 11, the 82nd Airborne Division said in a press release that another young infantryman, Specialist Terrance Salazar, from San Antonio, Texas, had been "found in his room unresponsive." Again, no cause of death was given, but Salazar's casualty report shows that he was killed by the depressive effects of combining cough syrup with alcohol.

Michael Tardie, a first sergeant in the 505th Parachute Infantry Regiment, from Yuma, Arizona, ingested a fatal dose of fentanyl while drinking alcohol on December 12. One week before that, Zachary Bracken, a Green Beret trainee from Norfolk, Virginia, who aspired to become a special operations medic, had died from the same combination of alcohol and fentanyl. "Although they expressed sympathy," said his mother, Andrea Bracken, "the Army had no real interest in how he died. I have many unanswered questions, but nobody seems to give a shit."

Fentanyl, a fully synthetic drug, is less expensive to procure than heroin made from poppy plants, more easily smuggled and trafficked, more powerful, and more addictive. In a nation primed for opiate addiction by two decades of easy availability of inexpensive heroin from Mexico and Afghanistan, "fentanyl just took hold everywhere," said Dr. Nora Volkow, director of the National Institute on Drug Abuse. By 2021, fentanyl was "absolutely the number one cause of death," she told me, among American adults aged eighteen to forty-five. The medical literature that she reviewed showed a "fast and dramatic" rise in fatal overdoses "among military men." Yet even amid this unprecedented surge in overdoses in both the general population and the armed forces as a whole, the per-capita OD rate at Fort Bragg substantially exceeded both the national average and the military mean.

According to the Pentagon's own calculations, the annual fatal overdose rate at Fort Bragg was 36 per 100,000 soldiers, versus 28 per 100,000 people in the U.S. population as a whole. The only other major base where soldiers were more likely to die of a drug overdose than the average American was Fort Campbell, Kentucky, which is not only near Fort Bragg geographically but also home to very similar units: the 101st Airborne Division, the Army's main fighting force besides the 82nd Airborne; the 5th Special Forces Group, which did as much time in Afghanistan as 3rd Group, if not more; and the 160th Special Operations Aviation Regiment, the main aviation element of JSOC.

FUELED BY RAMPANT drug use, the wave of criminality in the special operations community during the first Trump administration had not ended with the killing of Logan Melgar in Mali, or the shambolic Eddie Gallagher trial. With Trump fanning the flames by pardoning war criminals and clashing with military leaders trying to rein in rogue troops, the meltdown in special ops had only worsened during the second half of his term.

August 2018 had seen the bust of Dan Gould and Henry Royer, the Green Berets caught in the attempt to load forty kilos of cocaine onto a

U.S. military flight out of Bogotá. The story barely made a ripple in the English-language press but was big news in Colombia. "Dan's face was all over," said Esteban Hurtado, the U.S. Army infantry captain stationed at the American embassy who detected Gould's scheme and turned him in to the DEA. "They did magazine articles on it," said Hurtado, whose first language is Spanish. "They did prime-time shows." An article by the investigative unit at El tiempo, Colombia's leading newspaper, noted that Gould had been in the Colombian city of Cali on a solo plainclothes mission, passing for an American tourist. "Was I motivated for extra money? Sure, but it wasn't a necessity so much as something to do," Gould wrote in a letter from prison in which he ascribed his actions to the long spells of boredom inherent in clandestine operations. "And living in Cali, Colombia," he continued, "finding cocaine is as easy as finding a loaf of bread!"

In December 2018, in Cedar Rapids, Iowa, a former Army Ranger named Drew Blahnik had stabbed to death a man in a contract killing over a drug debt. The following month, in a brawl outside a bar in Erbil, Iraq, two Marine Raiders and a Navy corpsman had pummeled to death a contractor for Lockheed Martin named Rick Rodriguez, an ex–Green Beret who lived in Fayetteville. Days after Eddie Gallagher's trial concluded in July 2019, a member of SEAL Team Seven had bitten a female sailor in the face in the course of an alleged sexual assault during a boozy party thrown on a base in Iraq to celebrate Gallagher's acquittal. A few weeks after that, Navy Times had published an exposé of widespread cocaine use on SEAL Team Ten, quoting members of the team who derided the Navy's drug-testing protocols as laughable. "I never once got piss-tested on deployment or on the road, where I was using most often," one SEAL told investigators.

In November 2019, Trump had issued a pardon clearing a Special Forces officer named Mathew Golsteyn of summarily executing a suspected member of the Taliban, a murder to which Golsteyn had admitted on live television. Six months later, a trio of ex–Green Berets led by Jordan Goudreau, a veteran of Iraq and Afghanistan, had tried to overthrow the government of Venezuela in the absurd but deadly "Bay of Piglets" coup attempt for which the Trump administration disavowed responsibility.

President Joe Biden had been elected in November 2020, one month before Billy Lavigne and Timothy Dumas were murdered, and one of his first acts in office was to direct the Pentagon's inspector general to conduct an inquiry into potential war crimes committed by elite soldiers. The inquiry "could have seismic repercussions in the special operations community," *The New York Times* reported.

So far, Fort Bragg as an installation had not come under any especially heightened scrutiny. But the brass knew that they could be the next Fort Hood. Spurred by the Lavigne/Dumas murders, the Enrique Roman-Martinez case, and the Sarah and Keith Lewis murder/suicide, as well as a sharp spike in fatal overdoses, Army commanders quietly drew up a plan to crack down on drug trafficking by soldiers in the Special Forces and the airborne corps. It would not be very successful.

THE ANTIDRUG MEASURES implemented at Fort Bragg in 2021 included training more officers to administer urine tests, a requirement that all visitors to the base undergo a background check, and the deployment of more drug-sniffing dogs to the gates. The authorities also moved to arrest drug-dealing soldiers who in the past had been given get-out-of-jail-free cards by departments of police and courts of law reflexively deferential to men in uniform.

One repeat offender was Master Sergeant Martin Acevedo III, a forty-year-old artilleryman in the 82nd Airborne Division who had done five deployments in his career, including a tour in Iraq during the surge of 2007 and in Afghanistan during the 2012 surge. In July 2018, he had been arrested in Orlando, Florida, for dealing heroin but was turned loose by the local cops, who decided not to press charges "after learning he was in the Army," according to a report received by CID.

After that, Acevedo grew more reckless. In May 2021, the HSI office in Puerto Rico intercepted a package containing two kilos of cocaine addressed to Acevedo at his actual home address on Green Heron Drive in Fayetteville, one street over from where Billy Lavigne had lived on Anhinga Court. Federal agents backed by sheriff's deputies carried out a controlled delivery on May 27, raided the house, arrested Acevedo, seized two bricks of cocaine, multiple firearms, and $100,000 in cash.

Acevedo pleaded guilty to trafficking cocaine, but medical records and character references that he introduced into evidence under seal bought him a remarkably light punishment in federal district court. He was sentenced to thirteen months in prison, was released early after a mere seven months behind bars, and went straight back to serving on active duty at Fort Bragg.

DAYS AFTER HSI took down Acevedo in Fayetteville, the HSI-led task force investigating Freddie Wayne Huff had arrested him along with Jaime Rosado and Rahain Deriggs in Lexington. The cocaine withdrawals that Huff suffered in the Davidson County lockup, where he was initially jailed, were nothing compared with his wild fiending for tobacco. "I'd been smoking cigarettes since I was eighteen," he said. "It was by far more difficult to quit."

Huff had struggled with bipolar disorder all his life, and the sudden involuntary detox plunged him into the deepest depression that he had ever known. He repeatedly suffered seizures and had to be hospitalized. He tried and failed to hang himself with a bedsheet. Eventually, a sense of resignation set in.

Huff knew that the authorities had him dead to rights for trafficking cocaine and that he could also be charged with armed robbery involving a controlled substance, which is punishable by as much as twenty-five years in prison, as well as kidnapping with a firearm, which carries an even stiffer maximum penalty. Armed with punitive antidrug statutes, prosecutors could have hit him with a kingpin enhancement and put him away for life. His best shot at leniency was to cooperate. "At that point, when Freddie decided he wanted to spill the beans," said Patrick Doyle, a Davidson County sheriff's deputy who was present at Huff's initial interrogation, "he was brought to our offices to be interviewed."

Doyle said that federal agents questioned Huff about the murders of Billy Lavigne and Timothy Dumas, but only in passing. "Freddie said he had met the Delta guy a couple of times," said Doyle, "but didn't know him."

When questioned about Dumas, Huff became emotional, Doyle said. "He got upset and started crying." Newly sober, Huff now understood that the animosity he'd borne toward his former partner had been the product of pure paranoia. In reality, Dumas had been his truest friend. Their heyday slinging bricks together, making money hand over fist, had been the high point of Huff's life. "It was fun," he told me. "I never had that much fun with anybody."

IN SEPTEMBER 2021, the commander of Army CID, Major General Donna Martin, failed up to a three-star position following withering congressional criticism of CID for its inability to solve crimes at Fort Hood, whose travails continued to overshadow events at Fort Bragg in the mainstream media. The following month, a *New York Times* reporter paid a rare visit to Fayetteville, to canvass locals' attitudes toward an impending name change to Fort Bragg, and in an aside on soldier-involved violence near military bases, she wrote that "Fort *Hood* [emphasis mine] has been associated with several brutal crimes in recent years." In the three weeks before the article was published, on October 1, 2021, one Fort Bragg soldier had shot himself in the head, one had been charged with two counts of first-degree murder, one had been gunned down in a parking lot by unknown assailants, and two had died from fentanyl overdoses, but the reporter seemed oblivious to *these* brutal crimes and deaths of despair.

Behind the scenes, though, the Fort Bragg leadership knew that they continued to have a problem. In October, the top brass convened a confidential meeting with its CID office, and Special Agent Maegan Malloy was among the attendees. Beforehand, she had been given the task of analyzing hundreds of pages of spreadsheets containing crime statistics and intelligence reports from every unit. The purpose of the review, she said, was to "see where our stats were compared to the Fort Hood report."

General Erik Kurilla, commander of the XVIII Airborne Corps, wasn't pleased with Malloy's findings, which showed soaring crime, a backlog of unsolved cases, and high turnover among military police officers, many of whom lacked requisite training. "Fix it," was the message conveyed to CID, in Malloy's recollection of the closed-door meeting. "Fix it before we get investigated."

Like all cops, CID agents cut deals with minor crooks in order to net bigger fish. "We want you to work for us undercover," Malloy explained, paraphrasing the spiel she might give a junior trooper who's been busted for possession. "No one will know about it. Your name's not going to be put in any databases. We're going to have secret code names for each other. We're only going to meet in these places. Here's a cell phone for you. Keep in touch. If you're able to set us up with an undercover buy, we'll pay you up to $500 cash."

During sting operations, Malloy would often pass for a young civilian woman visiting a brother or boyfriend on base. In that guise, she went to a barracks party in mid-2021 and, while another undercover agent surreptitiously took photos, bought prescription painkillers from a twenty-six-year-old MP named Jacob Dickerson, who was known to be dealing oxycodone and Percocet from his police vehicle at intersections and parking lots around Fort Bragg.

This was nothing out of the ordinary. On Fort Bragg, even the police deal drugs. "Several other MPs were also buying and selling and using, from all ranks," said Malloy. "We were investigating damn near every MP company there." Before Specialist Dickerson, "we'd investigated five other MPs that piss-popped for cocaine," she said. "They all became snitches for us."

Dickerson belonged to the 21st Military Police Company, 503rd Military Police Battalion. From June until September, Malloy and her colleagues steadily built a case against him, another MP from the same company, and two others from the 118th Military Police Company, which belongs to the same battalion. Agents set up or surveilled five drug deals, then swept in and stitched them all up. Dickerson "cried like a bitch," said Malloy, when they slapped on the cuffs.

Despite CID's painstaking work, Army prosecutors quietly dropped all of the trafficking charges and let three of the crooked MPs go. Only Dickerson, who failed a drug test in October and then crashed his car while reeking of alcohol in December, was brought up before a court-martial, and then he was merely charged with wrongful possession and dereliction of duty. As punishment, he received a relative slap on the wrist: ten weeks in the stockade and a dishonorable discharge.

TWO HUNDRED AND SIXTY-FIVE paratroopers from the 82nd Airborne were expelled from the Army for drug-related misconduct in 2021, and 209 Fort Bragg soldiers were court-martialed for narcotics offenses, yet the crackdown didn't seem to pay any immediate dividends. "We've observed an over 100 percent increase in drug-related crime on the installation," the provost marshal, Major Travis Hallman, said in an interview with a local television news reporter in October 2021.

On June 11, a pair of radarmen from the 319th Field Artillery Regiment, Specialists Joshua Diamond and Matthew Disney, died almost simultaneously after taking counterfeit pills, supposedly oxycodone but really fentanyl, that they'd bought from another soldier in their regiment from whom Diamond had previously purchased LSD and steroids. "Matt, my son, was not a drug user," Disney's mother, Racheal Bowman, insisted. Disney knew all about prescription painkillers and their dangers because his little sister suffered from a rare intestinal disorder and had undergone dozens of surgeries in childhood. "Fentanyl, ketamine, Narcan, laudanum, Percocet, morphine," his mother recalled. "These are drugs that we talked about on a very regular basis." However, she said, "the one conversation I never had with my kids about drugs was counterfeit pills. I had never heard of a fake Percocet that looked legit from a pharmacy until my son took one and it killed him."

The soldier who had sold Disney and Diamond the deadly pills was investigated but not prosecuted for negligent homicide. Bowman tried without success to learn his identity. "The Army was just like, 'Here, go tie ribbons on trees,'" she said. "They don't want to acknowledge that there's a problem. It's all very secretive. It's all swept under the rug."

The deaths of Diamond and Disney were the only overdoses that Fort Bragg disclosed in 2021, but many others quietly took place with no public notice. The day after Diamond and Disney died, June 12, a staff sergeant in the headquarters company of the 1st Special Forces Command, Angel Manuel Acosta Melendez, was found lifeless while on leave to Long Island, New York. Medics administered Narcan, but he couldn't be revived.

On August 13, Specialist Mikel Rubino, an infantryman originally from Oroville, California, died from fentanyl toxicity somewhere on post. Specialist Matthew Meadows, a former Boy Scout and Christian missionary from Arlington, Texas, nodded off in the back seat of a taxi a month later, just outside Fort Bragg's main gate. "He had a whole lot to live for," Meadows's tearful brother told me. "He had just gotten engaged."

Six weeks later, Sergeant David Mazzullo, a signals intelligence analyst from Rochester, New York, passed away after taking heroin cut with fentanyl. On October 4, Sergeant First Class Michael Brett Hamilton, an artillery spotter from Plano, Texas, died from a toxic combination of fentanyl, alcohol, and kratom. Eight days after that, Staff Sergeant Van-Michael James Ellis, from St. Louis, became the third Special Forces trainee to die from a drug overdose in little more than a year and a half, killed by a lethal mixture of fentanyl, alcohol, and cocaine. The final fatal overdose of the year occurred on December 14, when Specialist Norwayne Reid, an infantryman originally from Jamaica, died from mixing alcohol and fentanyl.

ANOTHER NINETEEN FORT BRAGG soldiers died by suicide in 2021. Sixteen shot themselves in the head, one shot himself in the chest, one hanged himself, and one deliberately overdosed. The grim litany of soldiers killing themselves was unbelievably relentless and demoralizing. "We just had three suicides on post this past week," Enrique Roman-Martinez's high school friend and fellow Fort Bragg soldier Christian Romero told me on January 30, over breakfast at the McDonald's off Bragg Boulevard. "It's been a rough year," he said. We went out to the parking lot where greasy wrappers scuttled across the asphalt in the bleak winter sunshine, and he showed me the license plate just issued to him by the North Carolina Department of Transportation, in which he read a demonological portent: HEL-6666. "Fort Bragg is a depressing place," Romero said, getting into his brand-new Ford Mustang. "Everyone hates it."

The spate of murders at Fort Bragg that began in late 2020 also continued unabated into 2021, accelerated throughout the year, and then redoubled again. Over the next twenty-seven months, ending March 2023, only one Fort Bragg soldier would die in combat, while *fifteen* would be murdered or accused of murder stateside.

Not all of the Fort Bragg murders had an obvious connection to drug crime. At least as many were affairs of the heart, or the product of mental illness. On May 7, 2021, Tiara Nicole Vinson, a twenty-six-year-old soldier in the 519th Military Intelligence Battalion, walked up to a motor pool clerk four years her junior named Kelia Olivia Horton, her rival for the affections of a third soldier in the same unit, and shot her multiple times in the face. "I'm seriously fucked up in my head emotionally," Vinson's penultimate post to social media read.

Two more murders followed in September and October. Specialist

Tavis Rhodes, a young reservist on active-duty orders, was gunned down September 18 in the parking lot of a football stadium in Durham, North Carolina, in a double homicide for which no one was ever convicted. Two weeks later, Staff Sergeant Alonzo Dargan Jr., a radio operator who'd served at the Kandahar airfield during the Afghanistan surge, committed a drive-by shooting on a woman whom he'd impregnated, killing her and their unborn child.

It wasn't until August 26 that Fort Bragg recorded its first and only overseas fatality of the year. Staff Sergeant Ryan Knauss, an information warfare specialist assigned to the 8th Psychological Operations Group, was killed by a suicide bomber during the evacuation of the Kabul airport that marked the long-postponed end of the war in Afghanistan, the lengthiest armed conflict in American history.

THE WITHDRAWAL FROM AFGHANISTAN, which had to be done but needn't have been carried out in such an incompetent fashion, was a logistical debacle as well as a total collapse of American foreign policy. As tens of thousands of Afghans thronged the garbage dump of an airfield in the blazing heat of summer, desperate to secure a berth on one of the departing planes, President Ashraf Ghani fled the country in a helicopter crammed full of bags of cash. His feeble regime, propped up for twenty years by the Green Berets, had long served as a conduit for washing trillions of dollars out of the tax bases of Europe and America and channeling the money into the offshore coffers of transatlantic security contractors, who in turn funneled a portion to the corrupt politicians in D.C. who kept the war going. For nearly as long, the Afghan client state had functioned as the world's biggest drug cartel, responsible for producing at least four-fifths and more like nine-tenths of all the heroin consumed during the global opioid epidemic. Facing a certain wipeout by advancing Taliban, the infamous NATO protectorate, which was also deeply inculpated in child sex trafficking and roundly despised by the Afghan people, fell to pieces and dispersed. The Taliban, which by this time controlled all the checkpoints into Kabul, actually assisted NATO forces in attempting to make an orderly withdrawal, but were unable to prevent a strike by a newly emergent "affiliate" of ISIS known as the Islamic State of the Khorasan Province, or IS-K.

The shadowy terrorist group, an enemy of the Taliban, was composed in substantial part of remnants of the American client state's Tajik-heavy security forces. Based in the north of Afghanistan, near Tajikistan, IS-K was led by a man of uncertain national origin named Shahab al-Muhajir, who like his father before him had a history of working for narco-warlords sponsored by the CIA. Identification cards and other documents obtained by Afghan journalists and posted online show that al-Muhajir worked security for Rashid Dostum, JSOC's favorite drug lord, who had a whole exhibit set up in his honor at the Airborne and Special Operations Museum in Fayetteville. Al-Muhajir was also employed by Amrullah Saleh, who as head of the Afghan National Security Directorate was the CIA's right-hand man in Afghanistan, supplier of the remorseless Afghan assassins who made up the American spy agency's death squads, known as Zero Units. On August 26, 2021, a suicide bomber dispatched by IS-K, which in the future would commit devastating terrorist attacks against official enemies of the United States like Russia and Iran, slipped past the security cordon around the Kabul airport and detonated an explosive belt by one of the gates, killing about 170 people, including 12 marines and a corpsman, as well as Ryan Knauss.

Three days later, the JSOC-led special operations task force carried out a drone strike on a car in Kabul thought to be carrying the perpetrators of the airport attack. Based on flawed intelligence, the missile killed no militants, only an innocent Afghan aid worker, two bystanders, and seven little children. The Pentagon initially defended the bombing as a "righteous strike," only to admit, days later, that it was a "tragic mistake," marking a grimly demoralizing but bleakly fitting end to the long, hard-fought, morally injurious, and ultimately failed campaign, in which Fort Bragg soldiers were the very first to arrive and the very last to leave.

THE DAY AFTER the Kabul airport bombing, the Coast x Coast motorcycle club set out from Marina del Rey, California, on their eighth annual Ride for the Fallen. Their honorees that year included two Green Berets killed in an insider attack in Nangarhar, Afghanistan, and a pair of Marine Corps special operators who were the latest casualties of Iraq War III, which JSOC would continue to wage in total secrecy for years to come. On August 31, 2021, as the Hamid Karzai International Airport fell to the Taliban, the Coast x Coast club visited the grave site of Ryan Savard in Albuquerque, New Mexico. On September 7, the Taliban announced that they had taken Panjshir, the only province of Afghanistan that had remained outside their control. The next day, the Coast x Coast club made their usual stop at Mac's Speed Shop in Fayetteville.

On the back patio, under a faint drizzle of warm rain, the grizzled ex-operators with their tired faces, puffy eyes, and sleeve tattoos stood beneath a red pavilion emblazoned with the club's crest of crossed axes, where they had set up a booth to solicit donations and raffle off a custom Glock painted in the colors of the American flag. The noticeably tall and heavy-limbed white men on the young side of middle age, all of whom had dedicated most of their adult lives to waging foreign wars, Afghanistan above all, milled around double fisting pints of beer, smoking cigarettes, and chatting with other patrons at the outdoor bar. One had on a screen-printed shirt that said TALIBAN HUNTER over a grinning skull and crossed rifles.

The person who seemed to be in charge of the event at Mac's was a towering, barrel-chested man of about forty, the tallest person in the establishment, whose long and scraggly beard was streaked with gray. He was courteous, with an iron handshake, and gave his name as Joe

Mooney. I asked if Cris Valley was around. "No," Mooney replied. "He's at home, doing work shit."

Mooney said that he had known Billy Lavigne. "He was a great dude," he said. "He came with us, rode the ride. Or actually, he drove the truck." Other than that, he told me, "I don't think you're going to get any comment from anybody around here."

I tried to broach the topic of Lavigne's unsolved murder, about which the FBI had said absolutely nothing for the past eight months, but Mooney advised against asking such questions. "This is not a place you probably want to be doing that at," he warned. "It's done. It's over with. It's unfortunate."

SOON IT WOULD all be over for Cris Vallejo, too. His last Ride for the Fallen was in 2022. The following year, according to a post by the Coast x Coast club, as well as an obituary attached to an online fundraiser that collected more than $100,000 for his wife and newborn son, Vallejo was killed in a car crash near Albuquerque, New Mexico, shortly before the Fourth of July. He must have been in a car or truck at the time of the reported wreck, not on a motorcycle, because he had the family dog with him. The dog, named Dale, also died.

"It's been a rough year for the Coast x Coast family," a member of the club named Johnny Wilson said in a video posted online. "We've had a number of suicides," he said. "I won't get into many details, but on July second, one of our founders, Cris Vallejo, was unexpectedly killed on Interstate 40 in New Mexico. Many assumptions could be made about that," he added without elaborating.

Twenty-Two

PERMANENT WAR

Since the early '00s, Americans had been confidently informed by the most credible, respected, and prestigious institutions of media and government that the thousands of tons of pure heroin produced in occupied Afghanistan and exported all over the world were the work of the "narco-terrorist" Taliban. That had always been a vague claim, and an ahistorical one, but had been hard to disprove, thanks to the blackout on independent reporting imposed when the GWOT became an all-SOF affair under President Obama.

Now the misleading narrative, a species of that damnably effective propaganda tactic of blaming your enemy for exactly what you are doing, became wholly unsustainable as the Taliban consolidated control over Afghanistan and reinstated the same prohibitions on drugs as they had enforced from 2000 to 2001. In the spring of 2022, the Taliban decreed that year's poppy harvest illegal, along with alcohol, hashish, and methamphetamine. All traffic and trade in narcotics was banned. The stringent Islamist regime also reintroduced harsh restrictions on women's freedoms, surprising many who had thought that they would soften their oppression of women in a bid for international recognition. In addition, the Taliban outlawed the wicked and despicable practice of *bacha bazi* and suppressed child sex trafficking, which the State Department had finally denounced in a very belated report quietly issued one month before the American withdrawal, formally acknowledging, for the first time, that the U.S.-backed client state had exhibited "a government pattern of sexual slavery in government compounds."

In an exact repeat of the eradication feat that they had accomplished from 2000 to 2001, the Taliban proceeded to destroy Afghanistan's entire opium harvest in the span of a single growing season, from 2022 to 2023. Using low-tech methods that ranged from tractors to till up poppy fields to whacking sticks to beat down the plants, gangs of Taliban enforcers spoliated nearly a quarter million acres of opium crops. Few farmers resisted, and there were scant reports of violence. It was "the most successful counter-narcotics effort in human history," said an expert quoted in *The Telegraph*. "For the first time in several decades," the Taliban's interior ministry said in a statement corroborated by satellite imagery and certified by the United Nations, "the phenomenon of drugs has been eradicated across the country."

But millions of Afghans remained addicted to drugs. Under U.S. occupation, Afghanistan had come to have the highest rates of addiction of any country in the world, bar none. To deal with the problem, a source of profound misery and blight, the Taliban launched a massive rehabilitation program and rounded up thousands of homeless, derelict, emaciated, unwashed junkies and petty heroin dealers from under bridges, in fetid alleyways, and on raw street corners where skeletal opium smokers crouched in their filthy rags around sooty trash fires. The Islamic cops forced the hapless addicts onto buses, transported them to austere concrete detox wards, shaved their heads and beards, made them bathe, fitted them in clean clothes, and obligated them to stay for forty-five days, undergoing a forced cold-turkey quit for which no medicine was given aside from regular meals, cold water, and sunshine.

The Western reaction to the Taliban's involuntary rehab program and its poppy eradication campaign was surprisingly overt in its opposition and hostility. The line taken by nearly all think tank types, neoliberal academics, and international humanitarian organizations was that the poppy ban, coming at a time of severe drought, would devastate the Afghan economy. There was much hand-wringing in wealthy donor countries over the plight of the poor Afghan dirt farmer. THE TALIBAN'S SUCCESSFUL OPIUM BAN IS BAD FOR AFGHANS AND THE WORLD, read the headline of a typical think piece, published by the United States Institute of Peace. "Poppy has been replaced by wheat, a low-value crop, boding ill for the economy," wrote the author, a Harvard economist who had been the World Bank's country manager for Afghanistan. But according to a UN report issued in 2021, the Afghan people themselves earned only a few billion dollars a year from the drug trade, much less than the sum of hard currency that the sore-loser Biden administration stole from Afghanistan's central bank in the process of withdrawing. According to the UN, most of the revenues raised by the traffic in Afghan heroin went to "illicit drug supply chains outside Afghanistan," that is, international drug cartels in countries like Pakistan, Tajikistan, Turkey, and the United Arab Emirates.

AT FORT BRAGG, the mortality crisis that had coincided with the U.S. withdrawal from Afghanistan continued to play out with no respite. On January 6, 2022, Sergeant Layne Coleman Jones, a paratrooper from Frederick, Maryland, who according to his sister had "questioned his spirituality when he came back from Afghanistan, due to the troubling occurrences that he witnessed while deployed," including "prisoners being tortured, bodies being burned in a pit, and animals being hurt for no reason," shot himself in the head at his apartment in Fayetteville, becoming Fort Bragg's first suicide of the year. Sergeant Jones, aged twenty-four, belonged to the 82nd Airborne Division's 505th Infantry, a storied paratrooper regiment that's been particularly hard hit by the Army's twin epidemics of addiction and self-harm.

His mom, Lanna Jones, refused to believe that he'd taken his own life. "The story was an absolute fabrication," she insisted. Faintly but distinctly, she heard her son's voice speaking to her in the darkness of night. "Mom, I didn't do this," the voice said. "Don't give up on me."

Certain elements of the story didn't add up. Jones supposedly shot himself with a Glock in his left hand, but he was right-handed, and his daily carry was a Springfield XD. Other dubious forensic details had to do with the pattern of blood spatter on the wall, the erratic trajectory of the bullet through his brain, and a "stovepipe" malfunction of the pistol's ejection mechanism, which can occur when a handgun is fired from under a pillow.

Lanna's daughter, JoLynn Jones-Kerschner, a military policewoman in the Marine Corps, went down to Fort Bragg to investigate. She found no concrete proof that her brother's suicide had been staged, but was appalled by the open-air drug dealing that she saw all over Fayetteville. Fort Bragg had always been a place associated with druggy, dropout soldiers who hung around using and dealing after their service was up, and the pandemic years and the implosion of the war in Afghanistan had worn the social fabric even more ragged. "Right outside the police department," she said, "I had three people ask me for a dime piece, fentanyl, and cocaine, so nonchalant, like it was normal." One had a high-and-tight haircut and looked to be a soldier. Another was "a person in a clown outfit," she said, "with no pants on."

JoLynn took custody of her brother's phone and found that he often texted other soldiers in the 505th Infantry Regiment about buying, selling, and using cocaine. She confronted a sergeant in his platoon, and he "spilled the beans," she said, admitting to her that cocaine use is widespread in the 505th. He told JoLynn that the coke is mainly sourced out of Raleigh, transported down Interstate 95 by drug runners, and brought on base by members of "units who consider themselves above the law, who are free of oversight," said JoLynn, naming the usual suspects: "Delta, Special Forces, paratroopers."

JoLynn went on investigating, assembled hundreds of pages of files, and wrote a forty-page report of her findings. Eventually, she persuaded the state medical examiner to change Jones's official manner of death from suicide to "undetermined."

THREE WEEKS AFTER JONES DIED, the 95th Civil Affairs Brigade, the former employer of Timothy Dumas and Keith Lewis, lost another soldier under murky circumstances related to drug use in the unit. Sergeant First Class Christopher Calascione was found dead from an overdose on the floor of his house in Pinehurst.

Calascione was a thirty-four-year-old artilleryman from Staten Island, New York, who had done two tours of duty in Iraq. His wife, Sylvia Jablonowska, says that Iraq War II left him deeply afflicted by moral injury. He had been a Howitzer gunner, and memories of dead children crushed under broken rubble haunted his dreams. "He was having nightmares and night sweats," she said. "I caught him many times waking up from a nap or from sleep, looking a little bit scared. He had this *fear* in his eyes."

In 2013, Calascione transitioned to the anodyne-sounding but recondite world of active-duty civil affairs, the softer arm of the Green Berets. He was assigned to the 95th CAB, whose personnel undergo language training and cultural instruction and are taught "to map the civil human terrain and then identify the civil vulnerabilities that can be exploited." Trained to speak Russian, Calascione underwent courses in "NATO strategic operations," "intelligence studies," "joint information operations planning," and "Special Forces network development," his enlisted record shows.

In these capacities, Calascione did three deployments to Poland, which is where he met his wife, a flight attendant for a Norwegian airline. "He was this big loving bear," she said, but struggled to keep his drinking under control. He had come back from his last tour in Iraq with a prescription for oxycodone, and Army doctors now had him on several antidepressants as well as the sedative clonazepam, which left his pupils alternately constricted to pinpoints or widely dilated. "What's up with your eyes?" his wife would ask him. "I took a muscle relaxer," he'd say.

In between rotations to Poland, Calascione deployed to Hungary, Slovakia, and Lithuania. In 2018, he was sent to Ukraine, where four years earlier the democratically elected government of Viktor Yanukovych had been overthrown in a coup that was openly backed by the United States. "He was in Ukraine," said Jablonowska, "working secretly with the government. He was taking supplies to some area that was in need, the Donbas, I believe. He was doing a lot of stuff on boats, surveillance tasks very close to the Russian border."

In 2021, a drunk-driving accident in Stuttgart, Germany, derailed Calascione's career. He lost his security clearance and returned to Fort Bragg deeply depressed. Relegated to desk duty, he started using cocaine. An involuntary stint in military rehab seemed to help him regain his bearings. Then, in the last week of January, while his wife was out of the country at a fertility clinic in Poland, where she successfully became pregnant with his child, Calascione stopped answering his phone. He was dead from acute cocaine and fentanyl toxicity. The dog-sitter found his body.

"Chris didn't look like your typical drug user," Jablonowska said. "He had many people fooled, including me. Now, looking through his medical records, I see the red flags and how he was struggling in silence."

Jablonowska was "speechless and broken," she said, about how badly Fort Bragg and Fayetteville authorities bungled the aftermath of Calascione's death. "The police investigation was nonexistent and sloppy," she said. "There was no autopsy, either. They found needles, and basically wrote him off. Then the Army was relying on the police investigation, which was a joke."

The Army determined that Calascione's death was due to his own willful misconduct, meaning his wife could not collect the $400,000 in life insurance money that normally goes to the next of kin of service members who die on active duty. All the family members of overdose victims whom I spoke to inveighed against this injustice, with many saying that their loved one never had a drug problem until he joined the Army and was stationed at Fort Bragg.

ONE DAY BEFORE Chris Calascione died, on January 26, 2022, the United States, at the direction of President Joe Biden, rejected a Russian ultimatum demanding that Ukraine be excluded from NATO and that threatening military operations on Russia's borders come to an end. The Russian president, Vladimir Putin, responded to Biden's refusal to commit to Ukrainian neutrality by launching a ground invasion of eastern Ukraine, a major escalation of the armed conflict that had been simmering there for the past eight years.

Reporting on the war for *Harper's Magazine*, I spent a night in Rzeszow, a city in the southeast of Poland where some five thousand American soldiers had been sent to backstop the Ukrainian army. Nearly all of them were paratroopers from Fort Bragg under the command of Major General Chris Donahue, who had been Billy Lavigne's commander from 2013 to 2015, and now commanded the 82nd Airborne Division. Just six months earlier, Donahue had contrived to have himself photographed in a dramatic, green-tinted night-vision image, widely distributed by the Pentagon and dutifully published by every major media outlet, billed as "the last American soldier to leave Afghanistan." Now he was leading the charge in the latest permutation of the forever-war paradigm, in which the new enemies are Russia and China.

Arriving in Rzeszow in a rental car on March 17, I drove around an airport and sports arena where the American troops were based and saw an array of truck-mounted surface-to-air missile systems known as Patriots, their boxlike batteries pointed at the sky. That night, I walked around a sterile galleria in downtown Rzeszow, drifted in and out of brightly lit stores, and mingled wordlessly among scores of uniformed

American soldiers, with their backpacks, water bottles, buzz cuts, and chrome domes. Most wore the patch of the 82nd Airborne Division or the XVIII Airborne Corps on their shoulder.

On my way to the front lines, I spoke on background to a well-informed source who told me that JSOC operators were then physically present in Ukraine. Specifically, the source said, an "Advance Force Operations" team, or AFO, including operators from Delta Force and SEAL Team Six, was on the ground doing "operational preparation of the environment," an obscure military term of art, the exact definition of which is classified, that describes covert activities exempt from congressional oversight. The presence of American, British, and French special operators in Ukraine was confirmed a few months later by *The New York Times* and *The Washington Post*, based in part on classified documents leaked to a server called Discord.

Over the next year, in and around Russian territory, unexplained fires and explosions damaged or destroyed many pipelines, oil and gas facilities, railroads, fuel dumps, power plants, and shopping malls, while several pro-Russian propagandists, politicians, and generals were killed or injured by car bombs. Although it failed to forestall Russia's territorial acquisition of the Donbas and a land bridge to Crimea, the underreported campaign of covert action suggested that in the future the American way of war will be characterized, to an even greater degree than before, by the use of special operators, contractors, proxy forces, drones, spies, saboteurs, and hackers, all acting against the backdrop of an English-language media environment dominated like never before by propaganda produced by the military and State Department and disseminated by wire services, public radio, and the newspapers of record.

AS A MEAT-GRINDER of a war whose estimated casualty count would eventually approach one million raged in Ukraine, Fort Bragg was in the middle of the biggest cluster of military suicides ever recorded.

Eight soldiers killed themselves in one eight-week stretch beginning in mid-May, for a total of fifty-one suicides since the start of 2020.

There was no cessation, either, of the homicidal, soldier-involved violence. On January 6, a military policewoman from the 503rd MP Battalion, Specialist Yunique Weathers, killed a woman execution-style in the middle of an irrigated crop field just across the state line in Horry County, South Carolina. She then cleared her weapon, tossed it aside, and surrendered to the police who were converging on the rural location. The victim was a twenty-one-year-old woman named De'Erica Fisher. A motive was never disclosed.

The next killing occurred on July 23. A twenty-five-year-old-civilian, Malik Williams, allegedly shot up a party gathered at a house on a dirt road called Primrose Path in the Moore County town of Pinebluff. He wounded four people and killed Staff Sergeant Keith Wright Jr., a twenty-nine-year-old support soldier in the 3rd Special Forces Group who left behind four kids.

Two more Fort Bragg soldiers were killed in September and October. Sergeant Nicholas Antonio Bobo, a military warehouseman from Memphis, aged twenty-two, was shot multiple times in front of a Fayetteville apartment complex called the Enclave at eleven o'clock at night on September 13, allegedly by a pair of local teenagers. On October 19, Staff Sergeant Nikko Brown, an artilleryman from Chicago, aged thirty-three, was shot and killed in Hope Mills around two o'clock in the morning. Brown was the third young black male soldier from Fort Bragg to be gunned down at an apartment complex or house party in as many months, but his murder was different from the others. Police say the perpetrator was his brother.

IN THE MIDST of these late-summer shootings, a particularly cruel murder occurred that was disconcertingly reminiscent of the series of wife killings that had roiled Fort Bragg twenty years earlier. The perpetrator, David Jensen, was a lifelong Delta Force man.

Born in 1975 in a small town in South Dakota, Jensen had ridden with the Northern Alliance into Afghanistan in 2001 and deployed to Iraq in the opening salvos of the 2003 invasion. His daughter, Jaleigh, born in 1995, spoke poignantly about being raised in the Delta Force community. At the private schools she attended in Moore County, everybody's dads were always away, off on deployment or detached to the Pentagon or someplace in Florida. Her father joined a private military company founded by unit veterans called Triple Canopy in 2004 and for the next decade deployed more often than he had on active duty. Every time he came home from overseas, he seemed to have grown more hostile, controlling, and abusive toward his wife, a sweet-tempered and demure interior designer named Amber who had been his high school prom date.

To manage his black moods, Jensen depended on alcohol and pills originally prescribed to him by the Army after he was injured in a rocket attack on Bagram Airfield. "He tried to fight it," Jaleigh said. "He was sober for about ten years. But at the same time, it was just in him, this darkness."

Jensen went back to drinking around 2019. He had no close friends, was extremely paranoid and suspicious, and spent all his time alone, holed up in his garage, tinkering with guns. "He had a gun on him at all times," said Jaleigh. "More guns than I've ever heard of anyone else owning," she said. "A gun stashed in every room of our house."

The night of September 6, 2022, David and Amber Jensen had an argument. It began when he capsized his kayak on Thagard Lake, a short distance from their home in Whispering Pines, and she could not help but laugh at him, injuring his pride. The bickering that ensued dragged on for hours, escalated in rancor, and culminated in her vowing to leave him, not for the first time. He grabbed her arm and struck her in the face, leaving the bedspread splashed with blood. She took refuge in the master bathroom, bringing her ten-pound dachshund, Greta Bean, with her. As she frantically attempted to book a hotel room on her computer tablet, he kicked down the locked door and stomped the little dog to death, even though by all accounts he loved Greta Bean more than any other member of the family. As Amber cowered between the bathtub and the toilet, he took aim and shot her in the head, killing her. After taking a good long look at what he had done, he put the barrel of the pistol in his own mouth and pulled the trigger.

After the murder and suicide, the Moore County community, steeped in quiet loyalty toward the Special Forces, reflexively came together to protect Jensen's posthumous reputation and ensure that his actions were not permitted to reflect poorly on the unit, whose name was kept out of the matter entirely. An article in *The Pilot*, published September 7, did not make clear who had been murdered and who had died by suicide. Local authorities treated the incident, which was scarcely reported outside Moore County, as a tragedy for which no one was really to blame. "Nothing like this matches up with their character and prior behavior," the Whispering Pines police chief said, eliding the distinction between victim and perpetrator.

THREE WEEKS LATER, on September 26, 2022, Freddie Wayne Huff II was finally indicted in federal court. Nearly two years had gone by since the still-unsolved murders of Billy Lavigne and Timothy Dumas, and now it became clear that the FBI did not suspect Huff of being the Third Man. Though he had confessed to committing armed robberies and kidnappings and had millions of dollars' worth of meth in his possession when arrested, he was charged with a single count of trafficking cocaine, as well as conspiring with Jaime Rosado and Rahain Deriggs to do the same. He also caught an ancillary gun charge.

Huff waived his arraignment and, angling for a better plea deal, told federal agents about the drug ring in the Special Forces that had counted Timothy Dumas and Billy Lavigne among its members. He told them that with Dumas as a go-between, the Fort Bragg cartel had absorbed fully half of the cocaine that he had imported from Texas and Florida between 2018 and 2020, a quantity that amounted to at least a hundred kilos, probably more than a thousand kilos, and possibly as much as five *tons* of coke. Huff described the blackmail letter that Dumas had written and told the agents where they could find it, but to his surprise, they seemed uninterested in this information. They asked no follow-up questions and didn't review the thumb drive that remained under lock and key in the evidence room of the Winston-Salem Police Department. "It almost seemed to me like they didn't give much of a fuck," said Huff. "They just wanted to push it under the rug. Like I said," he added, "Fort Bragg has a lot of secrets."

He wasn't wrong about that. Two months before Huff was indicted, in July 2022, a very strange event had occurred that only added to Fort Bragg's store of undisclosed secrets and unsolved mysteries. It had to do with a small, privately owned airport immediately south of Fort Bragg, known as the Raeford Drop Zone, that for decades had been a Delta Force training ground, and for just as long had been rumored—truthfully, it turns out—to be a hotbed of regional and international drug trafficking. A man literally fell out of the clear blue sky.

Twenty-Three

FORT LIBERTY

Emily Osborn, of the oddly named but perfectly ordinary small town of Fuquay-Varina, an hour north of Fayetteville, was working from home the afternoon of July 29, 2022, when she was interrupted by the sound of tree branches snapping in her backyard, followed by a dull thud. Thinking little of the noise, she turned her attention back to her work. Then police vehicles, fire trucks, ambulances, and helicopters began to converge on the ordinarily quiet cul-de-sac in a wailing maelstrom of emergency sirens.

Lying under a broken tree in Osborn's densely wooded backyard was the dead body of a young man from Connecticut named Charles Crooks. An aviation enthusiast from a young age, Crooks had recently obtained his pilot's license and a job working for Rampart Aviation, a secretive, Colorado-based company that holds multiple lucrative contracts to support the airborne operations of the Army's Special Forces, as well as the Navy SEALs. Crooks had somehow fallen, jumped, or been thrown from a small turboprop plane that Rampart had put in the service of USASOC. No parachute was found anywhere near his body. He had departed the airplane, a stubby CASA C-212 Aviocar, in his street clothes alone.

Crooks's plane had taken off that day from the 5w4 P K Airpark, a dual-strip airfield within Fort Bragg's restricted airspace commonly called the Raeford Drop Zone, that has a long and checkered history, dating back to the 1980s, of fatal accidents, suspicious fires, unexplained burglaries, and acts of suspected sabotage. The original owner and operator of the airpark was Gene Paul Thacker, a first-generation Special Forces soldier and legendary veteran of the wars in Korea and Vietnam who had served in the CIA's opium-fueled shadow war in Laos. Returning from doing black operations in Southeast Asia with a sniper's bullet lodged in his shoulder and a Purple Heart pinned to his chest, Thacker settled in Raeford, bought the municipal airport and surrounding land, and for decades used the facility for two main purposes, one of which was quite illegal.

Leveraging his connections with the Special Forces, Thacker rented the airpark out as a training facility for the newly created Delta Force, as well as the Golden Knights trick parachuting team, also based at Fort Bragg, which counted Thacker among its original members. Ever since then, Green Berets stationed at Bragg have used the Raeford Drop Zone to practice the risky and difficult techniques of high-altitude, high-opening parachute jumping, or HAHO, which is a core competency of elite commandos, because it allows special operators to insert behind enemy lines from heights above the reach of radar systems and antiaircraft guns. "I can confirm that USASOC routinely uses the airport and has done so for quite some time," said Lieutenant Colonel Michael Burns, the chief spokesman for the Special Forces.

Declassified FBI files and court records dug up from the recesses of dusty old archives show that Thacker, a daring pilot and expert parachutist, also used the Raeford Drop Zone and the small fleet of turboprop airplanes that he maintained there to smuggle a staggering weight of cocaine into the United States, making frequent under-the-radar flights down to Florida and the Caribbean and back in stripped-down, blacked-out aircraft, at times carrying up to a thousand pounds of drugs in the cargo hold. A wily old outlaw with a bull neck, jug ears, a flattop haircut, and a devious twinkle in his eye, gifted with a shrewd hillbilly cunning inherited from his moonshine-distilling Kentucky kinfolk, Thacker had a preternatural ability to evade the law and was mixed up with some of the most notorious ex-military drug traffickers of his era. "I grew up," said his son, Tim Thacker, born in 1963, "around a bunch of smugglers."

Thacker's many accomplices included Andrew Carter Thornton II, a former Fort Bragg paratrooper, often spotted near the Nicaraguan contras' bases in Tegucigalpa and Ilopango, who had a law degree as well as a pilot's license, thought of himself as a New Age ninja warrior, collected Nazi regalia, consistently claimed to be an agent of the CIA, and in the course of his audacious criminal exploits inspired the "Cocaine Bear" myth; as well as Adler "Barry" Seal, a daredevil, barnstorming pilot and veteran of the 20th Special Forces Group who smuggled many tons of the Cali Cartel's cocaine into the United States, associated with right-wing causes, became an asset of George H. W. Bush's boys in the DEA and CIA, and was instrumental in an attempt by the Reagan administration to frame the Nicaraguan Sandinistas for alleged dealings with Pablo Escobar. But while Thornton died in a botched parachute jump with duffel bags full of cocaine strapped to his waist and Seal was gunned down by Colombian hit men outside a halfway house in Baton Rouge, Gene Thacker never got caught slipping. He walked away from every caper, always a step ahead of the cops. He was charged in 1984 in a Florida state court case described by the Associated Press as "the biggest cocaine indictment ever," but was acquitted after a procession of Golden Knights took the witness stand and testified one by one to the uprightness of his character, swearing under oath that they had never seen any planeloads of cocaine, or any other drug, being unloaded at the Raeford Drop Zone. According to Tim Thacker, whose allegations were corroborated by contemporaneous reports in the Raeford News-Journal, local lawmen resorted to sabotaging Thacker's airplanes in an extrajudicial effort to put a stop to his incredibly prolific smuggling.

"Thacker is widely known in the Raeford area for trafficking by air narcotics," wrote an FBI agent in the bureau's file on Andrew Thornton. "Raeford Aviation has been raided for drug runs by the Hoke County Sheriff's Department on numerous occasions, but almost always comes up empty."

Gene Thacker passed away peacefully in 2012 and was buried with full military honors. Responsibility for managing the Raeford Drop Zone devolved onto to his son, also a pilot and accomplished parachutist, who carried on the family business, licit and illicit. While continuing to operate the airpark as a Delta Force training ground, Tim Thacker also kept up its usage as a base for a long-running international drug-smuggling conspiracy, but with methamphetamine taking the place of cocaine. Brad Knott, a federal prosecutor in Raleigh, described the younger Thacker as "a very committed and very proficient drug trafficker," and a "career criminal," who was responsible for "pumping methamphetamine into North Carolina like we haven't seen before." From 2012 to 2018, Thacker bought and sold small airplanes; traveled all over the world following a low-flying, continent-hopping route that did not result in stamps on his passport; forged relationships with cartels in Mexico and Colombia; and was a principal supplier of ice that was 95 percent pure to street gangs in Sampson, Duplin, Hoke, and Cumberland Counties. In this, Thacker told me, he was driven by his own addiction to crystal meth. According to Michelle Moore, his much younger girlfriend, "His true addiction was to the art of the smuggle."

Billy Lavigne, who completed the four-week HAHO course in 2011 and went through the military free-fall jumpmaster course the following year, qualifying as a HAHO instructor, worked at the Raeford Drop Zone from 2017 to 2018. After his tours in the war against the Islamic State, amid his descent into severe meth and crack addiction, the unit took him out of rotation and posted him there to teach HAHO to other special operators. It was the last job that he held as a member of Delta Force. Lavigne also belonged to a civilian skydiving club based at the Raeford Drop Zone known as Paraclete XP. "Billy wasn't operating at that time," said Jordan Terrell. "He was on jumpmaster orders, getting guys trained up to do HAHO." He added, "I think that was how he was able to spend so much time with Mark."

Lavigne and Thacker worked at the Raeford Drop Zone together at the same time that both were dealing meth in Fayetteville. In November 2017, the cops nabbed a courier for a drug gang in the small town of Garland, and she fingered Thacker as the gang's wholesale supplier. That was the beginning of the end for Thacker. After being indicted in May 2018, he fled the state and had to be pulled naked from the crawlspace above a motel room in Oklahoma by federal marshals. He was twice offered leniency in exchange for cooperation with law enforcement but blew both chances after he was caught selling meth while out on bond and even while locked up in jail. He eventually pleaded guilty to trafficking and firearms charges, heightened by a kingpin enhancement, and was sentenced to a crushing forty years behind bars. "Thacker utilized a local, private airport," the Department of Justice said in an August 2019 press release announcing his conviction, "to open Eastern North Carolina to out of state, large scale methamphetamine suppliers."

BUT NONE OF THIS HISTORY of the Raeford Drop Zone, which is now owned by Gene Thacker's widow, Tim's mother, Billie Thacker, figured into the NTSB's investigation of the bizarre death of Charles Crooks, which took more than a year to complete. In its anticlimactic and inconclusive final report, released in December 2023, the NTSB found that there was "insufficient evidence" to support the account of the sole eyewitness, the chief pilot of Rampart Aviation, who'd been at the controls of the plane at the time of Crooks's aerial defenestration. His uncorroborated version of events was all that the board had to go on.

According to Rampart's chief pilot, who was not publicly named, he and Crooks had already flown two runs out of the Raeford Drop Zone on July 29, 2022, and were descending to pick up a third group of skydiving Delta Force operators or Special Forces soldiers, with Crooks at the controls, when sudden wind shear caused the plane's tricycle landing gear to clip the runway, knocking off the right wheel. Crooks immediately pulled back on the throttle and initiated a climb. The chief pilot took over, circled the plane around, and radioed the Raleigh-Durham airport to request permission to land there, where emergency services waited on standby. Air traffic controllers gave the go-ahead. It was then that Crooks met his inexplicable fate.

For the first twenty minutes of the flight to Raleigh-Durham, Crooks and the more senior pilot reviewed emergency landing procedures and planned how they would put the plane down with only one wheel. Then, according to the chief pilot, Crooks suddenly became upset, said that he was going to be sick, and lowered a cockpit window as if to vomit. He also pulled the handle that opened the rear ramp of the plane, which took a full nine seconds to lower. He then "disconnected his seat belt, dropped his headset, and ran out the back of the airplane toward the fully open ramp in a headfirst dive."

The unfortunate Charles Crooks plummeted three thousand feet through the wide-open void of hazy air above the patchwork of green fields and gray subdivisions studded with small artificial lakes that is Wake County, North Carolina. As the squiggly streets and curved roads spun in dizzying circles, one green patch in the center grew bigger and bigger. It was the backyard of Emily Osborn.

The NTSB report, which was not a police investigation but an administrative safety review, implies that Crooks was so upset over the hard landing at the Raeford Drop Zone that he was overcome by an irresistible suicidal impulse. "The pilot's subsequent decision to leave his seat in flight," it states, "resulted in his fall from the airplane."

A spokesman for the NTSB, Peter Knudson, described Crooks's death, which was ruled an accident, as a "freakish occurrence." Incidents of people falling from airplanes without a parachute, he said, are "vanishingly rare."

A LOT OF STRANGE things happen around Fort Bragg and are never explained. It's characteristic of life in this part of North Carolina, adjacent to a garrison of thousands of men trained for irregular warfare, many of whom have dedicated their lives to covert action, that anomalous events emerge, cause a brief stir, then subside into the past, never to be fully elucidated or resolved.

Shortly after nightfall on December 3, 2022, one or more gunmen armed with high-powered rifles severely damaged two Duke Energy electrical substations in Moore County, knocking out the power in Southern Pines, Pinehurst, and Whispering Pines and causing the death of at least one person, who depended on an oxygen machine to breathe at night. The fatality was ruled a homicide, the governor of North Carolina declared an emergency, schools closed, and people shivered in their unheated homes for the next four days as technicians worked around the clock to repair the deadened grid. The FBI opened an investigation into the deadly act of sabotage, which coincided with a controversial drag show scheduled to premiere at the Sunrise Theater in Southern Pines, but never made an arrest.

That's another thing you see around Fort Bragg quite a lot: investigations that go on forever and peter out inconclusively. On the afternoon of January 5, 2023, military police officers armed with fifteen warrants took up positions at Fort Bragg's Longstreet Gate on the road to Southern Pines, the start of a major crackdown on drug crime that initially seemed to promise dramatic results. In the ensuing dragnet, which caused a traffic jam memorably described by the reporter Jack Murphy, quoting an unnamed source, as "a trail of tears and douche bag cars," the MPs arrested more than a dozen USASOC soldiers on suspicion of trafficking narcotics and human trafficking. Green Berets from 3rd Group, psychological operations soldiers, and at least one Delta Force operator were reportedly among the suspects. "Panic began within the Special Forces community over the weekend," Murphy reported, with soldiers flushing their drug stashes, deleting incriminating text messages, and "rumors swirling that the arrests are also connected to various murders around Fort Bragg in recent years."

"The U.S. Army Special Operations Command is aware of the allegations of drug involvement from Soldiers assigned to USASOC units on Fort Bragg," Lieutenant Colonel Mike Burns said in a statement. "We take all allegations seriously and are fully cooperating with the Criminal Investigation Division."

Within days, though, the whole matter was overshadowed by yet another streak of murders. Twenty twenty-three was the first year since 9/11 that USASOC added no new names to its memorial wall, but stateside six Fort Bragg soldiers were murdered or accused of murder in the first four months of the year alone.

On January 18, a Delta Force support soldier, Staff Sergeant Brandon Allen Amos-Dixon—one of the unit's cooks—allegedly fired ten shots at his fiancée and her baby and then tracked down and killed Staff Sergeant Jimmy Lee Smith III, a cook in the 3rd Special Forces Group. On March 12, Sergeant Junando Recardo Dawkins, an Afghanistan veteran from upstate New York, was taken into custody on Fort Bragg as he was about to deploy overseas and charged with murdering a man who in the past had done federal prison time for trafficking cocaine behind a record label called Outta They League. Ten days later, an infantryman named Josef Nehemiah King Jr., who had recently washed out of Special Forces training, was charged with beating his girlfriend's toddler to death. Then, on April 2, another 3rd Group support soldier, Rolondo Martice Boone, allegedly shot and killed a man in a wild exchange of gunfire that spilled out of a Fayetteville hookah lounge, becoming the third Fort Bragg soldier in nearly as many weeks to be accused of first-degree murder.

The chaos at Fort Bragg, combined with the ongoing travails of the Navy SEALs, who'd recently been hit with another *New York Times* exposé of their "culture of brutality, cheating, and drugs," contributed to a growing impression that the special operations community was coming apart at the seams. "Does ARSOF have an ethics problem?" the editor of *Special Warfare* magazine, a publication put out by USASOC, asked in an issue wholly dedicated to addressing "moral drift" in elite units. "More and more, people are saying yes."

At a March meeting of the Senate Armed Services Committee, Senator Ted Budd of North Carolina questioned the SOCOM commander over "a series of concerning incidents" at Fort Bragg, including "suicides, murders, overdoses, [and] drug trafficking." General Bryan Fenton replied that he was "very angry when we get reports like that," which he admitted were "corrosives toward the trust and confidence" placed in elite troops. "We're laser-focused on eradicating that from [the] SO-COM enterprise," Fenton said.

In May, Senators Edward Markey and Elizabeth Warren of Massachusetts introduced the Department of Defense Overdose Data Act of 2023. The bill, which became law in December, requires the Pentagon to accurately report to Congress all fatal and nonfatal overdoses in each of the service branches every year and to come up with a plan for dealing with bases that have overdose rates that exceed the national average, such as Fort Bragg and Fort Campbell.

In July, President Joe Biden signed an executive order implementing a set of reforms to the military justice system long championed by Senator Kirsten Gillibrand of New York. In the past, the power to charge a soldier with a serious felony was entrusted to his or her brigade or division commander, creating an obvious conflict between the public's interest in the impartial administration of justice and the commander's career-driven interest in suppressing knowledge of criminal wrongdoing in that brigade or division. Now, in cases of serious offenses including rape and murder, the prosecutorial discretion will rest with the independent Office of Special Trial Counsel. However, unit commanders will retain their authority to scuttle drug-smuggling investigations and exonerate soldiers suspected of trafficking narcotics without any outside oversight or notice to the public.

That implicit veto power was evident in the case of the January 5 Longstreet Gate bust. Whether to charge any of the Special Forces soldiers suspected of trafficking drugs and people depended on the evidence gathered by CID and the recommendations of Army prosecutors, but the ultimate authority to convene courts-martial was vested in the chief of USASOC, Lieutenant General Jonathan Braga, a former Delta Force commander known as an advocate for increased psychological operations, such as a covert propaganda campaign that he spearheaded in the Philippines during the pandemic to spread disinformation about China's COVID vaccine. Under Braga's watch, not one of the fifteen suspects was prosecuted by military authorities, although two of them, a Green Beret from 3rd Group and a member of the 4th Psychological Operations Group, did catch felony drug possession charges in Harnett County.

ANOTHER MILITARY REFORM seen in 2023 was the rechristening of a number of bases named after Confederate generals. Among them was Fort Bragg, named after General Braxton Bragg, a native son of North Carolina who suffered heavy losses to his forces during the Civil War and is generally ranked by historians among the worst tacticians of his era.

Fort Bragg has a shameful legacy of vicious hate crimes committed by bigoted soldiers. In 1993, an Army sergeant angry about gays in the military got blackout drunk and committed a senseless mass shooting at a randomly chosen Italian restaurant. Two years later, a pair of neo-Nazi paratroopers shot and killed a couple walking down the street just because they were black. Fayetteville itself is built around an arcade and clock tower that used to be a slave market.

Considering this ugly history, few people in the community vociferously opposed stripping the base of its anachronistic appellation. Most were open to some kind of change, including the possibility of rededicating the base in honor of Braxton Bragg's more distinguished cousin, Edward Bragg, a Union Army officer, congressman, and diplomat. Instead, the commission appointed to the task by Congress renamed the base Fort Liberty, a surprisingly uninspired and generic choice that reminded me of nothing so much as "Freedom City," the mock Iraqi town built out past Spring Lake for troops to practice reacting to ambushes. Even the new signs looked cheap, with warped sheets of laminated polymer replacing the sturdy old wooden beams.

The renaming ceremony was held on the afternoon of June 2, a warm and muggy Friday. Beneath blue and yellow tents, a few dozen local dignitaries, retired officers, and Gold Star mothers had gathered to observe the final casing of the Fort Bragg colors. A sergeant major barked "at ease," and everyone stood at attention and saluted as the "Demon's Battery" of the 319th Field Artillery fired off their deafening howitzers. The band played "The Star-Spangled Banner" and "The Army Goes Rolling Along," the chaplain of the XVIII Airborne Corps offered up a brief nondenominational prayer, and then the ubiquitous Chris Donahue, Billy Lavigne's former commander, who had received his third star after the 82nd's deployment to Poland and would soon receive a fourth, gave a short commemorative speech, unremarkable in content except that he repeatedly referred to Fort Bragg, now Fort Liberty, as "the center of the universe."

Afterward, Donahue stood for a press scrum and took questions from reporters from the Associated Press, *PBS News Hour*, *The Fayetteville Observer*, and *Task & Purpose*. When my turn came, I tried to ask General Donahue about the Longstreet Gate bust, about which there had been no word since January, and the Lavigne/Dumas murders, which by this time seemed likely to remain forever unsolved, but Colonel Burns, the chief of public affairs, wouldn't let me finish. He rushed over to hustle me away on the grounds that I wasn't on the approved list of journalists, and six military policemen swiftly arrived to escort me off the premises of the installation now known as Fort Liberty.

OVER THE COURSE of the following year, instances of drug trafficking and gunrunning continued to emerge at a rate that for any other military base would be very abnormal.

In January 2024, a Fort Liberty medic originally from Virginia named Gordon Ray Custis, an Iraq War III veteran, was sentenced to fifteen years in federal prison for trafficking ketamine into the United States from the West African country of Cameroon. Like Master Sergeant Martin Acevedo III, Specialist Custis, a tall white man with a big beard who was enrolled in the special operations medical training course at the time of his crimes, used the international mail service to have commercial quantities of narcotics delivered to him at his house on Daharan Drive in Fayetteville. In this he had two military accomplices, a medic and a medical logistics specialist, all of whom had at one point belonged to the 44th Medical Brigade. A raid of Custis's house, the culmination of an investigation that began with a tip-off from French customs in West Africa, turned up digital scales, a heat press, vacuum sealers, packaging materials, a money-counting machine, sales ledgers, various firearms, and more than sixty pounds of ketamine.

Another Fort Liberty–based smuggling scheme with a connection to West Africa was adjudicated in April 2024, when a federal jury found Major Kojo Owusu Dartey, an airborne infantry officer known by the street name Killa K, guilty of trafficking guns internationally and dealing arms without a license. A DEA agent stationed at the port of Tema in Ghana had learned that Major Dartey, who served at the Kandahar airfield in Afghanistan in the same era as Timothy Dumas, used straw buyers to purchase semiautomatic handguns, assault rifles, fifty-round magazines, muzzle suppressors, and combat shotguns, which he smuggled in barrels of rice and clothing on ships embarking across the Atlantic from the Baltimore harbor. The conspiracy was based out of a church popular with Ghanaian immigrants in Fayetteville and involved at least one other Ghana-born American soldier who was stationed at Fort Campbell.

The following month, a long-serving sergeant major in the headquarters company of the Fort Liberty–based Army Forces Command, Jorge Esteban Garcia, whose many deployments went all the way back to Somalia in 1993, pleaded guilty to importation and possession of a controlled substance with intent to distribute. The previous May, he'd been caught at the San Ysidro border crossing between the United States and Mexico at Tijuana with eleven kilos of meth in his possession. Besides drug trafficking, Sergeant Major Garcia was accused of "active participation in a criminal gang," according to the charge sheet filed against him at his court-martial, and "wrongfully engaging in cyber-related activities in support of a criminal gang," in the knowledge "that such activities involve an extremist cause." Garcia had been an Army career counselor for twenty years and was the top career counselor at Fort Bragg, later Fort Liberty, responsible for coaching retiring soldiers on their post-military employment options.

Twenty-Four

THE THIRD MAN

On August 1, 2023, the other shoe finally dropped in the Lavigne/Dumas case, and the FBI implicitly broke its silence, as federal prosecutors unsealed an indictment against a young black man named Kenneth Maurice Quick Jr., alleging facts that painted him as the Third Man and accusing him of both murders. The U.S. Attorney's Office for the Eastern District of North Carolina also charged Quick with trafficking cocaine, plus two counts of obstruction of justice: one for attempting to dispose of Lavigne's body in McArthur Lake and the other for firebombing Dumas's truck.

Quick, who never served in the military and had no apparent connections to Fayetteville or Fort Bragg, was born on Christmas Day in 1999 and raised in Laurinburg, North Carolina. His home of record was on Pankeytown Road, a long strip of unpaved macadam where single-wide trailers sit on acre-sized lots amid widely spaced pine trees. He left school in the eleventh grade and worked for a time at Perdue Farms, but his lengthy rap sheet suggests that he preferred the drug game, with all its attendant risks, to the dangerous, odiferous, and gory work of processing poultry for low wages.

In his late teens, Quick was a whip-thin, dope-dealing hellion who tore around Laurinburg in a Ford Crown Victoria carrying two Glocks, one with an extended magazine, and his pockets stuffed with sacks of weed, coke, and MDMA. In January 2016, while still a minor, he shot up a house party, hitting three teenagers in the legs with bullets. Police officers responding to a shots-fired call in April 2020 accused him of resisting arrest. Then, on February 11, 2021, sheriff's deputies found him among three men lying wounded or dead in and around a mobile home on Blakely Road with no furniture and walls painted black that had been the scene of a close-range shoot-out among half a dozen men who had convened there for a five-figure drug deal. After Quick recovered from his injuries, he was indicted for the murder of Monterrio Dejuan Taylor, a dreadlocked Atlanta man who had died in the doorway of the trailer with two guns in his hands.

While out on bond for Taylor's murder, Quick sped off from a traffic stop and led officers on a high-speed chase that ended only when his Crown Victoria bottomed out in a field of cotton. The district attorney hit him with another slew of state charges, with spoliation of crops tacked on for good measure. Then Quick was indicted federally for trafficking cocaine and fentanyl. He was in jail awaiting trial in six separate felony cases, any one of which could have put him away for decades or life, when the Department of Justice stuck him with the murders of Lavigne and Dumas.

The cryptically phrased, bare-bones indictment against Quick, which is unusual in that it identifies the victims only by their initials, does not spell out what evidence the FBI has gathered of his guilt. According to a motion filed by a defense lawyer, the government's case comprises sixty-eight thousand records, a terabyte of information including video and audio recordings, but so far none of it has been made public.

Lavigne's mother attended Quick's initial detention hearing. The federal courtroom was surprisingly small, and Judy was only a few feet from the man who prosecutors say shot her son five times in the back. "I glared at him," she said. "He didn't look at me once."

Judy was somewhat troubled by the incongruity between her physically formidable son and a stripling like Quick. "Billy was very well trained," she said. "Many people tried and could never take him out. The Taliban, ISIS, whoever. And then this scrawny little punk of a kid does it?"

Judy was hoping to see Quick convicted, yet there was a sense in which she couldn't help but feel for the defendant, who spoke softly and politely when called upon by the judge. "The sad part is," she said, "he looks like one of the kids I work with at Walmart."

"Given this guy's record," said Ben Boden, Lavigne's high school friend, "I can see why they would pin the murders on him. That being said, I feel like he may just be an easy out for the government. I don't know his skills and abilities to fight and kill someone, but I did know Billy's, and I find it hard to believe that this guy would be able to take him out by himself, even if Billy was intoxicated."

Quick's young age led some, including Dumas's son, to doubt that he could have been responsible. "Why the fuck," Dumas Jr. angrily exclaimed, "would this twenty-year-old be on Fort Bragg hanging out with my father, who's forty-four years old, and William Lavigne, who's also up there in age? That don't sound right. Why is he with a group of Special Forces guys?"

The younger Dumas was even more incredulous the first time he saw a picture of Quick, who appears gaunt to the point of emaciation in his mug shot. "This skinny little motherfucker don't look like he's capable of taking the license plates off a vehicle and then burning it," T.J. said. "What does this boy have to do with anything? How are they so sure that he killed my father? I want to know the proof. It just seems like they're throwing somebody under the fucking bus."

BEFORE HE WAS INDICTED for allegedly killing Lavigne and Dumas, Quick had already been sentenced to fifty-seven months in federal prison for possessing a firearm as a felon. He is not going anywhere anytime soon, and there is no telling how many more times his trial will be delayed. As of February 2025, pretrial motions, responses, and replies are not all due in the case until May 28, 2025. But come what may, even if Quick pleads out or is convicted on the basis of incontrovertible evidence, a great many people in Fayetteville will be left unpersuaded of his guilt.

Courtney Williams, unsurprisingly, did not believe the official story. "I assume that *they* had him killed," she said, meaning Delta Force or corrupt elements within it. "No one will ever be able to prove it," she said, "but I guarantee it's what happened."

She added, "They are so well trained at diversion and misinformation. They are experts at covering things up. I would not put anything past them. They have no morals. They think they have no accountability, because they don't."

For years, Williams's job had been to assemble and curate fake identities under cover of which Delta Force operators entered hostile foreign countries guarded by paranoid counterintelligence agencies, carried out lethal covert missions, and then left without being detected. She knew that the unit was keenly practiced at psychological operations and capable of controlling media coverage of its activities. "The news lies all the time," she said. "We were trained that way in our signature reduction training. The news is fed false information on purpose."

For the past two decades, Delta Force has functioned as a high-tech death squad dedicated to covertly liquidating the male population base of recalcitrant ethnic and tribal groups that resist U.S. military occupation. That rogue members of such a monstrous institution might quietly *put down* one of their own, even on American soil, does not overly strain the imagination. I never uncovered any proof of such, but it did not surprise me that so many people, easily the majority of those I interviewed in Fayetteville and Moore County, reflexively assumed that Lavigne and Dumas were trash taken out to the curb, so to speak, by vigilante operators, if not the Special Forces command itself. Understandable suspicion also lingered around Mark Leshikar's former teammates in A Company, 1st Battalion, 19th Special Forces Group, although no evidence of their involvement ever came to light either.

"When I found out that Billy died," said Jordan Terrell, "I was pretty much convinced that Mark's team did it. Or one of his own unit guys, because he was fucking up quite a bit."

Perhaps the only scenario that local folks were unwilling to entertain and dismissed out of hand, was the one presented by the Department of Justice: that two long-serving special operations soldiers, hardened veterans of many years at war, both of whom trafficked narcotics by the kilo and dealt with international drug cartels, were done in by a reckless delinquent of twenty who lived two counties over and was already facing up to life in prison for unrelated crimes. "I don't believe that for a second," said Terrell, who, like T.J., found the expert sterilization of the crime scene and the firebombing of Dumas's Dodge Ram to be telling details. "It's really hard to burn a truck unless you have some sort of incendiary device," he said. "There's just no way some random gangbanger off the street is going to have that type of wherewithal."

WHILE THE INDICTMENT alleges that Quick "did unlawfully kill" Dumas "with premeditation and malice aforethought," the carefully worded language used to charge him with Lavigne's murder says that he used a firearm to "knowingly cause" the latter's death. A spokesman for the U.S. Attorney's office said that this conspicuous difference in phrasing is down to the legal niceties of federal jurisdiction over the crime of murder.

Murder is a common-law offense usually prosecuted at the county level, in state court. But it is a federal crime, specifically enumerated in the United States Code, to murder someone on U.S. government property. Because Quick allegedly killed Dumas on Fort Bragg, the federal murder statute applied. It did not apply, however, to Quick's alleged killing of Lavigne, because that is believed to have taken place elsewhere and not on government land. So prosecutors charged Quick with a separate federal offense, that of causing the death of a person through the use of a firearm in the course of trafficking drugs, a somewhat convoluted backdoor equivalent to a murder charge.

This may be a legal technicality, but it points to a real oddity in the notion of Quick in the role of the Third Man. If he did kill Lavigne, why would he choose to go onto Fort Bragg, of all places, to dispose of the body? McArthur Lake may be accessible to the public, not fenced in, but one would have thought that a pistol-packing young drug dealer from a small town an hour away would have instinctively kept his distance from a special operations base crawling with security guards and commandos. It's not as if the southern lowlands of North Carolina have any shortage of back-roads reservoirs.

The lake off Manchester Road could only have been Dumas's suggestion, because he lived in the area and knew Fort Bragg well. Assuming that the FBI adopted and built upon CID's theory of the case, they think that Dumas and Quick teamed up to kill Lavigne over a drug debt, then had a falling-out when it came time to sink his body. But that seems strange too, considering Dumas's established propensity to partner with older, more experienced men who had been soldiers or police officers.

Freddie Wayne Huff said that he never met Quick, never heard his name or saw his face until he read of his arrest in the news. "I believe that Tim found out or truly believed that Will was an informant," said Huff. Dumas must have hired Quick to serve as a wingman and as backup in his planned ambush of Lavigne, he said. Dumas and Quick baited Lavigne with four kilos of coke, killed him for being a rat for the FBI, then drove his body out to McArthur Lake to facilitate his sleeping with the fishes. Once the truck got stuck and problems arose lakeside, Quick must have started to look askance at Dumas. It dawned on the hired hit man that there were no witnesses around, and if Dumas were out of the picture, the cocaine would be all his. "Then Quick probably killed Tim and just took the dope," Huff said. "He got $160,000 right there."

But Quick's police record firmly establishes that he favored a

9-millimeter Glock, a firearm that he was charged on three separate occasions with unlawfully possessing. At the trailer park shoot-out in which Quick caught a bullet, the floor of the mobile home was found littered with .40- and .45-caliber handgun casings and brass from an AR-15. Among the gun-toting gangsters he ran with, an assault rifle or high-capacity automatic sidearm was the norm. He was never arrested with a small-caliber ankle gun such as the kind that Huff favored and that Dumas was killed with.

Huff's sentencing hearing was held two months after Quick was indicted. Taking notice of the "huge, large scale" of Huff's trafficking, and the fact that it had involved "guns, threats, robberies, and kidnappings," the judge in the case, the Honorable Catherine C. Eagles, said that federal sentencing guidelines called for a punishment of life in prison. But on account of Huff's "extraordinary cooperation," she sentenced him to a moderately lenient twenty-one years. He was never charged with any crime of violence.

In some of our conversations, Huff was speaking to me over a video call on a contraband cell phone rented from another inmate, and I was able to see him in his prison garb, looking neatly barbered with his hair combed, inside the penitentiary at Fort Dix, a minimum-security correctional institution nested in an Army base in New Jersey. "This place is awesome," he said, accepting a basket of fried fish handed to him by someone off-screen. "This is not a prison." A plentiful variety of hard and soft drugs, he said, were available for purchase on the inside. "The COs right now," he said, referring to corrections officers, "are bringing in huge amounts of cocaine, marijuana, meth."

When we last spoke, Huff had high hopes of getting out of prison well before his 2039 release date, thanks to his continuing collegial contacts with federal law enforcement. "I can move like a UC in here," he said, meaning an undercover cop. He went on to detail a number of sting operations that he said the FBI and DOJ were planning with his participation. "We might be looking at three, four, five, six years off my time," he said. Assuming that the controlled buys went smoothly and the targets were inculpated, "there's a slim possibility that I can be free."

HUFF WAS ONLY one of four people—who were not in contact with each other and had no apparent motive to lie—who told me about the blackmail letter that Dumas supposedly wrote after his expulsion from the military describing a cartel-like structure on Fort Bragg. "It was a community distributing drugs throughout the base," Huff said, an "unspoken, unnamed organization," including Dumas and Lavigne, "that would enforce actions against other soldiers. There's been lots of murders chalked up to that," he said.

Maegan Malloy, one of the CID agents who initially investigated the Lavigne/Dumas case, said that she learned of the existence of the text from a colleague. "Dumas was in the process of writing a book about the cartel," she said. "That was pretty well known."

Dumas made little secret of his plan to pressure the Special Forces command. "He never told me what was in the letter," Brianna Woods recalled, "but he said he was going to write one." She had not really believed that Dumas would dare to extort such a formidable institution. "I didn't think he was that dumb," she said.

"I always knew about the letter," said T.J., who remained certain that his father's murder, which he called "strategic" and "thoroughly planned," was an inside job. "My dad was considered a national threat to public security," he said. "He was writing a book on all them motherfuckers. He was going to find the truth and put it on the news. He threatened them, and they killed him for it. Now they're covering this shit up. And they're doing a great job. His death is not getting solved. It's all being hidden. My dad's killer is still out there. Or killers."

In March 2024, Detective Chris Luper of the Winston-Salem Police Department confirmed that their forensics unit was in possession of Huff's personal computer, three cell phones that had belonged to him, and two thumb drives. One of the thumb drives was full of Mike Sosa's family photos and appeared to have been among the loot scooped up from his house when he was robbed by Huff and Rahain Deriggs disguised as federal marshals. The other was found right where Huff said he stashed it, in the drawer of a minibar in the basement of his house in Lexington.

With Huff's permission, I requested that the police department turn over the thumb drive on the grounds that the case against Huff had been fully adjudicated and the device was his personal property. Somewhat to my surprise, both Winston-Salem and the federal prosecutor who had put Huff behind bars agreed to produce not the drive itself but a digital copy of its contents.

A few days later, Detective Luper told me that he had bad news. When he went to effectuate the digital transfer, he said, he found the drive empty of any files. There was nothing on there. The device was completely blank.

The thumb drive, and the forensic information stored on its circuit boards, remain locked away in the Winston-Salem Police Department's evidence room. No other copy of the letter that Dumas wrote is known to exist.

EPILOGUE

In his 2014 retirement speech, Admiral William McRaven, the former JSOC commander, called the era of the global war on terror the "golden age of special operations." But the wars that won him and his privileged ilk so many encomiums were, for the rest of the nation, an era of cataclysmic abasement. The wars that made SOCOM a budgetary and bureaucratic juggernaut were not worth fighting, in the opinion of a majority of Americans, including supermajorities of combat veterans. In Afghanistan, Iraq, Yemen, Somalia, Libya, Syria, and now Ukraine, the United States failed to achieve its stated ex ante objectives and succeeded only in killing millions of people, displacing tens of millions, squandering trillions of dollars, and making America the great villain of the twenty-first century in the eyes of most of the world. Ten years after McRaven's speech, the iconic archetype of the rugged special operator no longer occupied the same vaunted position in the cultural firmament. The prototypical figure of the bearded commando had taken on a grittier, dirtier, darker cast in the popular imagination.

"You start to see behind the curtain," said the former Delta Force soldier and Army Ranger Tyler Grey to the podcast host Sean "Buck" Rogers, an ex–Green Beret, of his service alongside the CIA in Iraq and Syria. "Dude, this is not what I thought it was," Grey realized. "We're not who I thought we were. We're not doing it for the reasons I thought."

Over time, the suspicion that the Americans might actually be the bad guys "just continues to grow," Grey said, speaking in 2023. "To where now I see why veterans of wars, when they're older, feel a certain way," he said. "I'm starting to be that guy."

Grey went on to say that if he could speak to a young person thinking of joining the military and pursuing a career in special operations, he'd be tempted to tell the kid, "Don't do it. It's a trap. Run, go live your life, man." He added, "Don't trust your recruiter. Don't believe them."

IN 2021, for the first time since polling began, less than half of respondents in the United States said that they placed a great deal of faith in the armed forces, an unprecedented result replicated by follow-up polls in 2022 and 2023. Partly as a result of the military's steep decline in public esteem, all four service branches missed their recruiting targets in 2022 and fared little better in 2023 and 2024. The Army raised the maximum enlistment age, temporarily dropped the requirement of a high school diploma, streamlined the naturalization process for immigrants, overlooked previously disqualifying hand and neck tattoos, and offered signing bonuses of up to $50,000, yet still fell the furthest short.

BETWEEN JANUARY 2017 and September 2022, a total of 15,293 active-duty service members suffered drug overdoses, and 322 of those were fatal, according to statistics compiled by the Department of Defense. The data showed that Fort Bragg had far more overdoses than any other military base, in both absolute and per capita terms, and that Fort Bragg soldiers were significantly more likely to overdose and die than the average American.

PRESIDENT JOE BIDEN cut the United States' losses in Afghanistan. But the myopic, blithely confident, and pathetically inept national security officials who ran his administration otherwise racked up a foreign policy record as execrable as any of his recent predecessors, provoking and then losing a proxy war with Russia over Ukraine that was as pointless as it was bloody, presiding over apartheid Israel's unspeakable genocide in Gaza, and—in the catastrophic finale of Iraq War III—causing the remnants of the Syrian state to fall to an affiliate of al-Qaeda notorious for chopping people's heads off and stoning women to death.

THE SOCOM WAR crimes review that Biden had ordered days after his inauguration, which *The New York Times* had predicted, too optimistically, might cause "seismic repercussions in the special operations community," produced no such dramatic results. The report, quietly issued by the Pentagon's inspector general later that same year, turned out to be a tedious and legalistic review of whether SOCOM had in place proper policies and procedures for personnel to report war crimes up the chain of command. Its only recommendations were minor tweaks to obscure administrative regulations.

THERE WERE AT least twenty-four murders involving Fort Bragg soldiers between 2020 and 2024. Many remained unsolved years after the fact.

ON MAY 3, 2024, a utility worker named Ramzan Daraev, a Muslim immigrant from Chechnya with a permit to work in the United States, was conducting a survey of high-speed internet cables in Moore County, and in order to photograph a power pole located on a utilities easement off Dowd Road in Carthage, went onto private property owned by Lieutenant Colonel Galen Legrand Huss, a Special Forces officer in command of a training battalion at the JFK Special Warfare Center and School. Colonel Huss got into an argument with Daraev, who was unarmed and carrying no tools, then pulled out a gun and shot him four times: once in the hand, once in the face, and twice in the back. Moore County's district attorney promptly determined that it was a case of justified homicide.

ON JANUARY 1, 2025, at a quarter past three in the morning, before New Year's Eve revelers had gone to bed, a former paratrooper in the 82nd Airborne Division named Shamsud-Din Jabbar plowed a rented pickup truck flying an ISIS flag into a New Year's Eve crowd gathered in New Orleans's French Quarter, killing fourteen people on Bourbon Street and injuring more than thirty before he was shot down by police. Jabbar, aged forty-two, a native of Texas who was raised Christian and converted to Islam, had been an IT technician in the Army and, like Enrique Roman-Martinez, an HR specialist.

Seven hours later, a Tesla Cybertruck parked in front of the Trump Hotel in Las Vegas exploded in a fiery ball of flaming debris. In the charred driver's seat, police found the dead body of Master Sergeant Matthew Livelsberger, an active-duty Green Beret in the 10th Special Forces Group who had deployed to Afghanistan five times during his lengthy military career, as well as to Tajikistan, Ukraine, Georgia, and the Congo. Authorities said that Livelsberger, aged thirty-seven, had shot himself in the head just before he detonated the bomb. A few bystanders were injured, but no one else was killed. "I needed to cleanse my mind of the brothers I've lost and relieve myself of the burden of the lives I took," Livelsberger, an enthusiastic Trump supporter, wrote in a note made public by the FBI. "Our soldiers are done fighting wars without end states or clear objectives."

Both Jabbar and Livelsberger were former Fort Bragg soldiers. Both served in Afghanistan in 2009, and both lived in Fayetteville around 2012. The sheriff of Clark County, Nevada, told reporters that the "very strange similarities" between the two and the uncanny joint timing of their mindless acts of domestic terrorism, were probably just a coincidence. ·

PRESIDENT DONALD TRUMP, whose malignant and maladroit leadership during his first term in office had precipitated the crisis of ethics in special operations, both at home and overseas, was sworn in to a second term on January 20, 2025. For a national security adviser, Trump chose Michael Waltz, a thuggish warmongering dullard who holds the distinction of being the first Green Beret elected to Congress. Aside from being the first former Special Forces officer to hold a seat in the House of Representatives, Mike Waltz was a wealthy man. He made tens of millions of dollars running a private company that trained special operations units of the drug-trafficking Afghan army. Waltz, a passionate advocate for war with China, has said that he expects the GWOT to last a hundred years.

For a secretary of defense, Trump chose Pete Hegseth, a dipsomaniacal former National Guard officer and opportunistic ex–Fox News host. Hegseth, the author of *The War on Warriors*, was known for his operator-style tattoos as well as his vociferous on-air defense of the most toxic figures in the special operations community, including unrepentant murderers like Eddie Gallagher and Mathew Golsteyn. One of his first acts in office, carried out on February 10, 2025, was to direct the Army to change the name of Fort Liberty back to Fort Bragg. "That's right," Hegseth said, holding up a copy of the signed order. "Bragg is back."

ACKNOWLEDGMENTS

This book exists thanks to Allison Lorentzen, my editor at Viking Books, who heard me talking about Fort Bragg on a podcast and got in touch to suggest the idea. Allison guided the project from inception to completion with a rare mix of creative vision and professional diligence, and her revisions to the manuscript were unfailingly thoughtful, intelligent, and astute. I am deeply grateful to her and her equally able colleague Camille LeBlanc.

My agent, Rafe Sagalyn, read my reporting on Fort Bragg in *Rolling Stone* and also encouraged me to develop the story into a book. I am indebted to Rafe and his colleague Dan Kirschen not only for their advocacy but also their frequent feedback on creative aspects of the project.

I am thankful to Sean Woods, my longtime editor at *Rolling Stone*, for his support and encouragement over the course of three magazine articles about Fort Bragg, and to Jason Fine, director of content development at *Rolling Stone*, with whom I consulted closely as the story unfolded. Thanks also to *Rolling Stone* editors Phoebe Neidl and Patrick Reis.

Kelsey Baker, a graduate student at Northwestern University's Medill School of Journalism and a reserve officer in the U.S. Marine Corps, provided invaluable research assistance and also helped with interviews in Fayetteville. Julia Gledhill, a researcher at the Stimson Center in Washington, DC, also provided research assistance on especially thorny topics such as the DEA's heroin tracing programs and federal court cases against alleged Taliban drug traffickers. Ahmed Jallow, a journalist at NC Newsline who shared my interest in the career of Freddie Wayne Huff, collaborated with me in conducting interviews with federal prisoners, notably Jaime Rosado.

In my day-to-day reporting, I often relied on articles published by the *Fayetteville Observer*, especially the work of Rachael Riley, who was on the Fort Bragg beat. Jack Murphy, a former Green Beret and a podcaster popular in the special operations community, was the first to report on the suspicious circumstances around the death of Mark Leshikar. Jack and I occasionally compared notes and swapped tips as we separately pursued the story, and I am grateful for the leads that he provided.

Special thanks to Brace Belden, Liz Franczak, and "Yung Chomsky" of the *TrueAnon* podcast, who hosted me on their show several times to discuss events at Fort Bragg and related topics such as the history of the Los Zetas cartel in Mexico and the Afghan heroin trade. Sincere thanks is due as well to Mark Ames and John Dolan, a.k.a. Gary Brecher, of the *Radio War Nerd* podcast, and Will Menaker, Felix Biederman, Matt Christman, and Chris Wade of the *Chapo Trap House* podcast, for providing a platform to discuss my reporting on Fort Bragg.

Senator Edward Markey of Massachusetts was instrumental in obligating the Department of Defense to release comprehensive data on overdoses across the armed forces, which greatly enlarged the depth of my reporting. I am grateful to Senator Markey and his press secretary, Ahmad Ali, for taking the problem of overdoses in the military seriously and for spearheading the passage of the Department of Defense Overdose Data Act of 2023. Thanks also to Senator Elizabeth Warren of Massachusetts, who co-sponsored the bill.

The Yaddo retreat for artists and writers in Saratoga Springs, New York, provided a six-week residency in which I was able to complete an early draft of the manuscript. The New America foundation in Washington, DC, provided a generous grant as well as a like-minded community of writers and documentarians. Many thanks to the Future Security Initiative at Arizona State University for sponsoring my fellowship at New America.

ACKNOWLEDGMENTS

Most of all, I am grateful to the family members of soldiers who died at Fort Bragg who took the time to speak to a reporter in the midst of their grief and loss. Mark Leshikar's mother, Tammy Mabey, and his sister, Nicole Rick, were the first to open my eyes to the sorry state of affairs that prevailed at Fort Bragg in early 2021, and without their honesty, moral clarity, and generosity with their time, this exposé would have never come to fruition. The same goes for Billy Lavigne's mother and father, his childhood friend Ben Boden, Enrique Roman-Martinez's sister Griselda, Sarah Lewis's mother, Rhonda Phillips, and her aunt, Tammy De Mirza.

As time went on, I interviewed many other bereaved family members who had the courage to speak out, with the result that there are too many to name here. It is my hope that this book will contribute to a reformation of the armed forces and a fundamental rethinking of American foreign policy, so that in the future, fewer soldiers' loved ones will have to suffer through the same grief and pain that they have endured with poise and grace.

NOTES

Chapter 1: I Kill People for a Living

3 where both men were stationed: Leshikar was not stationed at Fort Bragg as an active-duty soldier but told his family that he had a desk job there working for the Special Forces, an assertion that USASOC refused to confirm or deny.

4 that was freely distributed: A Pentagon spokeswoman, Heather J. Hagan, told me in an email sent February 7, 2023, that tramadol is no less controlled in the military than in a civilian setting. But there's no shortage of anecdotal evidence of loose prescribing practices around tramadol. See, for example, David Philipps, *Alpha: Eddie Gallagher and the War for the Soul of the Navy SEALs* (Crown, 2021), 158–61, 198.

7 defined under federal law: 50 U.S.C. § 3093(e).

16 he said to Lavigne: The quotations attributed to Mark Leshikar and Billy Lavigne in this passage were actually spoken by Jordan Terrell, who heard from Lavigne a paraphrased version of the argument in the car on the way home from Disney World.

Chapter 2: They Do What They Want

22 The field manual: Army Field Manual No. 21-150, *Combatives*, 5-17 through 5-30.

Chapter 3: Fayettenam

34 Delta Force became operational: Details on the formation of Delta Force and the career of Col. Charles Beckwith come from a one-page biography published by the Special Forces Association, available at www.swcs.mil/Portals/111/sf_beckwith.pdf.

34 a catastrophic debacle: Note that failed hostage rescue attempts would continue to dog Delta Force throughout its existence. The Joint Special Operations Command's ratio of successes to failures when it comes to rescuing hostages is no better than fifty-fifty. See Sean Naylor, *Relentless Strike: The Secret History of Joint Special Operations Command* (St. Martin's Press, 2015), 146, 371, 383, 403–5, 412–13, 425–26, 435–36.

35 There was no ceremony: Naylor, *Relentless Strike*, 3–14.

36 the official story: Gen. Stanley McChrystal, the JSOC commander during the Iraq War, repeats the Operation Eagle Claw origin story several times in his memoir. Stanley McChrystal, *My Share of the Task* (Portfolio, 2013), 23–25, 34–36, 45, 51, 60, 179, 270.

36 The Senate Select Committee on Intelligence: Senate Resolution 400, May 19, 1976.

36 Its counterpart in the House: House Resolution 658, July 14, 1977.

37 was activated four months later: Denise Goolsby, "Palm Springs Man Was Army Delta Force Co-Creator," *Desert Sun*, July 14, 2016.

37 The Intelligence Oversight Act: Senate Bill 2284, 96th Cong. (1979–80).

37 **Congressional regulation of covert action:** The Intelligence Authorization Act of 1991, for example, exempted covert operations carried out by the Department of Defense from the requirement of a presidential finding if the secret missions were defined as "traditional military activities" connected to "ongoing" or "anticipated" hostilities. Mark Mazzetti, *The Way of the Knife: The CIA, a Secret Army, and a War at the Ends of the Earth* (Penguin Press, 2013), 77.

37 **Colombia, Haiti, and Grenada:** Naylor, *Relentless Strike*, 23–25, 46, 53, 57.

38 **A classified White House memorandum:** Mazzetti, *Way of the Knife*, 57.

38 **the memo authorized killing:** A declassified, partially redacted copy of the executive order, National Security Decision Directive 138, can be viewed on the website of the Reagan Library at reaganlibrary.gov/public/archives/reference/scanned-nsdds/nsdd138.pdf.

38 *The New York TImes* **belatedly:** Jeff Gerth and Philip Taubman, "U.S. Military Creates Secret Units for Use in Sensitive Tasks Abroad," *New York Times*, June 8, 1984.

38 **"covert operations in Central America":** Gary Webb, *Dark Alliance: The CIA, the Contras, and the Crack Cocaine Explosion* (Seven Stories Press, 2014); Alfred W. McCoy, *The Politics of Heroin: CIA Complicity in the Global Drug Trade* (Lawrence Hill Books, 2003), 488–500; Peter Dale Scott and Jonathan Marshall, *Cocaine Politics: Drugs, Armies, and the CIA in Central America* (University of California Press, 1992), 26–33, 151.

40 **members of the secret society:** Alexandra Robbins, *Secrets of the Tomb: Skull and Bones, the Ivy League, and the Hidden Paths of Power* (Little, Brown, 2002), 174.

41 **"It's crazy to shoot people":** Don Terry, "Standoff in Texas Goes on After Cult Chief's Broadcast," *New York Times*, March 7, 1993.

41 **heat-generating gas canisters:** David Stout, "F.B.I. Chief Says He Supports an Outside Inquiry on Waco," *New York Times*, Sept. 1, 1999.

41 **Declassified SOCOM documents:** Philip Shenon, "Documents on Waco Point to a Close Commando Role," *New York Times*, Sept. 5, 1999.

41 **Photos in the custody:** Jim Yardley, "Tenacity of 2 Played a Role in Reviving Inquiry on Waco," *New York Times*, Sept. 2, 1999.

41 **the *Times* ran an editorial:** Charles McCarry, "Waco, Forever Unresolved," *New York Times*, Sept. 5, 1999.

42 *Charlie Wilson's War:* George Crile, *Charlie Wilson's War* (Grove Press, 2003).

42 **Ali Abdul Saoud Mohamed:** For a full-length book on Ali Mohamed, see Peter Lance, *Triple Cross: How Bin Laden's Chief Security Adviser Penetrated the CIA, the FBI and the Green Berets and Paved the Way for 9/11* (Regan, 2006).

42 **fluent in Arabic, English, and Hebrew:** Lawrence Wright, *The Looming Tower: Al-Qaeda and the Road to 9/11* (Knopf, 2006), 204.

42 **born in 1952:** Combating Terrorism Center at West Point, "Ali Mohamed: A Biographical Sketch," 1, ctc.westpoint.edu/a-profile-of-ali-mohamed.

42 **attending a program:** Pete Blaber, *The Mission, the Men, and Me: Lessons from a Former Delta Force Commander* (Berkley Caliber, 2008), 182. Other sources say that Mohamed completed the Fort Bragg exchange program in 1981. See, for example, Tom Hays and Sharon Theimer, "In a Life of Double Crosses, Egyptian Worked with Green Berets and bin Laden," Associated Press, Dec. 26, 2001.

42 **he was approached by the CIA:** Combating Terrorism Center, "Ali Mohamed," 2.

42 **soon became an asset:** Peter Dale Scott, *The Road to 9/11: Wealth, Empire, and the Future of America* (University of California Press, 2007), 153.

42 **he joined Egyptian Islamic Jihad:** Hays and Theimer, "In a Life of Double Crosses, Egyptian Worked with Green Berets and bin Laden"; Scott, *Road to 9/11*, 152.

43 **with CIA sponsorship:** Combating Terrorism Center, "Ali Mohamed," 3; Scott, *Road to 9/11*, 153, 338n14; Wright, *Looming Tower*, 205.

43 **"essential to the furtherance":** 50 U.S.C. § 403h.

43 **marrying an American woman:** Combating Terrorism Center, "Ali Mohamed," 3; Wright, *Looming Tower*, 205; Blaber, *The Mission, the Men, and Me*, 183.

43 joined the Special Forces: Hays and Theimer, "In a Life of Double Crosses, Egyptian Worked with Green Berets and bin Laden"; Wright, *Looming Tower*, 205; Blaber, *The Mission, the Men, and Me*, 183.

43 an Army record: Combating Terrorism Center, "Ali Mohamed," 4.

43 repeatedly traveled to Afghanistan: Blaber, *The Mission, the Men, and Me*, 183–84; Wright, *Looming Tower*, 205–6; Scott, *Road to 9/11*, 153; Combating Terrorism Center, "Ali Mohamed," 3–7.

43 the al-Kifah Refugee Center: Combating Terrorism Center, "Ali Mohamed," 5; Scott, *Road to 9/11*, 155–58; Wright, *Looming Tower*, 205–7.

43 religious schools known as madrassas: Steve Coll, *Ghost Wars: The Secret History of the CIA, Afghanistan, and bin Laden, from the Soviet Invasion to September 10, 2001* (Penguin Press, 2004), 86.

43 supplied hundreds of millions: Crile, *Charlie Wilson's War*.

43 had roads built: Coll, *Ghost Wars*, 85–88.

43 Gulbuddin Hekmatyar and Nasim Akhundzada: McCoy, *Politics of Heroin*, 462, 475, 478–81, 484–87, 514; McChrystal, *My Share of the Task*, 318–19; James Rupert and Steve Coll, "U.S. Declines to Probe Afghan Drug Trade," *Washington Post*, May 12, 1990.

44 kidnapping and rape of children: Chris Mondloch, "Bacha Bazi: An Afghan Tragedy," *Foreign Policy*, Oct. 28, 2013.

44 The Taliban forbade: Amir Shah, "Taliban Leader Outlaws Poppy Growing in Afghanistan," Associated Press, July 28, 2000; Barbara Crossette, "Taliban's Eradication of Poppies Is Convulsing Opium Market," *New York Times*, June 13, 2001; Mondloch, "Bacha Bazi" (discussing Taliban's outlawing of "boy play").

44 "the most dramatic event": Crossette, "Taliban's Eradication of Poppies Is Convulsing Opium Market."

44 transferred from active duty: Wright, *Looming Tower*, 180; Blaber, *The Mission, the Men, and Me*, 187; Combating Terrorism Center, "Ali Mohamed," 7.

44 fifty-eight trips abroad: Andrew Martin and Michael J. Berens, "Terrorists Evolved in US," *Chicago Tribune*, Dec. 11, 2001; Combating Terrorism Center, "Ali Mohamed," 18.

44 "The manuals were issued": Blaber, *The Mission, the Men, and Me*, 182.

45 taught the core leaders: Statement of Patrick J. Fitzgerald, U.S. Attorney, Northern District of Illinois, Before the National Commission on Terrorist Attacks upon the United States, June 16, 2004; Scott, *Road to 9/11*, 151–59; Blaber, *The Mission, the Men, and Me*, 188; Wright, *Looming Tower*, 206.

45 He personally trained Osama bin Laden: Interview with Jack Cloonan, *Frontline*, PBS, July 13, 2005.

45 bin Laden's whole security detail: Hays and Theimer, "In a Life of Double Crosses, Egyptian Worked with Green Berets and bin Laden."

45 bin Laden's house in Peshawar: Combating Terrorism Center, "Ali Mohamed," 10.

45 He literally wrote: Wright, *Looming Tower*, 205; Scott, *Road to 9/11*, 154; Dina Temple-Raston, *The Jihad Next Door: The Lackawanna Six and Rough Justice in an Age of Terror* (PublicAffairs, 2007), 84–85. One of the only native speakers of Arabic in the military, who was called upon by the FBI to help translate the manual, writes in his pseudonymous memoir that the job was "the easiest thing ever" because he had already memorized much of the material while in Special Forces training at Fort Bragg. Adam Gamal with Kelly Kennedy, *The Unit: My Life Fighting Terrorists as One of America's Most Secret Military Operatives* (St. Martin's Press, 2024), 111.

45 money from an unknown source: Combating Terrorism Center, "Ali Mohamed," 8.

45 phone calls were monitored: Combating Terrorism Center, "Ali Mohamed," 14.

45 released at the behest: Scott, *Road to 9/11*, 152–53; Combating Terrorism Center, "Ali Mohamed," 13.

45 took Ali Mohamed out: Lance, *Triple Cross*, 274–77.

45 the alias Abu Osama: Combating Terrorism Center, "Ali Mohamed," 10.

45 one of the al-Qaeda conspirators: Scott, *Road to 9/11*, 157; Wright, *Looming Tower*, 225–26.

45 anonymized federal court proceedings: Hays and Theimer, "In a Life of Double Crosses, Egyptian Worked with Green Berets and bin Laden"; Scott, *Road to 9/11*, 157–58.

45 bombed the World Trade Center: Hays and Theimer, "In a Life of Double Crosses, Egyptian Worked with Green Berets and bin Laden"; Scott, *Road to 9/11*, 139, 152, 160, 347n20; Combating Terrorism Center, "Ali Mohamed," 6, n40.

45 Abd al-Rahim al-Nashiri: Interview with Cloonan, *Frontline*.

46 employ of Bandar bin Sultan: Elsa Walsh, "The Prince," *New Yorker*, March 24, 2003; Lawrence Wright, "The Twenty-Eight Pages," *New Yorker*, Sept. 9, 2014; Catherine Herridge, "Newly Released Video Shows 9/11 Hijackers with Alleged Saudi Intelligence Operative," CBS News, April 27, 2022; Daniel Benjamin and Steven Simon, "New 9/11 Evidence Points to Deep Saudi Complicity," *The Atlantic*, May 20, 2024.

46 writes in his 2008 memoir: Blaber, *The Mission, the Men, and Me*, 190–91.

46 Bush signed a secret order: Mazzetti, *Way of the Knife*, 9.

47 heroin processing still flourished: McCoy, *Politics of Heroin*, 515, 518–21.

47 war criminals, ex-communists, smugglers: Craig Whitlock, *The Afghanistan Papers: A Secret History of the War* (Simon & Schuster, 2022), 20.

47 "The guard on my right": Blaber, *The Mission, the Men, and Me*, 207.

47 first official acts: The English-language news archives contain some diametrically contradictory reports about the legalization of poppy cultivation after the Taliban's fall, but U.S. government sources and the most well-informed reporters hold that the new Afghan regime immediately overturned the Taliban's prohibition on planting drug crops. See, for example, DEA National Drug Threat Assessment 2004, 67 ("The Taliban poppy ban was lifted in late 2001. As a result, Afghanistan reclaimed its position . . . as the leading heroin-producing country in the world."); Whitlock, *Afghanistan Papers*, 135 ("As soon as the U.S. military invaded and removed the Taliban from power in 2001, Afghan farmers resumed sowing their poppy seeds.").

48 writer for the Norfolk *Virginian-Pilot*: Dannis O'Brian, "'Fatalville, USA'— Fayetteville, NC, Home of Fort Bragg, Has Tried Time and Time Again to Shake Its Tough-Town Image. Last Summer's Slayings Didn't Help," *Virginian-Pilot* (Norfolk, Va.), Oct. 10, 2002.

48 She described Fayetteville: Catherine Lutz, *Homefront: A Military City and the American 20th Century* (Beacon Press, 2001), 4, 100.

48 Andrea Floyd's mother: Estes Thompson, "Military Wife Slayings Spur Review," Associated Press Online, July 26, 2002 (quoting the *Review* newspaper of Alliance, Ohio).

48 "A source close to members": Mark Benjamin and Dan Olmsted, "Third Bragg Soldier Took Malaria Drug," United Press International, Aug. 17, 2002.

49 the spooky effects: Mark Benjamin and Dan Olmsted, "Ft. Bragg Suspect Said to Be Delusional," United Press International, Aug. 31, 2002.

49 commander of a Green Beret: Benjamin and Olmsted, "Third Bragg Soldier Took Malaria Drug."

49 *Vanity Fair* article: Maureen Orth, "Fort Bragg's Deadly Summer," *Vanity Fair*, Dec. 2002.

Chapter 4: Don't Call Me Your Husband

50 During the very same week: Thomas E. Ricks, "U.S., Britain Bomb 5 Iraqi Sites," *Washington Post*, Feb. 17, 2001.

51 some 750,000 eye surgeries: Military Health System, "For Thousands of Troops, Eye Surgery Is Key to Vision Readiness," press release, Feb. 10, 2022.

53 International inspectors searched Iraq: Steve Coll, *The Achilles Trap* (New York: Penguin Press, 2024), 450, 458.

54 the reporter aptly described: Michael Gilbert, "As Targets Go, Cavalry Prefers to Be Moving," *News Tribune*, Dec. 24, 2003.

55 Christmas Eve 2003: The KIA were Sgt. Benjamin W. Biskie, Cpt. Christopher F. Soelzer, and Maj. Christopher J. Splinter. "More U.S. Troops Killed," *San Luis Obispo Tribune*, Dec. 27, 2003.

55 Insurgents picked off: The nine KIA were Pfc. Nathan P. Brown, Pfc. Shawn C. Edwards, Spc. Michael C. Campbell, Pfc. Samuel R. Bowen, Spc. Joseph M. Garmback Jr., Pfc. Collier E. Barcus, Sgt. Robert E. Colvin Jr., Spc. Sonny G. Sampler, and Spc. William R. Emanuel IV.

55 Eight more soldiers: Sgt. Jeremy J. Fischer, Sgt. First Class Linda Ann Tarango-Griess, Sgt. Tatjana Reed, Pfc. Torey J. Dantzler, Sgt. Armando Hernandez, Spc. Anthony J. Dixon, Pfc. Ryan A. Martin, and Lt. Charles L. Wilkins III.

55 a complex battle: Matthew Cox, "'They Weren't Going to Get This Bird.' Kiowa Down, Pilots Injured. Stryker Troops Resolve to Rescue Fliers and Keep Helo out of Enemy Hands," *Army Times*, Nov. 22, 2004.

55 took fire in Mosul: U.S. Department of Defense Information, Multi-National Forces, Iraqi National Guard Continue Operations in Tal Afar, Sept. 10, 2004.

55 the fifth of Lavigne's comrades: Michael Gilbert, "Accidental Explosion Kills Two U.S. Soldiers; Five Injured: One Victim Was with Stryker Brigade," *News Tribune*, Feb. 10, 2004; Carol Ann Alaimo, "Buena High Mourns Alum Killed in Iraq," *Arizona Daily Star*, Feb. 19, 2004; "American Deaths," *Boston Globe*, Sept. 18, 2004; "Stryker Officer Was Just Days from Homecoming," Associated Press State and Local Wire, Oct. 13, 2004.

Chapter 5: Pipe Hitters

58 "The hell that is Iraq?": Daniel Immerwahr, "Everything in Hand," *New Yorker*, June 17, 2024.

58 unwelcome media scrutiny: Campbell Brown, "New Front in Iraq Detainee Abuse Scandal?," NBC News, May 20, 2004.

59 The giant hangar: McChrystal, *My Share of the Task*, 150–51.

59 I was one of them: I was a private first class in the 277th Engineer Company, a U.S. Army Reserve unit out of San Antonio, Texas, that was mobilized to serve in Iraq and attached to the active-duty 84th Engineer Battalion out of Schofield Barracks, Hawaii. Our deployment lasted from December 2003 until March 2005, by which time I had been promoted to sergeant.

59 "For security and secrecy": McChrystal, *My Share of the Task*, 150.

59 On just one day: "Bloodshed in Iraq Continues," Associated Press, June 30, 2006.

60 accompanied by Ali Mohamed: McChrystal, *My Share of the Task*, 48. "Only years later did I learn of his subsequent membership in al-Qaeda," McChrystal writes of Mohamed, neglecting to mention that the Egyptian-born U.S. citizen was already by then a member of Egyptian Islamic Jihad, a close associate of Ayman al-Zawahiri's, and a CIA asset.

60 few foreign fighters: McChrystal, *My Share of the Task*, 171, 175.

60 most came from neighboring Syria: Michael Vickers, *By All Means Available: Memoirs of a Life in Intelligence, Special Operations, and Strategy* (Knopf, 2023), 343.

60 the term "al-Qaeda in Iraq": Abu Musab al-Zarqawi's group later adopted the name al-Qaeda in Iraq, but by that time JSOC had been using the term for nine months. McChrystal, *My Share of the Task*, 161.

61 Abu Musab al-Zarqawi: Stanley McChrystal himself admits that many analysts doubted that Zarqawi was in Iraq. McChrystal, *My Share of the Task*, 138. For background on the U.S. military's propaganda campaign to exaggerate Zarqawi's importance, including in making the Bush administration's case for war, see Thomas E. Ricks, "Military Plays Up Role of Zarqawi," *Washington Post*, April 10, 2006; Julian Borger, Richard Norton-Taylor, and Michael Howard, "Threat of War: Interrogations: Al-Qaida and Iraq: How Strong Is the Evidence?," *The Guardian*, Jan. 30, 2003.

61 McChrystal and his aides redefined al-Qaeda: McChrystal, *My Share of the Task*, 113–15. There might have been some communications between al-Zarqawi and the original al-Qaeda, and a tentative affiliation existed for a time, but Osama bin Laden's group soon disavowed Zarqawi for his extreme tactics.

61 In his memoir, McChrystal admits: McChrystal, *My Share of the Task*, 175.

61 In his memoir, Vickers recalls: Vickers, *By All Means Available*, 332–48.

62 Once limited to former regime officials: Vickers, *By All Means Available*, 337 ("We needed to take apart the enemy's network, not just his command-and-control nodes.").

62 Vickers calls this covert war: Vickers, *By All Means Available*, 334.

62 Vickers and McChrystal describe as "industrial": McChrystal, *My Share of the Task*, 179; Vickers, *By All Means Available*, 228. The press soon picked up the same terminology to describe the assassination program in Iraq. Gretchen Gavett, "What Is the Secretive U.S. Kill/Capture Campaign?," *Frontline*, PBS, June 17, 2011; Nick Turse, "The Secret War in 120 Countries," *The Nation*, Aug. 4, 2011.

62 ten per day: Vickers, *By All Means Available*, 336; McChrystal, *My Share of the Task*, 145.

62 Find, Fix, Finish, Exploit, Analyze, and Disseminate: Vickers, *By All Means Available*, 233 (borrowing language from McChrystal); Naylor, *Relentless Strike*, 265.

62 adoption of cell phones in Iraq: Naylor, *Relentless Strike*, 263, 309.

63 National Security Agency: Naylor, *Relentless Strike*, 263–65; Vickers, *By All Means Available*, 338–39.

63 a startling admission: McChrystal, *My Share of the Task*, 207.

63 "We were not death squads": McChrystal, *My Share of the Task*, 191.

63 fierce Kurdish mercenaries: Naylor, *Relentless Strike*, 258–59.

63 hundreds of thousands of war dead: The most conservative count of Iraq's war dead is 209,982, a compilation made by the Iraq Body Count project, which counted only named and confirmed victims of the war. *The Lancet* estimated the scale of Iraqi civilian deaths at more than 600,000. A poll by ORB International, which relied on telephone surveys of the Iraqi people, put the estimate at more than 1 million.

64 disguising themselves as Iraqis: Naylor, *Relentless Strike*, 261, 317.

64 They posed as: Naylor, *Relentless Strike*, 63, 75, 206–7, 317.

64 female support soldiers: Lt. Col. James Reese (Ret.), interview by author, July 17, 2018, Raleigh, N.C. For more on the role of female soldiers in Delta Force operations, see Naylor, *Relentless Strike*, 62, 66–67.

64 copied the enemy's tactics: Naylor, *Relentless Strike*, 306–8.

64 When they did wear uniforms: My description of the quasi-military attire worn by Delta Force operators is based on a review of numerous Iraq-era photos posted to Instagram in the early 2020s by the former Delta Force soldiers Jesse Boettcher and Chris VanSant.

66 "kept Ambien close at hand": McChrystal, *My Share of the Task*, 250.

66 McRaven also writes: William McRaven, *Sea Stories: My Life in Special Operations* (Grand Central Publishing, 2019), 201.

66 Attacks on foreign troops in Iraq fell: "'08 Saw Shift in Iraq, Afghan Troop Death Tolls," Associated Press, Dec. 31, 2008.

66 a truce that Iran brokered: Ali Akbar Dareini, "Officials Confirm Iran's Role in Brokering Truce Between Iraqi Government, Shiite Cleric," Associated Press, April 5, 2008.

66 alliance with Iraqi organized crime: Both Stanley McChrystal and Michael Vickers acknowledge that the Sunni tribes that allied with the United States against "AQI" were motivated by the desire to protect their smuggling routes, which the insurgents had suppressed. McChrystal, *My Share of the Task*, 241; Vickers, *By All Means Available*, 340.

66 "major strategic victory": Jennifer Loven, "Bush Touts Surge for 'Major Strategic Victory,'" *Chicago Sun-Times*, March 20, 2008.

67 nine times more heroin: According to the DEA's National Drug Intelligence Center, Afghanistan produced 630 metric tons of potential pure heroin in 2009, while the rest of the world combined produced 77 metric tons. Similarly, Craig Whitlock reports that at the close of 2007, Afghanistan was producing 90 percent of the world supply of heroin. Whitlock, *Afghanistan Papers*, 110.

67 **frequently too stoned:** Whitlock, *Afghanistan Papers*, 98.

Chapter 6: The Killing Fest

71 **redoubling of the pace:** Naylor, *Relentless Strike*, 354.

71 **rumored heroin addict:** Whitlock, *Afghanistan Papers*, 210.

71 **on the payroll of the CIA:** Matthew Rosenberg, "With Bags of Cash, C.I.A. Seeks Influence in Afghanistan," *New York Times*, April 28, 2013.

71 **Some of the top narco-bosses:** Kim Sengupta, "American Rift with Karzai Worsens over 'Drug-Dealer' Ally," *The Independent*, Aug. 29, 2009 (discussing Muhammed Fahim); McCoy, *Politics of Heroin*, 521–24 (discussing Hazrat Ali, Rashid Dostum, and Gul Agha Sherzai); Dexter Filkins, Mark Mazzetti, and James Risen, "Brother of Afghan Leader Said to Be Paid by C.I.A.," *New York Times*, Oct. 27, 2009 (revealing that Ahmed Wali Karzai was also a CIA asset). See also Whitlock, *Afghanistan Papers*, 123 (discussing Gul Agha Sherzai), 126 (Muhammed Fahim), 176 (Ahmed Wali Karzai).

72 **"durable drug cartel":** McChrystal, *My Share of the Task*, 319–20.

72 **"where he and his men stole boys":** McChrystal, *My Share of the Task*, 320.

72 **"corrupt and despised warlords":** McChrystal, *My Share of the Task*, 282.

72 **"a diverse taxonomy of groups":** McChrystal, *My Share of the Task*, 308. See also Michael Hastings, *The Operators: The Wild and Terrifying Inside Story of America's War in Afghanistan* (Plume, 2012), 97 (stating that the Taliban was not a hard-and-fast category but "a catchall phrase for local people who don't want foreigners in their valley"). See also Whitlock, *Afghanistan Papers*, 20–23 (reporting that the United States never knew who the "bad guys" were, and were so confused that the term "Taliban" had no real meaning).

72 **McChrystal pushed JSOC teams:** Naylor, *Relentless Strike*, 356, 359, 365.

72 **The pace of night raids:** Eric Schmitt and Richard A. Oppel Jr., "Elite U.S. Force Expands Hunt in Afghanistan," *New York Times*, Dec. 27, 2009 (stating that the pace of night raids rose dramatically); Naylor, *Relentless Strike*, 355 (describing a raid in which about 120 Afghans were killed), 365 (describing operations in which whole villages were leveled); Whitlock, *Afghanistan Papers*, 168 (describing Azizabad raid, which killed dozens of children).

73 **The error rate:** Naylor, *Relentless Strike*, 362, 367.

73 **Violent deaths in Afghanistan rose:** Michael Hastings, "The Runaway General," *Rolling Stone*, June 22, 2010.

73 **stop reporting body counts:** McChrystal, *My Share of the Task*, 313.

73 **scenes of him handing down tough truths:** See, for example, C. J. Chivers and Dexter Filkins, "Allies Attacking Big Taliban Haven in Afghan South," *New York Times*, Feb. 13, 2010; Hastings, "Runaway General."

73 **black-and-white video:** The video can be viewed at youtube.com/watch?v=itAuYiy PUqA.

74 **WikiLeaks released a document:** Cody Derespina, "WikiLeaks Releases 'Entire Hacking Capacity of the CIA,'" Fox News, March 7, 2017.

75 **How the CIA located bin Laden:** According to the Hollywood version of events, as recounted in the film *Zero Dark Thirty*, tough-minded CIA agents, including a red-headed girlboss played by Jessica Chastain, tortured Ammar al-Baluchi, a Pakistani citizen held at the Guantánamo Bay prison camp, until he gave up the key information that led to bin Laden's whereabouts. This is the story endorsed by the U.S. government. However, the investigative journalist Seymour Hersh reports that in August 2010 a senior Pakistani intelligence officer simply walked into the U.S. embassy in Islamabad and gave up bin Laden's location in exchange for a $25 million reward. The Pakistani general now lives in the Washington area, according to Hersh, and is a

consultant for the CIA. Seymour Hersh, "The Killing of Osama bin Laden," *London Review of Books*, May 21, 2015.

75 **an easy-breezy turkey shoot:** McRaven, *Sea Stories*, 271.

75 **With CIA assistance:** Ben Child, "Zero Dark Thirty's CIA Access Triggered Internal Agency Investigations," *The Guardian*, Sept. 11, 2015.

75 **a lengthy exposé:** Mark Mazzetti et al., "SEAL Team 6: A Secret History of Quiet Killings and Blurred Lines," *New York Times*, June 6, 2015.

75 **adapted into a book:** Matthew Cole, *Code over Country: The Tragedy and Corruption of Seal Team Six* (Bold Type Books, 2022).

75 **It revealed a penchant:** Cole, *Code over Country*, 172, 174, 176, 215.

Chapter 7: Alleged Mexican White

77 **the pace of night raids:** Rod Norland, "For a Long-Term Afghan-American Accord, Night Raids Are a Sticking Point," *New York Times*, Dec. 4, 2011.

77 **deadliest days of the Iraq War:** Eleven Delta Force soldiers died in Iraq or from wounds sustained there between 2003 and 2011, according to my review of casualty reports obtained from USASOC through FOIA.

77 **a two-day battle:** Barbara Starr, "Rare Glimpse into U.S. Special Operations Forces in Afghanistan," CNN, July 26, 2011.

77 **A total of nineteen:** Except where otherwise noted, all information on USASOC casualties comes from my review of a complete set of USASOC casualty reports from 2001 to 2021 that I obtained through FOIA.

78 **headquartered in Mazar-i-Sharif:** Naylor, *Relentless Strike*, 365.

78 **at nearby Kunduz:** Naylor, *Relentless Strike*, 366.

78 **based at Kandahar:** Naylor, *Relentless Strike*, 360.

78 **a rare visit:** Thom Shankar, "Special Operations Step Up in Afghanistan," *New York Times*, May 15, 2013.

79 **the world's leading narco-state:** Special Inspector General Report on Afghanistan Reconstruction, *Counternarcotics: Lessons from the U.S. Experience in Afghanistan*, June 2018, 5 (stating that poppy cultivation and opium production were the main economic activities under U.S. occupation, employed the most people, generated the most investments, and fueled the most construction).

79 **Within a year:** McCoy, *Politics of Heroin*, 522–25.

79 **"The significant increase":** Drug Enforcement Administration, National Drug Threat Assessment 2004, 60.

79 **The amount of Afghan land:** DEA, National Drug Threat Assessment 2005, 74.

79 **a mind-blowing 7,514 percent:** According to the CIA's Crime and Narcotics Center, heroin production in Afghanistan increased from 7 metric tons of potential pure heroin in 2001 to 526 metric tons in 2005.

79 **approached a *thousand* metric tons:** According to the DEA's National Drug Intelligence Center, Afghanistan produced 947 metric tons of potential pure heroin in 2007, while Mexico produced 50; "Burma" produced 24; and Colombia, 2.1.

80 **"Heroin from Afghanistan is our biggest":** Garrett Therolf, "Heroin from Afghanistan Is Cutting a Deadly Path," *Los Angeles Times*, Dec. 26, 2006.

80 **"China white" heroin:** Note that "China white" is a street term used inconsistently, often to refer to heroin from Afghanistan, but sometimes in reference to heroin from Southeast Asia, or fentanyl and possibly other synthetic opiates. Also note that some Afghan heroin is brown.

80 **nearly pure heroin was available:** DEA, National Drug Threat Assessment 2013, 5–7.

80 **"heroin signature program":** See, for example, DEA Intelligence Report, The 2015 Heroin Signature Program Report, Aug. 2017.

80 **the DEA cautions:** DEA, National Drug Threat Assessment 2007, 17 (stating that "the amount of Asian heroin," especially from Afghanistan, "transported to the United States is relatively unknown"); DEA, National Drug Threat Assessment 2008, 21

(stating that "no program currently exists that is designed to produce a nationally representative sample of heroin available in the United States"); DEA, National Drug Threat Assessment 2015, 30 (stating that since not all heroin seizures are submitted for analysis, the source area proportions should not be characterized as market share).

81 **"the amount of Asian heroin":** DEA, National Drug Threat Assessment 2007, 17.

81 **the heroin domestic monitoring program:** Office of National Drug Control Policy, Drug Availability Estimates in the United States (2012), 66, n54.

81 **"Alleged Mexican White":** The quotations in this sentence are from the DEA, National Drug Threat Assessment 2015, 28; and DEA, National Drug Threat Assessment 2016, 47.

81 **the authors of the paper wrote:** Office of National Drug Control Policy, "Drug Availability Estimates in the United States" (2012), 57–58.

82 **made no mention of Afghanistan:** Technically, the DEA's 2015 National Drug Threat Assessment did mention Afghanistan, in a brief footnote acknowledging that Afghanistan was a major source area for opium poppy.

82 **published a report:** James Risen, "Reports Link Karzai's Brother to Afghanistan Heroin Trade," *New York Times,* Oct. 4, 2008.

82 **"The extent to which the Taliban":** SIGAR, Counternarcotics, 76.

82 **"There was little consistency":** SIGAR, Counternarcotics, 170.

82 **"I personally never believed":** SIGAR, Counternarcotics, 35.

83 **Baloch drug lord:** James Risen, "Propping Up a Drug Lord, Then Arresting Him," *New York Times,* Dec. 11, 2010.

83 **SIGAR found ample evidence:** SIGAR, Counternarcotics, 1, 5–6.

83 **"Almost everyone in influential positions":** SIGAR, Counternarcotics, 5–6.

83 **"eroded the legitimacy of the Afghan state":** SIGAR, Counternarcotics, 1.

83 **Drug money flows from Afghanistan:** SIGAR, Counternarcotics, 72.

83 **were a complete failure:** SIGAR, Counternarcotics, 86–89, 146–47, 163–68.

83 **"detrimental to its mission":** SIGAR, Counternarcotics, 166.

83 **"The CIA instead prioritized":** SIGAR, Counternarcotics, 40. Note that the two men that SIGAR named as CIA assets had previously been accused by the Justice Department of being *Taliban*-affiliated drug traffickers.

83 **implicit U.S. policy:** SIGAR, Counternarcotics, 54.

83 **a quarter million hectares:** United Nations Office on Drugs and Crime, World Drug Report, 2023.

83 **Lal Jan Ishaqzai:** SIGAR, Counternarcotics, 79.

84 **"It was rarely mentioned":** SIGAR, Counternarcotics, 55.

Chapter 8: The Northern Distribution Network

85 **the fourth Delta Force soldier to die:** Besides Sgt. First Class Ryan Savard, the others were Master Sgt. Benjamin Allen Stevenson, KIA in the Paktika province on July 21, 2011; Sgt. First Class Ronald Aaron Grider, KIA in the Kunduz province on September 18, 2010; and Master Sgt. Jared Neville Van Aalst, KIA in Kunduz province on August 4, 2010.

85 **Sher Khan Bandar:** Yaroslav Trofimov, "As Trade Is Rerouted, a Border Town Booms," *Wall Street Journal,* June 11, 2012.

85 **the bridge's opening ceremony:** "U.S.-Made Tajik-Afghan Bridge Opens," BBC News, Aug. 26, 2007.

86 **the Northern Distribution Network:** "Road Blocks; Afghanistan's Northern Neighbors," *Economist,* March 7, 2009 (reporting that "America . . . is stitching together a 'northern distribution network' to bring non-lethal supplies such as water and fuel into Afghanistan through Russia and Central Asia").

86 **the armed forces of Tajikistan:** Joshua Kucera, "The Narcostate," *Politico,* March/April 2014.

86 Tajikistan's gross domestic product: Letizia Paoli et al., "Tajikistan: The Rise of a Narco-State," *Journal of Drug Issues* 37, no. 4 (2007) ("Tajikistan now rivals Afghanistan in being the country most dependent on the illicit drug industry.").

86 another three Green Berets: Cpt. Andrew Michael Pedersen-Keel, on March 11, 2013; Sgt. First Class James Floyd Grissom, on March 21, 2013; and Staff Sgt. Michael Harrison Simpson, on May 1, 2013.

87 Systematic analytical errors: Naylor, *Relentless Strike*, 362.

87 Enlisted operators reportedly felt: Naylor, *Relentless Strike*, 424.

87 a chilling murder mystery: Nancy McCleary, "Family of Slain Fort Bragg Soldier Asks for Help Solving the Case," *Fayetteville Observer*, Feb. 17, 2014. That Wells was shot in the head comes from his USASOC casualty report.

87 The crime was never solved: A man named Donovan Lamar Moon was eventually charged in the murder of Sean Wayne Wells, but his accomplice was never identified, and no motive was disclosed. Nancy McCleary, "Hoke County Man Charged in Fatal Shooting of Soldier," *Fayetteville Observer*, June 9, 2014.

89 a tepid address: Daniella Silva, "'We Are Safer': President Obama Marks Formal End of War in Afghanistan," ABC News, Dec. 28, 2014.

89 more opium and heroin than ever: United Nations data shows that the amount of land under poppy cultivation in Afghanistan reached nearly 240,000 hectares in 2014, a record high that would soon be surpassed during Donald Trump's first administration.

92 Five Green Berets in 3rd Group: Rachael Riley, "Ex-Bragg Soldiers Sentenced for Embezzling Funds During Afghan Deployment," *Fayetteville Observer*, Aug. 2, 2019; Reuters staff, "U.S. Army Green Berets Admit to Stealing $200,000 in Counter-Terrorism Cash," Reuters, Jan. 14, 2020.

92 two in 7th Group: "Former Fort Bragg Soldier Pleads Guilty to Fraud, Smuggling Charges," *Fayetteville Observer*, Dec. 13, 2011; "Washington: Former Army Sergeant First Class Sentenced on Government Theft Charges," *U.S. Official News*, March 8, 2014.

92 at least 115 service members: Julia Harte, "U.S. Troops Have Stolen Millions in Iraq and Afghanistan," *Slate*, May 5, 2015 (citing a tally of court records compiled by the Center for Public Integrity).

92 Whole pallets of shrink-wrapped cash: David Pallister, "How the U.S. Sent $12Bn in Cash to Iraq. And Watched It Vanish," *The Guardian*, Feb. 7, 2007.

94 a unique organization: Sean Naylor, "Demand Skyrocketing for Active-Duty Civil Affairs Brigade," *Army Times*, Oct. 13, 2008.

94 in the words of its plans officer: "U.S. Army Corps of Engineers, Civil Affairs Brigade Partner for Readiness Exercise," *U.S. Fed News*, Jan. 27, 2016.

94 killed by blast injuries in Timergara: The two KIA were Sgt. First Class Matthew Stephen Sluss-Tiller and Sgt. First Class David James Hartman. Both belonged to the 95th CAB's 96th Civil Affairs Battalion.

94 disguised as Pakistani men: Jane Perlez, "Soldier Deaths Draw Focus to U.S. in Pakistan," *New York Times*, Feb. 3, 2010.

94 killing all six occupants: Craig Whitlock, "Mysterious Fatal Crash Provides Rare Glimpse of U.S. Commandos in Mali," *Washington Post*, July 8, 2012.

94 A third American serviceman: Master Sgt. Trevor Bast, at the time of his death in Mali, was a communications technician assigned to the U.S. Army Intelligence and Security Command at Fort Belvoir, Virginia. SOFREP.com, a news blog popular in the special operations community, written by special ops veterans, said that Bast and one of the 95th CAB soldiers who died "were almost certainly members of the elite, but relatively unknown, Intelligence Support Activity."

96 a misconduct investigation: Drew Brooks, "Fort Bragg Soldier Relieved of Duties amid Misconduct Investigation," *Fayetteville Observer*, Feb. 27, 2014.

96 sergeant Christopher Mann: Melissa Stephenson, "Hampton Soldier Sentenced for Stealing Nearly $1 Million in Property from Fort Bragg," CBS3-WTKR, Oct. 26,

2016. Additional details on Mann's crimes come from a review of Army CID investigative reports.

97 **The New Yorker published:** Matthieu Aikins, "The Bidding War," *New Yorker*, Feb. 28, 2016. Accusations of fraud against Hikmatullah Shadman were first reported in August 2013.

97 **Staff Sergeant Tonya Long:** U.S. Attorney's Office, Eastern District of North Carolina, "Staff Sergeant Sentenced for Bulk Cash Smuggling," press release, March 4, 2013.

Chapter 9: Rise and Kill First

99 **born in May 2014:** The dates of Lavigne's marriage and the birth of his daughter are according to his mother, Judy Brandt. Other sources give different dates and the definitive vital records are protected from public disclosure under North Carolina law.

100 **"Al-Qaeda Network Execute Order":** Mazzetti, *Way of the Knife*, 128–29; Naylor, *Relentless Strike*, 164–69; Jeremy Scahill, *Dirty Wars: The World Is a Battlefield* (Nation Books, 2013), 169–71, 183.

100 **dozens of neoconservative pundits:** For one of the first uses of the term "Arab Spring," see George Packer, "Dreaming of Democracy," *New York Times*, March 2, 2003. For the chorus of neoconservative voices that began clamoring for an "Arab Spring" in March 2005, see, for example, Michael Hirsh, "Bush Bends," *Newsweek*, March 2, 2005 ("Bush arrived on the continent with the fresh wind of the Arab Spring at his back."); Martin Walker, "Walker's World: Will History Fail to Turn—Again?," *United Press International*, March 7, 2005 ("Iran's ayatollahs may have the power to stop this whole movement that the Middle East is calling 'the Arab Spring' dead in its tracks."); Jeff Jacoby, "The Arab Spring," *Boston Globe*, March 10, 2005; Editors, "Progress," *National Review*, March 10, 2005 ("The last two months have been an Arab Spring."); Stuart Taylor Jr., "Revisiting Iraq, and Rooting for Bush," *The Atlantic*, March 2005 ("The Arab spring has many causes, of course. But the big one was Bush's removal of Saddam.").

100 **activists and agitators:** Ron Nixon, "U.S. Groups Helped Nurture Arab Uprisings," *New York Times*, April 14, 2011 ("Interviews with officials of the nongovernmental groups and a review of diplomatic cables obtained by WikiLeaks show that the democracy programs were constant sources of tension between the United States and many Arab governments.").

100 **"shadow force of Westerners":** Mark Mazzetti and Eric Schmitt, "C.I.A. Agents in Libya Aid Airstrikes and Meet Rebels," *New York Times*, March 30, 2011.

101 **"some kind of stick or knife":** Tracey Shelton, "Gaddafi Sodomized: Video Shows Abuse Frame by Frame," *GlobalPost*, Oct. 24, 2011.

101 **Secretary of State Hillary Clinton:** A video of Clinton laughing over news of Qaddafi's death, a moment caught on camera between shots of an interview with network television, can be viewed on YouTube at youtube.com/watch?v=6DXDU48RHLU.

101 **"a shit show":** Tim Walker and Nigel Morris, "Barack Obama Says David Cameron Allowed Libya to Become a 'S*** Show,'" *The Independent*, March 10, 2016.

101 **roving jihadist bands:** For reporting on the lack of understanding that Pentagon officials have of Islamist militants in the Sahel and Sahara, see Mark Mazzetti and Eric Schmitt, "Mali Militants: U.S. Confronts a Hazy Threat," *New York Times*, Jan. 17, 2013.

101 **smoothly worded but logically slippery:** The transcript of President Obama's speech can be read at obamawhitehouse.archives.gov/the-press-office/2014/05/28/remarks -president-united-states-military-academy-commencement-ceremony.

101 **transatlantic cocaine trade:** For background on cocaine trafficking in the Sahel and Sahara, see Laura Burke, "Kofi Annan Tackles Drug Trafficking in West Africa," Associated Press, Jan. 31, 2013; Baba Ahmed, "Mali Mayor Accused of Drug Trafficking Arrested," Associated Press, April 11, 2013; Yochi Dreazen, "Welcome to Cocaine Town; Mali's Government Can Do Little to End the Alliance of Islamists and Drug

Lords," *Toronto Star*, April 26, 2013; Afua Hirsch, "Cocaine Flows Through Sahara as al-Qaida Cashes In on Lawlessness," *The Guardian*, May 2, 2013.

101 to stand up a "counterterrorism battalion": Eric Schmitt, "U.S. Training Elite Antiterror Troops in Four African Nations," *New York Times*, May 26, 2014.

102 more of a monitoring station: For an in-depth magazine report on U.S. military operations in Niger, see Caitlin L. Chandler, "Over the Horizon," *Harper's Magazine*, Dec. 2022. Journalist Nick Turse has also reported extensively on the same subject, for *The Intercept* and several other publications.

102 Advance Force Operations: To circumvent congressional oversight, obviate the need for a presidential finding, and frustrate other legal safeguards, Pentagon planners characterize AFO missions not as covert actions but as "traditional" or "routine" military activities to "prepare the environment" or "prepare the battlespace" for an imminent war. The underlying legal reasoning is tortuous and counterintuitive, but in Syria this technical talk of "operational preparation of the environment" proved to be appropriate because JSOC's activities there from 2003 to 2011 really were an overture to an overt war.

102 lock-picking kits and camera equipment: Naylor, *Relentless Strike*, 317–21.

102 cross-border strikes: Naylor, *Relentless Strike*, 226, 323.

102 the State Department channeled funds: Adam Zagorin, "Syria in Bush's Cross Hairs," *Time*, Dec. 19, 2006.

102 Washington's efforts to overthrow Assad: Regime change in Syria was official U.S. policy. President Obama said, in August 2011, that Assad had to "step aside," a call echoed by other close American allies, including Israel, whose president, Shimon Peres, had said one month earlier that "Assad must go." Hannah Allam and Adam Sege, "Obama, European Allies Say Syria's Assad Must Go," McClatchy-Tribune Service, Aug. 18, 2011; Daniel Estrin, "Israeli President Says Syrian Leader Assad Must Go," Associated Press Online, July 26, 2011.

103 a billion-dollar fiasco: Mark Mazzetti, Adam Goldman, and Michael S. Schmidt, "Behind the Sudden Death of a $1 Billion Secret C.I.A. War in Syria," *New York Times*, Aug. 2, 2017.

103 traffickers working for the CIA: See, for example, Sheera Frenkel, "Syrian Rebels Squabble over Weapons as Biggest Shipload Arrives from Libya," *The Times* (London), Sept. 14, 2012. See also Eric Schmitt, "C.I.A. Said to Aid in Steering Arms to Syrian Opposition," *New York Times*, June 21, 2012. The CIA-backed effort to funnel weapons from Libya to Syria was ultimately halted by the September 11, 2012, attack on the CIA station in Benghazi, which killed two former members of Seal Team Six. See Adam Entous, Siobhan Gorman, and Margaret Coker, "C.I.A. Takes Heat for Role in Libya," *Wall Street Journal*, Nov. 1, 2012.

103 the flood of black-market arms: See Conflict Armament Research, *Weapons of the Islamic State*, Dec. 2017. See also Mark Mazzetti and Ali Younes, "C.I.A. Arms for Syrian Rebels Supplied Black Market, Officials Say," *New York Times*, June 26, 2016; Phil Sands and Suha Maayeh, "Death of a Syrian Arms Salesman," *The National*, Aug. 7, 2016; Jim Michaels, "The US Bought Weapons for Syrian Rebels—and Some Wound Up in the Hands of ISIS Terrorists," *USA Today*, Dec. 14, 2017.

103 the core leadership of ISIS: First-generation Islamic State commanders who served in Saddam Hussein's military included Samir Abd Muhammad al-Khlifawi, formerly an army intelligence colonel; Fadel Ahmed Abdullah al-Hiyali, an ex–special forces officer; and Abu Abdulrahman al-Bilawi, an ex–infantry captain.

103 three hundred military advisers: Mark Landler and Michael R. Gordon, "U.S. to Send up to 300 Military Advisers to Iraq," *New York Times*, June 19, 2014.

103 Obama upped the number: Helene Cooper, "In Increase, U.S. to Send 130 Advisers to Aid Iraqis," *New York Times*, Aug. 12, 2014.

104 In the early morning hours of May 16: Helene Cooper and Eric Schmitt, "U.S. Commandos Kill an ISIS Leader in Syria," *New York Times*, May 17, 2015.

105 **Four Army Special Forces soldiers:** The four USASOC soldiers who overdosed and died in the eighteen-month period beginning November 2014 were Staff Sgt. Kevin Archer, from opiates and benzodiazepines, on November 12, 2014; Capt. Howard Wade, from acute butalbital, oxycodone, and zolpidem intoxication, on June 6, 2015; Staff Sgt. James Brackett, from methamphetamine and methylene, on June 6, 2015; and Sgt. First Class Anthony Munoz, from oxycodone, on April 26, 2016.

105 **only two fatally overdosed:** The two USASOC soldiers who overdosed and died in the first eight years of the GWOT were Sgt. First Class Case Hamilton Binion, from unspecified substances, on April 6, 2003; and Spc. Patrick John Sullivan, from combined oxycodone intoxication, on January 7, 2006.

106 **fifty special operators:** Peter Baker, Helene Cooper, and David E. Sanger, "U.S. Troops Sent to Syria to Aid Forces Fighting ISIS," *New York Times*, Oct. 31, 2015.

106 **established a cell in Tel Aviv:** Naylor, *Relentless Strike*, 165 (describing Israeli tutelage of JSOC), 305 ("In the middle of the decade, Delta established a cell in Tel Aviv specifically to exchange intelligence with Israel.").

106 **prolific extrajudicial executioners:** For background on Israel's assassination program, see Ronen Bergman, *Rise and Kill First: The Secret History of Israel's Targeted Assassinations* (Random House, 2018).

106 **sometimes wore the uniform:** Naylor, *Relentless Strike*, 314.

107 **Ashton Carter told reporters:** Helene Cooper, Eric Schmitt, and Michael S. Schmidt, "U.S. Captures ISIS Operative, Ushering In Tricky Phase," *New York Times*, March 2, 2016.

107 **doubled in size:** Compare Helene Cooper and Eric Schmitt, "U.S. Sees Elite Military Unit as Key to Bigger Push Against ISIS," *New York Times*, Dec. 3, 2015 (reporting that the ETF comprised a hundred operators), with Helene Cooper and Eric Schmitt, "Detainee Helps U.S. Destroy Chemical Arms Held by ISIS," *New York Times*, March 10, 2016 (two hundred).

107 **the operational tempo surged:** All assertions in this paragraph, other than the first sentence, are based on interviews with Courtney Williams, a civilian intelligence specialist who worked for Delta Force during the deployment of the Expeditionary Targeting Force.

109 **complex federal regulations:** For a discussion of these "force management levels" in the context of U.S. military operations in Syria, see U.S. Government Accountability Office, Testimony Before the Subcommittee on Oversight and Investigations, Committee on Armed Services, House of Representatives, Overseas Contingency Operations: Observations on the Use of Force Management Levels in Afghanistan, Iraq, and Syria, Dec. 1, 2016.

109 **deployment orders of less than 180 days:** Lt. Col. James Reese (Ret.), interview by author, July 17, 2018, Raleigh, N.C. Other sources say that the cutoff point is ninety days.

109 **a press conference in Baghdad:** Andrew Degrandpre, "Top General Says 4,000 US Troops Are in Syria, Though Pentagon Says Only 500," *Washington Post*, Oct. 31, 2017. See also Idrees Ali, "Pentagon Likely to Acknowledge 2,000 US Troops in Syria," Reuters, Nov. 25, 2017.

111 **some of the craziest people:** Eric Schmitt, "Clinton and Trump Each Lay Claim to Military Brass," *New York Times*, Sept. 7, 2016.

111 **The White House announced:** W. J. Hennigan, "Trump Administration Stops Disclosing Troop Deployments in Iraq and Syria," *Los Angeles Times*, March 30, 2017.

111 **a specific threat to Americans:** For a discussion on how the rules of engagement changed for special operators following Trump's election, see Rukmini Callimachi et al., "'An Endless War': Why 4 U.S. Soldiers Died in a Remote African Desert," *New York Times*, Feb. 20, 2018. See also Dave Philipps, "Pentagon Begins Independent Inquiry into Special Ops and War Crimes," *New York Times*, Jan. 28, 2021.

111 **The pace of bombing increased:** Jim Michaels, "U.S.-Led Coalition Increases Airstrikes by 50% against Islamic State," *USA Today*, May 23, 2017.

111 **killed hundreds of civilians:** Tim Arango and Helene Cooper, "U.S. Investigating Mosul Strikes Said to Have Killed up to 200 Civilians," *New York Times*, March 24, 2017.

111 **the largest nonnuclear bomb:** Mujib Mashal and Fahim Abed, "'Mother of All Bombs' Killed Dozens of Militants, Afghan Officials Say," *New York Times*, April 14, 2017; Eric Schmitt and Helene Cooper, "Trump Unleashes the Generals. They Don't Always See the Big Picture," *New York Times*, April 20, 2017.

111 **a JSOC raid in Yemen:** Eric Schmitt and David E. Sanger, "Raid in Yemen: Risky from the Start and Costly in the End," *New York Times*, Feb. 1, 2017.

111 **"the Candy Man":** Jared Keller, "Ronny Jackson Was Allegedly Known as 'Candy Man' for Doling Out Prescriptions. He'll Fit Right in at the V.A.," *Task & Purpose*, April 26, 2018.

112 **"awash in speed":** Noah Shachtman and Asawin Suebsaeng, "Trump White House Was 'Awash in Speed'—and Xanax," *Rolling Stone*, March 3, 2024. Note that modafinil, Xanax, morphine, hydrocodone, diazepam, lorazepam, fentanyl, and ketamine all have legitimate medical uses. However, the law forbids their distribution without a prescription.

112 **called down a bunker-buster bomb:** Dave Philipps, Azmat Khan, and Eric Schmitt, "A Dam in Syria Was on a 'No-Strike' List. The U.S. Bombed It Anyway," *New York Times*, Jan. 20, 2022.

113 **American and European volunteers:** Seth Harp, "The Anarchists vs. the Islamic State," *Rolling Stone*, Feb. 14, 2017.

115 **ten operators were seriously injured:** Eric Schmitt, "U.S. Soldiers Injured in Syria Were Part of Commando Unit," *New York Times*, June 13, 2023.

115 **fifteen hundred Fort Bragg soldiers:** Kathryn Hubbard, "Fort Liberty Announces 1,500 Troops to Deploy Under 'Combined Joint Task Force,'" CBS17.com, Aug. 29, 2023. Note that Fort Bragg's name had been changed, at this time, to Fort Liberty.

Chapter 10: Cover Girls

123 **decrepitude and disrepair:** See Todd South and Davis Winkie, "Army Buildings Need Work, but These Two Bases Need the Most," *Army Times*, Dec. 1, 2022.

129 **The Army as a whole:** See "The Changing Profile of the U.S. Military: Smaller in Size, More Diverse, More Women in Leadership," Pew Research Center, Sept. 10, 2019.

129 **In a telling passage:** McChrystal, *My Share of the Task*, 97–99.

130 **"The top tier of operators":** Assertions in this chapter, including those regarding G Squadron, come primarily from interviews with Courtney Williams and Esther Licea, but Sean Naylor also writes about G Squadron and describes the compartmented element in similar terms. See Naylor, *Relentless Strike*, 307, 432 (describing G Squadron as an "AFO-type squadron," and stating that it was "the most prestigious squadron to command").

131 **"sensitive compartmented information":** A useful overview of the process by which access is granted to sensitive compartmented information facilities and special access programs can be found on the website of a company called DC Security Clearance Consultants, available at www.dcsecurityclearanceconsultants.com/sensitive-compartmented-information.php.

135 **a confused exchange of gunfire:** Michael R. Gordon and David D. Kirkpatrick, "Libya Holds Four American Military Personnel for Hours," *New York Times*, Dec. 27, 2013; Michael S. Schmidt and Michael R. Gordon, "Shots Fired Before 4 Were Held in Libya," *New York Times*, Dec. 28, 2013.

136 **the Libyans posted pictures:** Jim Hoft, "Libyans Seize Passports of Two Americans," *Gateway Pundit*, Dec. 27, 2013.

Chapter 11: Warehouse 13

142 **military-adjacent motorcycle clubs:** See Jana Winter and Jordan Smith, "Exclusive: Leaked Report Profiles Military, Police Members of Outlaw Motorcycle Gangs," *The*

Intercept, May 22, 2015. One of the "key findings" of a 2014 report by the ATF on out-law motorcycle gangs' infiltration of the military, leaked to *The Intercept*, was that ex-plosives had been found in the house of a Delta Force soldier affiliated with an unnamed outlaw motorcycle gang in the Fort Bragg area. However, in response to a FOIA request, the ATF's Office of Strategic Information and Intelligence told me that it had been unable to locate any record of this event. Email from Adam C. Simple, chief of ATF's Information and Privacy Governance Division, April 21, 2023.

143 **thrown out the first pitch:** A video of Cristobal Vallejo throwing the ceremonial first pitch of a San Diego Padres game on August 23, 2016, can be viewed on the website of Major League Baseball, available at mlb.com/astros/video/8-23-16-cris-throws-first -pitch-c1094257183.

143 **In Colorado Springs:** Angela Case, "Coast to Coast Ride for the Fallen Coming Through Colorado Springs," FOX21 News, Sept. 23, 2015.

150 **Angel Martinez-Ramos:** *United States v. Angel Martinez Ramos et al.*, No. 13-3823 (S.D. Fla. filed Dec. 24, 2013).

150 **James Matthews, a former SEAL:** See "Former Navy SEAL Arrested with 360 Pounds of Marijuana Pleads for Legalization at Sentencing," *Governance, Risk, and Compliance Monitor Worldwide*, Dec. 5, 2016.

150 **James Dennis Smith Jr.:** *United States v. Carl Rye, Bryon Rye, James Dennis Smith Jr.*, No. 1:17-mj-149 (D. S.C. filed June 16, 2017). For details on Smith's past paramilitary service, see John Monk, "Former Navy SEAL and C.I.A. Special Agent Charged in S.C. Federal Drug-Smuggling Case," *The State* (Columbia, S.C.), June 19, 2017.

151 **who trafficked drugs by air:** Smith's use of his private plane for trafficking drugs was detailed in the federal court case against him. Matthews told me that he did the same, but ultimately found that it was more economical to move drugs across the country with a truck and trailer.

151 **arrested for driving under the influence:** "Navy SEAL Who Claimed to Kill Bin Laden Arrested for DUI," ABC News, April 9, 2016. The charge against Rob O'Neill was dropped in the end.

151 **an Army Ranger out of his mind:** Alexis Krell, "Ex–Army Ranger Gets 6-Year Sentence for Shooting Man in Tillicum," *News-Tribune* (Tacoma), Feb. 15, 2017.

151 **two SEAL Team Six operators:** Details on the Logan Melgar case come primarily from the extensive reporting done by Spencer Ackerman and Kevin Maurer and published in *The Daily Beast* from 2017 to 2019. See, for example, Kevin Maurer and Spencer Ackerman, "Green Beret Discovered SEALs' Illicit Cash. Then He Was Killed," *Daily Beast*, Nov. 12, 2017; Kevin Maurer and Spencer Ackerman, "Navy SEALs, Marines Charged with Green Beret Logan Melgar's Murder," *Daily Beast*, Nov. 15, 2018; Kevin Maurer, "Slain Green Beret's Widow Speaks: 'I Knew They Were Lying,'" *Daily Beast*, June 25, 2019.

152 **exonerated of murder:** Adam Matthews, one of the SEAL Team Six operators who caused Logan Melgar's death, pleaded guilty to conspiracy, unlawful entry, hazing, obstruction of justice, and assault with battery, and was sentenced to a year in prison, but was released early after nine months. According to a November 23, 2022, email from Lt. Andrew Bertucci, a U.S. Navy spokesman, Matthews was released on February 18, 2020. Tony DeDolph, the SEAL operator who physically ended Melgar's life by choking him unconscious, was initially sentenced to a solid ten years behind bars, but in 2022, after media attention to the case had died down, the Navy's highest criminal court quietly overturned his sentence on a minor technicality and released him from prison pending a new trial. See Ben Finley, "Navy SEAL Wins Appeal of Sentence in Hazing Death," *Marine Times*, Nov. 22, 2022; Kevin Maurer, "Killer Navy SEAL Hires Trump Lawyer to Reduce His Jail Time," *Daily Beast*, March 3, 2023.

152 **a group of Navy SEALs came forward:** For details on the Gallagher case, see Philipps, *Alpha*.

152 **Delta Force had been implicated:** Josh White, "U.S. Generals in Iraq Were Told of Abuse Early, Inquiry Finds," *Washington Post*, Nov. 30, 2004.

153 **published on a local news site:** Ted Strong, "NC Soldier Charged with Rape," CBS17 News, Sept. 30, 2016.

156 **who later made public comments:** Two years after Vallejo's court-martial, Nance was called before a Pentagon advisory committee on sexual assault in the ranks. Asked by one of the panel members if he could explain the very low conviction rate of soldiers accused of rape, Nance replied, in essence, that many rape cases are factually weak because commanders, kowtowing to political and media pressure, are liable to recommend soldiers for rape charges even in the absence of convincing proof of their guilt. As a result, he said, very often it's a "bad case" with "bad facts," and "you're going to get an acquittal." "Sexual Assault in the Military, Former Military Judges Panel," C-SPAN, Feb. 14, 2020, c-span.org/program/public-affairs-event/sexual-assault-in-the -miltary-former-military-judges-panel/541590.

157 **an ABC News article:** Ella Torres, "Army Officer Says She Was Raped, but Supreme Court Ruling Blocks Her from Justice," ABC News, Jan. 21, 2020. The reporter who wrote this story evidently obtained Vallejo's enlisted record and, misled by the unit's change of name to the 3rd Operational Support Group, wrote that Vallejo had formerly belonged to Delta Force.

Chapter 12: He Was Seeing Bad Things

165 **had dropped felony charges:** In his only comments about Lavigne to the press, years later, Billy West told the *Fayetteville Observer* that someone else—he didn't say who— had taken responsibility for the drugs being manufactured in Lavigne's house. Rachael Riley, "Death of Special Forces Soldier Found on Fort Bragg Ruled as Homicide," *Fayetteville Observer*, Dec. 30, 2020.

166 **changed its official name:** In mid-2016, William Lavigne, Cristobal Vallejo, and other Delta Force operators whose enlisted records I obtained were transferred nearly simultaneously from the "1st SFOD-D (DELTA FORCE)" to the "3D OPL SPT GRP (ABN)," without any change in their military occupational specialties or duty titles. Employees of Delta Force who worked at the unit at the time of the transfer said that the 3rd Operational Support Group was simply a new official name for the unit.

166 **the commander of the headquarters company:** For clarity, concision, and the avoidance of acronyms, I have lightly edited the written comments made by the commander of the USASOC headquarters company on the challenges presented by incorporating former Delta Force soldiers into the unit. The officer's name and rank were redacted in the copy of the report that I obtained through FOIA, and the quoted comments might have been made by multiple officers in the company command group, though I have presented them as coming from a single speaker.

167 **first Green Beret to die:** According to his casualty report, Staff Sgt. Joshua Townsend died of tramadol toxicity in Tarin Kowt, Afghanistan, on January 16, 2009.

169 **his rap sheet in North Carolina:** Although Timothy Dumas Jr. was arrested many times in North Carolina, it is not clear from court records that he was convicted of any of the charges aside from larceny, which was downgraded to shoplifting. T.J. did not directly respond to questions about the circumstances of his many arrests, but did say that he had spent some time in jail.

Chapter 13: You Can't Make This Shit Up

174 **The original members of the GAFE:** An FBI memo dated April 22, 2005, and made available by the National Security Archive, states, "The original Zetas are former members-turned-deserters of Mexico's elite Airmobile Special Force Group (GAFE), trained in the U.S. at the School of the Americas at Fort Benning, GA." In 2010, Al Jazeera reported that some members of Los Zetas had been trained at Fort Bragg, based on an interview with Craig Deare, a former American special operations com-

mander with deep experience in Mexico. Chris Arsenault, "U.S.-trained Cartel Terrorises Mexico," Al Jazeera, Nov. 3, 2010. In 2012, the International Consortium of Investigative Journalists further detailed the GAFE's American training and substantiated reports that they had been trained at Fort Bragg as well as other U.S. bases. International Consortium of Investigative Journalists, "U.S.-Trained Forces Linked to Human Rights Abuses," Sept. 26, 2012. See also Ioan Grillo, "Special Report: Mexico's Zetas Rewrite Drug War in Blood," Reuters, May 23, 2012 ("A 2009 U.S. diplomatic cable published by WikiLeaks shows that at least one Zeta, former infantry lieutenant Rogelio Lopez, trained at Fort Bragg in North Carolina. Declassified U.S. training manuals used for Latin American officers include sections on combat intelligence and use of informants, both strong points of the Zetas."). In 2018, on condition of anonymity, I interviewed one of the original members of the GAFE in the Mexican city of Puebla, and he told me that he and his comrades, including Heriberto Lazcano, had been trained at Fort Benning and at a military base in New Mexico, and had also received training from Israeli instructors.

174 **A sophisticated criminal militia:** See Guadalupe Correa-Cabrera, *Los Zetas Inc.* (University of Texas Press, 2017).

175 **Spanish-language sources:** See, for example, Jesús Baldenea, "'El Talibán,' el sicario inspirado por el medio oriente que traicionó a Los Zetas y fundó su grupo criminal," *Infobae*, Nov. 8, 2023 (reporting that the "Taliban" nickname derived from Velásquez's penchant for beheading people).

180 **all four branches:** See, for example, U.S. Attorney's Office, Southern District of California, "Two National Guard Soldiers Plead Guilty to Trafficking Firearms to an Undercover Agent Posing as a Member of a Mexican Drug Cartel," press release, Jan. 14, 2016 (Army perpetrator); U.S. Attorney's Office, Eastern District of Virginia, "Two Men Sentenced to Prison for Illegal Firearm Purchases," press release, Jan. 6, 2020 (Navy); Briana Erickson, "Nellis Airman Sentenced for Selling Drugs, Firearms," *Las Vegas Review Journal*, July 13, 2021 (Air Force); City News Service, "Ex-Marine from Whittier Pleads Guilty in Gun-Smuggling Scheme for Cartel," *Los Angeles Daily News*, May 31, 2022 (Marine Corps).

180 **to name a few cases:** "Former Marines Held in Pasadena Weapons Case," *San Gabriel Valley Tribune*, Nov. 9, 2010 (detailing Florencia 13 case); Tim McGlone, "Former SEAL Gets 18 Months for Selling a Machine Gun," *Virginian-Pilot* (Norfolk, Va.), Dec. 4, 2010 (Mongols); Frank Main, "9 Chicago Men Accused of Buying Guns from US Soldiers in Kentucky," *Chicago Sun-Times*, March 31, 2022 (Gangster Disciples).

180 **"river of iron":** See, for example, James LaPorta and Jason Dearen, "How Brothers in Arms Plotted Theft, Sale of US Army Weaponry," Associated Press, Dec. 16, 2021 (assault rifles and accessories); Guillermo Contreras, "Bail Denied for Man Accused of Trafficking Guns," MySA.com, Dec. 13, 2018 (.50-caliber rifles); Doug Saunders, "Military Arms Get Out on San Bernardino County Streets," *San Bernardino Sun*, July 8, 2012 (AT4s, howitzer rounds); Johnny Johnson, "Devices Were Intended for Gang Members, Document States; Police Say Vet Planned to Sell Explosives," *Oklahoman*, Dec. 25, 2008 (custom-built roadside bombs); Seth Harp, "Arming the Cartels," *Rolling Stone*, Aug. 2019 (miniguns); and "Ex-Marine from Whittier Pleads Guilty in Gun-Smuggling Scheme for Cartel" (miniguns again). See also Southern District of California, "Two National Guard Soldiers Plead Guilty to Trafficking Firearms to an Undercover Agent Posing as a Member of a Mexican Drug Cartel"; "Army Sergeant in Texas Admits Funneling Weapons to Cartel," Associated Press International, Dec. 14, 2016; Guillermo Contreras, "Ex-GI Gets 17 Years in Weapons Case," *San Antonio Express News*, Nov. 4, 2017.

180 **attempted to sell:** LaPorta and Dearen, "How Brothers in Arms Plotted Theft, Sale of Army Weapons."

180 **a single pistol stolen from Fort Bragg:** Kristin M. Hall et al., "Some Stolen U.S. Military Guns Used in Violent Crimes," Associated Press, June 15, 2021.

Chapter 14: That Man Worked for the Cartel

186 Whittington, Anderson, and Tostado: Tostado and Anderson were indicted on October 14, 2021, for trafficking methamphetamine and pleaded guilty. Anderson was sentenced to twenty-two years in prison, Tostado to ten years. See United States v. Anderson et al, No. 5:21-cr-00383-FL-1 (E.D.N.C. filed Oct. 14, 2021). Whittington was charged in state court in January 2021 with drug trafficking and sentenced to eight years, according to Cumberland County court officials whom I spoke to by phone.

188 100,000 deaths in a single year: Josh Katz and Margot Sanger-Katz, "'It's Huge, It's Historic, It's Unheard-Of': Drug Overdose Deaths Spike," *New York Times*, July 14, 2021. See also Anh Truc Vo et al., "Illicit Substance Use and the COVID-19 Pandemic in the United States: A Scoping Review and Characterization of Research Evidence in Unprecedented Times," *International Journal of Environmental Research and Public Health* 19, no. 14 (2022).

188 a lengthy exchange of text messages: Jamie Carter read these text messages to me over the phone in early 2023. I have lightly edited her paraphrased verbal versions for concision and clarity.

Chapter 15: Freddie Had Everything Under Control

202 Lavigne really was an FBI informant: The Charlotte office of the FBI did not respond to an inquiry asking whether Lavigne ever worked for the bureau as an informant. The FBI also denied my public records request for files related to Lavigne, including the forms used to record contacts with confidential human sources.

202 Darren Griffin, a former Special Forces soldier: Erica Blake, "'The Trainer' Begins Terror Trial Testimony," *Toledo Blade*, April 3, 2008.

Chapter 16: Until Valhalla

204 published a memoir: Eric L. Haney, *Inside Delta Force: The Story of America's Elite Counterterrorist Unit* (Delacorte Press, 2006), 18.

206 Lavigne had been stripped of all clothing: One source, Special Agent Jeremy Speer, said that Lavigne was fully dressed in street clothes at the time that he was found dead. It is possible that crime scene technicians removed his clothes before Malloy and another CID source saw him naked except for running shorts.

206 shot at least three times: Judy Brandt said that federal agents told her that Billy Lavigne had been shot five times in the back. That is not necessarily inconsistent with Malloy's observation that he had been shot in the chest, groin, and leg, because bullets can cause entry and exit wounds.

209 a CBS News story: David Marin, "Foul Play Suspected in Deaths of Master Sergeant and Veteran at Fort Bragg," CBS News, Dec. 4, 2020.

210 *The New York Times* published an article: Michael Levenson, John Ismay, and Kwame Opam, "Army Investigates Deaths of Green Beret and Veteran at Fort Bragg," *New York Times*, Dec. 7, 2020.

210 read his obituary: Staff writer, "William LaVigne II," *The Pilot* (Southern Pines, NC), Jan. 12, 2021.

210 "an amazing father": The quotations in this sentence are taken from Lavigne's written obituary. Staff writer, "William LaVigne II."

213 On February 1, 2021: See "FBI Joins Investigation into Two Bodies Found on Fort Bragg," Associated Press State and Local Wire, Feb. 2, 2021.

214 James Comey was a frequent visitor: Courtney Williams, the signature reduction specialist who worked for Delta Force from 2010 to 2018, recalled seeing the former FBI director James Comey at the unit's compound and overhearing him boasting about his supposed college basketball career to the then-colonel Chris Donahue, who played football at West Point. In his memoir, the six-foot-eight Comey admits to having lied about playing college ball. See Ron Elving, "In 'A Higher Loyalty,' James Comey Describes an 'Unethical, and Untethered' President," NPR, April 13, 2018.

Chapter 17: The Thumb Drive

217 **"obtaining large quantities of illegal narcotics":** The quotation is from Huff's presentence investigation report, in which it is not attributed to any individual. See United States v. Freddie Wayne Huff II et al, No. 1:22-cr-00303-CCE (M.D.N.C. filed Sept. 26, 2022). The presentence investigation report was filed under seal and is not publicly accessible but Huff provided me with a copy.

219 **"This type of bulk monies":** César Rodriguez, "Sheriff's Office Traffic Stop Yields More Than $200K," *Laredo Morning Times*, March 29, 2021.

Chapter 18: Acid Is Life

230 **The password to his email account:** Except where specifically attributed to another named source, all assertions about the Enrique Roman-Martinez case in chapters 18 and 19 come from Army CID's 1,065-page-long investigative file, a redacted copy of which was obtained by Dustin Collier, a lawyer for Roman-Martinez's family, and made available to me.

231 **In the 1950s:** William Carlsen, "Army Data Describe LSD Test on Soldier," *New York Times*, Oct. 7, 1977; Thornwell v. United States, 471 F. Supp. 34 (D.D.C. 1979) ("Operation Third Chance was a covert program designed to test the utility of a psychedelic chemical, lysergic acid diethylamide, as an aid to interrogation.").

234 **ghost stories, tall tales:** See John Harden Sr., *The Devil's Tramping Ground and Other North Carolina Mystery Stories* (University of North Carolina Press, 1949).

236 **"A man was sitting at a table":** Carlsen, "Army Data Describe LSD Test on Soldier."

Chapter 20: Roid Rage

252 **I sued them in federal court:** *Harp v. United States Army Special Operations Command*, No. 1:23-cv-00106 (W.D. Texas, filed Feb. 1, 2023).

252 **he was charged:** Staff Sgt. David Rankine pleaded guilty to committing a violent domestic assault, aggravated assault, illegal use and importation of anabolic steroids, illegal use of cocaine, and violations of a military order not to consume alcohol and not to contact his spouse. Elvia Kelly, "Trial Results for Special Operations NCO for Domestic Dispute," SOCOM press release, June 2, 2022.

256 **SOCOM's directorate of science and technology:** David B. Larter, "'Performance Enhancing Drugs' Considered for Special Operations Soldiers," *Defense News*, May 16, 2017.

256 **no less than in the Navy SEALs:** See Dave Philipps, "Death in Navy SEAL Training Exposes a Culture of Brutality, Cheating, and Drugs," *New York Times*, Aug. 30, 2022.

Chapter 21: Withdrawal Symptoms

259 **a staggering two-year total:** Note that of the 109 soldiers assigned to Fort Bragg who died in 2020 and 2021, about 10 were reservists on active-duty orders. All the rest were active-duty personnel.

260 **at least nineteen articles:** Christina Morales, "Family of Fort Hood Soldier Who Disappeared in April Seeks Answers," *New York Times*, June 19, 2020; Johnny Diaz, "Arrest Is Made in Connection with Missing Fort Hood Soldier," *New York Times*, July 1, 2020; Johnny Diaz, Maria Cramer, and Christina Morales, "What to Know About the Death of Vanessa Guillen," *New York Times*, Nov. 30, 2022; Christina Morales, "'An Empty Presence in My Chest': Vanessa Guillen's Family Calls for Change in the Military," *New York Times*, July 6, 2020; Christina Morales, "They Grieve for a Soldier, and 'Heaven Has an Angel,'" *New York Times*, July 7, 2020; Jennifer Steinhauer, "A #MeToo Moment Emerges for Military Women After Soldier's Killing," *New York Times*, July 11, 2020; Christina Morales, "'You're a Warrior': Vanessa Guillen Is

Memorialized," *New York Times*, Aug. 14, 2020; Allyson Waller, "Family of Fort Hood Soldier Found Dead Demands Congress Investigate," *New York Times*, Aug. 26, 2020; Helene Cooper, "Army to Investigate Chain of Command's Actions at Fort Hood After Killing," *New York Times*, Sept. 1, 2020; Helene Cooper, "Army Inquiry into Soldier's Killing Expands to Base's Chain of Command," *New York Times*, Sept. 2, 2020; Manny Fernandez, "A Year of Heartbreak and Bloodshed at Fort Hood," *New York Times*, Sept. 9, 2020; Azi Paybarah, "Vanessa Guillen Died 'in the Line of Duty,' Army Officials Say," *New York Times*, Oct. 21, 2020; Sarah Mervosh and John Ismay, "Army Finds 'Major Flaws' at Fort Hood; 14 Officials Disciplined," *New York Times*, Dec. 8, 2020; Jennifer Steinhauer, "With Biden's Backing, Austin Prepares to Tackle Military's Sexual Assault Problem," *New York Times*, Jan. 26, 2021; Jennifer Steinhauer, "After Failures to Curb Sexual Assault, a Move Toward a Major Shift in Military Law," *New York Times*, April 27, 2021; Dave Philipps, "Military Missteps Allowed Soldier Accused of Murder to Flee, Report Says," *New York Times*, April 30, 2021; Editorial Board, "The Two Men Blocking Military Sexual Assault Reform," *New York Times*, June 19, 2021; Jennifer Steinhauer, "Biden Endorses a Major Change in How the Military Handles Sexual Assault Cases," *New York Times*, July 2, 2021; Melinda Wenner Moyer, "'A Poison in the System': The Epidemic of Military Sexual Assault," *New York Times*, Aug. 3, 2021.

260 **a months-long bureaucratic ransacking:** See Emma Platoff and Shawn Mulcahy, "Fourteen U.S. Army Leaders Fired or Suspended at Fort Hood," *Texas Tribune*, Dec. 8, 2020; Tara Copp, "U.S. Army to Replace Criminal Investigations Chief in Wake of Guillen's Death," *Defense One*, April 26, 2021.

261 **on the decline nationwide:** According to the Centers for Disease Control, the suicide rate per 100,000 Americans declined from 14.2 in 2018 and 13.9 in 2019 to 13.5 in 2020. Suicide Data and Statistics, Centers for Disease Control, Oct. 29, 2024, cdc .gov/suicide/facts/data.html.

261 **28.7 per 100,000:** Department of Defense, Annual Suicide Report 2020, 6.

262 **"found unresponsive in his barracks room":** Kyle Rempfer, "Special Forces Candidate Dies While Assigned to Med Group," *Army Times*, March 18, 2020.

262 **the 82nd Airborne Division said:** Kyle Rempfer, "Fort Bragg Infantryman Dies in Barracks," *Army Times*, Nov. 16, 2020.

263 **36 per 100,000 soldiers:** Gilbert R. Cisneros (undersecretary of defense for personnel and readiness) to the Honorable Edward J. Markey (U.S. Senate), Feb. 10, 2023.

264 **barely made a ripple:** Apart from a blurb on the website of NBC News, the Gould/ Royer case was reported only by *Army Times* and a handful of local Florida news outlets. See Courtney Kube, "U.S. Soldier Charged with Smuggling 90 Lbs. of Cocaine from Colombia to Florida," NBC News, Aug. 17, 2018; Meghann Myers, "Former Army Green Beret Sentenced in Colombian Cocaine Smuggling Plot," *Army Times*, May 1, 2019; "Man Gets 9 Years for Flying Cocaine into Elgin," *Pensacola News Journal*, May 2, 2019; Jim Thompson, "Ex–Green Berets Get 9 Years for Cocaine," *Northwest Florida Daily News* (Fort Walton Beach), April 30, 2019.

264 **investigative unit at** *El tiempo***:** Unidad Investigativa, "De héroe de guerra de EE. UU. en Afganistán a narco," *El tiempo*, Aug. 26, 2018 ("Gould, un ingeniero de 35 años, ingresó este año tres veces a Colombia, dos de ellas por Cali. Se movía con un pasaporte ordinario y andaba de civil.")

264 **Army Ranger named Drew Blahnik:** Trish Mehaffey, "Cedar Rapids Man Charged in Chris Bagley Killing Wants Trial Moved Out of Linn County," *The Gazette* (Cedar Rapids, Iowa), July 27, 2021.

264 **outside a bar in Erbil:** Thomas Gibbons-Neff, "Two Marines and Navy Sailor Are Investigated in Contractor's Death," *New York Times*, Jan. 7, 2019; Adam Rawnsley and Spencer Ackerman, "Ex–Green Beret Pummeled to Death in Apparent Fratricide," *Daily Beast*, Jan. 9, 2019; Nick Coffman, "MARSOC 3 Trials Postponed Indefi-

nitely," United American Patriots, April 16, 2021 (discussing evidence that tended to indicate that Rick Rodriguez was the initial aggressor in the brawl).

264 **bitten a female sailor in the face:** Dave Philipps, "More Details Emerge in Removal of SEAL Unit from Iraq; Allegations of Rape, Alcohol Use Reportedly Under Investigation," *San Diego Union-Tribune*, July 26, 2019; James Laporta and Julia Watson, "Former Sailor Details Misconduct by SEALs; in Rare Move, SEAL Team Was Pulled from Iraq After Allegations Came to Light," *Navy Times*, Aug. 21, 2020.

264 **an exposé of widespread cocaine use:** Geoff Ziezulewicz, "Internal Report Exposes Cocaine Abuse, Lax Testing, Inside SEAL Team 10," *Navy Times*, July 22, 2019.

265 **"Bay of Piglets":** Linda Pressly, "'Bay of Piglets': A Bizarre Plot to Capture a President," BBC News, July 29, 2020.

265 **an inquiry into potential war crimes:** Dave Philipps, "Pentagon Begins Independent Inquiry into Special Ops and War Crimes," *New York Times*, Jan. 28, 2021.

265 **"could have seismic repercussions":** Philipps, "Pentagon Begins Independent Inquiry into Special Ops and War Crimes."

266 **Federal agents backed by sheriff's deputies:** Mitchell Willetts, "Fort Bragg Soldier and His Son Arrested on Cocaine Trafficking Charges, Officials Say," *The News & Observer* (Raleigh, N.C.), May 27, 2021.

266 **serving on active duty:** Willie Harris (government information specialist, U.S. Army Human Resources Command) to author, Sept. 1, 2023.

267 **a rare visit to Fayetteville:** Jennifer Steinhauer, "Ed or Julia? Freedom or Valor? Army Base Names Are Changing. But to What?," *New York Times*, Oct. 1, 2021.

269 **a relative slap on the wrist:** Email from Capt. Matt Visser (deputy director of public affairs, XVIII Airborne Corps) to author, July 27, 2022.

269 **"We've observed an over 100 percent increase":** Andrea Blanford, "Fort Bragg Sees 100 Percent Increase in Drug-Related Crime on Installation," ABC 11, Oct. 14, 2021.

272 **no one was ever convicted:** Aaron Sánchez-Guerra, "Man Charged with Murdering Two People on NC Central Campus Found Not Guilty," *The News & Observer* (Raleigh, N.C.), Sept. 21, 2023.

272 **Staff Sergeant Alonzo Dargan Jr.:** Simone Jasper, "NC Soldier Shot Mother of His Unborn Child as She Drove on Georgia Road, Cops Say," *Columbus Ledger-Inquirer*, Oct. 6, 2021; Jatavia O'Neal, "Alonzo Dargan Jr. Sentenced to Life for Murder of Pregnant Troup Co. Woman," WTVM9, Jan. 27, 2023.

273 **The shadowy terrorist group:** Yaroslav Trofimov, "Left Behind After U.S. Withdrawal, Some Former Afghan Spies and Soldiers Turn to Islamic State," *Wall Street Journal*, Oct. 31, 2021.

273 **like his father before him:** Shahab al-Muhajir's father fought for Gulbuddin Hekmatyar, according to reporting in Persian-language sources.

273 **known as Zero Units:** See Lynzy Billing, "What We Know About U.S.-Backed Zero Units in Afghanistan," *ProPublica*, Jan. 5, 2023.

273 **a "righteous strike":** Matthieu Aikins, "In U.S. Drone Strike, Evidence Suggests No ISIS Bomb," *New York Times*, Sept. 10, 2021.

Chapter 22: Permanent War

276 **the Taliban decreed:** Associated Press, "Taliban Outlaws Poppy Harvest," *Los Angeles Times*, April 4, 2022.

277 **"a government pattern of sexual slavery":** U.S. Department of State, 2021 Trafficking in Persons Report: Afghanistan.

277 **"most successful counter-narcotics effort":** Samuel Lovett, Sarah Newey, and Ben Farmer, "How the Taliban Launched the 'Most Successful Counter-Narcotics Effort in Human History,'" *The Telegraph* (London), July 3, 2023.

277 **"For the first time in several decades":** Afghanistan International, "Taliban Rejects SIGAR Report on Drug Trade in Afghanistan," Aug. 8, 2024.

278 **a typical think piece:** William Byrd, "The Taliban's Successful Opium Ban Is Bad for Afghans and the World," United States Institute of Peace, June 8, 2023.

278 **"Poppy has been replaced by wheat":** William Byrd, "Understanding the Implications of the Taliban's Opium Ban in Afghanistan," United States Institute of Peace, Dec. 12, 2024.

278 **the sore-loser Biden administration stole:** Michelle Nichols, "U.N. Warns Afghanistan Needs Money to Prevent Total Breakdown," Reuters, Sept. 9, 2021 (reporting that "much of the Afghan central bank's $10 billion in assets are parked overseas, where they are considered a key instrument for the West to pressure the Taliban").

278 **"illicit drug supply chains":** Associated Press, "Taliban Outlaws Poppy Harvest."

280 **Eventually, she persuaded the state medical examiner:** On December 23, 2024, Dr. Craig Nelson, associate chief medical examiner in the North Carolina Office of the Chief Medical Examiner, determined that Sgt. Layne Jones died of undetermined means, changing the death certificate that had previously indicated suicide as the manner of death, according to emails and other documents provided by JoLynn Jones-Kerschner.

280 **"to map the civil human terrain":** Naylor, "Demand Skyrocketing for Active-Duty Civil Affairs Brigade."

282 **rejected a Russian ultimatum:** Yuliya Talmazan, Tatyana Chistikova, and Rebecca Shabad, "U.S. Offers Russia 'Serious Diplomatic Path Forward,' but Rejects NATO Ban on Ukraine," NBC News, Jan. 26, 2022.

282 **paratroopers from Fort Bragg:** Monika Scislowska and Czarek Sokolowski, "U.S. Airborne Infantry Troops Arrive in Poland amid Tensions," Associated Press, Feb. 6, 2022.

283 **"operational preparation of the environment":** See Joshua Kuyers, "'Operational Preparation of the Environment': 'Intelligence Activity' or 'Covert Action' by Any Other Name?," *American University National Security Law Brief* 4, no. 1 (2013). Note that these activities are sometimes called "operational preparation of the battlespace."

283 **estimated casualty count:** Bojan Pancevski, "One Million Are Now Dead or Injured in the Russia-Ukraine War," *Wall Street Journal*, Sept. 17, 2024.

284 **Specialist Yunique Weathers:** Danny Kelly, "S.C. Woman Sentenced to Life in Prison for Murdering 21-Year-Old in Horry County," *Post and Courier* (Myrtle Beach, S.C.), Dec. 21, 2023.

284 **Staff Sergeant Keith Wright Jr.:** Chloe Rafferty, Rodney Overton, and Dolan Reynolds, "Greensboro Man Arrested in Connection to Fatal Shooting of Fort Bragg Staff Sergeant, Deputies Say," WAVY10, July 27, 2022.

284 **Sergeant Nicholas Antonio Bobo:** Lexi Solomon, "Teens Arrested in Fatal Shooting of Fort Bragg Soldier," *Fayetteville Observer*, Sept. 24, 2022.

284 **Staff Sergeant Nikko Brown:** Kathryn Hubbard, "Hope Mills Man Arrested for Killing His Brother, Police Say," CBS17, Oct. 20, 2022.

287 **didn't review the thumb drive:** Detective Chris Luper (Winston-Salem Police Department), interview with author, April 28, 2024.

Chapter 23: Fort Liberty

288 **she was interrupted by the sound:** Colleen Hammond, Teddy Rosenbluth, and Korie Dean, "After NC Co-Pilot 'Exited' Plane, Questions Remain, Sadness Lingers Where He Was Found," *The News & Observer* (Raleigh, N.C.), Aug. 1, 2022.

288 **multiple lucrative contracts:** See, for example, "Rampart Aviation Gains Share of $450 Million Contract Modification," Targeted News Service, May 23, 2022.

289 **opium-fueled shadow war:** For background on this topic, see Jack Anderson, "U.S. Is Backbone of Laos Drug Trade," *Washington Post*, Sept. 9, 1977. Undated black-and-white photos of Gene Thacker in his Golden Knights gear show him meeting the debonair Prince of Laos, whom French customs officials caught with $13.5 million worth of heroin in his suitcase at the Paris airport in 1971. See McCoy, *The Politics of Heroin*, 283–84.

289 a Purple Heart pinned to his chest: Except where otherwise indicated, all assertions about the career of Gene Paul Thacker come from telephone interviews with his son, Tim Thacker, who was incarcerated at the maximum security federal correctional institute in Sumter County, Florida.

290 Andrew Carter Thornton II: For the most complete account of Thornton's military and criminal career, from which I have drawn this description of him, see Sally Denton, *The Bluegrass Conspiracy: An Inside Story of Power, Greed, Drugs and Murder* (Doubleday, 1990).

290 the "Cocaine Bear" myth: Thanks to a wildly off-the-mark Hollywood movie called *Cocaine Bear*, released by Universal Pictures in 2023, many recent articles on Andrew Carter Thornton II recycle an old story according to which a black bear in the Chattahoochee National Force overdosed and died after eating a bunch of cocaine that Thornton had thrown from an airplane, intending to collect it later. See, for example, Amanda Holpuch, "Yes, 'Cocaine Bear' Was Real. Here's the Back Story," *New York Times*, Dec. 1, 2022; Leo Sands, "'Cocaine Bear' Is Based on a True Story: Pablo Eskobear, Who Overdosed," *Washington Post*, Dec. 1, 2022. Readers interested in the real story would do better to consult contemporaneous news reports, which strongly suggest that the far-fetched tale was a fabrication concocted by Georgia state police as a cover for their theft of the bag of cocaine, one of many that Thornton tossed out on his final flight, which collectively were worth something like half a billion dollars. See Steve Baker, "Drug Parachutist Adds New Twist to Old Smuggling Game," Associated Press, Sep. 22, 1985; "GBI Investigating Cherokee County Parachute Find for Thornton Links," Associated Press, Oct. 17, 1985; "Bear Believed to Have Overdosed on Cocaine Dropped by Parachutist," Associated Press, Dec. 22, 1985; "Autopsy Will be Performed on Bear that Overdosed on Cocaine," United Press International, Dec. 23, 1985; "Medical Examiner Says Bear Did Not Consume All of Missing Cocaine," Associated Press, Dec. 24, 1985. Note also that the FBI's file on Thornton makes clear that the bureau suspected Gene Paul Thacker of having supplied the mil-spec cargo parachutes that Thornton used to jettison the bags of cocaine.

290 Adler "Barry" Seal: See Michael Hanion, "A Sting Avenged," *Toronto Star*, March 29, 1986; Frank Greve, Ken Fireman, Alfonso Chardy, "Suspects Boast Bush Knew of Private Iran Arms Deal," *Miami Herald*, Nov. 30, 1986; "Federal Informant Gunned Down in Parking Lot," Associated Press, Feb. 20, 1986; Scott Parks, "Talk Lingers of CIA Link in Arkansas; Agency Says It Never Hired Drug Trafficker," *Dallas Morning News*, Nov. 10, 1996. A video of Reagan's address to the nation in which he touted a photo taken by Seal that purported to show Sandinista officials off-loading drugs at a military airfield outside Managua, which was later shown to be a hoax, can be viewed on YouTube at youtube.com/watch?v=QaJQFor6KhQ.

290 "biggest cocaine indictment ever": "42 Charged in Indictment Said to Be Largest Ever," Associated Press, May 3, 1984

290 but was acquitted: Details on the outcome of Gene Thacker's court case in Florida come from the FBI's file on Andrew Thornton, as well as telephone consultations with Javier Angel Garcia, an archival specialist in the office of the clerk of court in Palm Beach County, Florida.

290 local lawmen resorted to sabotaging: See Sherry Matthews, "Plane Crash Photos Taken In Break-In," *News-Journal* (Raeford, N.C.), Dec. 22, 1983; Sherry Matthews, "Raeford Airplanes Sabotaged," *News-Journal* (Raeford, N.C.), Dec. 22, 1983; "FBI Nosing Around Airplanes' Sabotage," *News-Journal* (Raeford, N.C.), Jan. 12, 1984.

291 "Raeford Aviation has been raided": The FBI's file on Andrew Thornton, from which this quotation was taken, can be accessed on the website of the National Security Archive, a nonprofit organization based at George Washington University.

291 "very proficient drug trafficker": Assistant U.S. Attorney Brad Knott's comments about Tim Thacker were made during Thacker's sentencing hearing held August 6,

2019. See United States v. Timothy R. Thacker, No. 7:18-cr-00095-D-1 (E.D.N.C., filed May 15, 2018).

292 **she fingered Thacker:** Details on the police investigation of Tim Thacker and his arrest and conviction come from court documents filed in the federal case against him. See United States v. Timothy R. Thacker, No. 7:18-cr-00095-D-1 (E.D.N.C. filed May 15, 2018).

292 **August 2019 press release:** U.S. Attorney's Office, Eastern District of North Carolina, "Hoke County Man Sentenced to Forty Years for Drug Distribution," press release, Aug. 22, 2019.

292 **anticlimactic and inconclusive final report:** National Transportation Safety Board, "Aviation Investigation Final Report, Accident No. ERA22LA348," Dec. 14, 2023.

294 **causing the death of at least one person:** The death of Karin Zoanelli, aged eighty-seven, was ruled a homicide by the chief medical examiner of North Carolina.

294 **reportedly among the suspects:** Jack Murphy, "Panic Grips Special Forces Community amid Investigation into Drugs, Human Trafficking," Connecting Vets, Jan. 12, 2023.

295 **Brandon Allen Amos-Dixon:** Joe Jurney and Judith Retana, "Fort Bragg Soldier Jailed on Murder Charge in Shooting of Fellow Soldier in North Carolina," WBTW, March 20, 2023.

295 **Sergeant Junando Recardo Dawkins:** Dawkins and his brother were convicted of murder and sentenced to twenty-five years to life in prison. Ulster County, "Two Brothers Convicted of Murder Following 11-Day Jury Trial in Ulster County Court," press release, April 29, 2024.

295 **Outta They League:** Kathy Reakes, "15 in Drug Ring That Used Music Company as Front Charged in White Plains," *Peekskill Daily Voice* (White Plains, N.Y.), Oct. 13, 2016.

295 **Josef Nehemiah King Jr.:** Lexi Solomon, "Fort Bragg Soldier Accused of Beating Toddler to Death," *Fayetteville Observer*, March 23, 2023. King's enlisted record shows that he became an "SF STUDENT" in March 2022 but returned to the regular infantry four months later.

295 **Rolondo Martice Boone:** Joseph Pierre, "Fort Liberty Soldier Arrested in Deadly April Hookah Lounge Shootout," *Fayetteville Observer*, Aug. 29, 2023.

295 **another *New York Times* exposé:** Philipps, "Death in Navy SEAL Training Exposes a Culture of Brutality, Cheating, and Drugs."

295 **"Does ARSOF have an ethics problem?":** Janice Burton, "From the Editor: Is There an Ethical Crisis in Army Special Operations?," *Special Warfare*, March 2022.

296 **a March meeting of the Senate:** Rebecca Kheel, "Special Operations Boss Vows to Stamp Out 'Corrosive' Misconduct After String of Problems," Military.com, March 7, 2023.

296 **Department of Defense Overdose Data Act:** S. 1766, 118th Cong. (2023).

296 **championed by Senator Kirsten Gillibrand:** Office of Kirsten Gillibrand, U.S. Senator for New York, "Gillibrand Statement on President Biden Signing Executive Order Implementing Military Justice Reforms," press release, July 28, 2023.

296 **commanders will retain their authority:** Vianna Davila, "Military Justice Reforms Still Leave Some Criminal Cases to Commanders with No Legal Expertise," *Texas Tribune* and *ProPublica*, Feb. 13, 2023 (reporting that "commanders continue to decide whether to prosecute offenses such as robbery, assault and distribution of controlled substances").

297 **a covert propaganda campaign:** Chris Bing and Joel Schectman, "Pentagon Ran Secret Anti-Vax Campaign to Undermine China During Pandemic," Reuters, June 14, 2024 (reporting that "General Jonathan Braga pushed for the Pentagon's secret propaganda campaign").

297 **felony drug possession charges:** The two soldiers charged with possession in Harnett County were Sgt. First Class Ryan Wallen, aged thirty-seven, a 3rd Group communications sergeant; and Staff Sgt. Travis Rahmer, aged twenty-nine, a member of the 4th Psychological Operations Group. Rachael Riley, "Fort Liberty Special Operations Sol-

diers Arrested in Harnett County on Drug Charges," *Fayetteville Observer*, Oct. 25, 2023.

297 **a senseless mass shooting:** Estes Thompson, "Man Who Admitted Shooting Up Restaurant Convicted of Four Counts of Murder," Associated Press, April 1, 1994.

297 **a pair of neo-Nazi paratroopers:** Eric Harrison, "3 White G.I.s Held in 'Hunt' That Left 2 Blacks Dead," *Chicago Sun-Times*, Dec. 10, 1995.

298 **the mock Iraqi town:** "Iraqi Village Recreated at New Bragg Training Site," WRAL News, March 3, 2009.

299 **Gordon Ray Custis:** Rachael Riley, "Former Fayetteville Soldier, Veteran Accused of Money Laundering," *Fayetteville Observer*, March 30, 2023; U.S. District Court for the Eastern District of North Carolina, "Former Soldier Receives 15 Years in Federal Prison for Drug Trafficking Ketamine and Laundering More Than $700,000," press release, Jan. 26, 2024.

299 **Kojo Owusu Dartey:** U.S. Attorney's Office for the Eastern District of North Carolina, "Jury Finds U.S. Army Major Guilty After He Smuggled Guns to Ghana in Blue Barrels of Rice and Home Goods," press release, April 29, 2024.

299 **Jorge Esteban Garcia:** Rachael Riley, "Meth, Gang, Night Club: Fort Liberty Leader Faces Multiple Charges," *Fayetteville Observer*, Feb. 13, 2024. Other details about Garcia come from a review of his enlisted record and the charge sheet.

Chapter 24: The Third Man

302 **a close-range shoot-out:** Katelin Gandee, "February Homicide Has Led to Several Arrests," *Laurinburg Exchange*, April 12, 2021. Additional details come from an indictment filed against Shavonte Jarrel McBryde in the U.S. District Court for the Middle District of North Carolina on March 20, 2023.

302 **a motion filed by a defense lawyer:** Rachael Riley, "Attorney Injury Delays Federal Case of Man Accused in Killings of Green Beret, Army Veteran," *Fayetteville Observer*, June 11, 2024.

302 **five times in the back:** Note that while federal authorities told Judy Brandt that her son had been shot five times in the back, CID agents who worked the murder scene described Lavigne as having been shot multiple times in the chest and leg. Because bullets can cause entry and exit wounds, these descriptions are not necessarily inconsistent.

307 **"The COs right now":** Huff's allegation about drug trafficking by Fort Dix prison guards was corroborated by recent press reports. See Michael Balsamo and Michael R. Sisak, "Workers at Federal Prisons Are Committing Some of the Crimes," Associated Press, Nov. 14, 2021; Jim Walsh, "Second Guilty Plea in F.C.I. Fort Dix Drug-Smuggling Scheme," *Courier Post* (Cherry Hill, N.J.), Jan. 10, 2022.

307 **his 2039 release date:** Huff was sentenced to twenty-one years in prison in 2023, but was eligible for five years of supervised release. Accordingly, the Bureau of Prisons set his release date for 2039 rather than 2044.

Epilogue

310 **"golden age of special operations":** Dan Lamothe, "Retiring Top Navy SEAL: 'We Are in the Golden Age of Special Operations,'" *Washington Post*, Aug. 29, 2014.

310 **supermajorities of combat veterans:** Ruth Igielnik and Kim Parker, "Majorities of U.S. Veterans, Public Say the Wars in Iraq and Afghanistan Were Not Worth Fighting," Pew Research Center, July 10, 2019.

310 **"behind the curtain":** A video of Tyler Grey's interview with Sean "Buck" Rogers can be viewed on YouTube at youtube.com/watch?v=V2WLaB1QHRM.

311 **less than half of respondents:** Brad Dress, "Trust in Military Remains Below 50 Percent: Survey," *The Hill*, Dec. 1, 2022; Leo Shane III, "Trust in the Military on the Rise, but Still Below Pre-Pandemic Levels," *Military Times*, Dec. 4, 2024.

311 **all four service branches missed:** Khaleda Rahman, "US Army Shrinks to Smallest Size Since WW2 as It Struggles to Find Recruits," *Newsweek*, Oct. 5, 2023; Ben Kesling,

"The Military Recruiting Crisis: Even Veterans Don't Want Their Families to Join," *Wall Street Journal*, June 30, 2023; Thomas Novelly et al., "Big Bonuses, Relaxed Policies, New Slogan: None of It Saved the Military from a Recruiting Crisis in 2023," Military.com, Oct. 13, 2023. The Army claimed to have met its recruiting target in 2024, but only after setting a lower goal. Lolita C. Baldor, "Military Recruiting Rebounds After Several Tough Years, but Challenges Remain," Associated Press, Sept. 26, 2024.

312 an affiliate of al-Qaeda: That the Sunni extremists who took over the remnants of the Syrian state in 2024 were an affiliate of al-Qaeda is to adopt official U.S. government terminology. In 2017, the Department of Justice put a $10 million reward on the head of Muhammed al-Jawlani, "the senior leader of . . . al-Qaeda's affiliate in Syria," known as Hay'at Tahrir al-Sham.

312 chopping people's heads off: See, for example, "Syrian Islamist Militant Group 'Publicly Stones Three Women to Death' in Idlib," *New Arab*, March 30, 2021; "Syria Conflict: Boy Beheaded by Rebels 'Was Fighter,'" BBC News, July 21, 2016 (detailing atrocities committed by the Nour al-Din al-Zinki movement, which later merged with Hay'at Tahrir al-Sham).

312 The SOCOM war crimes review: Inspector General, U.S. Department of Defense, "Evaluation of U.S. Central Command and U.S. Special Operations Command Implementation of the Administrative Requirements Related to the Department of Defense's Law of War Policies," Nov. 16, 2021.

313 a note made public: Griffin Eckstein, "'This Was a Wake Up Call': Letters from Las Vegas Cybertruck Bombing Suspect Shine Light on Motive," *Salon*, Jan. 3, 2025.

313 both lived in Fayetteville around 2012: Caitlin Doornbos, "Revealed: New Orleans ISIS Terrorist and Cybertruck Bomber Both Served at Fort Bragg," *New York Post*, Jan. 2, 2025.

313 "very strange similarities": Ricardo Torres-Cortez and Richard N. Voletta, "Las Vegas Sees Increased Police Patrols After Trump Hotel Bombing," *Las Vegas Review-Journal*, Jan. 2, 2025.

314 He made tens of millions: Lee Fang, "Congressman Seeking to Relaunch Afghan War Made Millions in Defense Contracting," *The Intercept*, Aug. 20, 2021.

314 he expects the GWOT to last a hundred years: Kris Osborn, "Green Beret: U.S. Fighting 100 Year War," *National Interest*, Jan. 13, 2017.

314 *The War on Warriors*: Pete Hegseth, *The War on Warriors: Behind the Betrayal of the Men Who Keep Us Free* (Broadside Books, 2024).

INDEX

INDEX

100 YEARS of PUBLISHING

———◇———

Harold K. Guinzburg and George S. Oppenheimer founded Viking in 1925 with the intention of publishing books "with some claim to permanent importance rather than ephemeral popular interest." After merging with B. W. Huebsch, a small publisher with a distinguished catalog, Viking enjoyed almost fifty years of literary and commercial success before merging with Penguin Books in 1975.

Now an imprint of Penguin Random House, Viking specializes in bringing extraordinary works of fiction and nonfiction to a vast readership. In 2025, we celebrate one hundred years of excellence in publishing. Our centennial colophon features the original logo for Viking, created by the renowned American illustrator Rockwell Kent: a Viking ship that evokes enterprise, adventure, and exploration, ideas that inspired the imprint's name at its founding and continue to inspire us.

———◇———

For more information on Viking's history, authors, and books, please visit penguin.com/viking.